NOTHING'S BAD LUCK

NOTHING'S
BAD LUCK

THE LIVES OF
WARREN ZEVON

C. M. KUSHINS

Da Capo

Da Capo Press
Hachette Book Group
1290 Avenue of the Americas, New York, NY 10104
dacapopress.com
@DaCapoPress, @DaCapoPR

Printed in the United States of America

First Edition: May 2019

Published by Da Capo Press, an imprint of Perseus Books, LLC, a subsidiary of Hachette Book Group, Inc. The Da Capo Press name and logo is a trademark of the Hachette Book Group.

The Hachette Speakers Bureau provides a wide range of authors for speaking events. To find out more, go to www.hachettespeakersbureau.com or call (866) 376-6591.

The publisher is not responsible for websites (or their content) that are not owned by the publisher.

Print book interior design by Jeff Williams.

Library of Congress Cataloging-in-Publication Data
Names: Kushins, C.M. author.
Title: Nothing's bad luck : the lives of Warren Zevon / C.M. Kushins.
Description: First edition. | New York, NY : Da Capo Press, 2019. | Includes
    bibliographical references and index.
Identifiers: LCCN 2018057389| ISBN 9780306921483 (hardcover : alk. paper) |
ISBN 9780306921476 (ebook : alk. paper)
Subjects: LCSH: Zevon, Warren. | Rock musicians--United States--Biography.
Classification: LCC ML420.Z475 K87 2019 | DDC 782.42166092 [B]—dc23
LC record available at https://lccn.loc.gov/2018057389

ISBNs: 978-0-306-92148-3 (hardcover), 978-0-306-92147-6 (ebook)

LSC-C

10 9 8 7 6 5 4 3 2 1

For M

CONTENTS

Overature   1

PART ONE: SONG NOIR

Chapter One (1903–1966)   7

Chapter Two (1966–1970)   27

Chapter Three (1970–1976)   41

Chapter Four (1977–1979)   77

Chapter Five (1979–1980)   115

Chapter Six (1980–1983)   155

PART TWO: HEAVY METAL FOLK

Chapter Seven (1983)   187

Chapter Eight (1984–1987)   207

Chapter Nine (1988–1990)   247

Chapter Ten (1990–1995)   267

PART THREE: ADULT CONTEMPORARY

Chapter Eleven (1995–2002)   305

PART FOUR: THE LAST TEMPTATION OF WARREN WILLIAM ZEVON

Chapter Twelve (2002–2003)   331
Chapter Thirteen *A Leaf in the Wind*   353
Coda   359

Discography, 365
Sources, 373
Acknowledgments, 382
Index, 385

An old man told his grandson, "My boy, there is a battle between two wolves inside us all. The first one is Evil. He is anger, jealousy, greed, resentment, inferiority, lies, and ego. The second is Good. He is joy, peace, love, hope, humility, kindness, empathy, and truth."

The boy thought about this for a moment, then asked, "Grandfather, which wolf wins?"

The old man replied, "The one you feed."

—TWENTY-FIRST-CENTURY AMERICAN FOLK TALE

Ah-Hoooooooooooo!!!

—WARREN ZEVON

OVERATURE

SUMMER, 1978

THE ROAR OF THE REVOLVER WOKE HIM.

It had been a dream, yet an awful, familiar one. The echo of the hand cannon resounded in his ears. Warren's eyes stared at the ceiling and he labored to think back through the hangover, scanning the details of the night. It had been the third time the recurring dream had taken hold of him—and with it, fevered shakes throughout his body.

He had awoken in the dream, too, blurring the line between reality and alcohol-soaked slumber. There, as in waking life, he had slowly picked himself up and out of bed, trying his hardest not to rattle the heavy head on his body. Everything ached, every muscle. The throbbing in his temples pulsated with each small move. He trembled in the dark.

Still waking up in the mornings with shaking hands.

As if by instinct—or was it the skilled muscle memory of a piano player?—Warren reached out in the darkness, to his left, and found the heavy weapon in its usual place on the nightstand. The gun rested beside his eyeglasses, pills, and a cocktail glass—empty but for the languid millimeter of melted ice. He pulled the gun to his body and his hand brushed against the warm glass. At least he had used one, he thought, instead of just chugging straight from the bottle. And ice? Warren never usually cared that late at night.

The lucidity forced Warren to pause and sit up on the edge of the bed. He reconsidered the reality of the moment, the *now*. Was he awake, or was this the same old familiar dream starting again like a Möbius strip?

Gun in hand, he stumbled up and out of the bed, cautious not to wake Crystal. She had finally gotten to sleep, too, and rested silently in a fetal position. He watched her body rise and fall. By the window, Ariel's bassinet was bathed in moonlight.

The combination of hangover and darkness left Warren fumbling toward the door on the legs of a toddler taking its first steps. He was bare-chested but had passed out wearing a pair of denims. He extended his free hand out to find the bedroom door and his toes side-stepped the books, pages of sheet music, empty bottles, and baby toys littered around the carpet. The weight of the .44 Magnum pulled his left hand straight toward the floor. The gun always felt heavier than he remembered.

He made his way down the stairs and felt for the broken section of bannister near the bottom. He let the splintered cavity guide him to the front door, then lumbered across the front yard. The cool air parted like a soft curtain. Warren breathed in slowly through his nostrils to calm his stomach muscles, trying not to vomit. Not quite dawn, the night was dark as the bedroom. He could just make out the shapes of palm trees swaying in the distance, tall and vague. They danced, silhouetted aberrations against the blue-black of the sky.

He would later write, "Don't the trees look like crucified thieves?" And they did.

Clutching the heavy gun, Warren walked down the driveway and angled his body toward the road. His head wobbled atop his six-foot-tall, wiry frame, and his trademark wavy blond hair—worn long to his shoulders—was matted to the side of his face. Despite the Santa Barbara breeze, he was caked with sweat. He wiped the wrist of his gun hand across his forehead and let the moonlight lead him. The Magnum hung at his side and he imagined he was James Bond. Warren smirked as he mimicked the debonair strut of the secret agent walking within the iconic gun barrel of an unseen enemy's scope—ready to turn and fire first.

Paul would certainly approve of the cinematic image. He'd have to share that with him, next time in New York.

Warren found a worthy spot just beside the mailbox. There, he slowly took to one knee, careful not to topple over on his side. He brought the gun up to eye level, a perfect military stance. His left hand, still shaky with the weight, cradled his right. Warren brushed his hair back with his shoulder. He took aim at nothing, just the abysmal darkness of the road. Although scarce at this hour of night, a car would be sure to pass at some point.

Featherhill Road, located in the heart of Montecito, ran roughly half a mile from east to west, its most eastern section becoming a straight line before merging into a sharp curve south for the rest of the road's length. Facing both sides, Warren felt the perspiration dripping down his brow as his arms grew tired. He swallowed hard, his mouth dry and with the staleness of an ashtray coated in whiskey.

Any minute now, a license to kill.

Ahead and to the left, the opaque rows of valley oaks and manzanitas that lined the road were beginning to lighten. The diffuse lights of an oncoming car leaked across the branches like a stain. The car slowly snaked down Romero Canyon Road from the east. Warren knew it was just around the bend. He readied himself and felt his arms and legs stiffen. A Smith & Wesson Model 29 .44 Magnum, truly as Dirty Harry claimed—the most powerful handgun in the world. It was worth the extra effort to cradle and aim. With the barrel over eight inches long in front of his face, he could barely make out a clear shot. The illuminated trees continued to reveal about fifty yards in front, allowing Warren's eyes to quickly adapt and sharpen behind his glasses. And no matter who was driving the oncoming car—man, woman, or child—a moving target was a moving target.

Finally, the white dots of the headlights rose above the curve. Warren's heart beat faster, his hand shaking but his aim true. He watched intently as a black sedan smoothly curved up and straightened in his direction. Only seconds away. The shape of an anonymous figure began to grow clearer behind the windshield as the sedan gained momentum. Warren squinted into the growing high beams and took a deep breath. He felt his eyes tighten, the driver nearly distinguishable. From the height above the steering wheel, it was a man. His finger tightened on the trigger.

In the flash of an instant, the face behind the wheel became clear in the murky moonglow. The halo of shoulder-length blond hair was the first tell, then the finite glint of a bespectacled face.

It was him. Driving the car, it was Warren himself.

Without hesitation, Warren sucked in a deep breath and fired. The discharge filled his vision with white light. He felt his body give out and was thrown backwards with the kickback.

Then, he awoke, the shot's roar still echoing in his head.

It took a few seconds in the silence for Warren to be sure it had all been a dream. He kept his eyes shut tight. He counted to ten. Out of habit, he reached to his left to find the gun, ready to check the chamber for a missing round. Instead, Warren's arm bumped into a wall. Then, it all came back. He wasn't home. He wasn't in his bedroom or camped out on Jorge's couch or in Phil's guest house. Any sense of relief was instantly replaced with one of defeated misery. Just as he had for the past two weeks, Warren slowly opened his eyes to the sterile white walls of a private hospital room.

The kill mission may have been a dream, but nonetheless, Warren Zevon awoke to a very real nightmare. He knew what today was. The reality of it made him shiver. What did the doctors call it? *Intervention therapy.* Well, if it was good enough for Billy Martin . . .

After the last bender in New York, Crystal had finally reached her wit's end. She had called Paul, desperately pleading with him for help. He, in turn, had called Jackson, desperately pleading with him for help. Without all hands on deck, they knew Warren would be dead within the year. Two quarts of vodka a day—plus all the drugs. What was he trying to prove? The album was selling so well this time. Eight years of blood, sweat, and tears and he finally had scored a genuine hit. What was he so unhappy about, anyway?

With a little research and a few phone calls, Crystal had found Pinecrest Rehabilitation Center. It was the only place in California, one of the first in the entire country, that offered the experimental therapy that Warren was about to receive. Under doctoral guidance, every person dear to Warren would gather together at the hospital, each clutching a laundry list of infractions that he had caused in their lives. Then, in order, they would read it aloud. Every detail and every wound—one by one. The drinking, the drugs—the lawyers, the guns, the money. The ego and the self-loathing. And Warren would to be forced to listen. To understand. To accept.

It was, by definition, a last-ditch effort to save Warren Zevon from himself.

He had been feeding the wolf for a long time.

Part One
SONG NOIR

CHAPTER ONE

(1903–1966)

WARREN WILLIAM ZEVON WAS BORN ON FRIDAY, JANUARY 24, 1947, in Chicago, Illinois.

It was the city that his father had long considered a spiritual home. As a professional gambler with ties to organized crime, many of William Zevon's closest associates and business contacts were based there. Although his much younger bride, Beverly, would have preferred to stay near her family in Fresno, California, she had abided by her husband's wishes. The move was just one of many facets of their relationship that enraged her parents, strict Mormons who had always tried to instill in their daughter the same devout faith and moral dogma by which they lived. Ellsworth and Helen Simmons made no secret of their disapproval in their daughter's choice of a suitor. But while much of the Mormon doctrine had sunk in, Beverly just couldn't be persuaded.

In later years, if Warren Zevon displayed signs of duality in both his life and music, one need not look much further for explanation than in the "opposites attract" dichotomy of his parents.

When William was only two years old, his father, Ruven Zivotovsky, had uprooted the family from their home in Kiev for a new start in America. Hopeful at the prosperity that the journey promised, Ruven also sought an escape from the rampant anti-Semitism that plagued the Ukraine. For nearly a century, the Judaic community remained the target of widespread pogroms—bloody riots primarily enacted as retribution for the 1821 death of Greek Orthodox patriarch Gregory V. Many

Ukrainians continued to resent the Jews for forcibly carrying out Gregory's execution, and by the time Ruven could transport his family to
America in 1905, there had been over two hundred such riots throughout the country. Although his family would still be poor upon arrival,
the New World would, at least, guarantee them their religious freedom.
Upon arriving in New York, Ruven attempted to westernize his family as
best he could, changing his own name to the less ethnic *Rubin* and the
family's surname to the more palatable *Zevon*. They settled in Brooklyn
only to find that, while they had successfully escaped the bloodshed of
Kiev, their new home presented the obstacles of severe poverty and social
indifference.

Violence and desperation would follow the Zevon family for generations, later becoming major recurring themes in Warren Zevon's music.
When Warren was still a child, his father pulled him aside and reminded
him of the stigma attached to their family's humble roots. "You are a
Jew," he told the boy. "Don't ever forget that."

∞

In Brooklyn, Rubin Zevon had six mouths to feed: his wife, Sadie, and
sons William, Murray, Al, Lou, and Hymie. By his own admission,
William Zevon and his family endured the typical immigrant experience—a life of squalor that he would later succinctly deem as "shit."
The five boys shared the same bed, each sleeping along the mattress's
width. William later admitted that his best memory as a child was receiving a cucumber for his birthday.

"Their father—my grandfather, Rubin—was a tough guy," remembered Murray's son, Sandford Zevon. "And Uncle Willie was also a
tough guy, a pugnacious guy. They called him 'Stumpy' because of his
height, but he would protect my father if there were any problems in the
neighborhood. He worked at the reputation."

To further his image as a young man not to be trifled with, William countered his small physical stature by taking up boxing. He also
made no secret of his aim to escape the poverty in which his family
lived. Seeking prosperity elsewhere, he and his brother Hymie left home
while still in their teens. They headed to Chicago, where it didn't take
long for the brothers to become enamored with the danger and glamor
that the city offered. It was, after all, the home of Al Capone's criminal
empire. Known to law enforcement as the "Chicago Outfit," Capone's

underground conglomerate included bootlegging, prostitution, gambling, and other nefarious activities. Upon arriving in Chicago, William Zevon befriended two up-and-comers within that network—Mickey Cohen and Sam Giancana.

According to Sandford Zevon, it was Giancana who put the ambitious Zevon boys to work running numbers for the mob. "They both became involved with [Giancana], the mafia boss in Chicago," he recalled. "Uncle Willie told me much later, when I visited him, that they were so young at the time, Giancana said they could work for him, but 'no guns.' They could only do book-working and running kinds of stuff, but only because they were still just kids."

During World War II, William and Hymie headed to California. In the eyes of the American public, Hollywood was a glamorous juxtaposition to the war abroad. Much like movie moguls, underworld leaders played into the public's romantic visions of flashbulbs, colorful stucco homes, palm trees, and cool desert winds. The numerous gangsters who had set up camp out west acted as prospectors to an opening market, albeit a criminal one. Arriving in Los Angeles, William reconnected with old friend Mickey Cohen, who was then working under Las Vegas founder Bugsy Siegel. Often portrayed by the media as a sort of criminal "matinee idol," Cohen's picture ran in the Los Angeles society pages almost as often as the celebrity glitterati. He soon put William to work running numbers and collecting gambling debts. Over time, the two became close, and when Cohen got married in 1940, William served as his best man. In his jailhouse memoir written years later, the mobster even recalled assigning William the task of keeping his dog, Toughie, at bay during the midnight wedding ceremony.

William and Hymie opened carpet stores in various western towns, including in Arizona and Fresno, California. At one point, Mickey Cohen's former bodyguard Sam Farkas owned a stake in their Wilshire Boulevard location, fueling rumors of underground dealings happening behind the storefront. Eventually, the brothers had a falling out, leaving William as the chain's sole owner.

Although William was arrested many times for suspicion of racketeering, he always eluded conviction. In his later years, William even entertained his grandchildren by referring to Capone as "Uncle Al" and telling them the infamous mob leader had actually been "a really nice guy."

It was while running the Fresno store that William first met the young woman who would become his unlikely bride and mother to his only son.

∽

Beverly Simmons was exactly half William's age when their courtship began, but being willingly romanced by a fast-talking, forty-two-year-old New York Jewish bachelor was precisely the sort of rebellious act that had been brewing within her. Born on May 30, 1919, she was the product of a strict Mormon upbringing, complete with all its dogmatic tradition. Her parents, Ellsworth Blythe Simmons and Helen Nicholson Cope, were not pleased upon meeting "Stumpy" Zevon, who was easily the most colorful character ever to sit at their kitchen table.

Unlike Jewish immigrant William, Beverly could trace her heritage back decades—a fact that the Simmons family took great pride in acknowledging. All of her great-great-grandparents had either been first-generation American citizens, or were a mere step away from their Anglo-English roots. As practicing Mormons, the Cope-Simmons family tree could even be authenticated to Joseph Smith's initial founding of the Latter-day Saints movement.

Beverly's mother, Helen, was a woman who took her spiritual responsibilities and religious practices very seriously, viewing both as cultural moral codes. Like her own parents, her husband, and her daughter, Helen had been born in Salt Lake City. She married Ellsworth the day after Valentine's Day in 1916. Their first child, Warren, was born the following year. When Beverly was born two years following Warren, it was discovered that she suffered from a crippling congenital heart condition, a fact that fueled her parents' overprotective natures.

In 1946, while the Simmons family was living in Fresno, Beverly met William Zevon at one of his carpet stores. She was quickly drawn to the smooth-talking older man. To the chagrin of her parents, the blushing Anglo-Saxon Mormon girl quickly agreed to marry the wise-cracking Jewish salesman with rumored ties to the mob. At the groom's urging—and against the vehement wishes of Ellsworth and Helen Simmons—the newlyweds relocated to Chicago. The honeymoon was short-lived. Beverly had abandoned her parents' wishes for a traditional Mormon family life, yet the young bride still yearned for a semblance of normalcy to which William never quite related. Years of hard living on the road—drinking, gambling, and fending for himself—had shaped her new husband into a stubborn lone wolf. His personality and unorthodox lifestyle blurred the fine line between self-reliance and selfish bachelorhood. It was the latter which kept him out all night, playing marathon poker games and carousing until the wee small hours of the morning. None of that had changed by the time Beverly gave birth to Warren the following year.

William may have made it a point to instill in his son a self-awareness of his Judaic heritage, but the reverent tradition associated with it never seemed to factor into his roles as husband and father. Instead, young Warren was often subject to the fruits of his mother's own strict childhood. The theological aspects, however, never truly sank in. "I was brought up with religious beliefs, Christian religious beliefs," Warren later remembered. "But it's one of life's great searches and I don't like talking about it. And I don't like talking about it more than I do in my songs."

In later years, he would be significantly more candid discussing the internal conflicts and personal demons that plagued his adulthood, attributing them to his ancestral namesake: Beverly's older brother, Warren Cope Simmons, who had been born on the Fourth of July and later gave his life for his country as a member of the 30th Infantry Regiment—killed in action on November 10, 1943, while on a tour in Italy. The elder Warren's legacy had been immortalized in a painting that hung in Ellsworth and Helen's home. Like a specter, it had haunted the younger Warren throughout his youth. "Uncle Warren was sort of the dead figurehead of the family, and I was brought up to follow in his footsteps," he later claimed. "My ideal was supposed to be a dead man—with my name, looks and career intentions. A dead warrior who'd been waylaid by his heroism. I guess that kind of background gave me the idea that destroying myself was the only way to live up to expectations."

During Warren's adolescence, his parents separated and reconciled nearly as often as they changed their place of residence. Although born in Chicago, Warren was primarily raised by Beverly in Fresno, where she eventually returned to live on the same street as her parents. Ellsworth and Helen Simmons refused to let their daughter live down the strange life that she had chosen for herself, making Warren witness to the verbal venom often directed toward his mother and absentee father. As Warren later claimed, "They treated him like a vagabond and a roustabout. It must have been terribly uncomfortable for him, so he wasn't there a lot of the time. I wouldn't have been either, if I'd had a choice."

Having already weathered a long string of fights and separations from her husband, Beverly saw the darkest side of William Zevon one Christmas morning when Warren was nine years old. The couple was in the midst of one of their frequent separations and William arrived at the house unannounced to see his son. He had been up all night playing poker and had won Warren a Christmas present—an upright Chickering piano. Reluctant for Warren to be influenced by his father in any way, Beverly was adamant that the piano had to go. But for the child, the piano was a special gift that his father had specifically won just for *him*. It was the first musical instrument the boy had ever gotten his hands on and he was instantly fascinated by it. As Warren watched, his father ran to the kitchen and, like a circus performer, hurled a carving knife across the room. Missing Beverly's head by barely an inch, the blade impaled the wall behind her. More terrified than angry, she fled to her parents' house down the street.

William, however, calmed himself and sat Warren down on the piano bench. "Son, you know I gotta go," he told the boy. "She's your mother, so I guess you gotta stay."

Warren was left behind to be raised in the forced regimentation and cold tradition of his mother and her parents. As irresponsible as he was, William had been Warren's greatest champion, the parent who envisioned big things for his son's future. The gift of a piano had proven the faith he had in the boy.

The Christmas episode would always hold a lasting impression on Warren. Not only had that morning ushered in an era of fatherless adolescence, but it had provided him a ringside seat to a first glimpse at real violence. And it had all been over a piano, no less. *His* piano—the first one he had ever touched.

For Warren Zevon, music and danger would forever be entwined.

∞

Although William wasn't present during much of his son's youth, his intuition regarding Warren's potential rang true. Throughout his elementary school years, Warren sat at the piano every chance he had, displaying a prodigious gift for recognizing and replicating melodies. An imaginative and intelligent child, he was soon using music as an escape from the turmoil of his home life. His passion for the instrument was to the apparent resentment of Beverly, who saw much of her husband's personality in their young son. Begrudgingly, she slowly learned to accept it. When Warren was old enough to purchase his first guitar, she watched as he mastered that instrument, as well. By the time William could charm his way back into her life a few years later, their son had become an accomplished musician.

Granting William one more chance, Beverly moved into his ocean-front house in San Pedro and enrolled Warren in the local junior high school. There, Warren threw himself into the musical program. Although the piano and guitar were his true extracurricular passions, Warren's ambition for a well-rounded education in music theory was quickly established; in a group high school yearbook photo of the program's "Wind and Percussion Section," a young Warren is posed clutching a clarinet, although his interest in mastering that particular instrument soon waned.

Quickly recognizing the young man's talent, the school's band teacher pulled some professional strings and arranged for Warren to visit the West Hollywood home of famed Russian composer Igor Stravinsky. Now thirteen years old, Warren found himself discussing music theory with Stravinsky and his protégé, Robert Craft. In later years, Warren was often asked about this influential encounter by numerous journalists. "[I was brought to a session] by the band teacher at Dana Junior High School," he claimed. "He was a classical session player, a trumpet player. He took me to a Stravinsky–Robert Craft session, and after that, I corresponded with Robert Craft and he invited me to come and visit them—which I did. So, I met Stravinsky, but I was in no way friends with him or anything."

Craft, a renowned composer in his own right, also enjoyed young Warren's precocious nature and maturity. "Though [Warren] seemed much younger than I anticipated," he later recalled, "he was self-possessed and articulate beyond his years. After some conversation, I played recordings of contemporary pieces, not available commercially and unknown to him. He was keenly attentive and his responses were unambiguous; very young people are always judgmental, of course, but he supported his judgments with acute arguments . . . Mr. Zevon, on that first visit, reminded me of my own first meeting with Stravinsky, though I was ten years older and much less intelligent."

Stravinsky and Craft had lasting impressions on Warren. At the time, he had been tempted to drop the piano to devote himself fully to the electric guitar. But the two composers successfully instilled in Warren a new love of classical music equal to his ongoing passion for rock and roll. He dedicated himself to studying advanced music theory, poring over original Stockhausen scores and listening to obscure German radio performances alone in his bedroom. He soon began working on an ambitious symphony of his own, titled simply *Symphony No. 1*— a project that he would tinker with for decades. Much to his disappointment, however, the visits with Stravinsky abruptly ended when Beverly left William for the final time and dragged him back to Fresno.

As Warren later remembered, "Nobody ever told me anything, and my parents' marriage has been a mystery to me all my life. They didn't even let me know that they'd gotten a divorce until long after the fact."

Ties to his father's lineage weren't completely severed. Just prior to the return to Fresno, Warren had finally met his Uncle Murray's son, Sandford. Then undergoing a medical school residency in nearby San Francisco, Sandford wanted to introduce his new wife, Madeline, to his notorious gangster uncle. He had also heard much about his talented younger cousin. The newlyweds took a daytrip to William's Fresno home for what would be a memorable visit. "My Uncle Willie, who was pretty well-off financially at the time, had a beautiful home on the cliffs overlooking the Pacific Ocean," Sandford remembered. "I knew of Warren, but I didn't meet him until then, when he was about twelve years old and I was about twenty-eight, or something like that. Uncle Willie was very proud of him and he thought he was a genius and had him play the piano for us. To my ears, it sounded crazy—Warren banging away at the piano—but I remember my uncle yelling, 'He's great!'"

The cousins didn't see each other again until Warren was in his late teens, then only bumping into each other at a family bar mitzvah. At that point, Warren was already a recording artist and laying the groundwork for his first solo album. Years later, however, Sandford would become a crucial emotional resource to Warren and the two would remain close for decades.

☙

Against Warren's wishes, Beverly enrolled him in McLane High School the following year. He hadn't taken the move back from San Pedro well, feeling the sting of losing his father for the second time. Adding insult to injury, Beverly now had a new man in her life, a local handyman named Elmer Reinhardt who had been hired to fix their roof. The decision to enter into a new relationship not only severed any chance of her reconciling with William again, but also created a rivalry for her affection between son and suitor. Once Elmer moved in, it was accepted that Warren would be treated like an unwanted stepchild, and the new man of the house had no bones about making the boy feel like an intruder. Desperate to make this new relationship last, Beverly allowed Elmer to constantly demonstrate his indifference toward Warren and was soon enacting a form of it herself.

Now in his teens, Warren began to show signs of becoming a rebellious loner like his father. Pockmarked and inherently shy, he used both his musical skills and sarcasm as tools to win friends and attention from girls. He donned faded jeans and T-shirts and coupled his new image with a bad attitude and growing affection for rock music. Although his love of classical music was strong as ever, he downplayed it for the sake of popularity among his peers. He could often be seen around the schoolyard with his guitar, showing off his ability to play popular rock-and-roll tunes by ear. Claiming to hold one of the highest IQs ever recorded in the Fresno school system as a badge of honor, Warren proudly toed the line between class clown and stifled intellectual. When he wasn't out goofing off with his buddies, he was usually alone in his bedroom, poring over books. A vivacious reader since childhood, Warren now devoured everything from great literature to dime-store pulp novels—all of which would have lasting impacts on his lyrics and musical themes.

When word eventually got home that his behavior had grown disruptive in the classroom, the beatings from Elmer began. Ever resilient, Warren took the blows that his stepfather doled out and began spending as little time at home as possible—usually just long enough to swipe booze from Elmer's private stash. At fifteen years old, he was drinking regularly. His nights were spent carousing with friends, attempting to pick up girls, and jamming with the few other students who shared his love of music. Coming into young adulthood, Warren was honing his skills in two areas—songwriting and smooth-talking his way out of trouble. He was soon a master of both.

∞

William Zevon eventually adhered to Warren's pleas to get him as far away from Beverly and Elmer as possible. He reappeared in his son's life just long enough to put him in touch with a business acquaintance in San Francisco—an aspiring music producer named Ben Shapiro. As a favor to William, Shapiro agreed to act as benefactor to Warren and his bandmates, staking them with new instruments and an apartment of their own. In exchange, the boys were to grind out quick, commercial fare that could be presented to various record companies. Warren leapt at the chance to record original material and quickly gathered his neighborhood crew—David Cardosa on drums, John Cates on bass, and Glenn Crocker on keyboards. Early the next day, the boys loaded up the car and headed south.

After only a few weeks, the boys concluded that Shapiro had fewer contacts within the music industry than they'd believed. When the boys' demos failed to yield a quick buck, he immediately cut off their funding. It made little difference to Warren. The relationship with Shapiro had, at least, earned the band new gear and a few precious weeks in a five-bedroom loft on Thirty-Fifth Avenue—a far cry from living under Elmer's roof. Warren was determined never to return to that situation. Weeks before, as he and his friends had loaded up the car for San Francisco, Beverly had made it perfectly clear that there was no love lost between them. She had not seen them off, or uttered a word of goodbye.

He started telling new friends and acquaintances that his mother was dead.

∞

Needing a place to stay, Warren again contacted his father. William Zevon had since moved to Culver City, and viewed his son's request as an opportunity for the two to make up on lost time. He obliged, and was soon indulging Warren the best ways he knew how—doling out wads of his poker winnings and buying him a yellow Corvette Stingray. William's chain of carpet stores—coupled with his full-time gambling and part-time bookmaking—had grown successful enough for father and son to then relocate to Los Angeles. There, Warren planned to focus on a real future in the music industry.

Believing in his son's talents completely, William would often drive him to San Francisco, enabling the young troubadour to bum around Haight-Ashbury and play in local folk clubs. Warren was in his element. But while his aptitude for devouring books, culture, and classical music was one thing, putting that intelligence to use in the classroom was quite another. His capability to excel musically, while still partying all night, had proven just that. Ever since getting his first piano, the one consistency in Warren's life had been a passion for music. But mastery required time. While far from lazy, he was slowly displaying the first signs that his creative process required a benefactor—financially or emotionally, or both. He had no problem if someone else could keep the lights on, thus clearing his schedule for rehearsal time and musical woodshedding.

Warren's tendency to allow someone else to foot the bills and responsibilities, leaving him free to focus his creative energies, would become a trend throughout his life. As he approached adulthood and his seriousness toward a career in music grew deeper, who better to provide that support than the one person who had always believed in him—his gangster father?

∞

Leaving Fresno may have liberated Warren from Beverly and Elmer, but it had also meant abandoning his neighborhood friends and bandmates. When he entered Fairfax High School as a sophomore in the fall of 1964, he became a loner once again. Without an audience to play to, the class clown routine largely subsided. It was replaced by a brooding, pensive demeanor and a growing maturity toward his musical ambitions. As William spent most of his nights carousing and gambling, he'd be at home sleeping throughout the day. In order to focus on new songs and avoid his father's hangover, Warren hung around the school after classes let out. Most afternoons, he could be found alone in the courtyard, strumming his acoustic guitar and working out song ideas.

One afternoon that spring, he caught the attention of a pretty transfer student. Like Warren, Violet Santangelo was new to Fairfax. She had already attended three different high schools in that year alone and the transient nature of her adolescence had hit her hard. As she spied him noodling with his guitar, she sensed a kindred spirit. "I was sitting on the grass and Warren had his guitar and, call it 'divine intervention,' I went right over to him," she remembered. And while it was uncharacteristic of her to initiate a conversation with a boy she didn't know, in doing so, the shy seventeen-year-old (who would later adopt the stage name "Laura Kenyon") inadvertently launched both of their careers in the music industry.

Kenyon's family had just relocated from Chicago and the sunny atmosphere of Los Angeles presented a fair amount of culture shock. The former East Coast Italian girl found it difficult to relate to the laid-back, blond surfer types who seemed to be everywhere. "When I got to California, the kids were sitting around during fourth period and I asked, 'Why aren't you in class?' They were all sitting around eating fruit and one of them said to me, 'Well, it's Nutrition Period.' And I thought, 'Oh boy, this place is serious.'"

Coming from a playful and sarcastic family, Kenyon wasn't taken aback by Warren's initial standoffishness or his quips directed toward her. Instead, she played along. Her ability to grasp his dry humor—and even give it right back—was a trait that immediately won him over. "I also had that streak," she remembered, "and maybe he noticed that I had been sitting all by myself, too. But our connection happened right away."

While Warren was no stranger to cruising around to pick up girls, he was unaccustomed to one making the first move. His awkwardness came out as both boyish charm and some of his father's old-fashioned chauvinism. As he took Kenyon for a ride in the Corvette Stingray, he tried to play it cool, feigning disgust at the classical music that popped up on his car radio. "I hate that shit," he barked. It was obviously for her benefit, but that reflexive temper made a lasting impression on her. "That was one of the first indications I had about him," she recalled. "Here was a strong person who was angry. Coming from the family that I had, I could handle it and maybe Warren knew it. When you're young, you just sense all that, and I sensed an inner anger."

Warren took her back to the apartment he shared with his father. Things didn't go smoothly, as William Zevon was recovering from another booze-soaked gambling marathon. "When I walked in, his father was sitting right there," Kenyon remembered. "He was wearing a beige shirt and rumpled pants and looked really disheveled and unshaven and looked like a really miserable man."

Soon after, Kenyon would learn just how miserable William was capable of being. During a visit to the Zevon home a few weeks later, she and Warren entered to find that William was stone drunk in the middle of the day. "He called me a 'whore' and a 'snake' and suggested I dig a hole in the ground and crawl into it," she recalled. To her surprise, Warren merely laughed it off. She then understood that much of Warren's own temper stemmed from his father.

Kenyon recalled that Warren's bedroom was in a constant state of disarray and always appeared "transient" in its neglect. Books, notes, and record albums littered the floor and unmade bed. As music was his only priority, Warren just couldn't be bothered to face any responsibility that he viewed as mundane, such as tidying up or folding clothes.

That afternoon, they sat on his bed for hours, singing Beatles songs together and trying out two-part harmonies. Warren was excited to discover that Kenyon shared his passion for music and was quite a natural singer, and she was instantly impressed with his original songs and his guitar playing. Although it was still uncertain if she viewed him romantically, Warren seemed at ease knowing he might have found a potential collaborator. While all his buddies had returned home following the Ben Shapiro fiasco, he had remained steadfast in his commitment to get recorded. A new partner could be a great find.

The two made plans to jam together again. This time, however, at her house.

ᚙ

For the next few weeks, the two met every day after school. They usually ended up at the Santangelo home, where her parents were delighted to hear the duo rehearsing together or to watch Warren perform on the family's sixty-six-key piano. As both he and Kenyon were originally from Chicago, they bonded over shared memories of the Clark Theater, as well as their mutual interests in jazz, folk music, literature, and movies. Although platonic, it was the first intimate relationship for either of them. "There was a love between us," Kenyon remembered. "It was so innocent and sweet."

Sweet as the love may have been, Warren was, nonetheless, a teenage boy. One afternoon, he made his lone attempt to make the relationship physical. When Kenyon rebuffed his advances, Warren offered a glimpse of the anger she had long suspected he suppressed. "He tried to kiss me one time," she recalled, "but I didn't have those feelings for him. He was hurt and embarrassed and called me a lesbian. We eventually made up and our time together continued." Having met Warren's father and experienced his volatile demeanor firsthand, she tried hard to understand Warren's constant angst. "But that was the hardest part about knowing him. That was the person that had turned the radio off in the car and cursed the music our first afternoon together. That anger was always there."

Warren made amends with Kenyon by offering her the greatest compliment she would ever receive from him. "You know what I like about you?" he had quietly asked her. "When you're seventy, you'll still have something to say."

And moments like that kept her at his side.

⁂

One night while visiting Kenyon's home, her family asked the duo to perform some of their songs for the evening's dinner guests. It was the first time they had been asked to show off their well-rehearsed skills and, at least in Kenyon's case, to perform for an audience of any size. Confident as ever, Warren picked up his acoustic guitar and the two ran through a few favorite Beatles tunes. Unbeknownst to either, there was a special guest in attendance that night.

"My older sister was dating a former child actor named Michael Burns," Kenyon remembered. "His mother worked at White Whale Records, which had discovered the Turtles, and was dating one of its founders, a man named Lee Lasseff. Michael came up to us after we had performed for everyone and said that he wanted to tell his mom all about us. Warren and I were absolutely ecstatic." True to his word, Burns was able to set up a meeting between Lasseff and the young folk duo later that same week.

Lasseff and business partner Ted Feigin had founded White Whale Records in 1963 following a visit to the Revelaire Club in Los Angeles. There, they had seen a performance by a local surf rock band calling themselves the Crossfires. Recognizing potential in the group, Lasseff and Feigin signed them as White Whale's first artists. In turn, the band's leaders, Mark Volman and Howard Kaylan, had taken a cue from popular radio favorite the Byrds and retooled their sound for a more folkish quality. Renamed the Turtles, the band recorded a cover of Bob Dylan's "It Ain't Me, Babe" and scored the burgeoning record label an instant hit. Having hit pay dirt, White Whale's founders continued to produce more Turtles singles, all of which cracked the Top 30 during the label's first year.

Not wanting their overnight success to quickly fade, the two founders were on an active lookout for new talent. With a youthful innocence reminiscent of other successful boy-girl folk duos such as Ian and Sylvia, Warren and Laura Kenyon (still known by the exotic-sounding Violet Santangelo), perfectly fit the bill.

In preparation for their meeting at White Whale, Warren and Kenyon decided they needed to name their act. They sat at the Santangelos' kitchen table and brainstormed for hours. Warren was an admirer of e.e. cummings and opted to mimic the poet's stylish discounting of capitalization for his stage name, then coupled it with an homage to his favorite color at the time—green. Kenyon, for her part, drew inspiration from her favorite French film, Serge Bourguignon's *Sundays and Cybèle*. A few days later, "lyme and cybelle" walked into Lee Lasseff's luxurious office on Sunset Boulevard.

"Lee Lasseff brought us into his office, a huge white room with a huge desk," Kenyon remembered. "It was surreal. You could sense this odd feeling, like a sleazy thing. It was intimidating for a shy seventeen-year-old." For the meeting, Lasseff was joined by Feigin, a significantly taller man who, when standing next to his partner, gave the two an appearance of a mismatched comedy act. They asked Warren and Kenyon to play some songs and were immediately pleased with what they heard, offering a contract on the spot for the release of at least one single. To Warren's additional delight, Lasseff and Feigin had expressed a particular enthusiasm for his songwriting abilities and instructed the duo to prepare an original song for the recording session. If the teens hadn't been intimidated before, they certainly were now. Up until that point, Kenyon had only sung for friends and family, while Warren acknowledged that this was his first real attempt at composing a professional piece of music. Both knew there was a lot riding on the opportunity.

Lasseff and Feigin began to scout for the appropriate producer to helm lyme and cybelle's debut. They chose Dayton "Bones" Howe, a twenty-eight-year-old sound engineer who had previously worked with Elvis Presley and the Mamas and the Papas. For the latter, Howe had engineered "California Dreamin'" earlier that same year, quickly establishing himself as a major studio presence. The White Whale moguls yearned for that same kind of success, while Howe was looking for advancement as a producer. He had also co-produced White Whale's biggest hit, "It Ain't Me, Babe," and felt his reputation warranted such a leap. When Lasseff and Feigin approached their promotional team for a recommendation as to who should helm lyme and cybelle's first track, Howe was unanimously selected.

"At the time, I was an independent studio engineer," recalled Howe. "I had engineered a lot of records by then and quite a few turned out to be hits. People began to talk about me—first the musicians, whom I worked well with, and then people in the industry. I saw the lyme and cybelle debut as an opportunity to get another song on the radio while I was still dealing with the insanity of the Turtles." He met with Warren and Kenyon at White Whale a few weeks later and was enthralled with the raw talent that he heard, comparing Kenyon's voice to "freshly fallen snow." Howe also felt a connection with Warren's hunger for perfection.

∽

With a recording contract in hand, Warren borrowed enough money from his father to rent an apartment in the Hollywood Hills. The small bachelor pad, located on Orchid Avenue, soon became his personal think tank, a haven where he could play as loudly as he wanted, whenever he wanted. The threat of Fresno had been permanently extinguished, as had any intention of returning to school in the fall. While most sixteen-year-olds were contemplating upcoming vacations and their first summer jobs, Warren had a record contract and a place of his own. As far as he was concerned, his childhood was happily over.

Before he could enjoy all the freedoms that living alone afforded, however, Warren threw himself into finishing his first assignment for White Whale. Fueled at the prospect of having a song on the radio, he wracked his brain for an idea that he and Kenyon could present to the label. Always with a guitar he began to develop a simple riff that he had already been toying with—something psychedelic that could be adapted perfectly for an acoustic duet. The composition also had the potential to work well if sped up, or if he were asked to make it "catchier" for the airwaves. His recent interest in "raga rock," the Indian-influenced, trippy sound that the Beatles would soon take into the mainstream, rounded out the unique tone.

Kenyon recalled that Warren was the first person she had ever heard experimenting with the Indian style. "That riff that he came up with, that was the thing that he was most interested in," she said. "The sounds themselves, that's what got him—and that's really what makes a real composer. They get something stuck in their head, a motif. And that was Warren. He looked at me and said, 'I have this thing I'm working on—now improvise over it.' I did, and I wrote those lyrics right on the spot." The two named their composition "Follow Me."

Throughout his career, many of Warren's best-known songs were collaborative efforts, although he would sometimes go to great lengths to conceal that fact. As his reputation as a songwriter grew, that trend would continue—sometimes to disastrous results. His youthful insistence on sole songwriting credit sometimes led to the termination of close friendships. At the time, however, he and Kenyon were both fresh blood in the music industry and shared an equal desire to deliver a quality song for White Whale as soon as possible. Kenyon was also nervous about disappointing Warren, whose ambition to be a professional musician predated their friendship. She was reluctant to offer any ideas he might consider subpar to his own high standards. "It was so scary because I didn't want to lose him," she later admitted, "and the whole idea of having a record contract was just too fabulous to ruin."

Only a few days after moving in, Warren invited Kenyon and Howe to his new apartment, presenting them with a polished version of "Follow Me." He also had a mixed bag of assorted compositions to show Howe and spent the evening jumping back and forth between his guitars and the new piano he had bought. The producer was truly impressed with the wide array of genres that Warren was capable of playing—jazz, blues, rock, and classical alike. But with "Follow Me," Howe believed that the duo had a real shot at a hit. "We went through a bunch of material and Warren came up with this thing, 'Follow Me,'" remembered Howe. "I thought that it had enough heat in it as a track to really get some attention." The following afternoon, the three of them presented it to a very satisfied Lasseff at the White Whale office. The recording session was immediately booked.

Just prior to the recording date, Warren crafted a new persona for himself, making his stage name "stephen lyme," complete with a new wardrobe entirely consisting of green garments. "He had decked the whole apartment in green, too," remembered Howe, "and even had a fake nickname to match, 'Sandy.' So it was sometimes 'Stephen,' with the small 's,' or sometimes 'Sandy.' I called him Warren to make it easier on us all."

The confusing, interchanging personas didn't last long. Warren remembered that his cousin, Sandford, was already his family's original "Sandy," and eventually considered that two stage names may be one too many. Processing an ever-evolving image, however, would last his entire career.

∽

Following White Whale's approval, turnaround became rapid. Howe brought Warren and Kenyon into Sunset Studios, believing that the song—which to him sounded "like a pipe dream come to life"—would eventually be viewed as the first true psychedelic record. A musician himself, Howe sat in for the sessions on drums, proving himself a perfect foil for the multitalented Warren. The two also shared an appreciation for using unorthodox instrumentation, demonstrated in Howe's suggestion to use a jawbone as part of the song's percussion section. "It was an easy record to make," recalled Howe. "[Warren and Kenyon] took direction in the studio very well and we basically built the song off of the rhythm section that I put together. We added their parts later, the way we often did in the studio at the time, and I was happy when it ended up having a kind of samba feel to it. Warren really got a kick out of that jawbone."

For the B-side, White Whale selected "Like the Seasons," another original that Warren and Kenyon had composed together. Increasingly afraid to lose Warren as a friend and partner, she held her tongue when it was released without her co-writing credit. That decision proved difficult when she learned that the Turtles were planning to cover it. Their front men, Howard Kaylan and Mark Volman, admired Warren's songwriting style and were soon introducing him around the Los Angeles music scene. With their influence, he was dually signed as a house songwriter to White Whale's affiliate division, Ishmael Music.

The new status earned Warren the recognition he had hoped for, yet came with certain personal repercussions. While it provided the leverage to compose more varied kinds of music for the company's other bands, it also gave him a stricter claim over any future songs that saw his name attached—something that could negatively affect his working relationship with Kenyon.

As "Follow Me / Like the Seasons" was only the seventh single that White Whale had released since the company's formation, Lasseff and Feigin wanted to push its chart potential. To generate a buzz, Warren and Kenyon were booked at a few local venues around Southern California, the largest of which was a national television appearance on the popular variety program *The Lloyd Thaxton Show*. For many teenagers, Thaxton dictated what was hot and hip and was regarded as Los Angeles's answer to Ed Sullivan. The Turtles, the Kingston Trio, and Marvin Gaye had all appeared on the program just prior to achieving larger fame. The night that Warren and Kenyon performed, they were joined by chart-topper Jackie DeShannon. "I had a friend do our costumes," remembered Kenyon. "We were incredibly nervous and Warren knew that we needed a unique look. I had these white stockings, knickers, and this cashmere suit. Warren wore the same colors and we looked really, really great when they brought us out to perform."

The exposure worked and, to the surprise of White Whale and the performers themselves, "Follow Me" cracked the local Top 10. More importantly, the track peaked at 65 on the national *Billboard* pop charts that April—a strong achievement for a new act's debut.

Eager to keep the momentum going, Lasseff and Feigin instructed Howe to get Warren and Kenyon back into the studio as soon as possible.

Initially, Howe wanted to produce a cover of Simon and Garfunkel's "The Sound of Silence" as the duo's second release, but the label nixed his suggestion in favor of Bob Dylan's "If You Gotta Go, Go Now." The switch was just fine with Warren, as Dylan was, and would remain, one of his songwriting idols. According to Howe, White Whale's priorities at the time had slowly shifted to reflect other companies within the music industry—pushing for full albums over singles, ultimately leading to larger profits. "That was the mentality," recalled Howe. "You know, you only made an album if you had a hit single that you could attach to it, then sell a few thousand albums and make some real money. White

Whale hadn't always been an 'album-oriented' company, but it changed after the Turtles' 'It Ain't Me, Babe.' So, we did a bunch of demos and 'If You Gotta Go, Go Now' was the only one that seemed like it had any possibilities. Unfortunately, it really didn't go anywhere."

The failure of lyme and cybelle's second single could largely be chalked up to bad publicity. Bill Gavin, a former radio personality and social commentator, had publicly denounced the song as "sexually suggestive," leading to criticism and boycotts. At the time, such a backlash wasn't uncommon; in 1957, The Everly Brothers' "Wake Up Little Susie" had been banned in Boston for similar innuendos and, in 1965, the Beatles' "Norwegian Wood" found widespread media opposition. But while those songs had gone on to prove their accusers wrong and become hits, White Whale was a small record label that didn't have the resources to push the song through the controversy. Ultimately, Warren and Kenyon's follow-up didn't even chart. "What was so sad about the whole thing was that our first song had shot up the charts in LA," recalled Kenyon. "This was real heartbreak for us."

The failure of the single posed a real problem for both White Whale and the duo—Warren in particular. While the song was a Bob Dylan composition, its B-side was a lyme and cybelle original entitled "I'll Go On." Without charting, the release did nothing to raise awareness about him as a songwriter.

His days as stephen lyme were numbered.

CHAPTER TWO

(1966–1970)

"WARREN WAS PROBABLY DRINKING BEFORE I MET HIM," remembered Kenyon, not knowing just how right she was. Warren had been no stranger to alcohol since early adolescence. He had taken his first underage drink in the home of Igor Stravinsky and, later, was regularly swiping booze from his stepfather's personal stash. By age eighteen, he viewed alcohol as old hat. As his adult years began—with a song on the radio, a television appearance under his belt, an apartment near the Sunset Strip, and a Corvette bought with his father's gangster money—Warren was getting his first taste of the rock-and-roll lifestyle. It wasn't long before harder substances became available to him.

By mid-1966, he was spending more and more time with other seasoned musicians, all of whom became powerful influences in fueling both his creativity and interest in mind-expanding drugs. The closest of these friends was David Marks, a founding member of the Beach Boys. According to Laura Kenyon, Warren became completely enamored of Marks's humor and experience, believing Marks to be "the funniest, smartest person he knew."

"I was driving around and heard that lyme and cybelle song—I think it was 'Follow Me'—playing on the radio," remembered Marks. "I found out that Warren was signed to White Whale, along with my friends in the Turtles, so I made it a point to stop down there. Warren and I became fast friends and, eventually, I started sleeping at his place on Orchid Avenue. I guess I was there so much that I even left my own mattress back behind his small kitchen near the bathroom." Within a few weeks, he and Warren were spending all their days and nights together jamming, talking art and philosophy, and sharing the hallucinogens that Marks seemed to always have on hand.

The Orchid Avenue apartment soon became an unofficial boy's club, further alienating the female half of lyme and cybelle. "[Marks] had a very strong influence on Warren, a bad effect, and I didn't think that Warren needed that," Kenyon recalled. "But those two had a communication with each other that was unbelievable. Warren kept saying how David was 'super brilliant' and quoting him and laughing at all of his jokes. I guess that the influence made Warren think differently about music and his own writing."

Kenyon added, "It was also around that time that White Whale dropped him as a writer."

The label's decision to release Warren from his writing contract may have come suddenly, but not as a surprise. Most record companies had a low tolerance for new talent that hadn't broken out quickly, and the faltering of lyme and cybelle's second single had shown the record executives the writing on the wall. By that point, a full-length album was already out of the question. But what most record executives had an even lower tolerance for was the excessive drug and alcohol use that, more often than not, accompanied musicians and their entourages. In the case of established stars, such behavior was strongly frowned upon, but reluctantly tolerated with the turn of a blind eye. In new artists, however, it was seen as a red flag. Warren still fell into the latter group. That combination, plus his growing insistence for more creative control, brought the hammer down on his association with Ishmael Music.

While the failure of "If You Gotta Go, Go Now" was not necessarily the end of lyme and cybelle, it was the beginning of the end for Warren and Kenyon's collaborative partnership. Having lost his credentials as a house songwriter, Warren's heart was no longer in lyme and cybelle. His time was now completely divided between working on his own solo compositions and carousing with his powerful buddies around Los Angeles's clubs and party scene. Kenyon, along with White Whale's executives, had noticed the shift in Warren's priorities. "He had just written a song called 'I See the Lights,'" she remembered, "and I was at the session for the demo, but there was this energy that I wasn't a part of. I was sitting alone in the booth and he was doing this quiet thing to me that Dylan probably did to Baez—I guess just a mood shift when you're a composer. You fly and leave people behind you. When our second song hadn't taken off, it was a drag, so he just started writing new material really fast. He didn't need me and made it quite clear. I couldn't connect with him anymore."

∞

"White Whale introduced us to Warren and we treated him like a kid, even though he was really one of our contemporaries," Turtles front man Howard Kaylan remembered. "But he was so talented and brilliant and such a nice guy, that we liked him immediately and took him under our wing. I, personally, got really close to Warren. We would hang out and drop tons of acid and go down to this seedy place called Pioneer Chicken and just get silly together. He was a kid, but his songwriting was incredible and I knew what he was writing was the sort of direction that the Turtles should have been going in."

The band had released their cover of "Outside Chance" as a lead single in early 1966 and, as a favor to Warren, repackaged it as a B-side only months later, over White Whale's objections. Toward the end of the year, they forced White Whale to release their version of lyme and cybelle's "Like the Seasons" twice consecutively—first as a B-side to "Can I Get to Know You Better," and then again as the flip for their biggest hit, "Happy Together." When that song proved an instant smash in February 1967, Warren scored his most profitable royalty check to date.

As Kaylan had anticipated, White Whale was furious at the band's stubbornness in recycling Warren's song as the flip side, but he knew the move would bring their new compatriot some much-needed revenue. Kaylan was right, as "Happy Together" became the label's greatest success, bumping the Beatles' "Penny Lane" from the Number 1 spot on the *Billboard* Hot 100 the following month. It was an incredibly rare case of the *artist* securing songwriter royalties—an appropriately flipped version of what was commonly known in the music industry as the "flip-side racket." In a flip-side racket, artists or their producers would intentionally place an "undesirable" track (such as an instrumental or a previously released track) as the B-side, therefore ensuring that the A-side would get the most attention. In this case, the members of the

Turtles pushed Warren's song to be the B-side, not so much to ensure the success of the A-side, but to guarantee that his track received royalties merely for its inclusion anywhere on the vinyl single.

"I don't think I have higher praise for anybody that I've met or encountered in this field than to say, 'I realize this is money that could be going into my pocket,'" Kaylan remembered, "'I'd rather it go into his.' Believe me, we were not always that selfless. I don't remember doing that again, even with an ex-wife. But, in Warren's case, he was a very, very special person. We wanted him to share in our good fortune."

Warren celebrated by replacing his Corvette with a brand-new Jaguar.

White Whale's second executive decision in their attempt to keep lyme and cybelle functioning was to replace Warren outright with another musician, manufacturing a doppelgänger to assume the stage name of "stephen lyme" while retaining Kenyon's services as the female counterpart. She had no say in the matter and knew that the record label was merely grasping at straws. The act's new incarnation, with former Monkees backup singer Wayne Erwin plugged into Warren's place, lasted only long enough to record a third and final single. "[Erwin] composed, he had a guitar, and he had had his own group," remembered Kenyon. "So, I inherited him—or he inherited me. Whichever it was, I didn't care for that feeling."

As far as Kenyon was concerned, the new version of lyme and cybelle had strayed too far from its original vision—two best friends having fun collaborating on folk tunes. Before long, new members were integrated into the act and Kenyon was relegated to standing on stage, shaking a tambourine. It came to a screeching halt one night following a gig at the Sea Witch, a popular Sunset Boulevard venue. Erwin pulled Kenyon aside and informed her that the band was going off on its own, without her participation. "Oh, great," she said to him. "You're firing me from my own band." The move left her confused and heartbroken.

At that point, her attempts to make contact with Warren had become futile. As the folk revival began to wane, the drugs, alcohol, and company that Warren kept all began to push him further into the world of harder-edged, experimental rock music. At no time was Kenyon more crushed than when, just over a year later, she came upon Warren's eventual solo debut. "There was a place on Hollywood Boulevard where you could take an album into a booth and listen," she remembered. "Warren's album had just come out and I went by myself and listened to it. It wasn't the Warren I knew."

The album's cover said it all—credited solely to "Zevon," it made no mention of his previous participation in lyme and cybelle, and with his hair grown long and bohemian, the shy blond boy from the schoolyard was all but unrecognizable. Kenyon sadly accepted that her partner was gone for good. At a friend's suggestion, she enrolled at the University of Southern California the following year, earning a full scholarship in the Theatre Arts department. She didn't see Warren again until well after her move to New York in 1970, where she was making her way as a Broadway performer. By then, Warren was on the cusp of stardom and the lyme and cybelle releases had gone out of print.

Save for a few commercial jingle gigs and a session appearance on Phil Ochs's *Pleasures of the Harbor,* Warren approached the end of the decade in a state of career limbo. While he had made some powerful friends in the music industry, he was without a solid recording contract of his own. Thanks to his growing reputation for literate and thoughtful songwriting, however, he had just enough money coming in to keep chasing the ghost.

Prior to exiting lyme and cybelle, Warren had already begun to polish material for Bones Howe and knew that if he could stick it out a little longer, a solo album would be in the cards. The personas of "stephen lyme" and "Sandy Zevon" were skins to be shed.

Warren Zevon was coming into his own.

That summer, his hard-partying lifestyle nearly came to a screeching halt.

One night toward the end of August 1967, Warren and David Marks had been carousing with the Turtles at the Whisky A Go-Go, when a surprise telegram arrived for the band. To everyone's amazement, it was a message from George Harrison. In a gesture of congratulations for having successfully bumped the Beatles at the top of the *Billboard* chart months before, the legendary guitarist had invited all Turtles members and their friends to his place on Blue Jay Way.

As always, Marks had come prepared, his pockets loaded with LSD capsules. What he and the group hadn't counted on, however, was the number of cars that lined the road leading up to Harrison's house, nor the valets that he had hired. "We got as far as where they were parking the cars and one of the attendants had an attitude," Marks recalled. "One of the guys in my car mouthed off to him and he ended up being an undercover cop. He dragged us all out of my car and lined us up."

As the officer slowly inched toward them, Marks suddenly realized he was still carrying copious amounts of illegal drugs throughout his clothes. With no other option, he reached into his pockets and quickly gobbled up every ounce of the hallucinogens, popping the last one just as he and the officer came face-to-face.

Knowing full well what effects drugs of that quantity were about to hit his friend, Warren had no choice but to skip out on Harrison's party and, instead, rush Marks to the safe haven of the Orchid Avenue apartment. For the next forty-eight hours, he stood guard as Marks suffered the worst psychotic trip he had ever experienced. "I just laid awake in a fetal position for, I don't know, maybe twelve hours," he recalled. "It took me several days to shake that huge shock to my system. I can remember Warren bringing people into the apartment, saying, 'Yeah, that's him,' like a zoo animal. I guess he was amazed that I had consumed so much and was still alive."

Warren's life following lyme and cybelle had been a whirlwind of hard living and creative energy. He had finally become the furious hybrid of Igor Stravinsky and Jim Morrison of his youthful ambitions.

With Marks as his tour guide, Warren threw himself into everything that the Los Angeles counterculture had to offer. The two spent hours together, taking drugs and experimenting with psychedelic sound collages. Prior to their friendship, Warren had been uninitiated to the soul of traditional blues greats like John Lee Hooker and Muddy Waters; Marks in turn got turned on to the classical music and advanced music theory that had enraptured Warren during his youth. "Warren was a genius when he was [a] kid," said Marks. "He introduced me to this thing called a 'work ethic,' an annoying thing where he'd want to work constantly. But he definitely taught me how to be a better artist, too, as far as expressing yourself and being uninhibited in certain creative areas. We learned a lot from each other."

According to Marks, the two believed that intellectual exploration and drugs went hand in hand. "Drugs are always part of the creative process," he claimed. "It's an experience that influences the artist and they have a very profound effect on the emotions and creativity. All the ones I know, have at least dabbled in it. . . . We listened to a lot of music centered around free expression, like Coltrane and George Harrison's Indian stuff, and we started to play with those sounds too. We would drop acid and create free expression sounds for hours, just going with it and losing time."

When Warren's old friend Glenn Crocker relocated from Boston and moved into the Orchid Street pad, the three jammed as an experimental trio and partied together on a nightly basis. Over the next few months, they took part in Marks's pet project, the Moon, and briefly started an ensemble of their own—a heavy-sounding psychedelic band called the Flies. Marks remembered, "The Rolling Stones' 'Satisfaction' had just come out and it was one of the first songs that had a distinct 'fuzz-tone' in it. Warren loved it and we started playing around with those sounds. He thought he sounded like flies buzzing around, so he named the band. We played a few live gigs, one at Bido Lito's and some other hippie clubs, but never really pursued it. We were content to just keep exploring."

Although the Flies' existence was short-lived, those experimental jam sessions would influence the artistic concepts behind Warren's eventual solo album.

∞

Warren's days as a carefree bachelor were soon over.

He had recently reconnected with Marilyn Livingston, a nineteen-year-old actress and model from San Francisco. "Tule," as she was known to friends, dressed like a flower child, yet carried herself like a femme fatale. She had first met Warren at a party in Haight-Ashbury and, according to his friends, it had been love at first sight for both. With strawberry blond hair, freckles, and a sarcastic intellect on par with his own, she was more than Warren could have asked for in a girl. The two lost touch following their star-crossed weekend together, although he hadn't forgotten her.

A year later, fate brought them together again. While joyriding around Laurel Canyon, he spotted her hitchhiking. After she happily climbed into his Jaguar, the two became inseparable. Before long, she was living with him on Orchid Avenue.

⁓

Following his work with lyme and cybelle, producer Bones Howe had gone on to several high-profile projects, scoring hits with the Association and Johnny Rivers. After Warren returned from a short stint in New York, where he had been testing new material around Greenwich Village, the two friends reconnected.

While Warren's creative evolution impressed him, Howe realized that his latest compositions were harder-edged and more avant-garde than the folk material of lyme and cybelle. Still convinced of his protégé's potential, Howe made a few phone calls and was eventually able to solidify a deal at Imperial Records. It was an opportunity Warren desperately needed, as Tule had discovered she was pregnant. The couple moved into a larger Mediterranean-style apartment on North Beachwood Drive, just beneath the Hollywood sign. The elegant building had been constructed during the 1920s, and with hardwood floors and a wood-burning fireplace, it would work as the couple's first true home as an expectant family. Warren soon traded in his Jaguar for a more-affordable VW bug. He knew more expenses were on the way.

Howe agreed to oversee some early demos, but believed that someone familiar with hard rock would be a more appropriate producer. He chose Kim Fowley, a promoter and notorious character from the local music scene whose passions were more in line with underground art movements. His flamboyant bravado had earned him a reputation as Los Angeles's answer to Andy Warhol. As unorthodox as his style could appear, his intuition for hot musical acts often attracted record executives.

In later years, Fowley would be best remembered for discovering Joan Jett and the Runaways, but in the late 1960s, he was still looking for a foray into studio production. "Kim was what I call a 'Sunset Boulevard character,'" remembered Howe. "He was hanging out in all the different clubs and pretended to be extremely intellectual. He would often call me or hang around my office scouting for acts to record. I thought that he and Warren might hit it off."

As Fowley recalled, "One day, Bones had me come over to his office and said, 'I want you to help me solve a problem—this is Warren Zevon.' And he played me some of Warren's work, which at that point was the lyme and cybelle stuff and some commercial stuff. He called Warren, 'a troubled, but brilliant guy,' and thought we might be a good fit together in the studio. After I heard the music, I said to Bones, 'Oh, he's literary, huh? So, I'll just let him be Ernest Hemingway with a slide guitar, or F. Scott Fitzgerald down in the Delta.'"

That initial impression of Warren wasn't far off. In the few years since lyme and cybelle ended, Warren had been writing new songs at a furious pace, always refining his style. He had matured as both a songwriter and as a composer. The new material ran the gamut from blues to folk rock, from classically influenced to experimental. His love of literature also influenced his creative evolution, with lyrics sometimes reminiscent of film noir atmosphere, but shot through with his own wry wit.

While many of those songs would never see the light of day, Warren used the best of the bunch for his Imperial demos. In the coming years, he would also use them as raw material for more mature work.

For his first meeting with Fowley, Warren presented the full cache. "I went over to Beachwood Canyon and there was Warren with Tule," Fowley remembered. "Tule was a beautiful, pale, redheaded goddess. Of course, Warren is drinking cognac at four in the afternoon and starts expounding on everything from Damon Runyon to Dashiell Hammett just to see if I'm literate or not. But, I am, and we were kind of like kindred spirits and, at first, we really got along. After he played all this material for me, I told him, 'Just be presumptuous in your lyrics and drink a lot and steal from black musicians in the Delta and you'll be fine.'"

Warren's synergy with Fowley was genuinely strong and the two began spending time together around Los Angeles, usually at the Whisky or the Troubadour. Fowley gave Warren session work on his own solo album *Good Clean Fun* and a project he was producing for the Underground All-Stars, *Extremely Heavy!*

On one occasion, the two attended a Doors concert at the Hollywood Bowl. It was Warren's only time seeing Jim Morrison in person, but the already-legendary rocker's poetic persona and swagger fascinated him. During their very first conversation, Fowley had asked Warren, "Are you prepared to wear black leather and chains, fuck a lot of teenage girls, and get rich?" While Warren most certainly wanted that kind of success, it was apparent that Fowley's vision differed from his own. Bob Dylan would never wear chains. In addition to coordinating the upcoming studio dates, Fowley attempted to play Pygmalion, giving instruction on how to dress and walk like a rock star. Egos began to clash as soon as the recording sessions began.

A number of seasoned musicians were brought into the studio to help out, including the Byrds' bassist Skip Battin and drummers Jon Corneal, Drachen Theaker, and Toxey French for various songs. Imperial hired LA-based photographer Richard Edlund to shoot Warren's headshot for the cover. Affectionately dubbed "Darkroom Dick," or "Dark," for short, Warren and Edlund would remain friends for years.

The strongest material for the album came from songs Warren had long been refining. "A Bullet for Ramona" and "She Quit Me" were compositions he had started just after leaving lyme and cybelle, while "Gorilla" and the heavy sound collage "Fiery Emblems" were products of his experimenting with David Marks. He had penned "Tule's Blues" for his muse, Marilyn. The influence of both classical composition and pulp crime literature was evident in the music and lyrics.

Although Warren had begrudgingly agreed to use one of Fowley's own songs as the album's title track, creative differences quickly became the unraveling of their collaboration. Fowley left the production of *Wanted Dead or Alive* with just over half of the sessions recorded. "Warren wanted to play all the instruments himself and couldn't take direction," recalled Fowley. "I eventually went up to him and I said, 'Warren, you're unproducible. Why don't you just produce this thing yourself and make it easier on everybody? No hard feelings.' I went home and called him the next day and told him I had the clap and needed to take a week off, so he should keep going without me. I told the label something like, 'Because of Warren's artistry, I think it's appropriate that he complete the album himself.' So I helped him select some of the songs and do some arrangements and he went off on his own. But Warren took forever to finish that record and took too long, spending too much of Imperial's money. It's not as good as his later work, but at least he indulged himself and got it finished."

Warren later claimed he had a different reason for wanting to finish the album alone. As he put it, he had suffered "a sudden attack of taste."

∞

On the morning of August 7, 1969, Tule went into labor. Warren helped her into the VW bug and rushed her downtown to Good Samaritan Hospital. He carried her up the steps, gave her a kiss, and—having a studio session booked for that afternoon—left her in the care of her mother, Mary. He then rushed to the studio and tried to focus on the recording at hand.

Mary called him there later that afternoon with news that he was now the father of a beautiful, healthy baby boy. Ecstatic, Warren ran out and bought cigars for all the musicians. While sipping the Boone's Farm wine that a bandmate had produced in celebration, Warren looked across the studio at the Jordan amplifier the band had been using and thought it had a nice ring to it. He had found the perfect name for his son.

Jordan Zevon immediately became his father's major incentive to make it big.

∞

Knowing that Warren would need more money to support Tule and their new son, Bones Howe pushed for one of Warren's songs to be incorporated onto the soundtrack for the upcoming film *Midnight Cowboy*. He selected "She Quit Me" as the submission, believing that its moody, noirish lyrics would suit the somber drama. The track was considered for the film's theme, but was ultimately bumped in favor of Harry Nilsson's "Everybody's Talking."

It was of little consequence to Warren. Although the song's title and lyrics were slightly retooled to match the gender of bluesy songstress Lesley Miller's cover version, the soundtrack became a bestseller and earned Warren his first gold record. He proudly presented the framed award to his father.

William Zevon displayed it on his wall for the rest of his life.

∞

No one was prouder of Warren's recent successes than his father.

William had since moved out of Los Angeles, taking an apartment in the suburban section of Gardena. There, he spent his days hanging around a few legal poker parlors—the Rainbow Club and the

Monterey—and was soon a known figure among the local underworld. In January 1969 he remarried, this time a young cashier from the Monterey named Ruby Collins. Ever the charmer, William doted on his bride with expensive jewelry and a brand-new Cadillac.

But that love of flash and high living came with a cost. William's recent exploits throughout Gardena's poker clubs soon brought more attention from law enforcement than he had received in decades. Only a few months into his marriage to Collins, an FBI informant claimed that William spent most of his time collecting gambling debts on behalf of Los Angeles mob boss Nicolo Licata. There were also mentions of loansharking and fencing stolen jewelry. Buying cars for his son and new wife hadn't helped matters. For the next year, he was under constant surveillance, with FBI agents monitoring his every move. When it got to be too much for Ruby Collins, she divorced him. But, like Beverly Cope before her, she eventually returned. After William suffered a massive heart attack in 1971 they remarried for a few years, although that second shot didn't last either.

Alone once again, William took both the FBI attention and the heart attack as warning signs. Now in his seventies, he was older and wiser. He retired from all the seedy activities that had previously defined him. For the rest of William Zevon's life, gambling remained a mere hobby.

Besides, he already had a lifetime of great stories to tell his new grandson.

Warren had become a father, but that did little to curb his penchant for late nights, booze, and drugs. He insisted they fueled his creative energy. Those activities had always been a part of his process, but with the stress of producing material for a follow-up album and two mouths to feed, they had become habitual. As the stress mounted, Warren's behavior sometimes took a dark turn. Some nights, he would disappear—usually crashing on friends' couches or checking into seedy motels with bottles of whiskey and hordes of drugs, immersing himself in the atmosphere that inspired his pulpish lyrics.

But the combination also had the potential to fuel his temper. "There was one time that Warren was arguing loudly with Tule in front of the Troubadour," remembered Fowley. "He was jealous of something and was calling her awful names and she was crying. I saw him walk away and leave her stranded and it's about two in the morning. So, I gave her a lift to my place and the next morning, made her breakfast and sent her home in a cab. I thought twice about that because Tule insisted Warren would hurt her. Warren found out from people at the club that she left with me and was furious. He calls me and insists that I'd slept with her, going, 'That's my girl, motherfucker.' I tried to calm him down, saying, 'I don't fuck my friends' girls, and besides, she's not dirty enough for me.' But he was convinced I slept with her. We didn't talk again for about twenty years."

Other friends had learned to weather the storms of Warren's erratic behavior—sometimes even enable it. Although David Marks had not played a part in Warren's first album, he had remained a close companion and creative sounding board. "That was around the time that Warren was living on and off in hotels and just not going home," Marks remembered. "If he wasn't crashing with me, he would end up at the Tropicana or the Hollywood Hawaiian, which was really dingy—the way he liked it, especially for his writing."

One night, Warren couldn't pay his bill at the Hollywood Hawaiian and called Marks for help. Ever the perfect partner-in-crime, Marks drove to the motel's back alley and watched as Warren threw his belongings out the window and snaked down the fire escape. The experience would lead to one of his best-known songs.

Years later, Warren made amends. He returned to the hotel and paid his longstanding bill, along with bestowing autographed copies of his album.

∞

Unfortunately, the success of *Midnight Cowboy*'s soundtrack did nothing for Warren's solo debut. As he would famously later recall, "*Wanted Dead or Alive* was released to the sound of one hand clapping."

His talents were evident to all his friends and collaborators, but mainstream success continued to elude him. Without a charting single and with dismal sales, the album was quickly forgotten. Frustrated, Warren knew it was time to buckle down once again. He had copious amounts of songs in progress, but focus would be crucial to landing a real hit on the radio—a mark of success that he had once briefly glimpsed with lyme and cybelle.

Yielding to Warren's pleas, Bones Howe convinced Imperial that he deserved a second shot at recording an album. Whereas Kim Fowley had helmed a good portion of *Wanted Dead or Alive,* for its follow-up, Howe was able to negotiate a deal that promised Warren the producer's chair from start to finish.

Many of the songs that Warren had in the bag were more melodic and lyrical, which marked a promising start on the early demos. But his love of experimentation was still strong as ever. With Marks on guitar and Warren himself utilizing a custom-made amplifier designed by "Darkroom Dick" Edlund, the entire second half of the sessions soon evolved into a lengthy instrumental steeped in ambient psychedelic sounds.

The title for the album remained up in the air. At one point considering the project to be an extension of "Fiery Emblem," the dissonant closing track of *Wanted Dead or Alive,* Warren toyed with naming his sophomore effort *An Emblem for the Devil.* Its other possible title, *A Leaf in the Wind,* came from a line in "Studebaker," a melancholy work-in-progress of which Warren was particularly proud. He could rock out when he wanted to, but the song's poetic lyricism demonstrated that, at heart, he could also write like a Tin Pan Alley poet laureate. Songs like "Steady Rain" and the Faustian "The Rosarita Beach Café" further displayed Warren's earliest fusions of romantic storytelling with Raymond Chandler's neon-lit lingo.

Howe joined in on the fun, taking to the drums on the folk-rock foot-stomper "You Used to Ride So High." Impressed with the early demos that he heard, the producer was nonetheless confused by the mix of genres that Warren was concocting. "Warren and I were not on great terms at that point because he was being rebellious," Howe recalled. "He really wanted to get away from being a pop artist and cut off any idea that he was pop-oriented. And with the tracks I heard, he had certainly done just that."

With a sizeable budget, the musicians had their jollies letting loose in the studio. All involved were shocked when Imperial's executives were less enthusiastic. To the group's great disappointment, the label abruptly canceled the album's release. The contract with Imperial was voided.

As a new decade was beginning, Warren knew he had to reinvent himself once again.

CHAPTER THREE

(1970–1976)

BONES HOWE HAD NOT BEEN ABLE TO SWAY IMPERIAL'S DECI-sion to cancel Warren's second album, but he soon received a phone call that validated Warren's growing reputation as a songwriter.

During his time producing the Association, Howe had crossed paths with a young representative from the William Morris Agency named David Geffen. The twenty-eight-year-old agent's smooth business savvy was matched only by his ambition to climb within the ranks of the music industry. When Geffen hadn't been able to secure a recording contract for his client, a young folk singer named Jackson Browne, he and fellow representative Elliot Roberts partnered up to form Asylum Records. Howe knew that the two were assembling their Asylum roster and were on the hunt for new talent.

Having heard about Warren's songwriting skills through the indus-try grapevine, Geffen wanted to sign him. "I still had a contract with Warren at the time," remembered Howe. "David called me up and told me he had heard Warren was a talented songwriter and he wanted to make a deal to have him write some songs for Asylum. After that last al-bum hadn't happened, I thought this was a good deal, so I arranged it."

Warren was in excellent company. Geffen's early list of talent was a veritable who's who of artists representing the currently popu-lar smooth California rock sound. Jackson Browne, the Eagles, Joni Mitchell, Linda Ronstadt, J. D. Souther, and Tom Waits—whose de-but Bones Howe was assigned to produce—all found artistic solace on

Geffen's songwriter-driven label. Warren's literate lyrics and complex, yet catchy, composition style seemed a perfect fit.

Geffen had also struck a deal for his new label to be distributed through Atlantic Records, guaranteeing his artists plenty of exposure. When Asylum was taken over by Warner Music Group in 1972, Geffen then arranged a merger with Elektra Records to form the Elektra/Asylum hybrid. The company, like its founder, was soon a powerhouse in the entertainment industry.

∞

Warren's status as a house songwriter for Asylum may have brought in some income, but the work remained sporadic.

Luckily, Bones Howe wasn't the only friend who had Warren's best interests at heart. The collaborations with David Marks may not have yielded any finished musical output, but their friendship soon led to another crucial connection. Aside from his eclectic musical projects around Los Angeles, Marks had wisely allocated some of his old Beach Boys residuals toward other financial investments. He had purchased an apartment complex in one of the more stylish residential areas north of Hollywood Boulevard and instilled his parents as the building's managers. Yielding to Tule's never-ending concerns about Warren's erratic behavior, Marks helped the couple set up camp in one of the Franklin Avenue apartments.

As part of his usual routine, Marks would often swing by the building to see that things were running smoothly. These frequent visits prompted many of his big-name friends to follow suit, casually dropping by on the chance that he might be around and inadvertently turning the property into an unofficial hot spot. One of the building's regular visitors was Phil Everly, who had become close friends with Marks and his parents. "Warren and Tule and Jordan lived in my apartment building for a while, right around the time that he was trying to finish that album and got dropped," remembered Marks. "Well, my mom was pals with Phil—he really liked my folks and would visit them there all the time. So, my dear little mother liked Warren and spoke to Phil and got him a job on the road with the Everly Brothers."

Phil and his older brother, Don, had enjoyed their greatest success years before the Beatles had crossed the pond and forever changed rock and roll. Hoping to recapture some of the old magic that had defined their heyday of the early 1960s, the Everlys had a major tour in the works. While there was still a demand for performances of their youthful classics like "Wake Up Little Susie" and "All I Have to Do Is Dream," the brothers were now in their thirties and their boyish innocence had long since worn thin; years of speed addiction and constant public bickering had hardened them both.

The siblings hadn't cracked *Billboard*'s Top 10 since 1962—almost a decade—and yearned for a comeback. Both were seasoned musicians, and neither had lost sight of the country sounds that had influenced them as teens. Their latest albums relied heavily on the music that they had grown up listening to with their father, guitarist Ike Everly, and the close family friend who had groomed them, Nashville legend Chet Atkins. As luck would have it, the brothers needed a piano player who could replicate that style for the upcoming tour.

Marks arranged an audition for Warren, who proudly unveiled his latest work-in-progress, "Hasten Down the Wind," a melancholy ballad written for Tule. Immediately impressed, Phil Everly's only question for Warren was if he could play like Floyd Cramer.

Of course he could. He was hired on the spot.

∞

A steady paycheck, the promise of future studio recording sessions, and the invaluable experience of networking with a few famed musicians were just the icing on the larger cake. As musical director, Warren could also flex his bandleader muscles. Working under tour manager Don Wayne, his first assignment was to assemble the brothers' new band. He reveled in the creative control he was given.

None of the musicians he hired were novices. Already familiar with the Everly songbook and style, bassist Robert Knigge was retained for the tour. On drums, Warren hired Gene Gunnels, an alumnus from a psychedelic rock ensemble called Strawberry Alarm Clock. Of course, Warren would be handling all keyboard duties, just leaving the crucial vacancy for a powerful guitarist.

∞

Robert Wachtel was born on May 24, 1947, in the Jackson Heights section of Queens, New York. When he was only six years old, his mother, Rhonda, died after a long battle with lung cancer. Devastated by his wife's death, Harry Wachtel adopted a stern approach to his two sons' upbringings. Although Robert and older brother Jimmy both had early aspirations toward art and music, their father pushed for more stable career paths. Even as a young child, Robert—or "Waddy," as he became known to friends—had been fascinated with the guitar and wanted one of his own. However, the last thing Harry Wachtel wanted for his son was the life of a professional musician. If it had been up to him, young Robert would have become a doctor.

"My first guitar was a Kamico," remembered Wachtel. "It was a gorgeous thing to me when I was a kid, and eventually my dad broke down and got me a Gibson L-7 hole guitar when I was ten. I always had it with me and about the next year, I convinced my father into getting me a Les Paul. I ended up using that one for years."

Although Waddy Wachtel was destined to raise hell as a rock and roller, his earliest musical influences came from brother Jimmy's extensive collection of jazz records and from a piano-playing cousin who showed him the basics of reading sheet music. A few years later, a guitar instructor named Gene Dell helped broaden Wachtel's appreciation for the electric guitar and taught the left-handed boy to adapt his playing backwards, "normal" in a right-handed world.

As Wachtel entered his teens, he attracted the attention of neighbor Rudolf Schramm, head of the NBC staff orchestra and music teacher at Carnegie Hall. Taken with the young man's natural talent, Schramm agreed to give instruction in music theory and composition three times a week. By sixteen, Wachtel was often "in the basement, smoking cigarettes and drinking ginger ale, writing a million songs." Wachtel found gigs around New York City before forming his own band, the Orphans, which toured throughout New England over the next few years. In 1968, he moved his latest band, Twice Nicely, to Los Angeles, and took his nineteen-year-old girlfriend, Crystal, along for the ride. By then, Wachtel had become an experienced gun-for-hire in the studio, solidifying his status as a go-to session man. With that reputation growing, he soon disbanded Twice Nicely and was a regular figure around the Los Angeles rock scene.

In 1971, he got wind that the Everly Brothers were scouting for a guitarist. "I got a call from a friend of mine to come over and discuss some recordings we were planning," Wachtel remembered. "We're in the middle of discussing a session that was coming up and all of a sudden, he goes, 'Oh, by the way, the Everly Brothers are looking for a guitar player.' And I just went, 'You gotta be kidding me? That's my gig! I know every song and every part.' So, he handed me a phone number and said, 'Yeah, call this guy—Sandy Zevon.'"

Wachtel had grown up loving the Everlys' music and knew all their tunes. He figured he was a shoe-in for the job, but it wasn't exactly love at first sight between him and the Everlys' new bandleader. The day of the audition, Wachtel showed up looking every bit the part of a rock and roller, sporting a ponytail, long beard, rumpled T-shirt, and clogs. "All of a sudden, in walks this guy wearing a seersucker suit and a fedora," Wachtel recalled. "Warren goes over all the songs with me and goes, 'You just listen and we'll play it—then you can play with us.' And I said to him, 'Well, okay, but we can skip this step, since I know all these songs.' Warren just looks at me from behind the piano and goes, 'No—you just listen,' really pissing me off. When we finally got to a song called 'Walk Right Back,' I knew Warren was playing it wrong because it has this really specific lick in it. So, I corrected him and that really pissed him off, and he goes, 'I know how this goes—I'm the band-leader!' But Bob Knigge, on bass, says, 'Hey, wait, I think this guy is right.' So for a while, there was this little rub between Warren and me."

Wachtel was confident that his ability to play all the Everly songs had earned him the gig, but Warren was sure to add a final jab at the end of the audition. Wachtel remembered, "Before I leave, Warren says to me, really irritated, 'You probably got the job, but one thing—you have to cut off the beard.' I went nuts. I said, 'What the fuck are you talking about? I'm not even working for you yet—and where are the fucking Everly Brothers, anyway?' 'Oh,' he goes, 'they're in the studio making an album.' So we went back and forth like that, and on my way out, Warren yells across the room, 'Okay, wise guy, what's this?' and plays, like, the one classical piece I knew. I yell back, 'That's Beethoven's Fourth in G, asshole,' and I walked out the door. That week, Warren had to call me to say that I got the job, and I knew it killed him to have to do it. We were like oil and water at the beginning, until we realized how great we worked together."

The strained nature of the relationship didn't last long. Once War-ren and Wachtel began playing together, their musical kinship became fiercely apparent. While the two musicians were masters of different instruments, both had been musical prodigies in their youth and shared a natural inclination toward theory and composition. When Warren sat at the piano and Waddy gripped his axe, the two seemed to communicate almost telepathically. Soon, mandatory rehearsal dates spilled over into all-night jam sessions.

Warren was still building up a repertoire of new material for a possible second solo album and soon viewed Wachtel as a confidante and collaborator. The guitarist became privy to Warren's latest musical sketches long before anyone else, often adding new ideas into the mix.

The tour launched at Knott's Berry Farm on September 3, 1971. With Warren at the helm, the Everly Brothers band then set off for a string of dates throughout Western Europe, beginning in Holland and cutting through England and West Germany. Being an integral part of the tour was a finishing school, of sorts, for Warren, who later claimed that the experience had acted as "a fantastic introduction to the road."

He took note of the professionalism that the brothers displayed night after night, as well as their indifference to such a transient lifestyle. One particularly turbulent flight to a gig booked at a ski resort seemed, for him, to sum up the life of a seasoned musician. "It was the kind of flight where they serve you coffee and a moment later, it's on the ceiling," Warren later recalled. "I looked around and Don was sitting in his seat with pitch-black, dark glasses on, calmly reading *Time* magazine—and the plane was all over the place. And I looked around the other side, and Phil—he was smiling. He had his camera out, taking pictures out the window of the engine that was failing. And I thought, 'This is cool.'"

Over the course of the tour, Warren and Wachtel also grew closer. Like David Marks, Wachtel opened Warren's eyes to new musical genres, particularly the country sounds that the classically trained pianist had often overlooked in his youth. "Late at night, back in the room, we would always talk music and argue," Wachtel remembered. "We were always talking and arguing about music. I'd play him some John Lennon song, and he'd have something to say about it, and I'd go, 'Man, you'll die never having written anything as good as that,' and we would laugh and jam. But, we always agreed on the Rolling Stones, we were both fans of them. At the time, Warren knew a lot more about blues than I did. Heavy stuff, way past just the British blues that had been popular."

Warren, in turn, continued to share his latest compositions. One of Wachtel's personal favorites was "Carmelita," a haunting ballad about love and heroin. He was soon putting together his own finger-style guitar arrangement of the tune and playing it for other people. Neither man was a stranger to the dark content of the song. Both musicians had already done their fair share of drugs in the past, indulgences that only increased as the Everly Brothers tour rolled on. While Wachtel had smoked plenty of marijuana, snorted cocaine, and dropped acid in his youth, he had never been much of a drinker. There, Warren had him beat.

Between Warren's growing dependency on alcohol and both Don and Phil Everly's own thresholds for all-night bar binges, it wasn't long before the substance abuse on tour was out of control. As had been the case with David Marks and Kim Fowley only a few years before, Warren's new bandmates noticed the shift in his demeanor when the drinking and drugs took hold. When the tour finally returned home for its US dates at the end of November, Wachtel finally saw, firsthand, the effects that drugs and alcohol could have on Warren's behavior and productivity. Warren, high on alcohol and Quaaludes, threw his acoustic guitar at Wachtel, who shrugged it off but didn't forget it.

It was the type of episode that had become all too common with Warren and his treatment of friends and family. Both his life and burgeoning career had slowly become defined by stretches of genuine warmth and creative genius, yet punctuated by jarring moments of extreme jealousy and ingratitude. In the end, Warren's charm and intelligence would always win out, bringing back those closest to him time and time again. The conflict made Warren's music deep and autobiographical, but his creative process dangerously self-destructive. This cycle would continue for years.

∽

After a few final stops in Ohio and Milwaukee at the beginning of December, the band made it home just in time for the holidays. For Warren, things with Tule were turbulent, at best. When the band landed at LAX, he surprised Wachtel by asking for a lift—but not home. Wachtel's girlfriend, Crystal, had come to pick him up. She had heard much about the infamous Warren Zevon.

"Waddy had called me all the time from the road and had already played me 'Carmelita' over the phone," Crystal remembered. "He was just enamored of the songs that Warren had been writing. When I went to pick him up at the airport, he told me that Warren was on the outs with his partner at the time, Jordan's mother, and asked if we could drop him off at the Tropicana hotel. I had this Chevy sports van and Waddy was sitting in the front seat, rolling joints, and Warren was in the back seat. We kept looking at each other in the rearview mirror and there were definitely sparks right away."

Crystal couldn't shake the instant connection she felt with Warren, who remained quietly seated in the back of the car. Save for a few wry quips, he certainly did not come off as the intellectual party animal that Wachtel had built up over the phone. Intrigued, she couldn't keep her eyes off the pensive wiseass in her rearview mirror. She was instantly hooked. Warren's attraction to Crystal was equally strong and just as fast. Unbeknownst to anyone involved, the seeds of a love triangle were already forming. Crystal's playful intelligence, combined with her acceptance of bad-boy behavior, made her the ideal companion for the likes of both Wachtel *and* Warren Zevon. She could keep up with the literary and intellectual banter going on around her, while dropping acid and giggling with even the brashest of the rock-and-roll roadies. Crystal later claimed that with Warren, it had been "love at first sight."

Although things with Tule were merely on the rocks, he lied to Wachtel's companion and claimed that he was already single. Crystal took note of the fib. When she bumped into Warren and Tule at a local grocer the following week, Warren lied again, sheepishly claiming that Tule had started dating Wachtel. "For the next few weeks, it seemed like I was bumping into him everywhere," Crystal remembered. "I'd see him at the supermarket, the dentist office—and this was LA, a very big town."

Between Warren's "aww-shucks" boyish charm and the flirtatious glances, both he and Crystal knew there was an unspoken chemistry. Wachtel was either oblivious to the attraction between his buddy and his girl, or—more than likely—indifferent to it. With his own career in the Los Angeles music scene taking off, he let the indiscretion slide.

�∞

Crystal Ann Brelsford may have been a true product of the 1960s, but she had been raised in a much more traditional household than her free-wheeling adulthood let on. The stable home-life provided by Clifford and Barbara Brelsford had instilled in their daughter a maturity and moral conservativeness that would often clash with the hedonistic surroundings of her young adulthood.

As a teenager, wanderlust had led Crystal to Sugarbush, Vermont, where she met and fell in love with Waddy Wachtel. When Twice Nicely moved to Los Angeles in 1968, she went along for the ride. For the brief period that the rock band was under the wing of Cowsills' patriarch, William "Bud" Cowsill, Crystal worked a job in the Cowsills' fan club office. Eventually, Wachtel began to rack up his fair share of groupies and Crystal grew disillusioned with the "openness" of their relationship. With two foster children in her care, she fled Los Angeles and attempted to start a new life in British Columbia. To remain there, Crystal married a Canadian citizen.

On her wedding night, Wachtel phoned, announcing that he had just gotten a plum gig as the new guitarist for the Everly Brothers and was about to head off to Europe on tour—even though the music director who hired him was kind of an asshole. Conflicted by the romantic feelings that Wachtel's call had stirred up, the now recently divorced Crystal returned to Los Angeles and the two reconciled. While on the road with the Everly band, Wachtel phoned nightly and shared stories and anecdotes about the tour.

Soon enough, Crystal noticed that the name Warren Zevon had become ever present in her boyfriend's adventurous tales.

Warren and Crystal's mutual attraction came to a head weeks later.

Wachtel had been booked to record an antiwar song at Sound City Studios for friends Keith Olsen and Curt Boettcher, a successful production duo that had previously scored hits for the Association and blues rockers Fleetwood Mac. For the session, Wachtel had invited as many friends as possible to add lush background vocals to the track. Amid the drunken chaos of the recording session, Warren strategically sidled next to Crystal, slyly putting his arms around her and making certain that they had to share a single headset. Once the recording was complete, the full group headed for Benny K's, a hip venue where Wachtel and his musician buddies played a regular gig.

Following the performance, Warren offered to drive both Crystal and Wachtel home, knowing that the guitarist had been crashing at the home of a mutual friend, Arnie Geller. He purposely dropped Wachtel off first, keeping his girlfriend all to himself. At the house, she had recently rented an upright piano for the benefit of her two foster children and invited Warren in to try it out. Knowing an opportunity when he saw it, he serenaded her all night—then the two finally consummated weeks of sexual tension.

"That night, we both found ourselves at the same place at the same time while Waddy was playing," Crystal recalled. "And that was that—it was very quick. He came home with me and had just started to write 'Desperadoes Under the Eaves.' We had this amazing, romantic night, but in the middle of everything, he'd suddenly come up with another line or another idea and then run to my piano! Then, he'd sit back down with me and we would be romantic again—and then he'd get up again and go back to the piano."

At dawn the following morning, Tule called the house looking for Warren. He took the call in the other room and, after a few moments, returned. He asked Crystal to drive him home to gather his things.

∞

The Everly Brothers band had a few precious weeks off before launching the extended US leg of the tour in January 1972. During the break, Warren officially set up camp at Crystal's home. He used the opportunity to get to know her foster children—Cindy and Bart—and to tinker with new songwriting projects on the house piano.

His drinking hadn't gotten any better. It wasn't long before Crystal realized that Warren viewed alcohol as a creative stimulant, like many of his literary influences. He was particularly amused by a nickname he had coined for himself—"F. Scott *Fitzevon*"—and rather than admit to the darker implications of addiction, he would often wear that persona as a badge of honor.

Crystal, however, didn't see much honor in how Warren's mood could shift while under the influence—especially with two small children in the house. Arguments were commonplace. Within the first few months of their relationship, she fell victim to his frequent verbal assaults, primarily regarding her former boyfriends. Booze and jealousy seemed to be the usual catalysts for Warren's rage and she learned to give him a wide berth. The couple separated more than once, with Warren again finding himself crashing on friends' couches or at the Tropicana.

During the first week of February 1972, Crystal saw him at his worst. He had a few weeks off between tour dates and spent those days at the piano, drink firmly in hand. One afternoon, another fight ensued and quickly escalated. As neighbors watched, an inebriated Warren threw the living room furniture out onto the front lawn before driving off drunk. Panic-stricken, Crystal sent their mutual friend, "Darkroom Dick" Edlund, to the Tropicana on a rescue mission. The concerned photographer rushed to the motel and found Warren passed out on the floor of his motel room. His skin was pale blue and his body cold to the touch. Terrified that his friend had fatally overdosed, Edlund put his ear to Warren's chest. He was relieved to find a heartbeat and labored breathing. Slowly helping Warren to his feet, he walked him around the room for an hour, successfully resuscitating him.

It had been Warren's closest call, but a dangerous precedent had been set. As many of Warren's oldest friends already knew, the singer-songwriter's lyrics about violence, depression, and living fast and dying young weren't just words. As Crystal and Edlund had seen firsthand, Warren seemed to have a genuine death wish.

In an effort to keep his demons at bay, Warren spent as much of his time as possible at the piano. Although no record contract was in sight, he continued to pump out new material. Amid the personal chaos, he refused to lose sight of his goals for another solo album and the ambitious symphony that predated the recording of *Wanted Dead or Alive*.

Still signed as a house songwriter for David Geffen's Elektra/Asylum label, he also wrote material with other performers in mind. One of Geffen's most popular clients had taken an instant liking to Warren at their first encounter years before and would soon become his greatest advocate—Jackson Browne.

Warren and Browne had first met at the Laurel Canyon home of mutual acquaintance Barry Friedman, a former producer who went by the hipper name Frazier Mohawk. Friedman had once worked at the Troubadour and handled the public relations for the Beatles' Hollywood

Bowl concert in 1964. Semi-retired, he remained a known figure around the Southern California music scene and often threw "listening parties" for his friends within the industry. Warren had been introduced to Browne at one of those parties the previous year and the two were now linked through the Asylum label.

Like Warren, Browne had started his career as a songwriter. Following a tenure with the Nitty Gritty Dirt Band, Browne had also played folk clubs around New York City's Greenwich Village area, building up a reputation for writing poetic lyrics and gorgeous melodies. By the time he returned to California at the end of the 1960s, his songs had been covered by Joan Baez, the Eagles, and Linda Ronstadt. He had then been helped in making the leap to popular solo performer by his agent, David Geffen.

Young, handsome, and with a major solo album in the works, Browne was held in high esteem among his peers. He wanted that kind of success for Warren and encouraged him to keep writing and keep honing his skills.

∽

When Warren's hands were idle, Crystal would often come home to find him sleeping late and watching television, usually with a drink in his hand. It became a routine and the fights continued. Depressed, Warren chiseled away at the songs he hoped would populate his next album—whenever that might be.

He finally caught a small break when the Everly Brothers asked him to help out on their first album in four years, *Stories We Could Tell*. Warren and Wachtel joined an esteemed roster that included Graham Nash and Ry Cooder, bringing a revamped, country-rock vibe to the Everlys' sound. In an attempt at mainstream crossover appeal, the sessions were composed of covers written by popular artists like Kris Kristofferson and Rod Stewart. When the resulting album was released in March, however, it was met with mixed reviews and underwhelming sales. Phil and Don were none too pleased with the dismal response from critics and fans, sparking strife among the siblings.

Warren was just glad for the work. The Everlys' tour had come to an end in August and with it, his steady paycheck. In the months that followed, he wrote, drank, and worked odd jobs to make ends meet.

∞

In June 1973, tour manager Don Wayne called to offer Warren a much-needed gig. Despite the lackluster sales of *Stories We Could Tell*, the Everly Brothers were booked for a series of shows in Las Vegas and wanted him to again act as music director.

The timing couldn't have been better, as Warren and Crystal had separated yet again. With Warren's drinking and volatile behavior set loose by the lack of work, Crystal had accepted a job at her father's insurance agency and moved to Aspen with both foster children. Alone, Warren moved into a cheap bachelor pad. Wayne's offer promised a paycheck and change of scenery, both of which seemed enticing. He leapt at the opportunity.

But if stability was what Warren had been seeking, performing with Phil and Don Everly during this period in their careers proved less than ideal. The hostility between the brothers had since mounted to legendary heights, igniting media speculation that their future as a duo was in jeopardy. While their shows continued to go on as planned, they nearly came to blows on numerous occasions.

During one rehearsal session at the old Sahara hotel showroom, the two got into a shouting match so intense, it soon spilled over toward co-headliner Nancy Sinatra. Due to her legendary father, the thirty-three-year-old was regarded as industry royalty. She was shocked as the country-rock siblings hurled insults at each other—then at *her*—before storming offstage to their separate dressing rooms. Sinatra was grateful that her father had not been there to witness her treatment at the hands of the former matinee idols. Following those tumultuous Las Vegas shows, Don and Phil officially called it quits.

At their own farewell concert only a few weeks later, the Everly Brothers finally imploded on themselves. Beginning July 14, the duo was booked for a three-night engagement at Knott's Berry Farm. The shows had been billed as the Everlys' swan song and welcomed a star-studded turnout. Warren had even persuaded Crystal to return from Aspen for the event. Once the evening's painful drama got underway, however, many in attendance wished they'd stayed home.

Much to Phil's dismay, Don had downed several margaritas prior to taking the stage. By the time the band started up, he was already visibly tipsy and forgetting words to his own classic hits. It wasn't long before Phil lost his patience, causing the two to mince words in front of the audience. The fight escalated, Phil finally smashing his Gibson guitar on the ground. The brothers swore they'd never again share the stage. True to their word, the two didn't speak again until their father's funeral over a decade later.

While the audience was aghast at the spectacle, Warren had been witness to the brothers' slow disintegration for over two years. Ultimately, he would remain friends with both—but for the time being, the golden goose had been slain. With the exception of Elektra/Asylum's intermittent songwriting assignments, working for the Everly Brothers had been Warren's bread and butter ever since *Wanted Dead or Alive* had tanked.

If he was ever going to get a record contract again, it had to happen soon.

∽

To the chagrin of her parents, Crystal returned to Los Angeles—and to Warren.

Much like his father before him, Warren had managed to completely alienate the family of the girl he loved. Clifford and Barbara Brelsford remained unimpressed with the strange young man who drank a lot and often sent their daughter into an emotional tizzy. Nor could they comprehend how she expected to provide a sense of normalcy for her foster children, especially with someone as seemingly irresponsible as Warren dictating the major decisions. They were vocal in their concerns. But, like his father, Warren had managed to bewitch the object of his affection. Crystal made endless excuses for his behavior, a task that only became more difficult as his career frustrations—and drinking—continued to mount.

The couple rented a small house in Sherman Oaks and Warren converted a backyard shed into a music studio. He attempted to buckle down, punching a mental clock each morning and anchoring himself in the makeshift workspace to focus on new material. Beginning only weeks after the move, however, Crystal would commonly return home from her job at a nearby insurance office to find Warren already drunk. Again, the fights continued.

The regular arguments reached a breaking point one afternoon when Crystal discovered that Warren had been hiding liquor bottles in young Bart's outdoor playhouse. Enraged by the accusation, Warren drunkenly dragged Bart out to Crystal's sedan and drove off. He immediately smashed into a number of parked cars, barely making it to the end of the block where he crashed into a neighbor's house.

The episode earned Warren his first arrest for drunk driving, along with three sobering days in jail. When he was released, Warren discovered that Crystal had taken the kids to stay with a friend. She vowed not to return unless he agreed to attend an Alcoholics Anonymous meeting. Warren complied, but like many early attempts at sobriety, the meeting did little to change his behavior. Nonetheless, Crystal kept to her word and returned, this time only with Cindy. Bart had been traumatized by the drunk-driving incident and asked to live with another foster family.

Warren, Crystal, and Cindy moved into an apartment in Hollywood. Without the luxury of a personal workroom, Warren was relegated to working on a portable electric piano in the corner of the living room, the noise of which upset their neighbors. He remained steadfast in his hopes of putting together enough material for a new demo tape, but quickly tired of their latest living arrangements. Temporarily, he left Crystal to stay with friend, Danny McFarland, up in the Berkeley Hills. He again believed a change of scenery would be good for both his writing and sobriety.

For a few weeks, Warren played small clubs and coffeehouses throughout the area. In need of extra money, he assisted McFarland in his part-time piano-moving business. During one delivery, Warren did his best homage to Jack Nicholson in *Five Easy Pieces,* hopping out of the truck's front cab and playing the piano stored in back all the way across town to the drop-off point.

He had more in common with Nicholson's cinematic character than he let on. Like the film's angst-ridden, emotionally frustrated protagonist, Warren was also a classically trained pianist, hiding from his personal turmoil by immersing himself in the world of the American blue-collar working man. An avid movie buff, Warren surely knew the image he conjured, climbing into the back of McFarland's truck and performing for the other drivers along the highway. But, unlike the fictional blue-collar virtuoso, Warren's problems were very real.

Determined not to run away from them forever, he soon returned to Los Angeles and immediately proposed to Crystal. Despite her better instincts and the wishes of her parents, she tearfully agreed. The couple dropped acid together and drove across the desert to Las Vegas. Warren, dapper in an ascot, crafted a wedding ring from the washer from the bathroom sink and presented it to his bride. They were wed at a twenty-four-hour chapel on May 25, 1974.

∽

The newlyweds returned home to find a pleasant surprise awaiting them.

Following the catastrophic public demise of the Everly Brothers nearly a year before, both Don and Phil were each making attempts for solo careers. Over a congratulatory dinner, Don asked Warren to act as bandleader on his first tour without brother Phil. As a wedding present, Crystal was invited to join them all on the road. Following a string of incidents of Cindy running away, and the unstable home life, she had been forced to forfeit custody of Cindy to the state, and the excitement of accompanying her new husband on the road promised to soften that emotional blow. The Zevons now had complete freedom in crafting their future together, beginning with the Don Everly tour and, following that, shifting major focus to getting Warren back on top.

Warren planned to use Don's band as session players for some new demos that he could shop around. When the tour quickly went bust due to poor attendance, Warren was, at least, able to walk away with a new band and a few bucks in his pocket to bring them into the studio.

Through Crystal's new job, she arranged for him to perform at a musical think tank called the Alternative Chorus Songwriters' Showcase. The offbeat venue was the brainchild of her employers, John Braheny and Len Chandler, former folk performers who operated as the showcase's curators. There, the two auditioned fresh musical talent and hosted the most promising artists for industry professionals. With the wealth of material that Warren had been working on for the past few years, he was a shoe-in.

Warren was meticulous in assembling his roster for the showcase. Ever since the Everly Brothers' 1970 tour, his old buddy Waddy Wachtel had become a hot commodity around town. Having just completed a major gig as Carole King's lead guitarist, he was available to come on board. Warren also solicited Everly Brothers compatriot Gene Gunnels on drums, and close friend LeRoy Marinell to play bass. The team rehearsed for a number of weeks, recording homemade demos that Warren would later use to shape changes to the songs. Later classics like "The French Inhaler" and "Poor Poor Pitiful Me" became more refined.

At the showcase, the group's six-song set was a smash. It immediately caught the eye of audience member John Rhys, a British-born producer who had moved to the United States as a child and grew up with a love of music. Beginning his own career as a session guitarist, Rhys had quickly climbed the levels of engineering and went on to produce artists Jerry Reed, Tommy Roe, and Joe South for a multitude of record labels. An entrepreneurial freelancer, he now scoured Los Angeles for new and a unique talent that he could produce. Warren—with his old-timey swagger, film noir lyrics, and Aaron Copland–esque lyricism— was nothing if not a unique talent.

Rhys was determined to get Warren recorded again, this time at a major label. He sold half of his own publishing company to raise the $30,000 needed to stake his new protégé's demo tapes. Rhys presented Warren with a handshake agreement that should a major record company offer a contract, Rhys could produce the final product. They had a deal, and the demos were booked for the cheap overnight hours at a local studio.

Elated at the opportunity, Warren immediately rounded up troops for the recordings. He retained his Everly Brothers lineup, with the exception of Gene Gunnels, who was swapped for Hollywood Central's house drummer Eddie Ponder. Between Wachtel's recent session friends and Rhys's own networking in the music industry, a host of all-star cameo appearances made up the final demo tracks. T Bone Burnett, Lindsey Buckingham, Barry Cowsill, David Lindley, and Stevie Nicks all swung down to the studio to drink, party, and lend a hand. Both Phil and Don Everly showed support, although their cameos were recorded separately. Jackson Browne, who had slowly become one of Warren's closest music companions and advocates, also visited the session. Enthusiastic at the new tunes that he heard, he became as adamant as ever in helping Warren land a solid contract.

Between 1973 and 1975, Warren had only been able to get into the studio a handful of times. He had aided in Phil Everly's string of solo albums for RCA: *Star Spangled Springer, There's Nothing Too Good for My Baby* (known in the US as *Phil's Diner* and featuring "It's True," which Warren co-wrote), and *Mystic Line*.

But these demo recordings were very different. With Rhys staking the recordings, Warren didn't have to borrow money from Crystal's parents or from his own father. The new demos proved to be Warren's first real return to the studio as the lead artist and true star in nearly six years. And despite the frustrations, disappointments, and substance abuse, the now twenty-seven-year-old Warren had spent the years following *Wanted Dead or Alive* penning dynamite songs—and everyone who heard them knew it.

∞

Immediately following the demo recording sessions, Warren, Crystal, and the band went off to finish the final leg of Don Everly's solo club tour. Warren left the demo tracks with Rhys. As 1975 ended, both men were determined to get the rough album into the hands of industry guru Clive Davis, who was slowly transforming Bell Records into his own flagship label, Arista.

Warren and Crystal remained optimistic that a record contract was only weeks away.

∞

Although success finally seemed to be on the horizon, Warren's darker habits were not easily curbed. When stagnant and frustrated, his depression often got the best of him and led directly to the bottle. When times were good, however, he would often consume just as much vodka or just as many margaritas—only this time in the name of fun. Moods shift and sour very quickly with an alcoholic, and Crystal knew enough to stay out of Warren's way when he was on a bender.

Just prior to the holiday season, Tule had announced that she was moving to New York to give her acting aspirations one more shot. She left Jordan, now five years old, in Warren and Crystal's care. Only a month and a half later, Tule's mother, Mary, secretly picked the boy up from school and jettisoned him to New York to be with his mother. Deceived, Warren went off the deep end. He made his way to the Troubadour, but was quickly ejected by the bouncers. The evening ended with his second drunk-driving arrest.

Although William Zevon begrudgingly paid his son's bail, Warren had gotten the family car impounded and Crystal needed a ride to the San Vicente station house. With no other option, she called up an old friend she knew from her time with Wachtel and Twice Nicely, a local musician named Jorge Calderón. Originally from Puerto Rico, Calderón was a singer-songwriter who had toured with Buckingham Nicks as a percussionist. When Crystal called him up for help with Warren, Calderón's sense of loyalty won out. He not only picked Warren up from jail, but aided the couple in breaking back into their own place, as no one had brought their house keys.

Warren and Calderón would become lifelong friends and consistent songwriting collaborators.

∞

While waiting for John Rhys's promise of a solo album to come through, Warren took a number of lowly lounge player gigs at various country clubs and the types of seedy bars that would have done Charles Bukowski proud.

He quickly tired of the indignation. Although not usually one for confrontation, Warren's frustrations with Rhys and his waiting game were at an end. There were already lingering squabbles over future profit arrangements between the two. Enough was enough. He called for a meeting and the two had a heated argument, resulting in Warren angrily cutting Rhys out of all future deals. But, in the heat of the moment, he had forgotten that Rhys had funded the initial demos that were still floating around town.

Having let his emotions get the best of him, Warren never saw the high-quality demo tapes again.

∞

The Rhys sessions had been a dead-end and the sporadic studio gigs had yielded no recording contract. Following Warren's mandatory court appearance at the beginning of March for the drunk-driving arrest, he and Crystal decided that there was nothing truly linking them to Los Angeles any longer.

For a few weeks, they crashed at Phil Everly's guesthouse, saving every penny while liquidating any assets of value. Most of Warren's instruments and equipment were sold off for quick cash. After looking through travel deals in the newspaper, the couple settled on the cheapest flight they could find: two one-way tickets to Madrid for the last week of May. Upon arriving, they had no future plans.

While on a layover in Denver awaiting a connecting flight, Warren's name was paged. To his surprise, it was old friend David Marks calling him at the terminal. "I hadn't spoken to Warren in a while," remembered Marks. "At a certain point, our addictions had become destructive and we, kind of, just parted ways. It was subtle. There had been one tiff over the phone that had been fueled by alcohol and cocaine, and [we] hadn't spoken since. But I heard he was leaving LA for another country and I found out the information and had him paged right there in the airport. I had to wish him bon voyage." The two made peace before Warren faced his uncertain future.

Hopping from Madrid to Barcelona, Warren and Crystal took a train southwest to Sitges, a small beach community often referred to as "little Ibiza" for its artsy, countercultural atmosphere. Warren was enthralled by the exotic surroundings.

Following a tip from the Canadian couple with whom they had shared a hostel, the Zevons sought out an Irish bar called Dubliners. The English-speaking pub was owned by David Lindell, a former American soldier of fortune who had moved to Spain following years of mercenary work in Africa. To Warren, Lindell was like a real-life Humphrey Bogart character. The two liked each other immediately.

Martin guitar in hand, Warren was made the Dubliners' musical entertainment for 200 *pesetas*—plus tips. For the remainder of the summer, he and Crystal lived as romantic expatriates. Each night, he entertained the Dubliners' regulars with his own songs and popular requests while Crystal sat beside him and passed the hat. Lindell and his German wife, Lisa, provided the couple with breakfast and dinner, and Warren's role as the pub's very own Hoagy Carmichael footed the room and board.

He reveled in the adventurous nature of the trip itself and the experience of the foreign land. Like the pulp novels and film noir movies he had gobbled up over the years, he was a stranger in a strange land, crafting his own mysterious travelogue. The Graham Greene and Ross

Macdonald paperbacks he had brought along for the journey only fueled the fantasy.

Nothing indulged Warren's love of intrigue more than the former mercenary he had befriended, the Dubliners' owner. Each night, Lindell shared tales of foreign combat with his inquisitive American friend and, before long, the two were sitting side-by-side after hours, toying with song ideas. Together, they came up with a macabre tale that was part pulp fiction and part ghost story: a catchy murder ballad about a headless mercenary who returns from the grave, seeking revenge on the men who had betrayed him.

Warren ran with the idea. The seeds had been planted for one of his most iconic and enduring compositions.

While there had been an air of hopelessness in Warren's exodus to Spain, back in Los Angeles, things were slowly moving in his favor.

Over the past few years, Jackson Browne had released a string of radio hits for David Geffen's label, and the charismatic young performer now carried his share of clout in the music scene. Under Browne's Asylum agreement, he had been given both the power to produce his own albums and to scout for other potential talent. With that in mind, he had never forgotten the literary, electric demon that was his friend, Warren Zevon.

Browne and Warren had stayed in contact for years and both knew many of the same musicians; a few of the session men on Warren's recent demo tapes had first appeared on Browne's previous two albums. It was only natural that, at some point, the mutually gifted singer-songwriters would collaborate.

Toward the end of July, Warren received a postcard at Dubliners. The card's face showed an idyllic California beach landscape while the flip side contained a single, handwritten message: "Come back home and there will be a recording contract." It was signed simply, *With love, Jackson.*

To Warren, Browne's dispatch wasn't just hopeful—it was a solid promise of success if he and Crystal were to abandon their newfound bliss abroad. Considering the melodramatics of the past few years, it wasn't an easy decision for either of them. The loss of both foster children had hit Crystal hard, while Warren's stagnant music career had affected both their finances and their relationship. Then, of course, there were his ongoing bouts with drugs and alcohol. All were burdens that Spain had helped to dull.

Crystal knew, however, that if Warren were to miss this opportunity, he would regret it forever—and deep down, he hadn't just been writing a wealth of new material for tourists. When a second message arrived, this time from Phil Everly, offering Warren work as an arranger on a solo album that he was completing in England, the Zevons tearfully said goodbye to Lindell and to Spain. They headed for England.

∞

Warren completed his work-for-hire duties on Phil Everly's *Mystic Line* by the end of August.

Other than the promise of Browne's postcard, he and Crystal had no further plans upon their return to Los Angeles. For the first few days, they crashed at his father's apartment in Gardena. Although William remained Warren's biggest champion, the tension between father and son quickly took its toll on both. Since Jordan was born, William had given Warren more money than he could remember—and there always seemed to be drama and arrests. Instead, William loaned the couple enough money to rent a small place of their own on North Cherokee Avenue and bought them a used car to get around.

With no job lined up, Warren immediately set to work pruning his cache of new songs to present to Browne. By the time he was ready to triumphantly proclaim his return from Europe, there was almost enough material to fill two albums. But, there was one small problem. Browne hadn't meant his postcard as anything more than mere words of encouragement between friends. Warren, however, had taken the message as a concrete promise of a record contract, something solid that would be put into motion upon his return from Europe.

Browne was forced to quickly make good on the insinuation and promptly went to David Geffen. It took some finagling to broker the deal. Despite Browne's insistence of Warren's talent, Geffen was convinced he was merely trying to help out a buddy in need. Ultimately, Browne was allocated $60,000 for the production of Warren's Elektra/Asylum solo debut. Geffen had one stipulation—Browne would have to produce the album himself.

Warren was given a $6,000 advance for signing, plus the option to renew the contract based on the debut's chart performance. He would soon be back in the high life.

⌥

Time couldn't move fast enough. While Warren waited for the advance to be finalized, money remained tight. Browne's Asylum connections had afforded the Zevons invitations to swanky Hollywood parties with the likes of Don Henley and Joni Mitchell, yet, to save every penny, the couple stayed home most nights and played cards.

Crystal's worst fears became realized when Warren quickly fell back into his old habits. He had now added pills to the steady mix of alcohol and recreational drug use, making for more fighting and more depression—especially as he waited for the Asylum studio dates to be announced. He had begun to consume vodka at a rate of a quart a day.

On the night Warren signed for his advance, an intense argument erupted that made Crystal finally realize the true extent of her husband's addiction. In a drunken rage, Warren hit her. The couple had already weathered more than their fair share of shouting matches, but it was the first time Warren had gotten physical. Shocked and confused, she summoned the police. Hoping to keep Warren out of jail, she immediately redacted her statement. Still terrified, however, she fled the apartment and hitchhiked to Phil Everly's house. He allowed her to stay for a few days while she ignored Warren's calls and contemplated her next move.

When she and Warren finally spoke, he swore he'd change. In an effort to keep his promise, the couple moved into a new apartment at the Oakwood Garden Apartments, signaling yet another fresh start.

Crystal soon learned she was pregnant.

⌥

A few weeks later, Jackson Browne showed up at the Zevons' new place with good news. Production on *Warren Zevon* was scheduled to begin the first week of November. The sessions would run throughout the holiday season, culminating in a summer release.

Elektra/Asylum's studios were located on North La Cienega in West Hollywood. With Browne at the production helm, many of his most talented and famous friends could be depended upon to stop by and make cameos. Like the John Rhys demos from the previous year, the sessions were booked for evening and overnight hours—only this time, by choice. Nighttime seemed to be the right time to get the likes of Lindsey Buckingham, Glenn Frey, Don Henley, David Lindley, Stevie Nicks, Bonnie Raitt, J. D. Souther, and Carl Wilson to swing down to party and jam. Warren also enlisted Phil Everly to add some backup vocals, along with new friend and songwriting collaborator Jorge Calderón. Every session, the full group would assemble for Browne and Warren to select the most appropriate lineup for each individual track recording.

Apart from Warren himself, no one knew the material better than Waddy Wachtel. Warren insisted on his old friend as the album's lead guitarist. "Warren had been playing a number of those tunes for me for a long time," Wachtel remembered. "Stuff like 'Hasten Down the Wind' and 'Carmelita,' I knew those back from the Everly tours. So, Warren pretty much put me in Jackson's face and said, 'He's got to be on this, he knows the songs and the parts.'"

It had been five years since Warren had entered the recording studio to lay down new material, yet he had never once stopped writing new songs. He entered the studio armed with a spectacular array of lyrics and compositions that critics and listeners wouldn't be able to ignore. Warren envisioned this new work as a "concept album," and experienced in chronological order, the songs told an entire epic of the American West.

Warren opened the album with a rollicking yarn of the frontier. He had originally written "Frank and Jesse James" in honor of Don and Phil Everly, crafting the story of the infamous bank-robbing brothers as a romantic metaphor for the Everlys' roles as aging legends in a changing musical landscape. The composition was heavily influenced by Warren's classical roots, and he deliberately incorporated complex syncopated chords for a playfully antiquated sound. It properly matched the throwback feel of the Old West itself. The composition was the closest to Aaron Copland that Warren ever got—whether he welcomed such comparisons or not. For the lyrics, he had pored over history books at the local library to get his facts straight on the lives of the real outlaws, and his ability to condense copious amounts of historical accuracy into such a structured pop framework proved a testament to his natural storytelling skills. More importantly, it was catchy. For the last year, Warren had even used "Frank and Jesse James" as a showpiece for friends and acquaintances to demonstrate his playing style. Especially proud of the song, Warren had initially recorded it on the Rhys demos over a year earlier.

Browne already considered "Frank and Jesse James" to be a potential radio hit. For this definitive recording, Browne enlisted seasoned pros Bob Glaub on bass and Larry Zack on drums. He rounded out the lineup with David Lindley, who added his distinctive flair to the track playing banjo and fiddle. Flattered as being inspiration for the song, Phil Everly came on board for background vocals.

Warren was never one to shy away from dipping into his own autobiography for lyrical content. Almost every love song he ever wrote had a specific girl in mind, and later, his own personal struggles seemed to be worked out therapeutically through his songwriting. "Mama Couldn't Be Persuaded," however, was not only the first true autobiographical song he completed; it was also the most humorously embellished for narrative's sake. He had the initial idea for the song a few years back while in Las Vegas for the Everly Brothers' doomed final tour. Inspired by Don Everly's casino winning streak, Warren scrawled the story of his own parents' courtship on hotel stationery. For the song, he shifted focus to William Zevon's professional gambler background, and Beverly's parents' lifelong disapproval of him. Life hadn't been easy for young, preadolescent Warren, but his song's rocking reimagining made the years of domestic squabbles fun to sing about. The lyrics painted a colorful portrait of the unnamed "gambling man" as a harbinger of the seedier side of life, while playing the role of the charming scoundrel; the "Mama" of the title can't resist the smooth-talking lothario, much to her family's dismay.

If *Warren Zevon* is to be taken as a spiritual chronology of the New West, "Mama Couldn't Be Persuaded" offered a look into the post-Depression era that linked the Old West of the James brothers to the modern neon landscape in which Warren and his generation now lived. For the track, the same studio lineup as "Frank and Jesse James" was used, creating a sonic continuity and further establishing the narrative structure that the full album would contain.

"Backs Turned Looking Down the Path" was a song written at a faster pace, but with no less autobiographical influence, than the other tracks on the album. Warren had started the initial work on it just prior to leaving for Spain with Crystal and had continued to tinker with it up until their first night in Madrid. At the time, he had confided to his new wife that it was the song he believed that he would be best remembered for. Although the song clearly reflected the hopeful wanderlust that Warren and Crystal had felt in leaving Los Angeles less than a year before, the resulting track was more reminiscent of his earliest style as part of lyme and cybelle.

Recorded at the end of January 1976, the folkish tune was one of the last tracks for the sessions and was given a more modern treatment with a switch in lineup: Lindsey Buckingham was brought in for additional guitar work, along with Browne himself, who played slide guitar; Marty David took over on bass and former Steve Miller Band player Gary Mallaber took over on drums.

"I knew Jackson for a while and had recorded with him on *For Everyman*," Mallaber remembered. "In LA, there was this amazing collective of songwriters and performers that kind of knew each other from hanging around the Troubadour and, eventually, all collaborating together. I got to be part of that 'roundtable' and then was brought in to meet Warren."

According to Mallaber, although it was Warren's album, Browne was the driving force in the studio. "Jackson, as a producer, always knew exactly what he wanted and who to use in chopping down that creative forest. So, for Warren's album, he really assembled the best collective that, I think, he knew would work. Much of the work was primarily divided between the other drummers and myself, and I think that Jackson and Warren always had it in mind to utilize certain players for their strongest suits on specific tracks."

In later years, Warren would joke that when he performed "Hasten Down the Wind" in concert, he could tell who his real friends were by counting the number of walkouts during the song. Not that it was a weak tune. On the contrary, it would later be heralded as one of his lyrical masterpieces. Originally written during his tumultuous split from Tule, Warren playfully explained later that the song was so personal, he had to write it in the third person. The ballad of lost, confused, young love did aim for the heart, especially presented as the first ballad introduced on the album. Its John O'Hara–inspired lyrics were enough to convince bestselling songstress Linda Ronstadt not only to cover the song later that same year, but retain the song's title for her own album. Waddy Wachtel played lead guitar on both versions.

For Warren's version, Wachtel was joined by the initial lineup of bassist Bob Glaub and drummer Larry Zack; Lindley added his slide guitar and Phil Everly contributed backup vocals.

Following the slow, mournful vibe of "Hasten," the next track brought listeners right back into the world of real rock and roll. Warren had recorded "Poor Poor Pitiful Me" as a demo track for John Rhys. The new, definitive version—with Browne at the production helm and a band twice the original size—rounded the rousing, tongue-in-cheek lament to bad relationships to new heights.

Warren later claimed that the song had been inspired by Desmond Dekker's reggae Rasta hit "Israelites," a song he sometimes covered years before with Danny McFarland during their Berkeley days. Laden with in-jokes and downtown Los Angeles references, the song's unnamed narrator makes his way across town where the girls only get fiercer and more dangerous, culminating in a humorous S&M episode at the famed Hyatt House. At that point in the track, Warren adds in dry spoken-word, "I don't wanna talk about it," before the band blazes back in before the fade-out. The core lineup was joined by Bobby Keys on saxophone and Lindley on fiddle. Jai Winding played piano to let Warren let loose vocally. For the rest of his career, Warren would often use the song as an encore to bring down the house.

Although vocally the two performers couldn't be less alike, it was songs like "The French Inhaler" that earned Warren early comparisons to fellow Elektra/Asylum artist Tom Waits. For this ballad, Warren offered a genuine "story song," a smooth yet lecherous come-on from one barfly (the song's narrator named Norman) to another (an unnamed aspiring actress, based largely on Tule). The dirty poetics, heavy in their innuendo and cynicism, come off as if Los Angeles skid row poet laureate Charles Bukowski had written "Eleanor Rigby." Warren's autobiography is also present in the fictional tale, as his references to the sad bar culture and the alcoholics that cohabit there—con men and washed-up wannabe starlets—were figures he had already rubbed elbows with in real life. The lyrics seem to exhume ashtray debris and Formica, and the tale's denouement is mournfully left open-ended.

The lush chorus of "The French Inhaler" was greatly aided by Eagles front men Glenn Frey and Don Henley, who popped into the studio to contribute vocals and rhythm guitar. Old Hollywood television composer Sid Sharp and his orchestra added the somber strings to both this track and the album's closing epic, "Desperadoes Under the Eaves."

Written at his in-laws' lodge during a visit to Aspen the year before, "Mohammed's Radio" was one of the first tracks laid down for the sessions and recorded the first week of November 1975. Warren constructed it as a gospel song, with the mellow, sing-song feel deliberately working its way up into becoming an adoring anthem for the love of music and all its healing powers.

Like the track before it, Warren created a tapestry of colorful fictional characters, all of whom are counted among the downtrodden: the local sheriff, the village idiot, and the rest of the young disillusioned baby boomers who can't pay for meat in the post-Watergate economy all switch on their radios for the solace and escapism that the soundtrack of the American airwaves provides. For the session, Warren was joined by the initial core band, plus Lindsey Buckingham and Stevie Nicks; Bobby Keys returned for the soulful saxophone breaks.

Warren's wiseass intellectualism could always be counted upon as a defining characteristic in his work. "I'll Sleep When I'm Dead" was a perfect example. The origins of the track's title stemmed from a sarcastic retort he had once given to Crystal when she had tried to help him relax at home. The two had both laughed so hard that the phrase quickly became both Warren's personal mantra and a song idea. Later, Warren would cryptically explain to interviewers that he'd written the song "on a practice drum set in the middle of the day at a friend's house in Death Valley."

He had envisioned it as a march that slowly built to a crescendo and incorporated the party atmosphere of the studio with all its lively, beautiful dissonance—whoops and hollers (many of which were provided by Jorge Calderón) included. The only catch was that he had, initially, insisted on playing drums for the track, although he wasn't much of a drummer at all. As a compromise, Browne recorded Warren doing his best John Bonham impression, then played that demo for professional drummer Gary Mallaber to use as the framework for the real recording. Mallaber, who had created the memorable jazz-infused high-hat intro to Van Morrison's "Moondance," easily replicated Warren's march concept and aided in crafting this song's signature cadence.

"Sometimes, you don't really know the strength or the endurance of the recordings that you're working on until after they hit," remembered Mallaber. "Then, you look back and say, 'Wow, this somehow became iconic.' I think that that was the feeling with my work with Van Morrison, and those recordings kind of got me the key to the city around LA, and at least, with Jackson's trust. I always believed that my work on Van's stuff made me a 'go-to' player for Jackson and, ultimately, the Warren tracks."

"On this song, Jackson had told me that Warren wanted to play the drums himself, but was talked out of it," Mallaber added. "Evidently, he had had fun going crazy demonstrating his ideas on the demos. But I was able to put that 'march' feel to it, really spirited, the way that Warren had envisioned it."

As far as the autobiographical quality to the song, Warren had begun collecting guns.

The gentle, Mexican-infused guitar opening to "Carmelita" was something that Waddy Wachtel had been refining ever since Warren first played the then unfinished song for him on the road with the Everly Brothers. Warren had also continued to refine the song over many years, recording numerous demos of alternate lyrics—even one with himself on lead guitar. In later years, Warren referred to the song as a "cheerful number about heroin," although that was one substance that, while he had sampled, he never abused. Other elements in the ballad, such as geographic references to the Pioneer Chicken Stand and Alvarado Street were real Los Angeles locations that he had frequented all the time. Aside from its tragic lyrics, the beautiful simplicity of the song would garner numerous cover versions in later years, starting with Linda Ronstadt's the following year—again featuring Wachtel on lead guitar. The stripped-down nature of the song contained the initial group lineup, plus Glenn Frey returning for some additional guitar.

In late November, just as the sessions were truly picking up steam, the group recorded one of the more soulful and funkier tracks on the album, "Join Me in LA." Warren had been sitting on the song for a while and had recorded a few demo versions in years past. Although not nearly as autobiographical as the rest of the songs, the track still fits into the chronological order of the full album by bringing the listener into the modern era of Los Angeles. Its "come hither" quality to the sin and promise of late-night Los Angeles oozes along a slow funk vibe. To fully capture the slow R&B tone of this atypical composition, Browne added a full section of female backup singers—Rosemary Butler, Stevie Nicks, and Bonnie Raitt. Bobby Keys again created the standout saxophone sections.

Like a great novel, *Warren Zevon* closes its final chapter in grand, epic style. "Desperadoes Under the Eaves" is Warren's magnum opus. Recorded near the album's home stretch in mid-January, the heartbreaking confessional on addiction, depression, and longing had been inspired by Warren's frequent solitary nights in seedy motels with no other company than his thoughts and his demons. And while it is clear that the song's narrator is shamefully hiding from the outside world, unable to face the judgment of the angry sun or the punishment of the threatening trees below, brilliant self-deprecation and Chandler-esque wit remind the listener that Warren is very much aware of *who* and *what* he is.

Although still under thirty, Warren wrote the song from the perspective of a man who has lived many lifetimes, condemned to repeat an entire stretch on earth over and over again until he gets it right. But it's as if his addictions follow him throughout every reincarnation. If the motel in which he is staying can withstand even the power of mother nature in order to keep running until the room bill is paid, then even death isn't an escape from the greatest of all Grand Inquisitors— himself. Warren would later admit that "Desperadoes" was, truly, the most autobiographical of all his songs.

For the operatic conclusion to the album, Warren and Browne brought back all key members of the band, plus Sid Sharp's strings, and enlisted Carl Wilson to help in arranging the all-important vocal chorus.

Wilson brought along his brother-in-law, Billy Hinsche, a Philippines-born session musician who had been one-third of the vocal group, Dino, Desi and Billy. "Jackson had contacted Carl Wilson, and Carl called me," Hinsche remembered. "He went, 'How would you like to be on a Jackson Browne album?' I loved Jackson's work, he's another LA guy, you know, so I was thrilled. We went down to the Elektra studios, which was really new and state-of-the-art at the time, and it was maybe nine at night. Jackson was in the booth with some other people—there were a lot of people at the session—but I had no idea that the session was for Warren. I hadn't heard of him at that time. Finally,

I see this guy come out of the booth, long hair and glasses, and he sits at the piano and starts yelling something to Jackson across the room. He goes, 'Forget playback—I'll show you!' and started demonstrating some changes right there on the piano. So, I laughed and thought, 'Now I get it.' But, really, that right there was my first impression of Warren— coming out of the shadows when coming to fit his vision."

Like Gary Mallaber, Hinsche observed that Browne seemed to take the lead in organizing the sessions' production and transitions. "Warren was very quiet, very focused, almost invisible," he recalled. "It seemed like it was Jackson's show until Warren had something that he was compelled to add in. Carl was brought in for 'Desperadoes' because of the gorgeous harmonies on it and, I think, had that Beach Boys type of harmony. I knew exactly what they were going for right there in the booth with my headset on. The arrangement is still one of my favorites."

Following the session, Hinsche and Warren became friends. "It was later that I really got to know Warren," he remembered. "There was one time when we were hanging out together, Warren and I, and we were in a Denny's in the middle of the night. We finished up and went outside and he flagged a cab. I said, 'Where are we going?' and he just smirked and said, 'You'll see.' So, he makes the cabbie take us out to the middle of nowhere, like a field or something, and he pulls a gun out of his jacket! He made this cabbie drive us to God-knows-where so he could show off shooting beer cans."

Warren again played the waiting game while the final recordings went into the postproduction stage.

In Browne's deliberate effort to establish Warren as a serious songwriter of true literary caliber, several of the tracks—the maudlin "Frozen Notes" and novelty songs "Excitable Boy" and "Werewolves of London"—were placed back on the shelf to be used at a later date. Biding his time, Warren kept himself busy by working on new songs and aiding a very pregnant Crystal settle into their new two-bedroom house in North Hollywood. Wanting his love of music to continue in both his children (son Jordan had, after all, been named after an amplifier), Warren played Beethoven and Beatles music against his wife's stomach, hoping for the baby to kick.

Browne was aided in the mixing by John Haeny and engineer Fritz Richmond. His intention was to unveil the finished album to Geffen and Elektra/Asylum president Joe Smith for a summer 1976 release. Just prior to that crucial meeting, however, personal tragedy struck. Browne, who was already in the early stages of recording his own new album, *The Pretender,* suffered a devastating blow when his young wife, model and actress Phyllis Major, committed suicide with an overdose of sleeping pills. While the glamorous couple had been dating ever since their chance meeting at the Troubadour in 1971, Browne and Major had only been married for four short months. Shocked and grief-stricken, the only twenty-eight-year-old Browne now found himself a widower and single father to their baby son, Ethan.

In an effort to stay on deadline, Browne enlisted the help of close friend Jon Landau, a fellow producer and manager who had been privy to much of *Warren Zevon*'s recording sessions. Landau's credits included not only managing up-and-comer Bruce Springsteen but also co-producing that artist's breakthrough album, 1975's *Born to Run.* Browne assigned the young producer to the all-important Geffen/Smith executive meeting on his behalf. A firm believer in Warren's work, Landau pushed hard at the unveiling, ultimately scoring *Warren Zevon* a release date for the second week of May.

Peaking at 189 on the Billboard charts, sales were underwhelming, but Warren's lyrics and composition—not to mention the lush arrangements and sleek production—made the debut a critical darling almost instantly. Robert Christgau of *The Village Voice* claimed he liked the way Warren resisted "pigeonholes like 'country-rock' while avoiding both the banal and the mystagogical."

Rolling Stone's Stephen Holden concurred, stating, "Zevon's style, however, is distinct. . . . Despite its imperfections, *Warren Zevon* is a very auspicious accomplishment. . . . Who could have imagined a concept album about Los Angeles that is funny, enlightening, musical, at moments terrifying and above all *funny?*" Kit Rachlis of *The New York Times* wrote, "Part of Zevon's appeal is the knowledge that he will only improve. He is already like a good boxer; he jabs with his romanticism, sits back on the ropes and challenges with his humor; his combinations are straight rock 'n' roll."

☙

The critics may have loved Warren's intellectual brand of rock and roll, but it was the album's commercial appeal that would ultimately dictate his future on the Elektra/Asylum label. Executives agreed that while the release of *Warren Zevon* warranted a tour, he was too new as an act to pack out a large house. They were forced to get creative in presenting him to the public, while still keeping travel and venue costs within check.

The label's solution was to book Warren and his band cabaret-style, in smaller clubs primarily along the East Coast, targeting venues that would appreciate his unique blend of story songs, biting lyrical humor, and—when the mood struck him—wild-child, piano-driven rock.

The gamble paid off. Under the guidance of road manager Howard Burke, the *Warren Zevon* tour—also referred to as the I'll Sleep When I'm Dead Tour—launched on June 11, 1976, with a kickoff performance at New York City's the Bottom Line, to great success. Word of mouth had spread of Warren's unique act and many of New York's biggest names came out for the debut gig. Not only was Bruce Springsteen spotted in attendance, but comedy bad boy John Belushi introduced the show and personally brought Warren out on stage.

There were compromises, however. Jackson Browne skipped Warren's tour, instead taking refuge from his wife's death in the studio to complete his own album. News of Waddy Wachtel's guitar prowess had spread far and wide and he was in demand more than ever; he was already off to Europe to back Linda Ronstadt's tour. In his place, American-born but England-raised rock guitarist Jerry Donahue took over the lead guitar duties, and longtime Jackson Browne veteran Mickey McGee was hired on drums. Warren was able to retain bassist Doug Haywood from the album sessions. The summerlong tour took Warren and crew south through Nashville and Philadelphia, then westbound again for final stops in Chicago and Denver. The roadshow made its triumphant ending back in Los Angeles at the Roxy.

As had been the case with the album he was promoting, Warren's live performances were the subject of almost unanimous critical praise. His greatest advocate was *Rolling Stone* staffer Paul Nelson. An aspiring novelist, Nelson's published criticism bordered on genuine literature, and the care he gave his output often gave his editors their fair share of headaches. Blurring the line between critic and artist, Nelson often sought out the performers with whom he was most enamored. While rock stars usually kept reporters at arm's length, Nelson could count Jackson Browne and Bruce Springsteen among his circle of friends. With Warren, Nelson immediately sensed a creative connection. While Warren was in New York for the album's tour, he took the time to dine with Nelson and the two became fast friends.

"They both had this affinity for Ross Macdonald and Lew Archer," explained Nelson's official biographer, Kevin Avery. "Their shared interests certainly helped propel the friendship forward. But, I think that Paul saw in Warren the same thing that Warren saw in Paul, and that was an understanding of what it was really like to be an artist. They both knew how difficult it is to take that vision that you have in your head—in Warren's case, setting it to music, and in Paul's case, putting it on the page. It wasn't easy for either of them."

Nelson quickly won Warren over with his own glowing review. "Although such oversimplification hardly does Zevon or the LP justice," he wrote, "it would suggest that he is a talent who can be mentioned in the same sentence with Bob Dylan, Jackson Browne, Randy Newman, Neil Young, Leonard Cohen, and a mere handful of others—no apologies necessary. If it doesn't, I'll come right out and say it: Warren Zevon is a major artist."

Many critics took note of Warren's onstage antics, not quite realizing that he was often very drunk during the performances. Alcohol had long been his solace during frequent bouts of depression, writer's block, and self-doubt. However, he could be just as indulgent, if not more so, when faced with the prospect of having to finally deliver the goods to a paying audience. Behind the scenes, the band, roadies, groupies, and celebrity admirers were always present to party and keep the drugs and booze flowing. With Warren, however, there were usually no limits, and his newfound success was proving an unfortunate catalyst in keeping his severe addictions going. Fortunately, he was able to perform as a functioning alcoholic and the show always went on.

For the time being, things were truly in Warren's favor. Only a few days after returning from the tour, Crystal went into labor and made Warren a father for the second time. Ariel Erin Zevon was born August 4, 1976.

Warren had made a vow that as long as the birth went well, and both his wife and child made it out okay, he would swear off vodka for a month. He kept the promise.

The record company had selected "Hasten Down the Wind" as the first single off the album, coupled with "Mohammed's Radio" as the B-side. It was followed swiftly by "I'll Sleep When I'm Dead." During the fall of 1976, it wasn't uncommon to hear these and other tracks off the LP in normal rotation on the radio, finding them in good company on the air with the likes of the Eagles, Elton John, and Linda Ronstadt. And, of course, Jackson Browne, whose album *The Pretender* was due out in November.

Still deep in mourning, Browne had been advised by family and friends to keep himself busy. Following that advice, he decided to go back on the road a month before *The Pretender* was due to hit, both as a strategy for early promotion and an effort to occupy his mind. He asked Warren to perform a series of joint concerts along the East Coast again during the month of October, and when those proved hugely successful, Warren was extended an offer to be Browne's opening act on a nine-city tour throughout Europe. As Browne had his three-year-old son to tend to and Warren and Crystal were nursing infant Ariel, Browne mandated that all friends and family were welcome on the tour, free of charge.

Although Warren wasn't the top dog on this tour, being Jackson Browne's opening act had its benefits. Everywhere they went, the group played to a packed house, meaning more and more ears were finally hearing songs that Warren had spent years crafting. Additionally, there had been a substantial budget behind the tour, guaranteeing numerous great musicians always on hand—as well as top-notch accommodations and plenty of press.

Under the arrangement, Warren used Browne's musicians during his opening set: guitarist Mark T. Jordan, bassist Bryan Garofalo, and drummer John Mauceri—all seasoned performers who could handle the material. After seven songs, Browne would take the stage and jam with Warren before going solo for the rest of the show. Browne had also taken to performing some of Warren's songs during his own solo portion, displaying Warren's songwriting abilities to new legions of fans.

Between late November and mid-December, the full band hit Stockholm, Manchester, Amsterdam, Oslo, and London. The seams of both performers were starting to unravel, however. As the pressures of being a headlining rock star, single father, *and* spiritual father figure to his ambitious musical friends all began to mount, Browne was not above lashing out at his hired hands and regretting his decision to tour so soon after his wife's death. Warren, on the other hand, soaked up whatever limelight had finally fallen his way. He not only traveled with a make-shift minibar in his luggage, but was usually fall-down drunk between gigs, leaving most domestic responsibilities on his wife.

When the tour finally ended, Warren and Crystal decided to kick around Europe a bit, stopping in to see old friend David Lindell in Spain. One night during the visit, Warren got loaded and Crystal made the grave mistake of trying to quiet him so that their infant daughter could sleep. Warren flew into a drunken rage that resulted in more vi-olence. He would tell Paul Nelson years later: "The first night there, I got into a fight with some drunken Spaniards over my version of 'Jingle Bells.' My glasses were smashed and my hands slashed by a broken beer mug. Things went downhill from here . . . "

Crystal frantically called the record label and begged for help and money. After emergency funds came through, Crystal returned to Los Angeles and took refuge at the home of Jackson Browne, who was al-ready well aware of the incident. With a baby of her own to care for, Crystal was determined not to take Warren back this time.

Warren had taken all of the money he and Crystal had in their hotel in Spain and—without bothering to pay the bill—purchased a ticket to Casablanca. "I decided to go to Morocco with a bag filled with Valium, vodka, and Fitzgerald," he later recalled. "Too much booze and not enough food. I've always figured that in dragging myself to Tangier and back, I squeezed the last drop of 'glamour' out of my rapidly worsening toxic condition."

Within a week of blackout drunkenness, the drugs and drink were gone, and Warren was flat broke. He tearfully called Crystal and begged for help to come home, claiming he had no recollection of how he ended up in Morocco. He simply didn't know what had happened.

But he did know that he was very much alone—and it had been of his own doing. After years of creative woodshedding and career hustling, the gods had seen fit to gift a handful of diamonds—a cache he was dangerously close to tossing away into the surrounding desert sands.

Hearing the shape he was in, Crystal acquiesced. Warren hung up the phone and waited for the money to come.

He looked east.

CHAPTER FOUR

(1977–1979)

WARREN RETURNED TO LOS ANGELES HAVING LEARNED A harsh lesson about his newfound fame and the effects it could have on his private life. Even with the recognition that *Warren Zevon* and its subsequent tour had brought, after Casablanca, he knew that he could lose it all—could find himself lost and alone, "figuratively and literally"—in the blink of an eye.

After the disastrous quarrel in Spain and having squandered the couple's very last cent in Morocco, Warren had to beg Crystal for financial help in getting back to the States. Once home, he sought refuge the best way that he knew how, forcibly submersing himself in the preparation for his follow-up album. It was a task that was easier said than done. Anxiety over both the critical and commercial receptions for this next record had driven much of Warren's erratic behavior in Amsterdam and Spain. *Warren Zevon*'s follow-up could assert his place as a rock-and-roll force with which to be reckoned; it could dictate staying power.

Whereas his debut had been entirely composed of songs years in the making, Warren now approached the follow-up effort with nearly nothing in the bag. Worse still, this new album was already highly anticipated by colleagues and critics, all viewing it as a legitimization of the promise that *Warren Zevon* represented. Although he had already been in the music industry for half his life, mainstream listeners saw Warren as a new kid on the block—and one who hadn't even scored a hit big enough to qualify him as a "one-hit wonder," should the next album flop. The pressure didn't need to mount; it was already there.

Aside from leftovers from the debut album and a few unfinished compositions that he'd started in Spain, Warren started from scratch. Creating enough new material to fill an entire LP, especially one hot on the heels of a critically acclaimed debut, quickly proved daunting and intimidating. *Warren Zevon* may have been imperfect, but *Warren Zevon* had been flawless—or at least as close to it as its eponymous creator, along with Jackson Browne, could muster.

The immediate pressure Warren felt upon his return from Morocco led to his first major bout with writer's block—a literary artist's greatest nemesis, which always seemed to lurk during the presaging season of urgency befalling a deadline. For his failing marriage, Warren found solace in music; for the failure of creative ability to meet the height of his own artistic standards, in drugs and alcohol.

From conception to postproduction, his first album benefited from the team of musicians and engineers who had come out of the woodwork to lend a hand. Whether or not many were there on behalf of Jackson Browne was irrelevant. The studio had been chock-full of talent and encouragement and the sonic quality of *Warren Zevon* was proof. Browne's stellar band of seasoned musicians had helped guarantee both the overall professionalism of the sessions and the balance between Warren's ego and perfectionism.

The new year, however, had brought tides of change. By this time, Waddy Wachtel was in constant demand as the "it" guitarist around Los Angeles and was frequently courted to tour with other acts. Browne, who'd had to contend with Warren's family problems in Europe on top of his own, now had *The Pretender* to promote. Both men would be around for the recording sessions, but as Warren faced the preliminary stages of the project, he was—as he had felt on the payphone in Casablanca—entirely alone. For an artist like Warren, however, there was liberation in this solitude. Crystal and Ariel had left him to his own devices and he wasn't expected to contact Browne until a collection of material was ready to be unveiled; he now had the autonomy that his creative duress required.

Warren Zevon had been full of gorgeous, poetically charged autobiographical songs of love, loss, and addiction. When crafting its final form, Browne had been very deliberate in holding back the more playful and commercial fare. In a bid to earn Warren recognition as a serious songwriter, Browne had remained steadfast in saving certain material he felt would muddle the album's literary tone—songs that critics, had they not already heard Warren's potential, might otherwise have regarded as minor: "Excitable Boy," a catchy 1950s throwback that contained, among other things, R&B backup vocals, saxophone breaks, and a narrative about a serial killer; an epic murder ballad about a dead mercenary that Warren had oh-so-proudly co-written in Spain with his buddy, a genuine soldier of fortune; and that funny novelty tune about a dapper, well-dressed werewolf. Convincing Warren of anything outside of this own creative vision was a notoriously difficult process, but, for the good of the album, Browne had been able to hold his ground.

Aside from being penned years before, those songs shared another characteristic—all were rare instances of Warren working with a collaborator. When Warren was writing songs of an autobiographical nature, setting his own thoughts and emotions to music came quite naturally. He was the sole author of every track that made up his first Elektra/Asylum release, rightfully deserving the album's eponymous title. When it came to mainstream appeal, however, he would often need a push toward a more commercial direction. Words like "quirky," "cerebral," and "esoteric"—dubious descriptors frequently recycled by critics struggling to pin him down—were not often associated with rock music, and certainly not viewed as a selling point to the youth market. Despite having had numerous discussions with Browne regarding the need for a radio-friendly track, Warren's writing was often accused of being over the heads of mainstream listeners. Even with "Hasten Down the Wind" and "I'll Sleep When I'm Dead" as two stellar singles, neither had charted. Browne had deliberately held back on the more commercial songs, but both he and Warren had believed in the tracks selected as singles. Their failure to find a mass audience came as a bit of a shock, leading Browne to reconsider the three track's he'd originally shelved.

David Geffen had been very adamant regarding Browne's active participation in the production of *Warren Zevon,* and for good reason. Browne's own self-produced releases had all been bona-fide hits and demonstrated his clear understanding of commercial appeal. He had shown that he was an artist of great integrity and his lyrics were uncompromised, yet they were catchy and accessible enough to enter frequent radio rotation. Browne had spent the last half decade writing songs that resonated with an entire generation—former flower children, now settling down and having families, nostalgic and disenfranchised by the failed ideals of the 1960s. His songs had meaning, but more important to the label, they charted well.

For Geffen, Browne was a shining example of the standards envisioned for Elektra/Asylum. This, and some haggling, had earned the green light to record *Warren Zevon* in the first place. But it had also come with Browne's dubious responsibility of having to produce it. Based on the enthusiasm and certainty with which Browne talked of Warren's talent, Geffen had expected not only a great record, but a great product. Besides, he had vouched for Warren, nearly pleading on his behalf. Let him put his money where his mouth was.

Warren, on the other hand, viewed his chief responsibility to be in the quality of his songwriting. The perfectionism with which he approached his writing was always a bid to meet his own self-imposed standards. This responsibility was the one he had to himself, the one for which he had always shirked other responsibilities throughout his life. Although he claimed to hold a genius-level IQ, he'd dropped out of high school to prove his worth as a musician. How many jingles had he pumped out in order to spend just a few precious hours in a professional studio? He had even been in the studio during his son's birth. How many friends' couches had he slept on, how many odd jobs had he worked to keep his instruments for as long as possible before the heat was turned off or the baby got sick? All his life, Warren had been told of his potential by key figures who continued to cast long shadows over his own musical standards. If this new work didn't deliver upon that potential, there had been no point to all the effort and sacrifice.

In later years, Warren would remark that his favorite albums were the ones that "were really the person," citing Bob Dylan's *John Wesley Harding* and Bruce Springsteen's *Nebraska* as examples. Here were instances where the final collection of songs formed a perfect, personal statement by a single artist. In that vein, *Warren Zevon* had truly been Warren Zevon. It was an ideal for which he reached: the musician-as-author. He may have chosen rock and roll as his primary medium of creative expression, but he revered writers and often related to the competitive temperaments of his literary heroes. Just as the psychedelic nights with David Marks on the Sunset Strip had been an attempt to capture the hedonistic enlightenment of Arthur Rimbaud and Jack

Kerouac, Warren viewed presenting new material to the likes of Jackson Browne and J. D. Souther as a challenge not unlike the rivalries between Ernest Hemingway, F. Scott Fitzgerald, and their fellow expatriates. For Warren, creating an honest song was as much of a battle as Hemingway's crusade for One True Sentence. It was an existential blood sport.

Only out of necessity did Warren seek fresh blood.

∞

Jorge Calderón had remained close to Warren ever since springing him from the San Vicente drunk tank in 1975.

Jovial and warm, Calderón carried a sharp wit and sarcastic sense of humor matched only by Warren's own. In the two years since helping Crystal post Warren's bail, Calderón's good nature and sense of loyalty had made him a consistent presence in the lives of the Zevons. Having grown up on the Latin sounds of calypso that embodied his native Puerto Rico, Calderón had first discovered rock and roll through the AM airwaves. He took up guitar and percussion and formed his first band while in his teens. After an unsuccessful bid for recognition in New York, the group relocated to Los Angeles in 1969. They disbanded when the city offered few opportunities, but Calderón opted to remain in Southern California to try his hand at session work. A multi-instrumentalist, it wasn't long before it achieved notice. Within a few years, he was touring with Lindsey Buckingham and soon made the acquaintance of Warren and Crystal.

Calderón had already worked in the studio with Warren a little, having added background vocals to numerous tracks on the debut album— most memorably yelling out Spanish phrases during the raucous "I'll Sleep When I'm Dead." As both a guitarist and percussionist, he also had a natural ear for melody, integrating a beautiful Spanish flair and lyricism to every song he touched. Most importantly, he had been introduced into the Zevons' lives as a friend first and musical colleague second, granting him rare immunity from Warren's sense of professional competition. Jorge was a man who could be trusted. And now, with so many of Warren's usual studio-mates out of the picture, he became the most logical partner for penning new material.

The first of what would be many collaborations between the two artists was "Veracruz." Written as one of Warren's favorite genres, the historical "story song," the ballad combined his love of research and natural literary abilities. For subject matter, the two chose an event that had, for all intents and purposes, been relegated to the footnotes of history: the 1914 US occupation of the eponymous Mexican city. Having caught a television documentary about Emiliano Zapata, Warren dug through biographies on the Mexican revolutionary at the Hollywood Library. When the seeds of the song were firmly in place, Warren had presented his findings to Jorge Calderón, who was already very familiar with the events and their historical and cultural significance.

Sung from the perspective of a Veracruz native struggling to keep his family intact amid the growing chaos, it was a profound and serious ballad for which the songwriters had brainstormed for accuracy and emotion. During the process, Calderón quickly demonstrated his value as a partner, not only writing the Spanish verses in their entirety, but infusing the song with the needed cultural perspective and emotion.

Additionally, working with Calderón had presented Warren with a healthy literary exercise. To that point, writing his other two story songs, "Frank and Jesse James" and "Roland the Headless Thompson Gunner," had yielded their own life lessons; the former had been Warren's first major foray into journalistic research, leading him to the library in search of Old West history and lingo, while the latter had proven he *could* collaborate with a writing partner—as long as that partner brought something special to the table. Through Calderón, Warren had been able to add another literary device to his songwriters' arsenal: using first-person perspective to re-create another culture. Like good historical novels, his previous tales had been safely written from the third-person perspective, allowing research to saturate the narratives with detail and atmosphere. Thanks to Calderón's own background and cultural knowledge, "Veracruz" rang with the honesty and emotion of a memoir. Whether the subject matter could be fit into a song that cracked the Top 40 was another matter.

For good measure, Warren and Calderón balanced this by making their second collaboration a disco tune.

Working together in close quarters, Calderón saw the full spectrum of Warren's personality. On some days, he saw the virtuosic bursts of energy and creativity that resulted in Warren's best work; on others, the intense episodes of drunkenness and mayhem that represented his worst behavior. During their collaboration, Calderón began to understand the complexities that drove Warren's creative process—and the dangerous game it was becoming.

On one memorable occasion, the two decided to catch Browne in concert at the Universal Amphitheatre. Warren had been drinking throughout their writing session that day, leaving Calderón to drive. It wasn't until they reached the arena parking lot that he realized Warren was packing a loaded .357 Magnum. He watched in disbelief as Warren leapt from the car and, waving the gun in the air, began shouting taunting rhymes about Browne at the top of his lungs. The spectacle quickly drew a sea of onlookers. After he belligerently attempted his way backstage, security forced him to leave.

As he turned thirty, not even the critical success of his first mainstream release or the birth of his daughter could properly curb the growing addictions. He and Crystal had finally reconciled, yet the few weeks of creative autonomy and unchaperoned bachelorhood she'd granted him hadn't merely focused his energies—it had left his substance consumption largely unmonitored. For Warren, the alcohol and drugs offered cures to too many of his maladies to quit cold turkey; booze provided him with the right level of arrogance and inhibition to sit and compose, while the drugs worked to spark his creativity and quiet the inner demons that made him second-guess his work. Introverted and shy throughout his youth, Warren had been using alcohol and drugs to struggle through social situations since high school. The only differences now were that the drugs were harder, the booze was top shelf, and he didn't need to sneak out of the house in order to enjoy it. Once reconciled, Crystal returned to a version of Warren no less out-of-control than the one she'd left in Spain. But at least he was working.

"Much of 1977 was a nightmare," Warren later claimed. "Crystal and I lived apart for several months, and I was seriously into the noir life—vodka, drugs, sex. Somehow, I got the songs written for *Excitable Boy*. Jackson begged me to get more sleep for my voice's sake. Waddy Wachtel looked like he wanted to tear his hair out for six months."

He added, "I thought my days were numbered in fractions."

∞

The following month, Browne asked Warren to play a series of benefit shows with him. Browne was known for his environmental advocacy and often volunteered to perform charity concerts and fundraisers. Drawing positive media attention to the philanthropic causes of his choosing, Browne would surprise the crowds by bringing talented friends and fellow rock stars onstage to lend a hand. Having not seen each other since their disastrous tour of Europe, he now reached out to Warren to get their chemistry flowing once again.

Browne had submersed himself in solitude while completing *The Pretender*. Using that time alone to grieve for his wife and re-prioritize his life and career, he now set out to tour again with a renewed energy and sense of focus. The sheer number of upcoming shows reflected the confidence Browne had in the tours to come. During the first week of February, he and Warren performed two shows dedicated to disarming the world of nuclear weapons, one show to save the whales, and another to benefit the United Farm Workers.

The charitable gigs were the sell-out smash Browne had hoped, garnering both performers solid press and critical accolades. With those US dates a success, Browne decided to take the show internationally, quickly agreeing to a two-night stint at Tokyo's Harumi Dome. Playfully entitled "The Rolling Coconut Review," the concert series also attracted big names such as Eric Andersen, Richie Havens, David Lindley, Country Joe McDonald, John Sebastian, and J. D. Souther—all of whom agreed to perform for free in what would become one of the first major all-star "Save the Whales" events in rock history.

Convinced that the drama that had plagued their European tour was behind them, Browne again extended the invitation to Warren. All was smooth until Browne revealed that the budget for such a charity tour wouldn't allow for Crystal and Ariel to come along. He explained that all performers were working for free—even close cohorts Waddy Wachtel and J. D. Souther—and any family members would be coming along out-of-pocket. During the previous tour, tensions had occasionally run high, leading to more than one altercation. Now, like a rewind of their arguments in Amsterdam, the two nearly went to blows.

Over their dinner with Don Everly later that week, Crystal made the grave error of admitting in front of a still-furious and heavily intoxicated Warren that she sympathized with Browne's position. They too went to blows—but with much worse consequences. Warren punched her before passing out cold. Crystal fled but returned in the morning. When Warren awoke hours later, she showed him the black eye, now swollen and raised. She had hoped the sight would be sufficient evidence of his addiction and the damage it caused. To her shock, he angrily accused her of lying. Warren refused to believe he could be capable of such violence, calling the act itself "evil." This time, he asked *her* to leave.

As she had made her way back into the house that morning, Crystal took note of their front lawn. It was littered everywhere with Warren's empties—liquor bottles and beer cans scattered throughout the grass. She hadn't noticed them the night before.

In the hopes of flexing some literary muscle, Warren decided to write a travelogue of his journey to Japan. He pitched his idea—a rock-and-roll chronicle in the style of "Gonzo" journalist Hunter S. Thompson, whom he admired—to *Rolling Stone*'s founding editor Jann Wenner. The young publisher not only agreed to run it, but also provided Warren with a young female editorial assistant to take on the trip.

When they returned from Japan, *Rolling Stone* rejected the article. Warren turned lemons into lemonade, the way he always did. He went home with the assistant.

As the clock ticked closer to the first few studio sessions, Warren drank with greater voracity. He had crashed at the San Francisco home of his *Rolling Stone* assistant for only a few weeks before returning to Los Angeles and taking a small apartment directly across from the Hyatt House. Rather than help his slipping focus, the new bachelor pad simply led to the continuation of Warren's binges—all-night parties, drugs, alcohol—and no shortage of friends and groupies to share in the illicit mayhem.

For Warren, it would take years of hard-earned sobriety before admitting the true depths of his self-loathing and denial.

Those closest to Warren would sometimes spy a crack in the facade—a brief glimpse of the fears and insecurities driving his dependency. Crystal had recognized the denial in his response to the black eye—going so far as to call the violence behind it "evil," yet still denying any responsibility for it. She understood now that Warren had no memories of his worst behavior. While part of him knew what he was, all of him seemed to deny it.

The latest estrangement from Crystal had granted him the time and flexibility to work at his own leisure, as well as the freedom to behave—or misbehave—as he pleased. But it provided none of the structure of marriage and family. Now facing a pending deadline, Warren found himself conflicted, needing a bit from both worlds. And instead of fueling his creativity, the isolation was fueling his addictions.

Warren called Crystal at her sister's home in Montana and begged her to take him back. She eventually agreed to a trial reconciliation. They would start with marriage counseling and then a family vacation to Hawaii.

Warren continued to pull creative teeth, using Stolichnaya as his proverbial novocaine. Needing a sense of balance between his personal and creative lives—and hoping to make good on his many promises to Crystal—Warren found them a new Spanish-style house in Los Feliz. Between the quiet, normal life symbolized by the new home with the liquor cabinets fully stocked, he believed he had finally found the balance he needed.

In Los Feliz, Warren found it easier to finish his work, but he had very little time left. The sessions for the newly named *Excitable Boy* were soon to begin.

∞

Warren's ongoing antics had taken their emotional toll on friends and family. Although no relationships had passed a point of no return, many had become strained in the years following production on *Warren Zevon* and the ill-fated tour of Europe. Having seen Warren at his worst, some musical cohorts were apprehensive about getting back into the studio with him.

Jackson Browne was the first to admit that the combination of helping Warren both personally and professionally had left him exhausted. He'd bent over backwards to get David Geffen in Warren's corner, had made Warren the opening act for *The Pretender* tour, and had even taken Crystal into his own home when Warren disappeared in Morocco. Last but not least, Browne had rolled with the punches when Warren was drunk and obstinate during the original recording process.

Waddy Wachtel later recalled, "Jackson brought me in, and he said, 'I need you to co-produce this record because Warren won't listen to me—anything I say. He'll give wise-guy cracks, but he won't listen. But he *will* listen to you—now, anyway. That'll change after *Excitable Boy*.' And he was absolutely right.' "

They set up camp at the legendary Sound Factory in Hollywood. With both Wachtel and Browne officially attached to the project, assembling a strong studio band became that much easier. As both co-producer and lead guitar, Wachtel was surrounded by stellar and familiar company: Russ Kunkel took on drums and Danny Kortchmar added additional percussion, while Jorge Calderón returned for background vocals and harmonies to the full album. Various bassists were used for different tracks, and—like *Warren Zevon* before it—*Excitable Boy* was chock-full of cameo appearances by renowned musicians.

They had even been able to land Fleetwood Mac's Mick Fleetwood and John McVie to add their respective drum and bass skills to one of the first songs to be cut—that funny werewolf song audiences found so amusing.

∞

The origins of "Werewolves of London" went back to 1974, during the earliest sessions for the notorious John Rhys demos. Warren had only just come off his stint with the Everly Brothers when Phil Everly offered the casual recommendation that the young songwriter come up with a playful tune that could inspire a dance craze. An avid movie buff, Everly took it a step further and suggested a possible title, cribbed from an old Universal horror film he had recently caught on television—*Werewolf of London*. The obscure thriller held the distinction of being the very first Hollywood film featuring the mythical monster. In a description that could also have been made of Warren, upon the film's 1935 release, *The New York Times* had called it "a charming bit of lycanthropy."

Throughout those years, he and Crystal spent many nights hanging out in the Venice Beach home of LeRoy Marinell. During one otherwise typical visit, the trio sat around smoking weed and horsing around when Warren decided to amuse Marinell with Everly's silly idea about a werewolf dance. They were still laughing when Waddy Wachtel—straight from the airport, having just returned from a gig in England—walked through the front door.

Warren later recalled, "Waddy walked in and said, 'What are you guys doing?' And I said, 'We're doing the "Werewolves of London."' And Waddy, without batting an eye, said, 'You mean, "Aah-Ooh!

Werewolves of London?'" And we said, 'That's right.' And he sat down and we wrote it in twenty minutes."

Marinell had been saving the song's now-signature guitar riff for years, and while there is no bridge or key change within the simple composition, its three-chord structure made it ripe for jamming. Wachtel wailed on his Stratocaster and, laughing, began to yell out a first verse about the werewolf seeking out Chinese food through the rainy streets of SoHo. "Yeah, passing a line from each of us around," Warren added. "I remember certain lines and whose they were. I think most of the first verse was entirely Waddy. I thought it was pretty remarkable that he spontaneously delivered himself of this sort of Paul Simon–esque verse."

Hysterical, Warren chimed in for the second verse and, finally, Marinell concocted the third verse about the "hairy-handed gent" running amok in Kent. They were done in twenty minutes, giggling, but not really thinking too much of the song. At Wachtel's request, Crystal had jotted down the lyrics in her steno pad—just for posterity.

The following day, Warren and Crystal stopped by the studio where Jackson Browne was tinkering with some of his own demos. In passing, Warren mentioned the novelty song, then sat at the house piano and performed a bit. Browne loved it and soon added it to his concert repertoire. When they had toured Europe together, Warren and Browne often performed it as a duet.

Encouraged to use it for *something*, Warren initially recorded a version for the Rhys demos, then later, the version Browne had shelved during the *Warren Zevon* sessions. During the many versions, multiple ensembles took a crack at the playful number, but none struck the recording team as a definitive—or rather, releasable—cut. Now feeling the crunch of meeting *Excitable Boy*'s studio deadlines, Warren decided to finally record that polished, definitive version.

Warren later recalled the long road that the song had taken in becoming an addition to *Excitable Boy*: "Well, that was the last of several different ensembles that played [the song]. And I don't remember how many we did, but I remember that Waddy said, 'I think we're done.' And Mick [Fleetwood] stood up and said, 'We are *never* done!' But we played it before. We'd recorded it with different groups. And I remember that Jorge Calderón said, 'I think you need a *real* band'. . . . And I said, 'Really? You mean like Buddy Rich?' I remember that. And Jorge said, 'No, I was thinking more like Fleetwood Mac.'" After Calderón made a phone call, Fleetwood and McVie agreed to come to the Sound Factory and help hammer it out.

According to Wachtel, the arduous recording session required for "Werewolves of London" was comparable to the infamous filming of *Apocalypse Now*. As co-writer, he had already performed lead guitar on every previously recorded demo. But now, with Browne at the switchboard and pros from Fleetwood Mac rounding out the band, the silly novelty tune from LeRoy Marinell's house slowly morphed into a promising rock-and-roll track.

By dawn, the group had cut sixty takes. They decided to use the second one.

Warren had specifically penned "Johnny Strikes Up the Band" to play as the album's opener. Led off by Wachtel's signature licks, the track kick-started *Excitable Boy* like a finger-snapping, toe-tapping call to arms. Its opening lines, "Dry your eyes, my little friend," playfully worked as a lyrical response to the heartbreaking fade-out coda of "Desperadoes Under the Eaves," marking the first of numerous instances where Warren seemed to thematically link the "omegas to the alphas" of consecutive albums.

Although the lyrics offer no direct identification of the "Johnny" in question, Warren often used certain first names for his characters more than once and with little explanation. Norman in "The French Inhaler" was one example. In the case of this song's eponymous "Johnny," various interpretations have made him a bandleader returning triumphantly to town, bringing with him the joy of music, or perhaps a drug dealer arriving with his long-awaited cache. In later years, Warren would also use "Johnny" as an endearing nickname for Jordan, as well as in other later songs.

As always, Warren liked to simplify things: "I appropriated the title from an opera, *Jonny Spielt Auf,* by Ernst Krenek," here referencing an obscure 1927 German opus that had been banned throughout Nazi Germany. As for the "Freddie" that is "getting ready," Warren claimed he'd had blues legend Freddie King in mind. For the album's master track, Warren and Wachtel were joined by Russ Kunkel on drums and Leland Sklar on bass, with Danny Kortchmar handling additional percussion.

Had Kurt Weill ever written a libretto based on works by Edgar Allen Poe, it might have come close to the macabre tone of Warren's prized collaboration with ex-mercenary and Dubliners owner David Lindell. "Roland the Headless Thompson Gunner" was another older composition that Warren had been sitting on for years, pre-dating his contract with Elektra/Asylum. Written during the Zevons' idyllic 1976 sojourn to Spain, Warren had used for inspiration Lindell's true stories of his time in Africa as a soldier of fortune. He had worked closely with Lindell to get his dark ghost tale about a betrayed gun-for-hire as accurate as possible in its historical references and portrayal of life as an international mercenary.

On the day of the recording, Wachtel had the band get to the studio earlier than scheduled, hoping to nail the song's theatrical, orchestra-driven ending before Warren arrived. Wachtel took to the engineering booth and led the musicians through the extra rehearsal time, with every member of the ensemble repeating the nuances of Warren's full arrangement until it was perfect. When Warren showed up, the band shocked him by executing it flawlessly on the very first take. As the crescendo of Russ Kunkel's drum march brought the song to its thunderous conclusion, Warren dramatically leapt from the piano, his arms in the air.

In later years, the song itself gained status as a supreme fan favorite, rivaled only by "Werewolves of London" as Warren's best-known work. He not only included it on nearly all future set lists throughout the remainder of his career, but it would one day hold the profound distinction of representing his swan song from public performance.

While the same profundity could not be said of the album's title track, the rollicking, piano-driven rock and violent, offbeat lyrics of "Excitable Boy" instantly made it a notorious requisite for nearly all future Warren Zevon concerts—not to mention providing yet another outlaw sobriquet for his ever-growing list.

An homage to classic R&B, "Excitable Boy" featured some of Warren's most bizarre lyrics yet. The tale of an adolescent sociopath and his grisly spree included scenes of assault, attempted cannibalism, murder, and necrophilia—all culminating with the construction of a cage fastened of human remains. While horrific in theory, the dark subject matter is instead infused with Warren's signature tongue-in-cheek humor and playful sense of shock value. And it was very catchy.

Like "Werewolves of London," the principal draft for "Excitable Boy" started during a visit to LeRoy Marinell's home in Venice Beach.

Warren and Crystal had recently returned from Spain and were still awaiting Jackson Browne's confirmation of the Elektra/Asylum deal. To celebrate their homecoming, Crystal had prepared Warren's favorite dinner, pot roast. She became hysterical as he expressed his gratitude— tearing off his dress shirt and rubbing the meat all over his bare torso. When Marinell coincidentally prepared the very same meal for them a few nights later, the couple burst out laughing and shared the story with their very amused host.

While jamming after dinner, Warren confided in Marinell his frustration that no one ever allowed him to play guitar on any of his tracks. When Marinell explained that that was due to Warren being a little "too excited" in his playing style, Warren leaned in and smirked. "Well, I'm just an excitable boy."

Undecided if the song was strong enough for his Elektra/Asylum debut, Warren tested the waters by performing it at parties for friends and guests. Usually, the piano-thumping yarn of rape, murder, and grave-robbing got an enthusiastic response—especially from those who were well accustomed to Warren's sense of humor. At one Los Angeles soiree, however, he was disappointed to learn folk songstress Joni Mitchell found the tune less than amusing—although it is not remembered if the version sung for Mitchell included the omitted verse that described tearing off the prom date's arm and fucking the cavity.

As a longtime appreciator of Warren's unique sense of humor, Browne loved it. Although it had been the plan to use Warren's first album as a showcase for the more serious side of his songbook, Browne nonetheless recorded a version during those sessions. Like the early cut of "Werewolves of London," the song was ultimately shelved for *Warren Zevon*'s follow-up. It was now decided that "Excitable Boy" would pair nicely with this album's edgier humor and darker themes. The title also worked well for the album itself, introducing the darkly playful side of Warren it was meant to represent.

For the definitive studio recording, Warren used the core lineup from "Roland the Headless Thompson Gunner," with a few additions to match his updated arrangement. Jim Horn was brought in to provide the song's R&B-infused saxophone break, while Linda Ronstadt and Jennifer Warnes provided the retro "girl group" backing vocals.

"Accidentally Like a Martyr" was a composite based on an older sketch Warren had been noodling with for years, coupled with additions reflecting the tumultuousness within his marriage. Dating back to the Rhys sessions, the song had started as an up-tempo pop number entitled "Why'd I Let You Get to Me Again." Warren had since renamed the song and slowed its pacing, transforming it into a proper ballad. It also featured some of his most emotional and reflective writing since "Hasten Down the Wind." For the studio session, Warren now used the same lineup as "Johnny Strikes Up the Band," inviting Karla Bonoff to provide the additional backing vocals.

Although recorded on separate dates and featuring different session players, both the songs Warren had written with Jorge Calderón were aligned consecutively on the album. The first, "Nighttime in the Switching Yard" was the disco song that the duo had penned to balance out the seriousness of "Veracruz" and its anti-imperialist social commentary. Once the two friends were satisfied in their collaboration—teaming up on a layered historical ballad with both lyrical and compositional complexity had been no easy task—offering up a radio-friendly disco track to the label seemed like a bargaining chip to guarantee "Veracruz"' for inclusion on the final release. And despite Warren's preference for penning more cerebral and literate fare, adding a funky song with a danceable vibe to his repertoire was a sure-fire way to get audiences on their feet during live performances.

While Warren and Calderón had been discussing possible material for their follow-up to "Veracruz," Warren shared with him some of ex-mercenary David Lindell's stories about the railroad switching yards and the men responsible for manually changing the tracks for each passing train. Over dinner with Calderón and Wachtel weeks before, Warren had explained his idea of using Lindell's stories as a starting point for a new song. Intrigued by the image of a mysterious track operator, alone at night with his trains, the three immediately began work on the track. Since disco was still a huge craze, the group jammed out by making Warren's concept as funky as possible. Calderón, who was not only a songwriter but a gifted percussionist, had suggested the syncopated a cappella sections to stand in for a proper chorus. When the session date for "Nighttime in the Switching Yard" finally arrived, Bob Glaub returned on bass and Danny Kortchmar accompanied Wachtel on second guitar; renowned drummer Jeff Porcaro came in for the track, only a few months away from establishing his own band, Toto.

As one of the last songs left to record, "Veracruz" featured an almost entirely different lineup from the sessions up to that point. Kenny Edwards provided bass and Rick Marotta, who would go on to form the band Ronin with Wachtel the following year, stepped in on drums. In order to capture the cultural flavor of the song, Warren included additional instruments into the composition: Jim Horn traded in his saxophone for the nostalgic tone of the recorder, while a Mexican harp, or *jarana*, and *requinto* guitar were added to flesh out the song's final, heartbreaking sound.

Two additional songs had been cut in demo form, but ultimately shelved: a maudlin ballad entitled "Frozen Notes" and "Tule's Blues," which Warren had already recorded in an earlier form for *Wanted Dead or Alive*. Although the songs had been slated to appear on *Excitable Boy*, both producers Browne and Wachtel were unsure of their inclusion—especially Wachtel, who hated both.

Everyone was exhausted when the *Excitable Boy* sessions wrapped. Warren and Browne were particularly ready and willing to consider the album complete. When Wachtel returned to the studio one night, Browne informed him that he and Warren were about to hold an impromptu "listening party," and had invited friends and family to hear *Excitable Boy* in its entirety. Once the guests arrived, Wachtel was immediately aghast. He watched as a small gathering shifted and yawned, fighting their boredom and indifference to the tracks. Once the final song had faded out, he checked his watch to find that the album was only twenty-four minutes from start to finish—barely long enough to qualify as a releasable LP. Furious, Wachtel grabbed both of his cohorts and dragged them back into the studio.

"I took Warren and Jackson and I told them we didn't have a finished album," Wachtel remembered. "There were two songs that I took off, 'Tule's Blues' and another one called 'Frozen Notes,' and I said, 'I'm sorry, guys, but neither of these songs fit on the record.' It wasn't that I didn't like them—I mean, we worked them and [Don] Henley did a beautiful harmony on 'Frozen Notes'—but, honestly, those two tracks dragged it all down. Jackson was surprised and said, 'What are you talking about, we have an album right here,' and I had to be honest. I said, 'You're fucking crazy.' And I had no problem telling Warren, they were 'duds' in the context of closing the album's second side. People at this party of theirs were on the phone, walking around, yawning."

According to Wachtel, he pulled the two men aside and made them peek into the living room to see the apparent boredom around the room. "I said to them, 'You believe me now? You see what's fucking happening in there? We *don't* have an album yet.'"

Wachtel gave Warren an ultimatum. He was booked to tour with Linda Ronstadt for the next three weeks and when he returned, he demanded two new songs written—both matching what he considered to be the same quality of the other material. Worn out from the pressures of meeting the *Excitable Boy* deadline, Warren begrudgingly agreed. As Wachtel recalled, "He just lowered his head and said, 'Alright, alright— fucking asshole, alright.' But that was us."

Initially, it had been *Excitable Boy*'s looming session dates that pushed Warren's recent openness toward collaborative writing. Regardless of its necessity, the process had yielded incredible results. Working alongside Jorge Calderón hadn't merely gotten Warren out of a creative jam; writing "Veracruz" together had been a productive and meaningful experience for both. It had proven that with the right partner, Warren's writing could expand in genre and instrumentation even further, sparking even more creative possibilities. With only mere weeks until Wachtel's return, he decided to team up with Browne to finish the album once and for all.

Although Warren's drinking hadn't curbed during the production of *Excitable Boy,* the daily creative regimen of the studio had kept the depression and self-doubt at bay. However, facing the new frustrations that yet another deadline presented, Warren's default creative process quickly led back into dangerous territory.

Only a few nights after the studio altercation with Wachtel, Browne received a frantic phone call from Crystal. Warren was on a drunken rampage. In fear—and at her wit's end—she pleaded for Browne's help. He immediately sped to their home in Los Feliz and spent hours calming Warren down. He later recalled, "I went over to his house because a bannister had been ripped off the wall. It was late when I got there, one or two in the morning, and he had no memory of doing this."

Getting creative in his effort to keep the peace, Browne suggested the best therapy he knew—working on their song. The two wrote into the late hours of the night, still drinking, but now with an air of creative camaraderie. "We sat down and started this song," Browne recalled. "I might have written the first two [lines]. Then I went down. When I woke up, it was a song. I don't know what the arc of his waking and sleeping was, but when I came up, it was done." To his astonishment, Warren— even in an inebriated state—had written a gorgeous and heartfelt song for Ariel.

"Tenderness on the Block" was the first true set of lyrics that Warren had penned for his infant daughter, writing from his own perspective as a proud father: possessing the knowledge that this new life will soon grow up to face the excitement and romance of becoming an adult, and the bittersweet frustrations that a parent faces in having to sit back and watch it occur. Rather than perform the gentle lyrics as a ballad, Warren composed a distinctive repeated piano lick throughout the chord progression, the playful light-rock vibe that was just what the album needed—and Wachtel expected.

Perhaps as a young single father himself, and with his position as Ariel's own godfather, Browne always deemed "Tenderness on the Block" among his personal favorites of Warren's songs.

There was still the matter of Warren's behavior, however. The cathartic creation of "Tenderness on the Block" had successfully brought him back down to earth during a particularly erratic, alcohol-infused episode, but Warren had apparently learned little from that night's drama. Having written the song following a period of blackout drunkenness, Warren had already forgotten the destruction he had inflicted upon the house. Much like Crystal's black eye of the previous year, Warren couldn't accept accountability for damages done.

Browne took the initiative in seeking more help, this time calling Elektra/Asylum head Joe Smith, who had replaced David Geffen in a bizarre turn of events that had seen Geffen temporarily retire during a highly publicized cancer scare. (Geffen was now vice chairman of Warner Bros.) Without emphasizing the gory details, Browne explained to Smith that Warren was burned-out from the stress of completing *Excitable Boy* and needed some time off to ponder the album's final cut. Sympathetic, Smith contacted the label's go-to A&R (artists & repertoire) man, Burt Stein, and asked the charismatic representative to accompany Warren on a brief retreat to Hawaii. With no time to lose, they left right away. While there, they got into a mess with a local waitress who coerced them into "visiting" a local friend—unaware that they were aiding her in breaking and entering. Warren wrote the song that night on a wet cocktail napkin. "Lawyers, Guns and Money" would become one of Warren's best-known songs and, much to his delight, the one most quoted by political commentators when analyzing foreign policy.

Wachtel called Warren as soon as he returned from his tour with Linda Ronstadt. "How'd we do?" he asked.

"I got 'em," Warren said.

Wachtel was rightly pleased with the material awaiting him. "Tenderness on the Block" was a lighthearted rocker, but a rocker nonetheless, with plenty of sonic meat for the ace guitarist to sink his teeth into. Additionally, the signature piano refrain provided a perfect counterpoint to Wachtel's incorporated licks. To Wachtel, this was "as good as it gets." He recalled, "We were all over the moon with that one—it had these little bits of classical, all with rock and roll." And "Lawyers, Guns and Money" not only offered up Warren's signature humor in its adventurous, yet self-deprecating, desperation, but it's hard-rock power chord structure drove the album to its thundering conclusion. Wachtel later recalled, "He wrote two incredible songs."

In order to get *Excitable Boy* completed in time for its January release, the three immediately headed back to the Sound Factory. In the whirlwind sessions for both tracks, they used the crew from "Nighttime in the Switching Yard," Kenny Edwards and Rick Marotta, on bass and drums, respectively.

With all players and crew satisfied, *Excitable Boy* was finally wrapped.

∞

As had been the case with *Warren Zevon* two years earlier, everyone was proud of the work, yet admittedly eager to move on. Wachtel had more gig offers than he could list—not only as a session man, but for various tours and further producing work—and Browne had all but washed his hands of having to guide Warren around professionally. It was uncertain if *Excitable Boy* would finally garner Warren the mainstream listeners Elektra/Asylum was hoping for, which would also dictate any preliminary plans for a promotional tour and potential third album. Regardless of the outcome, Browne had the postproduction of his new album to complete and a career to focus on. Warren had the tools to keep his career running; the ball was in his court.

For the cover of *Warren Zevon,* Wachtel's older brother, Jimmy, had acted as photographer and graphic designer, providing an iconic shot of a very dapper-looking Warren on the outside steps of the Palladium during that year's Grammy Awards. With the atmospheric tones of the spotlights in the background, the image had been a perfect fit for the new LP. Adding a tongue-in-cheek nod is the fact Warren hadn't even been invited to the awards ceremony he stood beside.

Jimmy Wachtel returned to design *Excitable Boy.* This time, however, Warren wanted to get even more conceptual. Although the primary photo shoot for the cover had yielded strong traditional headshots of Warren against a vibrant red background, at his insistence, Wachtel added multiple layers of retouches to Warren's face, making the singer appear as much as the titular "boy" as possible. The results presented Warren as a sort of mischievous bookworm, perversely innocent and cherubic given the thematic contents of the songs—particularly the album's title track.

To further the design's ironic motif, Crystal arranged the inner sleeve's design photograph: a plate of home-cooked side-dishes—potatoes, carrots, peas, and garnish—with a .44 Magnum hand cannon in place of Warren's beloved pot roast. She called the conceptual piece, "Willy on the Plate." Warren loved it.

That week, Warren made Howard Burke's wife and personal assistant, Claudia, drive him to a local gun shop. He had to have one for his home arsenal.

∽

As a collective, Warren, Browne, and Wachtel were all shocked when the label executives announced their intentions for the album's marketing campaign. While the team had successfully delivered the goods in time for a January 18, 1978, release, the three were furious when "Werewolves of London" was picked as the flagship single.

Wachtel recalled, "When they picked 'Werewolves' we were aghast— we were spitting and cursing, you know, 'What the fuck? "*Werewolves*"? Is that really what they want to hear?' I mean, we wrote it in like ten minutes on the run."

Warren and company hadn't agreed with Elektra/Asylum's choice for the first single, but the optimism for the album was apparent: in a push for major exposure, they planned to release five singles—a generous amount given the LP consisted of only nine songs.

Joining "Werewolves of London" as radio edits were "Johnny Strikes Up the Band" and "Excitable Boy," followed by "Nighttime in the Switching Yard" and "Lawyers, Guns and Money." As the label had anticipated, "Werewolves" proved the track with the most staying power, hitting 21 on *Billboard. Excitable Boy* itself proved a solid hit; on May 13, it cracked the Top 10 at a respectable Number 8. By April, the album was certified gold.

As had been the case with *Warren Zevon,* critics loved Warren's second effort, widely acknowledging his evolving presence as more than merely the songwriter of other artists' hits.

"The further these songs get from Ronstadtland, the more I like them," wrote Greil Marcus in *The Village Voice,* being one of many renowned cultural critics who continued to take Warren seriously as an artist. "The four that exorcise male psychoses by mock celebration are positively addictive, the two uncomplicated rockers do the job, and two of the purely 'serious' songs get by. But no one has yet been able to explain to me what 'accidentally like a martyr' might mean."

Barbara Charone of *Sounds* agreed with the addictive nature of Warren's harder-rocking efforts, writing, "Undoubtedly, *Excitable Boy* is one of the finest albums to emerge since Warren Zevon's first album surfaced over a year ago. It transcends California and all its smugness, America, the universe and punk rock too. In a word; it's brilliant."

Most critics were enthusiastic in the darkly humorous turn Warren's writing had taken with the new effort, and assured legitimization of Jackson Browne's intuition to save the fun stuff for the second album. Now that Warren's writing talents had been confirmed, there was an openness from critics and fans alike to see his more mischievous, and wilder, side.

"On the inner sleeve of Warren Zevon's *Excitable Boy* album is a picture of a .44 caliber revolver, and this foreshadows the performance by Zevon as he blows the audience away," wrote Chip Engemoen. "The lyrics from many of Zevon's songs conjure up images of Clint Eastwood meeting the Texas Chainsaw Murderer, but the music is incredibly fine in Zevon's piano-based rock. The lyrics are clever and the violence in them is tongue-in-cheek, reminding one of Monty Python."

Billboard, on the other hand, zeroed in on the more serious nature of Warren's ballads and more autobiographical tracks. "Zevon's second album proves to be a more balanced and cohesive set of true-to-life tales of day to day living," claimed its review. "His lyrics, no matter how morose and down, nevertheless reflect reality and the sad but true deficiencies in the human condition. Zevon's first album was critically acclaimed and this follow-up should add further credibility to the artist's songwriting ability."

During interviews, Warren made a habit of name-dropping his major literary influences and taking on a serious, theory-driven voice when speaking about his writing. The apparent dichotomy of a scholarly intellectual in whose chest beat a rock-and-roll heart soon crafted an undeniable mystique. It seemed to bring out the literary best in the major cultural critics who profiled him, many of whom were as excited by his approach to a "thinking-man's rock and roll" as they were confused by his conflicted personal nature.

Greil Marcus of *The Village Voice* was moved to write more than a usual review of the album, instead running a meditative essay on Warren's persona within the grander perspective of the contemporary music scene. By the end of his overtly cerebral ruminations on the meaning behind Warren's use of gun imagery, horror themes, and an apparent bloodlust, one is left wondering if Marcus approves or not.

"If Zevon opened his first Asylum album hanging himself with the same corny rope (in "Frank and Jesse James"), he cut himself down by the end (in "Desperados Under the Eaves")," Marcus wrote. "Right below the surface—with Zevon, the surface is usually a joke—Zevon's songs speak of a fascination with violence as a means to life, of a need to touch it, to come to terms with it."

Of the album's seemingly cavalier regard toward violence and death, Marcus added, "You won't get to the bottom of *Excitable Boy* simply by noting that its subject matter includes contract killing, the Congo civil war, revenge murder, psychos, the Mexican revolution, rape, the Symbionese Liberation Army, necrophilia, and mutilation, but you won't completely miss the point, either. *Excitable Boy* could just as well have been titled *Red Harvest*."

Less conflicted was tried-and-true friend Paul Nelson, who followed up his 1976 declaration that "Warren Zevon is a serious artist" with his reaction to *Excitable Boy*'s release. "Warren Zevon's *Excitable Boy* is the best American rock & roll album since Bruce Springsteen's *Born to Run* (1975), Neil Young's *Zuma* (1976) and Jackson Browne's *The Pretender* (1976)," he jubilantly declared in *Rolling Stone*. "If there's not enough firepower in that statement, let's cock the hammer on another. Thus far, the Seventies have introduced three major American rock & roll artists—Browne in 1972, Springsteen in 1973 and Zevon—and I have every confidence the music of all three will be even better in the future."

Like all critics who had taken note that Warren's fixation with guns seems to reach far beyond the marketing motif that identified his trade-marked persona, Nelson too relished in writing about a musical artist who seemed to have romantically swaggered out of a dime-store pulp novel. "Pictured on the inner sleeve of this album is Zevon's .44-caliber Smith & Wesson revolver resting on a dinner plate filled with his wife's cooking," Nelson noted. "The photograph is titled 'Willy on the Plate,' and it tells the whole story. Warren Zevon wants it all—and, on *Excitable Boy*, that's exactly what he gets."

In his own rumination on the Zevon mystique, Greil Marcus had found the gun's overwhelming omnipresence to be a somewhat darker specter, recalling a brief, yet ominous exchange with the artist: "Or as Warren Zevon said to me when I asked him if the gun pictured on the inside sleeve of *Excitable Boy* was his: 'Not that one.'"

∽

Warren's developing "bad boy" persona was further etched in an extended profile in *Rolling Stone,* coinciding with both the release of *Excitable Boy* and the start of its tour. "To me, *Excitable Boy* sounds ferocious, all growling guitars and driving drums," wrote Dave Marsh. "To Zevon, 'it's more wholesome than my last album. Because of the spirit of fun. Fun is my idea of art—fundamentally, I mean.'"

Marsh, like all writers before him, couldn't help but emphasize the duality that not only mystified Warren's audience, but often, seemingly, himself. "I'd call him a visceral intellectual," Marsh noted, "except that he reminded me earlier of [Raymond] Chandler's advice: 'Eddie, don't get complicated. When he gets complicated, he gets unhappy. When he gets unhappy, his luck runs out.'

"Zevon says life is much less complicated with notes, which may be why he's running in luck lately," Marsh added. "And to celebrate his 31st birthday, he bought a .44 Magnum. When he got home, he threw up. That excitable enough for you?"

∽

To promote *Excitable Boy,* the label had upped their stake in Warren, booking a string of larger venues than his previous promotional tour. With "Werewolves of London" quickly becoming a quirky radio staple and excellent critical word of mouth for the album itself, there were higher expectations for audience turnout.

Even amid all the positive early buzz, Warren had yet to prove himself as a genuine draw, leading to some mandatory budget compromises along the way. More importantly, the tour would be missing one of his most constant advocates: Jackson Browne, who opted to skip participation. After a falling out that all but entirely severed their professional working relationship, Browne had finally washed his hands of Warren's career moves. While their personal friendship would continue for years, the long string of drama and stress surrounding their two albums together had greatly strained the duo's collaborative projects.

With another production credit under his belt, Waddy Wachtel's reputation had grown and his schedule had continued to tighten. To compensate for the pay cut that came with accompanying Warren on the *Excitable Boy* tour, he asked for first-class airfare and more creative input. He also brought along ace drummer Rick Marotta, a partner on his new Ronin album project. David Landau, Jon's brother who had contributed to Browne's *The Pretender* tour, was enlisted for additional guitar work and, fresh off a longstanding gig with Peter Frampton, renowned bassist Stan Sheldon came onboard to round out the band. Up-and-coming comic Richard Belzer was handpicked to be the opening act.

It was a stellar lineup of seasoned professionals, but when it came to touring with Warren, no one knew what to expect.

∽

Like the tour before it, the *Excitable Boy* tour was slated to begin its string of nationwide appearances on the East Coast. After a few warm-up shows in upper New York, the true kickoff launched in New York City—at the Bottom Line.

For four months, they crisscrossed the United States, hitting some of the most notable venues available: Traxx in New York, Washington, DC's the Cellar Door, and once back in Los Angeles, the Universal Amphitheatre. At the end of the tour, Warren played his first gigs at Los Angeles's famed Roxy, which would later host one of his greatest recorded live performances. Throughout the spring, Warren and the band hit everywhere in between, usually playing sold-out shows to packed houses: Boston, Chicago, Dallas, Detroit, Kansas, and San Francisco were all enthralled with his unique blend of personal pyrotechnics and literary wit. Canada was also on the list, as Warren brought his cerebral circus to Calgary, Montreal, Toronto, and Vancouver.

Aside from an enthusiastic audience reception and a growing legion of fans, the success of "Werewolves of London" earned Warren professional recognition as an up-and-coming star. When he was booked to play the Academy of Music in Philadelphia during the first week of May, a congratulatory phone call from label head Joe Smith was waiting for him—along with a limousine outside. Warren and Crystal were shuffled to their swankier hotel across town, where caviar and flowers greeted them in their suite.

For all his apprehension over howling, it had made him a star.

The critics loved Warren Zevon the rock star, but they weren't privy to the offstage antics that were slowly signaling the unraveling of Warren Zevon the man. As the tour rolled on, his demeanor had noticeably shifted, the ultimate product of recent stardom and too many substances. By the time he and the band returned home in late July, Warren's addictions had become a ghastly spectator sport. Much to the dismay of his family and friends, Warren's alcoholism had shown itself, in grand scale, during numerous instances along the tour. Too many times on the road, he'd had to be propped up on stage, too drunk to play through his own material; Crystal sometimes idled by during performances to feed him lyrics he had forgotten. There were instances when he had to be carried offstage, and—in one memorable case—hadn't shown up at all.

In comparing his condition to that of James Dean's iconic fall-down drunk from *Giant,* Warren later took to calling this dark period "The Jett Rink Tour."

Much to the concern and annoyance of Wachtel and the full touring crew, Warren's condition not only dictated irresponsibility as the star attraction: the fame, success, and alcohol were fueling the temper he often kept suppressed. At a key performance in Washington, DC, road manager Jerry Cohen was abruptly fired on the spot for failing to notify Warren that fireworks would be accompanying that evening's rendition of "Roland the Headless Thompson Gunner." Warren's fit of rage frightened all those within earshot. Later, in San Francisco, he fell off his piano bench and, in Chicago, sprained both his ankles while gyrating around the stage during a performance of "Nighttime in the Switching Yard." He had also trashed several hotel rooms along the tour, leaving Elektra/Asylum to handle the bill.

Critics were taking notice of Warren's changing performance style, and more so, his public persona. What eccentricities were previously deemed electrifying were now often regarded as out-of-control and manic. Whereas Warren's first album for Elektra/Asylum had successfully earned him critical recognition years in the making, *Excitable Boy* seemed to signal a new, dangerous era. Warren sought to meet the expectations of his new fans, becoming the real-life "excitable boy" of his music. By only his second album, a growing number of listeners equated the artist himself with songs chock-full of mayhem, debauchery, wild living, and plenty of booze and late-night adventure. As the pressures of newfound fame and addictions allowed Warren to play along with the notorious rock-and-roll character for which he was now recognized, those fan expectations slowly became a reputation.

In the past, Warren hadn't been prone to such public displays of narcissism. Although he had finally achieved the recognition from critics and peers that had so long eluded him, he was slowly becoming another person, one that family and friends were often nervous to be around. When his estranged mother and grandmother attended one of his concerts, bringing with them young Jordan, Warren had been so inebriated he didn't remember they were there. And with only one hit single to his credit, Warren was expected to toe the line if he wanted to remain on top. Aside from his well-being, those in Warren's inner circle worried he was close to destroying the career he had worked so hard to build, tossing away opportunities not likely to be repeated.

∞

However, as far as Warren's behavior seemed to push his loved ones away, none had turned their backs on him. On the contrary, Warren's intelligence and charm continued to keep his friends and family coming back for more, regardless of what he dealt out to them. As had been the case during his rambunctious teen years, "The Offender" was able to talk his way back into the good graces of the offended.

Although critics remained well aware of Warren's behavior and habits, they often wrote it all off as little more than a mystique he had crafted for himself. Almost all his earliest reviews championed the literary romanticism with which he displayed his drinking, hard living, and machismo through both his music and his personal life.

The one critic who saw through the smoke and mirrors of the persona was old friend and *Village Voice* auteur music critic Paul Nelson.

Nelson had been enthralled with Warren's Elektra/Asylum debut, making it a point to rave about the album and the tour that followed. As Warren's biggest critical advocate, Nelson had deliberately set out to meet the artist, whom he considered a kindred spirit in literary and musical influences. By 1978, they had become close friends and confidantes.

The Minnesota-born Nelson had initially worked as an A&R label representative and prolific music critic for numerous underground magazines and newspapers. He was an early defender of Bob Dylan's electric period and gave newcomer Bruce Springsteen's some of his first positive critical appraisals, and his positive assertions of Jackson Browne, Leonard Cohen, the New York Dolls, the Ramones, Rod Stewart, and the Velvet Underground had aided in establishing them all as popular and important artists.

It wasn't long before what had begun as a mutual appreciation society became a genuine friendship. Only a few years older than Warren, Nelson shared many of the same passions: he was a devout film buff and lover of all things film noir and pulp; like Warren, he could gobble up hours of classic black-and-white mysteries and Westerns, binge dozens of paperback novels by Mickey Spillane and Ross Macdonald, and spend full weekends listening to the complete discography of a given artist. Whereas Warren would infuse the influences of all those same passions into his music, Nelson aimed to use the hardboiled literary tradition of Raymond Chandler and Dashiell Hammett to write exquisite feature stories and artist profiles. In the same way that "New Journalism" practitioners Norman Mailer and Hunter S. Thompson put themselves into the events they were covering, elevating journalism to the same standards as great literature, so Nelson pored over his own works of freelance criticism.

Just prior to Ariel's birth, Nelson had even arranged for the Zevons to accompany him to the Coral Casino Beach and Cabana Club in Santa Barbara to meet their favorite mystery writer, Ken Millar. Nelson had recently interviewed the legendary older writer, who was better known publicly by his pen name, "Ross Macdonald," unaware that his writing held special significance to Warren and Crystal; during the impoverished early years of their marriage, the two would often stay and home, reading his books to each other as cheap entertainment. In later years, Warren would speak fondly of that afternoon and what a life-changing experience it had been to meet one of his living idols. The gesture had also solidified Nelson's place within the Zevons' inner circle, much more than just another friendly member of the press.

During the early stages of Warren's third Elektra/Asylum release, his friendship with Nelson would be put to the test, ultimately establishing the journalist's place as interviewer, confessor, and finally, blood brother. As 1978 drew to a close, the effects of Warren's dependencies were brewing like a storm, threatening both his personal and professional lives. Nelson had come along just in time to find himself in its eye.

The true extent of Warren's personal demons was largely unknown to those outside his closest social circle and most intimate collaborators. The critics and fans still adored the outrageous and over-the-top spectacle that Warren embodied when onstage, backed up with his trademark humor and showmanship.

Yet even as Warren's sobriety and personal responsibilities continued to slip, his career was reaching its peak. Following another sold-out show at the Roxy in Hollywood, he was scooped up by the label for an extravagant celebration at the Chateau Marmont. Company president Joe Smith personally presented Warren with his first gold record to commemorate the success of *Excitable Boy*. It was his first such accolade since the inclusion of "She Quit Me" on the *Midnight Cowboy* soundtrack almost a decade earlier—and this time, it was for his own solo album.

While "Werewolves of London" had spent twelve weeks on the *Billboard* chart, peaking at Number 21 on May 13, the album itself had cracked the Top 10, spending twenty-eight weeks on the chart and ultimately placing at a respectable Number 8. Following the critical raves yet lukewarm sales of his previous album, the numbers for *Excitable Boy* were a promising improvement. The album had also been certified gold in Canada, marking the beginning of Warren's longstanding constituency with fans abroad.

At the tail end of the tour, Warren received his first truly negative audience response, taking some of the wind out of his sails. During the first week of June, he and the band had arrived back in California following a successful show in Dallas only to discover an enticing invitation waiting for them. With "Werewolves of London" in consistent rotation on the airwaves, the Grateful Dead had begun performing a jam-friendly cover as part of their set list. An outspoken admirer of Warren's songwriting, founder Jerry Garcia sent word that he wanted Warren to share the bill for an upcoming show in Santa Barbara. Following a marijuana smoke-out that also included reggae legend Bob Marley, Warren himself took the stage. Before an audience of hippies stoned on pot and acid, Warren unleashed the electric werewolf in all its glory—dishing out his signature blend of literary rock and over-the-top stage antics. But the audience wasn't biting. It was the first time he had ever been heckled. The following day, local critics detailed the onstage massacre in their equally scathing reviews.

Despite this singular incident of negative press, Warren and Crystal loved Santa Barbara itself. Having gotten their first taste of the sun-baked county's rustic beauty during their visit to resident Ken Millar, the couple were enamored with its rural and cozy elements. Most importantly, it was just far enough from Los Angeles to keep Warren from his usual distractions.

With the tour finally completed and a follow-up to *Excitable Boy* expected, domestic solace was just what Warren felt he needed. After shopping around, he and Crystal found a house in Montecito, an upscale Santa Barbara suburb that was home to many celebrities who sought to escape the spotlight among the peaceful, rural landscape. To help with Ariel and daily chores, Crystal hired an au pair and a housekeeper, while Warren converted the outdoor guesthouse into a private studio. He had it professionally soundproofed, sealing him off as far from the maddening crowd of Hollywood as he could get.

When all was said and done, Warren had made his best attempt at a quiet, normal life. But even in the isolation his backyard studio provided, Warren didn't need the help of outside influences to feed demons. In addition to amassing an extensive gun collection—all of which he kept loaded and casually spread throughout the house—he had started battling his chronic insomnia by bringing bottles of vodka to bed.

In an eight-page biography he later penned for Paul Nelson's epic *Rolling Stone* profile, Warren described his mental state at that time:

> It's quiet, peaceful, safe, beautiful. The air is fine.
> It makes me nervous . . .
> . . . I have the guest house professionally soundproofed and
> build a four-track 'writing studio.'
> The studio makes me nervous.

As worried as Warren's family was over his behavior, it was nothing compared to the fear he had of himself. He later admitted to Paul Nelson a terrifying secret that he'd kept of that time. On the rare occasions when he'd gotten a few precious hours of sleep, those nights were plagued with feverish dreams: leaving his bed in the middle of the night and exiting the house, walking to the curb on Featherhill Road with a gun from his collection in hand—then using the drivers of passing cars for target practice.

He further confessed the part that scared him the most. The dreams had been especially vivid, compelling him to check the chamber of whichever gun was beside him that night to be sure no bullets were missing. He had started to double-check his reality.

∽

It wasn't the gun collection itself that gave Warren's friends so much concern. More so that he had now taken to carrying them in public and waving them around in front of guests. Friends were terrified when he began firing them in the house. Only Crystal and a handful of close friends were aware that Warren's hobby of shooting at bugs and inanimate household objects had started in Los Feliz.

Having alienated Jackson Browne and Waddy Wachtel throughout the arduous *Excitable Boy* sessions and the tour that followed, Warren now sought Jon Landau to possibly produce the next album. Their first meeting had been a disaster, with Warren knocking back three martinis and slowly becoming belligerent by lunch's end. Although they had been friends for a long time, a disturbed Landau left the restaurant convinced he wouldn't be able to work with any musician in that condition.

Toward the end of that summer, Landau was in New York managing Bruce Springsteen's tour. At Crystal's suggestion, Warren hopped a flight to catch Springsteen's show at the Palladium and, hopefully, convince Landau to come aboard his next project. Joining them were Paul Nelson and film critic Jay Cocks. The old friends watched helplessly as Warren's drinking escalated over the course of the night; he nearly injured himself backstage, causing Springsteen himself to flag a ride for Warren back to the hotel.

The following evening, Nelson received a frantic phone call from Crystal. She had just gotten off the phone with Warren and the conversation had terrified her. Warren admitted having been so blackout drunk the night before, he couldn't remember attending the Springsteen concert or any incidents that his behavior had caused. It was one of the longest gaps in his memory brought on by drinking. Hearing this, Nelson cautiously shared with Crystal the lurid details Warren couldn't remember: how he had become further inebriated backstage and tripped all over Springsteen's expensive sound equipment; how The Boss had forfeited his own pre-show prep time to calm Warren down and help him find his seat; and, finally, how by an awful stroke of misfortune, Warren had been seated next to *Rolling Stone* publisher—and Nelson's boss—Jann Wenner. The publisher had gotten so aggravated by Warren's boorish behavior, he swore aloud he'd never again cover his musical career.

"I remember waking up in the hotel room feeling I was going to die," Warren later recalled. "I couldn't make it down the hallway. I knew I'd had it. I called Crystal in LA and told her I was ready to get help, but I wanted to see Bruce first. She said, 'Warren, you've already seen him.' The idea that I couldn't remember seeing someone I felt that close to was the most frightening thing of all. It was an abuse of our friendship and of my self-respect."

Crystal begged Nelson to help her get Warren into a rehabilitation clinic. She had already found a perfect facility in Santa Barbara that could take him. Warren, she knew, would fight it tooth and nail and—if the mere suggestion happened to spark his outrage—possibly become violent. His response would be unpredictable, and she desperately needed help. Nelson agreed, unsure of how to casually suggest to his dear friend that he commit himself into rehab.

Only moments after speaking with Crystal, Nelson heard a knock on his door: it was Warren. He told Nelson that he had spoken to Crystal and was ready to admit he may have a drinking problem. Like Jackson Browne before him, Nelson kept Warren company all night, distracting him with deep discussions on literature, music, and life. Warren was nervous, as always, about his next album—and the symphony that he never seemed to have enough time to complete. Nelson shared his ambition to break into writing literary detective fiction. They spoke about Ken Millar and they spoke about Clint Eastwood. For hours, they talked of everything—except alcoholism.

Halfway through the night, Warren looked at Nelson and pointedly asked for his opinion: did *he* think he had a drinking problem? Relieved that Warren had been the one to bring it up, Nelson appealed to his friend's sense of pragmatism—Warren had nothing to lose by getting sober, and everything to gain. After all, if it didn't work out, couldn't he always just go get another drink?

The logic behind Nelson's careful approach seemed to work. Warren returned to his room at dawn, playfully declaring he and Nelson "blood brothers."

∞

True to his word, Warren remained sober for the first few days back in Santa Barbara.

Hoping to bring an air of optimism into their new home, Crystal organized a housewarming party for some close family and friends. However, it was much harder for Warren to keep to the straight and narrow in a social atmosphere. Surrounded by his friends, sipping a few innocent beers quickly became a binge. By the end of the night, Warren was smashed. When the last guests left, Crystal brought up the rehabilitation hospital, inevitably sparking Warren's fury. Adamant he didn't need professional help, he angrily boasted that he could cure himself of drinking whenever he pleased. In tears, Crystal headed to bed as Warren stumbled out to the solace of his backyard studio.

It was two in the morning when the gunshots woke her. She had distinctly heard three of them; she bolted upright in bed, immediately knowing they had come from the backyard. Her instincts feared for the worst—that Warren had finally made good on his veiled threats, his years both mocking and courting death through his "bad boy" song lyrics. *"If I start acting stupid, I'll shoot myself,"* he sang, promising to sleep when he was dead—had he just put himself to sleep?

Crystal fearfully crept outside to the studio. Warren had left the soundproofed door wide open. He stood beside the couch in the middle of the room, the .44 Magnum at his side. She walked in and watched him put down the gun. Their eyes meeting, she saw that Warren's expression was completely blank. She looked toward the couch and found his target: there were three bullet holes through the cover of an *Excitable Boy* LP. Rather than the passing motorists of his nightmares, Warren had used his own face for target practice.

Crystal recognized that a terrifying part of her worst fear had still come true: Warren *had* killed himself—in effigy. But that was enough for her. He laughed nervously, attempting to play the stunt off as a morbid joke. But Crystal assured him that none of this behavior was funny. Not anymore.

The next morning, Warren agreed to enter the Pinecrest Rehabilitation Center for alcohol and drug treatment.

∞

Although "intervention therapy" has since become an accepted form of rehabilitation and conflict resolution, its early development was met with clinical skepticism. The very concept of cornering an individual, forcing them to face their addictions head-on, intimidated the friends and family members expected to participate. As Paul Nelson would later describe, it was "an execution with a happy ending."

But by that point, Crystal had tried everything else. An intervention may have been viewed as an unorthodox, unconventional method of rehabilitation—but nothing conventional had ever worked on Warren.

Those closest to him had witnessed the alcoholism for years, but between his constant excuses and the numerous times he had charmed forgiveness from Crystal and others, accepting his behavior had become a way of life. Living with Warren was synonymous with living with his addictions.

Now that his dangerous behavior had plummeted to a dangerous new low, Pinecrest's medical staff assured Crystal that a harsh, "no excuses" confrontation would be the wake-up call Warren desperately needed. As part of the radical new therapy, participants in the intervention would have to list all the occasions when Warren's addictions and behavior had directly affected them. Details and brutal honesty were mandatory, as were the hospital's instructions that Warren be approached by the full group, and as a surprise. As Crystal had been told, remaining a united front when confronting an alcoholic demonstrated to them how many people had been impacted by their addiction. It also showed how many people in their lives loved them enough to care.

But the administrators were adamant that the intervention's true purpose remain clear: first and foremost, it was a non-negotiable ultimatum. Warren would stop drinking, or he would no longer have anyone in his life to clean up his messes.

Following his most recent series of dramatic episodes—the "lost weekend" in New York, his "blood brothers" ceremony with Nelson, and finally, the backyard gun incident—Warren entered Pinecrest willingly and quietly. He held Crystal's hands as his information was processed. Before the orderlies showed him to his room, Warren had one final request. He asked Crystal to call Elektra/Asylum president Joe Smith and have him issue a press release; likewise, he asked that Nelson do a write-up for *Rolling Stone*.

In Warren's mind, if his fans knew he was trying to get sober, quitting would only let them down.

"When an alcoholic discovers that people care for him," Warren later said, "his whole way of thinking is threatened. Either you try to return that love by taking care of yourself, or you keep drinking and spend your life being insulated from the rest of the world."

∞

Crystal called Nelson right away, but not for the press coverage Warren had requested. Warren was unaware about the "intervention portion" of the facility's rehabilitation methods, and Crystal only had two days to gather as many loved ones as were willing to travel to Santa Barbara.

"He's dying, Paul," she had told Nelson over the phone. "Some days, he can't even dress himself." It didn't take more than those words for Nelson to hop a flight to Los Angeles. There, he and Jackson Browne drove to Pinecrest together, sharing their fears and concerns over the therapy session to come. At the hospital, they were met by Crystal and the other participants in Warren's therapy: her parents, Jorge Calderón, LeRoy Marinell, and Jimmy Wachtel.

The full group was briefed on the confrontational nature of the session to come. During what amounted to a "rehearsal" for the real intervention, each member read their own list of Warren's personal infractions toward them. According to Nelson, when they had all completed their turns—already apprehensive at having to share their most horrendous stories—the doctors insisted they get "a lot tougher and more explicit" for Warren's own good. Against every impulse that years of confused silence had worked to ingrain, they each took the next few hours to revise their lists. With each draft, the picture grew grimmer, the dark nature of Warren's addiction and his out-of-control spiral becoming clearer in the tapestry the lists formed.

They were already emotionally exhausted from the lengthy dry run by the time Warren came into the conference room.

"Oh, God," he said, shocked to find the room full of his loved ones. "I suppose you're all gathered to watch the execution?"

His assigned therapist brought him to his seat and explained how the intervention was going to work: how Crystal had gathered Warren's closest circle of loved ones to share their stories of his worst behavior; how he had hurt them emotionally and physically over the years, and had now become a danger to himself and those around him.

He was warned that it was going to be brutal.

Crystal's parents, Clifford and Barbara Brelsford, were the first in the group to share their horror stories. Paul Nelson was next in line and later admitted how sheltered he had felt in hearing the details of Warren's profound offenses—so much that he briefly reconsidered speaking in front of the group. Admittedly a member of Warren's life the briefest amount of time, Nelson tactfully emphasized how poisonous the alcoholism was to his friend's talent and ambition—the very things that had made them friends. He remembered the candid moments when

Warren had shared his fears and the pressures of writing. "It was very apparent then that the fear of being unable to write another album went incredibly deep," Nelson read aloud, "far deeper than I'd imagined." He recalled how Warren had then leapt onto the sofa and retrieved his copy of T. S. Eliot's *Four Quartets*—a personal favorite he reread once a year—and began to read aloud from its climactic final stanza: "Into the crowned knot of fire / And the fire and the rose are one." Of the fire and rose, Nelson told Warren, "You spoke movingly about wanting— with all your heart—both of them."

One by one, Warren's family and friends recounted their stories, Crystal's being the most profound and shocking to the group. Warren silently listened to the various infractions and offenses, lies and embar- rassments—all without protest. He didn't remember some of his worst actions and was aghast to learn he'd waved a loaded gun in the studio, pointing it, on separate occasions, at friends LeRoy Marinell and J. D. Souther.

When it was over, the doctors instructed the group to stand and put their arms around Warren. Fearful he would never speak to any of them again for the secrets they had revealed, all cried as he stood to accept their embrace.

"If I meant that much to people whom I respected," he later re- called, "I felt I no longer had the right to pronounce and act a death sentence on myself."

CHAPTER FIVE

(1979–1980)

THE GROUP'S TEARFUL EMBRACE MAY HAVE MARKED THE END of Warren's intervention, but it also stood as the mere starting point toward his sobriety.

In the two weeks prior to the intervention session, Warren had been tossed into the regimen required of Pinecrest's substance-abuse patients from day one, and the zero-tolerance standards by which they held their developing practices came as a shock to his already vulnerable system. Coming off a regular diet that began with vodka and orange juice for breakfast, the loss of independence and a forced hospital atmosphere made him prisoner to his own thoughts and fears.

"When I went in, I was still protesting fiercely," Warren would later recall. "For a couple of days, I paced constantly. Sometimes, I'd listen for traffic—a boulevard or highway nearby. I'd plan escapes. Of course, I could have walked out the front door anytime, but, sobered up, I was too scared to stick my nose out of the door."

Following the intervention, Warren's stay in Pinecrest's Chemical Dependency Unit lasted a month. It was the longest that he had stayed sober since the births of each of his children, only this time, the sobriety had been enforced. Nightly withdrawal symptoms and fevered dreams continued while in the hospital, along with the emotionally charged therapy sessions that brought him face-to-face with the demons he drank to silence. Slowly, they seemed to quiet.

Despite the emotional and physical anguishes of rehabilitation, the intervention itself had provided enough motivation for Warren to stick it out and earn his discharge. Rather than immediately return to the temptations and pressures that the new home in Montecito had come to represent, he and Crystal opted for an extended family vacation to Hawaii. Far from the stress and drugs that Warren believed fueled his creativity, the serenity of the islands allowed him to begin writing songs for the next album.

Viewing this seemingly blissful period as a "new beginning" for them both, upon returning from the trip, Warren and Crystal began attending regular counseling sessions and couples' retreats. For a few weeks, Warren was able to keep to the straight and narrow, focusing on completing the writing for newly titled *Bad Luck Streak in Dancing School*. Having proven to Crystal that he could buckle down and keep to his work, remaining sober and willfully continuing their marriage counseling, they celebrated the apparent stability with more trips to Hawaii. It had remained a favorite destination of Warren's; he credited its idyllic change of scenery with curing frequent bouts of writer's block. Two years earlier, it was there that he'd found the inspiration needed to pen "Lawyers, Guns and Money" on a wet cocktail napkin in his hotel bar. With another deadline looming in the background, Warren hoped the tropical surroundings would again spark his creativity.

The inspiration only went so far. Throughout the winter of 1979, Warren suffered numerous relapses, sneaking booze during the hours when he thought Crystal wouldn't notice. As the dependency came back, his behavior became more brazen. Soon, Crystal was once again bearing witness to him at his worst.

As the decade drew to a close, the optimism behind its most promising possible ending—Warren's acknowledgment of his alcoholism and the declaration that he would beat it—soon waned. With the contention mounting, she notified Warren's therapists at Pinecrest, who suggested that the couple try a separate vacation. Apprehensive about Warren's stability while away, she had nonetheless grown exhausted from the round-the-clock monitoring that he required, especially as the duration between his relapses became shorter and shorter. It had slowly reached the familiar point where he was unabashedly drunk during the day. After some deliberation, she agreed, planning a trip to Ireland for the end of January.

Feeling the familiar pressures of writing a full album's worth of new material, Warren opted not to take a traditional vacation. Rather, upon hearing that favorite actors Robert DeNiro and Robert Duvall were staying at the famed Chateau Marmont in West Hollywood, he checked himself in there, as well. Planning to use the notorious hotel as a dubious form of writing retreat, along with his instruments and audio playback equipment, he packed multiple bottles of vodka, various narcotics, and his .44 Magnum.

Crystal's parents had agreed to watch Ariel during their daughter's vacation. With her flight to Ireland booked the morning after Warren's thirty-third birthday, Crystal checked herself into a nearby airport hotel. She had wrapped an expensive Montblanc pen and silk pajamas, along with a small birthday cake, and invited Warren to meet her alone for an intimate birthday and bon voyage dinner. He showed up hours late, too drunk to drive and claiming that the limo outside was waiting for him—as was Bianca Jagger back at the Chateau Marmont.

Crystal flew to Dublin the next morning, convinced that it was over.

∞

Before she left for Ireland, Crystal had made a single phone call to put her own mind at ease over Warren's condition. With so many of Warren's family and friends still burned-out by the intervention, coupled with the knowledge that he hadn't been sticking to the promises he'd made that day, local guardian angels were now in short supply. She instead turned to the one friend who, thanks to both geographical distance and an intuitive compassion, had yet to let her down: Paul Nelson.

"I can't help him, Paul," she had confided over the phone. "I've tried, but now he's got to help himself." Nelson confirmed that he understood and hung up.

Taking his "blood brother" status to heart, Nelson had been planning to fly out to Santa Barbara almost immediately following Warren's intervention. The rehabilitation took time, however, and the commute from New York on a journalist's salary wasn't cheap. Warren remained unaware that Crystal had had to pay for Nelson's airfare to attend the intervention. This time around, Nelson had haggled with his bosses and saved every penny; he wanted to be there for Warren in his time of need.

With him, Nelson had taken an early cassette of Neil Young's yet-to-be-released *Rust Never Sleeps*. When he got to the album's center-piece, the haunting ballad "Powderfinger," Young's narrative of a man describing his own death, Nelson couldn't help but hear the brooding eulogy beneath the words. He thought of his friend and the intervention, fearful of what awaited him in Los Angeles.

"Perhaps I was being overly melodramatic," Nelson said later, "yet I had a terrible premonition of what I might find there."

Although Warren had checked into the Chateau Marmont under the pretense of woodshedding the songs for his next album, no one was fooled by his decision to "vacation" right on the Sunset Strip—least of all himself. Having brought both his mobile recording gear and *Fear and Loathing*–esque cache of substances, the easier path of temptation instantly proved too great. As Nelson would later describe it, Warren "ran amok in Los Angeles for a month." It was an understatement. At the time, Nelson could never have guessed the extent of the debaucheries that had taken place before his plane even touched down at LAX.

Immediately following Crystal's departure for Dublin, Warren initiated what David Landau described as a "three-day binge," starting with a phone call to Jorge Calderón. Warren's extended relapse had alienated him from his loved ones, yet again, and one by one, the participants in Warren's intervention had fallen off his radar. The naturally compassionate Calderón was an exception. The two had already begun writing a new song together for *Bad Luck Streak in Dancing School*, "Downtown LA," which Warren continued to tinker with while secluded at the hotel. When Calderón accepted an invitation to work on the tune at the Chateau Marmont, he arrived to find Warren already inebriated. Unwilling to open the door more than a quarter of the way, Warren spouted two brief lines that he had written for the song, then quickly shut the door in Calderón's face. As an angered Calderón turned to leave, he caught a glimpse of another room door partially cracked. Bianca Jagger was peering out of her room, watching for him to leave.

The binge didn't end until three days later when the police were called to have Warren's gun taken away. He'd been shooting at a billboard of Richard Pryor out his room window.

Nelson arrived in Los Angeles that week and the two met for dinner. By Nelson's own account, Warren was shaky, attempting to hide the recent binge-drinking by ordering a Coke with his meal. Any masquerade of false sobriety was immediately cast aside when they returned to the Chateau Marmont and Nelson got a look at Warren's room. "There were empty bottles everywhere," he later recalled. "Full ones, too. Neither of us knew what to say about it, so we didn't say anything. To me, the room reeked of death."

Although Nelson kept the thought to himself, the sight before him brought to his mind Van Gogh's own description of his *Night Café*: "I tried to show a place where a man can ruin himself, go mad, commit a crime." Again, Nelson didn't know how right he was, but the tumblers of straight vodka that Warren continuously drank in front of him gave a hint. For three days as his guest, Nelson watched as Warren vocally debated the necessity to return to Pinecrest, convincing himself more than Nelson that he could drink now because he was already cured.

With the help of a Pinecrest outpatient and Good Samaritan limousine driver, Nelson was able to subdue the mostly incoherent Warren to check himself back into the hospital.

By the time they arrived at the Montecito house for Warren to pack a few things, he was already changing his mind and becoming argumentative. "I've got this nice house," he told Nelson. "Why can't I stay here and enjoy it?"

Reaching the end of his seemingly endless rope, Nelson finally became furious. "Because you *don't* enjoy it!" he screamed at Warren. "And you never *will* enjoy it unless you quit drinking!"

For the second time under duress, the sheer logic of Warren's blood brother had won out. "You're right," Warren finally said. "I don't enjoy it. Give me a drink and we'll go."

He was released three days later, and Nelson hung around for a few extra days to keep watch. Realizing that his improvisational logic would only go so far in keeping Warren at bay until Crystal returned from Ireland the following week, Nelson organized a grand gesture in the hopes that it would shake Warren out of his emotional apathy. During another shaky afternoon of watching television and listening to records to keep the demons silent, Warren answered the doorbell to find Ken Millar standing in front of him. Shocked, he knew that Nelson had clearly pulled out all the stops to get their mutual literary idol to make a house call. Nelson tactfully put on his running shoes and left Warren alone with their hero.

Warren later remembered his encounter with the great writer to Tom Nolan, Millar's own biographer: "So I was sitting in my palatial shithouse in Montecito, in terrible Valium pain, with instructions not to miss therapy the next day. I was in really bad shape . . . Ken was wearing some kind of plaid fedora, like a private eye . . . Everything he said was informed by a tremendous amount of compassion."

"We writers are overcompensated in this society," Millar had said, sitting across from Warren. "In this house, at your age, you feel guilty."

Being addressed as a fellow writer by one of his own profound influences had proven the jolt Warren had needed. He admitted he understood the guilt Millar had described, subconsciously believing that he was justly punishing himself for all sins rendered with the self-abuse of drugs and drink. During a pause in their conversation, Millar spotted on the coffee table a large biography of Igor Stravinsky, Warren's earliest creative influence. Warren pointed the book out to Millar. "Here's a guy who lived to be eighty-eight. Worked up to his last day, never had a problem with alcohol and drugs."

Millar had looked at him. "Lucky," he said.

Warren later claimed, "Of course, that word stayed with me all my life."

"The scariest part about alcoholism," Warren told Nelson later of the revelation Millar had provoked, "about any addiction for that matter— is that you credit the booze for all your accomplishments . . . Ken Millar made me realize that I wrote my songs despite the fact that I was a drunk, not because of it."

When Warren soberly began composing on the piano that night, Nelson believed it was safe to return to New York before he lost his job.

While Crystal was due back in Santa Barbara the next week, her trip had proven a positive experience, both creatively as a writer and liberating as an individual. While in Dublin, her writing had earned an opportunity to travel to Belfast with a friend from the *Irish Times*. Worried about Warren, she was conflicted over extending the length of her trip—although being viewed as an individual rather than solely as

"Mrs. Warren Zevon" had made the offer tempting. When he got her on the phone, it only confused her further. He told her about returning to Pinecrest of his own volition and how Ken Millar had sat and counseled him, helping Warren dump out the remaining bottles of liquor. If she returned to Montecito with Ariel, he promised, she would find him clean and sober upon her return.

She kept her plans and flew home.

☙

Had Crystal seen Warren's condition during that week's wait, it might have swayed her decision to return.

As soon as he knew his wife and child would be returning to their Santa Barbara home, every doubt and demon that had drawn him to the Chateau Marmont seemed to claw at Warren at once. Even with genuine attempts to crank out work at the piano, the nights were plagued with the nightmares and terrors associated with withdrawal and the earliest stages of sobriety. No longer shooting at anonymous drivers, Warren would now hurl himself against the wall to shake from fevered bouts of sleep paralysis—escaping screaming fits that only resounded in his own head, and fluttering images of Paul Nelson dragging his filthy body out of a slimy construction pit amid a sea of laughing, maggot-ridden hags. With sleep offering no respite, Warren ran mad throughout the house during the daylight hours, gorging himself on sugary candy and ranting at photos of himself.

"You're not a fucking boy and you're not a fucking werewolf," he told his image. "You're a fucking man, and it's about time you acted like it."

With only days before Crystal's return, Warren's true resilience was put to the ultimate test when an old drug buddy rang him up. Working furiously to keep his focus on the upcoming recording sessions, Warren desperately explained his need to stay clean and keep the productivity going.

"So why don't I come there with a bunch of cheeseburgers, a bottle, and an ounce of blow?" Warren heard from the receiver. "A little vodka, a little cocaine, and you'll be fine in no time."

It took a moment, but he hung up the phone.

"If ever I believed that there was a God and a Devil—and that they were just guys, you know," he later told Nelson, "one with the tail and the other with a long white beard—it was at that moment. It was just a satanic temptation."

He had looked temptation in the face and bested it. That night, Warren sat and opened *Four Quartets*. He wanted to read about the fire and the rose.

∞

Warren picked Crystal and Ariel up from the airport. Under his arm was a huge bouquet of roses and throughout the house, he had left little hidden notes of affection for Crystal to find. "You'll always be mine and I'll always be yours," one read, and was signed, "Your loving husband." At Ken Millar's suggestion, Warren had booked for them a surprise return to Hawaii. Under the pretense of celebrating both Crystal's return and his own successful second stint in Pinecrest by returning to Hawaii, Warren also hoped that the destination would inspire the completion of *Bad Luck Streak in Dancing School* once and for all.

On this trip, however, inspiration proved harder to attain. Warren spent much of the trip complaining and telling Crystal how badly he needed drugs. He began getting snippy with Ariel, and when they finally flew home, Warren announced that he simply wouldn't be able to focus while living in the Montecito house any longer. And with the recording for the new album beginning in only a few weeks, the commute to Los Angeles would be unbearable. He explained that Karla Bonoff, the folk singer-songwriter who had made guest appearances on his two Elektra/Asylum releases, was moving out of her house on Mulholland Drive and it was available for rent. Without providing Crystal with all the gory details regarding why the Chateau Marmont was no longer an option, he pushed for Bonoff's house.

It was only with cautious optimism that Crystal went along with it, well aware of the temptations that Los Angeles offered—especially to one of its favorite sons.

As recording for *Bad Luck Streak* began, once again at the Sound Factory in Hollywood, Warren's return trips to Montecito became less and less frequent. If she wanted to see him, Crystal would usually travel into Los Angeles on the weekends, bringing along Ariel and their au pair. At first, the distance seemed to keep the peace, along with Warren's absence and seemingly shifted focus on his album's production.

Weeks into the recording, however, he called her in Montecito and asked that she visit that weekend alone, suggesting they spend the weekend shopping for curtains and new stereo equipment for the Santa Barbara home. Interpreting this as a sign of Warren's reaffirmed dedication to their marriage, Crystal was shocked when she arrived and found Warren already irritable and anxious. When they headed out shopping, he drove distractedly, running red lights until she pleaded for him to let her out of the car. After Warren apologized, they continued their errands and headed to Robaire's for dinner.

Over the meal, Warren took on a serious tone. "You know, we've just put so much into this relationship, and it's everything I've ever wanted," he said. It was a sobriety and sincerity she hadn't heard in a long time. "I don't know what happens to me when I go off in other directions, but I don't want other women. So, let's just make that commitment and not have to worry about it if we have a fight. It doesn't mean we're going to split up."

Confused, Crystal agreed. The two had a romantic evening at the Los Angeles house. They made love and watched *The Tonight Show*. Afterward, she helped Warren come up with comical names for a novelty song he was tinkering with about a riot in women's prison. So far, he'd gotten as far as plotting the inmates' ransom demands, including the lyric, "We'll give you the prison doctor back with his balls sewn shut in his mouth." They giggled before falling asleep.

The following morning, she came home from picking out fabric samples to find that Warren had downed a bottle of cooking sherry accidentally left behind in Bonoff's move. Immediately, Crystal could see that it was a different Warren than the one she'd spent the previous evening beside. "I looked in his eyes, and I *knew* immediately," she later told Paul Nelson. "There was a rage there that was like when he was drinking."

Before she knew what had hit her, Warren threw his coffee cup through a window, snatching the fabric from Crystal's hands and berating her with accusations of destroying a great artist, attempting to "turn Dylan Thomas into Robert Young." For the second time, he told her to leave—but this time, not to come back. His parting words to Crystal as she walked out the door was a reminder that he would never be her father. She spent the day wandering aimlessly, confused as to what could possibly have happened to Warren's willpower and love for her overnight. She had left him before but had always returned.

As she continued to walk and assess her conflicted emotions, Crystal stumbled upon a group of women gathered beside a burger stand, each discussing their own husbands' battles with addiction. She quietly interrupted and told them about Warren, about how she didn't know if she would walk back through the door, only to leave again. Would today be the last time she walked out of it?

This time, she decided it would be.

The most important people in Warren's life had orchestrated and participated in his gut-wrenching intervention. Within a year, almost all were out of his life. The emotional experience of that mass confession had not deepened their bonds with him, but rather had become a source of their undoing. Still in the throes of his addictions, and now in a greater state of denial, Warren had effectively turned his back on nearly all those who had been in attendance.

Outside of the disintegration of his marriage to Crystal, Warren's gradual excommunication of Paul Nelson became, perhaps, the most tragic and callous example of this new era of severing ties. While Nelson had nearly lost his job for dropping his responsibilities to be by Warren's side during both the intervention and first major relapse, when Warren discovered through a credit card bill that Crystal had paid for Nelson's ticket to be in attendance, he became enraged, and an alcohol-influenced resentment was harbored. "He felt if Paul was really a friend he should have paid for his own ticket," Crystal later said.

Although they would speak on and off for the next few years, culminating in the masterpiece feature profile on Warren that would lead to Nelson's own departure from *Rolling Stone,* the "blood brothers" would see less and less of each other. A few years later, Nelson would explain to a curious Clint Eastwood, "Everybody who was at that intervention and helped him, he's cut us off totally. I feel sorry for him. He's pretty alone . . . I'm afraid he's falling apart, but he won't even talk to me, so I can't find out."

Out of this dark period, however, at least one truly profound relationship would be fostered.

Warren had first been introduced to George Gruel in July 1978 by Warren's then manager, Howard Burke, during the I'll Sleep When I'm Dead Tour. At that time, Warren was booked for a show at the Berkeley Community Theater. Burke knew Gruel from his years as a photographer and roadie for numerous rock acts, and as a knowledgeable staple at the famed Westwood Musical Instruments in Los Angeles. Knowing that Warren would need a seasoned veteran on his crew for his first major tour, he had invited Gruel down to make an introduction. As a familiar face around the local music scene, Gruel was well aware of Warren's reputation on the road. Apprehensive, Gruel agreed, and worked his first gig for Warren at the Berkeley show. "It was just pure rock and roll, and instant camaraderie," Gruel later remembered. "We were friends instantly."

"He drank way too much, yet somehow he was able to stand with his back to the piano," Gruel also recalled, "reach backwards with his hands and played all the correct notes . . . The rest of the show was really awkward for all involved. I don't know why I worked for him after that, but it was a long and loving relationship."

Impressed with Gruel's work at the concert, Warren visited Westwood Musical Instruments the following week and, after trying a few guitars and making chit-chat with owner Fred Walecki—whom Warren warmly considered "a cross between Baudelaire and Johnny Rotten"—made his way to Gruel, persuading him to join the road crew permanently. "He came in one day," Gruel remembered, "we started talking and he finally said, 'Would you like a full-time job on my tour?' I said, 'Doing what?' And he goes, 'Taking care of me, basically.'"

Although he started off as a general crew member, Gruel's expertise from years of assisting other acts, such as the Grateful Dead, his impressive photographic work, and his overall kind and bawdy attitude quickly put him up in the ranks of Warren's team. By mid-1980, Warren playfully, yet honestly, referred to Gruel as his unofficial aide-de-camp—a badge of honor that the jovial man's man would wear proudly for his full tenure as road manager.

At thirty years old, Gruel had already lived a lifetime of travel, music, and art. Originally from Michigan, he had moved to San Francisco in 1971 by trading his Chevy Vega for a gram of LSD, which he flipped for a panel van and the open road. Upon his arrival in the Bay Area, he made the acquaintance of Grateful Dead guitarist Bob Weir. "I was shooting pool with Bob Weir's wife, Frankie, who was starting her own little country band," Gruel remembered, "and I got a job hauling equipment."

His second gig with Warren at the Universal Amphitheatre went off without a hitch, although seeing Warren on the road quickly gave Gruel a good idea of the experiences that awaited him within Warren's camp. "I'll never forget my first job on the road with him," Gruel later said. "I remember Warren's wife, Crystal, going down the hallway to get vodka for him out of the bar. He was in the middle of a very serious alcohol problem, but he still had this wonderful wit and humor about him that really was just *wonderful*."

Like all those who had slowly made their way into Warren's closest circle of friendship and trust, Gruel was characterized by his seemingly infinite patience and understanding of Warren's faults. As Paul Nelson had attested, "Gruel, who stands six-feet-five and weighs in at around 250 pounds, is so tough that you can strike a match on his muscles. After you've lit your cigarette, he's so polite he'll go get you an ashtray."

Gruel's appreciation for the music and culture Warren introduced him to solidified an admiration for Warren the artist, and a protective friendship toward Warren the man. At the Chateau Marmont, it had been Gruel who wrestled the .44 Magnum from Warren's hand and dealt with the police.

Within days of Crystal moving out, Gruel moved in.

∽

The ongoing turbulence and upheaval in Warren's private life had continued throughout the recording of *Bad Luck Streak*. During the album's production, Warren not only juggled the studio workload, but the disintegration of his marriage, and the dangerous freedoms that newfound bachelorhood presented. Pulling together the material for *Excitable Boy* had been difficult enough; this time, it had been a miracle Warren completed the work he did. And setting for himself the same high standards as the two previous endeavors, Warren would later claim his intention of using this album for "unifying the realms of classical music and popular song." With his hedonistic extracurricular activities well known in the press, his cerebral promises for *Bad Luck Streak* only added to the album's expectations. Fans and critics wanted to see what Warren had been cooking up throughout his year of debauchery.

Like every project Warren approached, *Bad Luck Streak* was, at its core, a concept album. As he had done with his previous Elektra/Asylum releases, Warren produced a balanced blend of tracks that ran the gamut of genre and intricate composition: traditional rockers, autobiographical ballads, a humorous sports biography, and an obligatory visit into foreign intrigue all made their way into his latest opus. In the wake of *Excitable Boy*'s success, Warren's struggles with addiction had been made very public, giving this new release an aura of "comeback" to many critics. To compensate, the rockers rocked harder, the ballads were more heartbreaking, and the injected humor ran deeper into the bizarre. With conscious efforts in "changing and experimenting with the form of the songs," he had also introduced the use of synthesizers into his instrumentation for the first time, making for a brilliant and strange juxtaposition with the samples of his *Symphony No. 1* woven throughout the album.

True to their word, Browne and Wachtel declined their previous roles as acting producers, although both would perform on various tracks. Instead, Warren opted to co-produce the album alongside Greg Ladanyi, giving himself just enough creative control to shape the finished version as he saw fit, while having Ladanyi's expertise and professional demeanor as anchors for the sessions' workflow. It was Warren's first attempt at such a working relationship since his aborted collaboration with Kim Fowley on 1969's *Wanted Dead or Alive*.

Much had changed in the decade since Warren's disastrous first solo attempt: he now not only had additional years of experience on the road and in the studio under his belt, but two moderately "hit" albums and a significantly larger budget with which to work. But much hadn't changed either, the least of which was the frantic egotism that could manifest when the booze and drugs flowed liberally throughout the studio. Without Browne or Wachtel to guide the new project's consistency and overall polish, the shape of *Bad Luck Streak* was left up to Warren's own whims, making for a finished collection that somehow autobiographically symbolized its creator's own mental state at the time:

conceptual and energetic, pensive and self-reflective—and with flashes of brilliant imagery, melody, and advanced composition. "He was very prepared when he went into that studio," George Gruel recalled.

In the end, the strongest material of *Bad Luck Streak* outweighed how uneven the album seemed to some, especially without the keen collaborative hands of Browne or Wachtel. If Warren was a perfectionist when it came to presenting a work that would meet his own standards, Browne offered the same creative obsession when presenting a finished product to the executives who had staked it.

But that wasn't to say that Warren hadn't written some new incredible material, miraculous considering the events surrounding the album's preproduction. From the very first moments of the album's title track, listeners of Warren's previous albums were made very much aware that they were still in capable hands. Following the opening bars of an idyllic stringed overture, the tranquility is abruptly halted by the unmistakable crack of two gunshots—Warren's trusty Smith & Wesson Model 29 .44 Magnum, fired off like a starter's pistol, signaling the grand commencement of his rock and roll.

The album's striking opening had been achieved with the creative use of Warren's gun fired directly into a wine barrel filled with sand. With a lot of trial and error—and plenty of nervousness on the part of producer Ladanyi—the team aimed multiple microphones at the receptacle and watched as Warren took aim himself, blasting the barrel as a wild substitute for a traditional handclap to start the song.

"Nobody had a clue if it would work," said George Gruel, recalling the anxiety that the improvised stunt caused among the crew members. "What if the sound concussion blows out the studio window between the console and the room? What will it do to the mics? Will the sand contain the 244 grains of lead? *Kaboom! Kaboom!* in perfect time with the track. Window still intact. Mics not smoking. Warren still standing. We dug through the sand and found the distorted blobs of lead. We did it."

As an opening track, "Bad Luck Streak in Dancing School" deliberately plays upon the bad-boy public persona that Warren had quickly cultivated as a traveling solo act, but with a pleading and regretful self-awareness of his crimes. "I been acting like a fool—I swear to God I'll change," plays more as a painful negotiation than a declaration of love, meshing the track's hard-rock sensibility with one of the artist's most vulnerable writings. No more universal than Eric Clapton's similarly gut-wrenching "Bell-Bottom Blues," Warren's musical cries to Crystal were transparent, despite the tongue-in-cheek meaning of the song's title: "dance academy" had been a nefarious euphemism for "brothel" since the mid-seventeenth century—much to Warren's intellectual amusement.

The dramatic incorporation of the gunfire had also been part of Warren's overall scheme to have a music video to accompany the album's release. Two years earlier, the label had green-lit the production for a modest promotional video to accompany "Werewolves of London," hoping the extra push would garner their flagship single even more attention. In a few simple takes, Warren and the band were filmed performing the song, the footage intercut with good-sport Jorge Calderón running amok through the street wearing a werewolf mask. With few television venues to screen the short film, it remained a fun experiment that had worked to entertain the participants more than attract viewership. Nevertheless, Warren had enjoyed the side project and saw both the creative and marketing potential in producing more videos. In his ongoing attempt to remain clean and relatively sober, part of his new regimen included martial arts training, as well as ballet lessons with JoAnn DeVito, the esteemed choreographer who had trained John Travolta in preparation for his career-defining turn in *Saturday Night Fever*. The latter of these two new passions would not only provide a suitable motif for the album's cover, but Warren found it equally perfect for a promo video that could be both elegant *and* titillating.

"The classical intro and the song were conceived together as a rock video, which no one would pay for, since no one seemed to know what a rock video was," Warren later recalled. Although music videos would soon become an integral part of the marketing and promotion of hot new music, the secondary project proved too expensive—at least to the increasingly impatient executives paying Warren's studio bill.

The majority of the album's sessions employed not so much a "core" ensemble, but a roster of familiar faces that were implemented from song to song, many of whom were freshly off of Jackson Browne's Running on Empty Tour. Although this practice would contribute to the negative criticism regarding the album's lack of continuity, cherry-picking his lineup gave Warren the opportunity to craft the individual sound of each track according to the unique musical sensibilities of each player. Rather than see this as a roadblock, Warren treated each track as the creation of a standalone entity, ultimately leading to a collection of well-polished gems that, unfortunately, lacked the tapestried sweep of *Warren Zevon* or the persona-defining *Excitable Boy*. Regardless of any shortcomings that A&R would find, the sterling collection nonetheless contained a few solid possibilities for airplay.

For the raucous title track, frequent collaborator Rick Marotta came straight off Warren's notorious "Jett Rink Tour" to perform his signature drums and percussion; likewise, David Lindley brought his lap steel guitar and Leland Sklar provided bass, both coming straight from Browne's road show. Following the positive experiences of working with the Sid Sharp Strings on the epic recording of "Desperadoes Under the Eaves" in 1976, Warren retained the ensemble to interpret the album's numerous orchestral compositions. More so than any previous jaunts into the studio, the recording of *Bad Luck Streak* gave Warren this rare opportunity to flex his arranger's muscles, and he pushed for as much time with the large string section as the budget would allow—including using the session as an excuse to record portions of his *Symphony No. 1*, long relegated as handwritten sheet music in the purgatory of his desk drawer at home.

In concert, Warren often performed covers of other artists' works, particularly the rock and pop songs that had ignited his imagination as a teen. Aside from the loving renditions of favorite Bob Dylan and Leonard Cohen compositions that he would incorporate into his set lists throughout the years, he would also occasionally perform some poppy bubblegum hit that was then tearing up the airwaves, a humorous jab at the mainstream appeal that always seemed to slip through his fingers. Now, in another first since his long-forgotten 1969 cover of the New Orleans Mardi Gras anthem "Iko Iko," Warren opted to cover a favorite from his youth: "A Certain Girl," an old R&B staple penned by hitmaker Allen Toussaint under his publishing pseudonym "Naomi Neville." It had first been a minor hit in 1961 for soul singer Ernie K-Doe, then a rock-infused B-side for the Yardbirds, featuring one of the earliest commercial recordings of Eric Clapton on lead guitar, three years later. Warren had performed his own wild rendition in concert throughout the *Excitable Boy* tour, using the song as an excuse to leap from his piano bench and offering audiences his own personal pyrotechnics, and making a studio arrangement all that much easier to produce.

For Warren's modernized and energetic recording, he pulled out all the stops in bringing the energy of his live version into the studio, making this session date a rare reunion of "the Gentleman Boys"—joining album constants percussionist Marotta and bassist Sklar were Jackson Browne, Jorge Calderón, and Waddy Wachtel, all of whom made themselves available for a brief return to the sonic symbiosis of the previous two albums. But despite his bustling schedule at the time, Wachtel recalled his confusion that Warren had retained Marotta for the album's sessions, yet had never attempted to persuade he and Browne to return as producers. "I remember saying to him, 'We just scored a hit record the last time out, and you only know Rick [Marotta] through me, but you'll fire me and Jackson?' He really wanted to do his own thing with the album, so I said, 'Good luck to you,' and Jackson and I came down for only a few songs."

George Gruel remembered that Warren would come into the studio fully prepared for the day's sessions with cassette tapes of his audible "sketches," or ready to demonstrate the intricate parts on the instruments available while Ladanyi and Wachtel looked on. "When [Warren would] play it," Gruel said, "I could already see Waddy thinking about the lead and rhythm parts. They'd start to jam on the song in the studio, this is where the magic happened."

As a bonus, Eagles alumni Don Felder stopped down for the "A Certain Girl" session, adding even more electricity to the lead guitar of Wachtel coupled with Jorge Calderón's rhythm work. In his selection of the song, Warren kept one other reason close to his chest: the song's signature refrain—"What's her name? / I can't tell ya!"—had become more autobiographical than some of the tunes Warren had written. He'd wasted no time in finding another woman in his life, and it wasn't long before the spare seat beside the engineer's console vacated by Crystal was taken over by twenty-four-year-old *Knots Landing* starlet Kim Lankford.

"Jungle Work" was a new collaboration with Calderón, giving listeners the rock and roll soaked in sweat, blood, and intrigue they'd come to expect from Warren. The instant fan favorite played as both a thematic sequel to "Roland the Headless Thompson Gunner" and one of his earliest experimental compositions from 1969's *Wanted Dead or Alive,* the psychedelic "Gorilla." Here, Warren told the gripping tale of a late-night siege undertaken by an airborne SWAT team, all armed to the teeth with M16s, Ingram guns, and a willingness to parachute into hell for their hard-earned pay. As spiritual descendants of the ghostly mercenary Roland, the guns-for-hire in "Jungle Work" express the morbid joy of their vocation with the primal chant that forms the stoic chorus: "Strength and muscle and jungle work!"

The session for "Jungle Work" featured the core lineup from "Bad Luck Streak in Dancing School," sans David Lindley's lap steel guitar; in his place, Joe Walsh lends a ferocious lead guitar—making him the second Eagle member to make an album appearance. The song's co-writer, Jorge Calderón, added more guitars and vocals, rounding out the mercenary anthem's thumping harmonies.

In what could be considered Warren's third great love ballad—after, chronologically, "Accidentally Like a Martyr" and "Hasten Down the Wind," both for Jordan's mother, Tule Livingston—"Empty-Handed Heart" was an unflinching letter of regret written specifically for Crystal. "Sometimes I wonder," its narrator confides, "if I'll make it with you," sadly accepting that with allowing the relationship to wither and end, they have "thrown down diamonds in the sand." With the parting words of advice—to "leave the fire behind you and start," presumably, a new life—Warren appeared to offer his wife a final farewell.

For the session, Warren gathered the closest he had to a "core" group—Rick Marotta, Leland Sklar, and himself on piano. In the second of two memorable appearances, Waddy Wachtel returned, lending a power-driven lead guitar to the song's bittersweet tone. Perhaps the most appropriate guest on the track, however, was Linda Ronstadt, who performed a heartbreaking descant against Warren's own primary vocal melody line. The result was a near-operatic conversation between two lovers, parting ways at the end of the affair.

While a four-bar classical overture opened the album itself, the twenty-six-second track entitled "Interlude No. 1" that followed "Empty-Handed Heart" was actually the first of two extended samples from Warren's extracurricular passion project, *Symphony No. 1.* Having the budget to enlist Sid Sharp's full orchestral string section had proved the perfect opportunity to have some of the work-in-progress performed and professionally recorded, and its inclusion on *Bad Luck*

Streak in Dancing School would finally demonstrate Warren's composing abilities for all to hear.

As an unfinished opus, Warren's symphony was the longest-running
project he'd ever worked on, having started toying with it in his late
teens. As the years passed and financial setbacks dictated the instruments and equipment available, Warren's classical composition had
mandatorily taken a back seat to more pressing projects. But with whatever downtime—and sobriety—his schedule allowed, Warren would sit
down at the piano and add to the symphony with incremental progress.
Still, the project haunted him like a ghost of his younger, purer self.

"[Classical] was his first love of music," remembered George Gruel,
who had settled into Warren's Los Angeles rental at this point, becoming both his closest confidante and personal assistant. "He'd work
endless hours on symphonies. I had the pleasure, more than once, of
lying flat on my back under the seven-foot Yamaha grand piano, in our
living room, and just listen to him play. Occasionally, he'd ask, 'Got
any more pot?'"

Gruel continued, "Before, or after, the session, Warren loved to go
into the studio and sit down at the ol' grand piano and drift off . . . I
loved watching Warren go off into that wonderful creative space where
nothing else in the world is going on."

Warren's early classical roots had been well emphasized in all press
coverage his career had yet garnered, particularly his teenage association with Igor Stravinsky. Throughout his career, interviewers would almost always bring up that biographical tidbit, inadvertently solidifying
Warren's enigmatic persona rather than calling for his classical works
to finally be heard.

Warren's closest friends and family were well aware how he longed
to complete the ambitious symphonic work. Soon after, in his published
Rolling Stone profile, Paul Nelson made it a point to demonstrate how
pervasive the project was in Warren's life: "Cassettes—Warren's and
mine—litter the living room. There must be 500 of them all over the
rug. Albums line the wall by the fireplace: Shostakovich, Mahler, Stockhausen, Bartok, and Stravinsky next to Eddie Cochran, Jimi Hendrix,
the Clash, the Sex Pistols, the Byrds, Dylan Thomas, the soundtrack
from Casablanca. There are guitars, a piano, a synthesizer, and a bass
signed by [Montreal Expos pitcher] Bill Lee. Plus, plenty of recording
equipment. A shoulder holster hangs over the arm of an easy chair."

He added, "Zevon tosses me a portfolio labeled 'Symphony No. 1,' which he works on nearly every night. I don't quite catch it, and the contents slide to the floor: pages and pages of meticulously annotated music and a dog-eared copy of *Soldier of Fortune* magazine. Perfect."

Nelson also noted that Warren truly "wanted to make his mark in classical music, as well as rock & roll," but, much like the gun holster on the armchair, the unfinished symphony hung "like a stone around his neck."

"I wanted nothing more than to be a classical composer and conductor," Warren later claimed. "That's what I believed would be rewarding, and every thought of it was fun and exciting, romantic, swashbuckling, whatever. The problem was that there was no such thing. And there really hasn't been any such thing since a cat named [Austrian composer and Arnold Schoenberg protégé] Anton von Webern was around. He was like, 'the last classical composer,' in the same way that maybe Samuel Beckett was the last traditional writer, or something."

Warren's own personal struggles, coupled with career stresses, made for less and less time devoted to his classical ambitions. Undeterred, he would adapt much of his knowledge in music theory into the intricate home recording that would liberate his later work—coincidentally making him one of the first rock artists to later professionally use digital recording technology.

In both theory and practice, Warren was able to intellectually legitimize his classical approach to composing rock and roll by viewing it through his larger perspective of the musical artists' place in society.

"So, what happens when there's no more literature is that there has to be something else," Warren later stated, extending his views on the place of the composer to that of all artists within the creative field. "What happens when there's no more classical music is that, all of a sudden, *bar* music becomes elevated to the artistic stature of what classical music was in the nineteenth century. So, a conglomerate like the Beatles and their producer becomes *every bit* as important and of the same caliber and quality, as the great classical composers of the century before. With certainly no depreciation in quality of artistic, spiritual, whatever."

He added, "So, what I'm getting at is, maybe rock 'n' roll is just running out. See, I think that these art forms, they run out. If you want to be a classical guy today and you want to write symphonies, like I wanted to do, then you pick the decade of the past that you want to write like. And you do some gimmick to 'put a spin on it,' as the critics say."

Although Warren's later views on the state of rock and roll seem to border on the fatalistic, he nonetheless would continue writing and composing songs of multiple genres—especially hard-driven rock—with equal lyricism and maturity for the rest of his life. By incorporating pieces of *Symphony No. 1* into *Bad Luck Streak,* he made his first and most pronounced attempt at blending the classical with the modernized sensibilities of rock-and-roll instrumentation.

On the album, Warren strategically placed his brief classical vignettes between two specific songs: the twenty-six-second "Interlude No. 1" preceded the raucous rock anthem "Play It All Night Long"; the extended one-minute-long "Interlude No. 2," which opens Side Two, softly led into the ballad "Bill Lee." In concert, the orchestral pieces were cleverly arranged for synthesizer, adding an adrenaline rush to the anthem's blaring opening chords.

For the session, Warren arranged and conducted Sid Sharp's fifteen-piece string ensemble—his first such opportunity to conduct since the 1975 sessions for "Desperadoes Under the Eaves."

"I'm no linguist," once remarked David Letterman, the late-night talk show host and future Warren compatriot, "but I believe Warren Zevon may be the only man in the history of human communication to use the word 'brucellosis' in a song."

Linguist or not, Letterman's observation was correct, and the aforementioned song, "Play It All Night Long," instantly achieved fan-favorite status. When performed live, it acted as the ultimate showcase for Warren's hardest-rocking abilities.

The song is also the closest Warren came to entering the "Southern Rock" genre until "Renegade" off *Mr. Bad Example* over a decade later. Here, however, he brought a razor-sharp commentary and overtly brazen humor, creating an unlikely hybrid of rock anthem and dark satire. His use of Lynyrd Skynyrd's "Sweet Home Alabama" was less a biting rip on the highly popular Florida-based blues rockers than a critique of the good ol' boy, Bo-and-Luke-Duke types who misunderstood the 1974 hit's meaning. It had originally been written by Lynyrd Skynyrd as a form of defensive response to two recent socially conscious ballads recorded by Neil Young, "Southern Man" and "Alabama," both of which dealt with the serious themes of racism and its pervasiveness within the American South. The members of Skynyrd wrote "Sweet Home Alabama" as a celebration of sorts, championing the positive aspects of the South's heritage, and the simpler pleasures that the rural lifestyle offered.

Depicting presumably typical scenes of stereotypical hillbilly living, the song includes, among other images, a family patriarch apathetic to his own incontinence, a shell-shocked veteran older brother, cancer, incest, sweat, piss, jizz, blood—and cattle dying of brucellosis. But the song rocked too hard to offend, or tread dangerously close to novelty. As Warren later recalled, the song had been "written really fast on marijuana around the synthesizer ostinato," referring to the song's signature repeated melody lick.

Although composed on the synthesizer, Warren would often alternate his lead instrument when performing the song live, demonstrating its unlikely interpretive versatility: a ballad-esque croon for solo piano, or a virtuosic showcase for his guitar skills when played using an arsenal of custom pedals. In the latter instance, Warren would memorably use the looped arpeggios created by the pedals to create a multilayered sound effect of his numerous guitar melodies at once, improvising over the sound-bed to simulate many guitarists playing in unison. On those occasions, "Play It All Night Long" could morph into a spectacular one-man jam session, demonstrating Warren's every artistic ability—the lyrics, humor, piano-based composition, and self-taught lead guitar mastery—in one act. When an encore, standing ovations were common.

As for the brucellosis: he'd found the term while reading Newton Thornburg's character-driven potboiler *Black Angus*. Set in the Midwest, Thornburg's quirky noir tale of a broke Missouri herder's desperate attempts to save his land, including a plot to fraudulently sell his dying cattle and a botched bank robbery, was well rooted in Zevon territory—but Warren never offered why he felt the rare cattle disease belonged in a rock-and-roll song.

When they recorded the no-holds-barred anthem in the studio, Warren played the core synthesizer ostinato and other postproduction instrumentation, while Marotta and Sklar returned. Just as Waddy Wachtel had made a solo appearance in addition to his reunion with Jackson Browne on "A Certain Girl," so Browne came back for his own vocal cameo, providing more layering to the song's background harmonies. David Lindley added a distinctive tone with his lap steel guitar, which Warren later claimed "make[s] it one of my favorite tracks."

The fourth adrenaline-fueled true rock-and-roll offering on the album comes in the form of Warren's famed collaboration with Bruce Springsteen, "Jeannie Needs a Shooter."

The collaboration was years in the making. Warren and Springsteen had met many times through their mutual friendship with Jon Landau, Springsteen's manager and chief architect of The Boss's public "blue-collar hero" persona. A few years earlier, Landau—who had long wanted to introduce the two songwriters—had mentioned to Warren the working title of a new Springsteen track, "Janey Needs a Shooter." Warren immediately loved the title, and was excited to hear that Springsteen hadn't yet penned the lyrics.

"I asked Bruce about it many times," Warren remembered later, "he finally said, 'You like it so much, why don't you write it?' I did write a few lines, T-Bone Burnett added something, I cut a track and actually put strings on it, then showed up at Bruce's house in Asbury Park in the middle of the night. He was asleep on the sofa in front of a videotaped baseball game. I roused him and played what I had for him. 'It's nice,' he said, 'but where are all the other verses?'"

In fleshing out the rest of the lyrics that night, Warren and Springsteen began a lifelong friendship and mutual admiration. A single listen to the finalized "Jeannie Needs a Shooter" and the author of its opening verse—and subject matter—is immediately apparent. Revisiting the American Old West for the first time since composing "Frank and Jesse James" during his stint with the Everly Brothers in the early 1970s, this time around Warren didn't attempt an epic story song; here, it is an old-time action Western in all its glory, summoning images of Alan Ladd on horseback, or a roguish Steve McQueen in mid-draw with his sawed-off Winchester Mare's Leg—like Warren, wanted dead or alive. Amid a motif of melodramatic Western saga, the Shooter relates his tale of forbidden love for the hardened daughter of a local lawman, and their tragic attempt to run off in the sunset together. But, in true Warren fashion, the story instead finds our hero alone in the darkness—penniless and bleeding to death from a single bullet. Jeannie and her father ride off into the night.

The recording took place during the same sessions as "Jungle Work," incorporating the core lineup of Warren, Marotta, and Sklar—and the added benefit of Joe Walsh returning, giving another thundering turn on lead guitar. Warren once again retained the Sid Sharp Strings for the song's stringed portions. George Gruel was able to snap a candid shot of Warren at the engineering console, a pack of Marlboros and the intricate sheet music for the "Jeannie Needs a Shooter" orchestral arrangement, remembering that studio session warmly as "perhaps one of Warren's all-time favorites."

There is a long tradition of great writers finding deeper existential meaning within the competitive nature of sports. As Hemingway, Fitzgerald, and Norman Mailer used boxing as a springboard for philosophical analogy, likewise troubadours and singer-songwriters have long followed in that literary tradition: Paul Simon had used the bare-knuckled vocation for the unnamed tragic hero of his eponymous 1969 "The Boxer," while Bob Dylan had successfully turned the controversial "rush to judgment" case of real-life middleweight contender Rubin Carter into a hit folk-rock murder ballad, 1975's "Hurricane." In the case of Dylan, the song not only heralded a return to socially conscious compositions, it also helped earn Carter a new trial and, ultimately, his freedom.

Warren's studio albums were always conceptual and consistent in their own individual themes, yet each contained songs varied in genre and tone, often making for a collection of short stories rather than a typical rock release. As a descendent of literary tradition, it was only a matter of time before Warren rose to the challenge of penning his own sports-inspired compositions—three total throughout his career. The first was unlike any sports biography ever set to music, wherein Warren depicted the inner thoughts of an active real-life baseball player, recognized more for his countercultural significance than athletic achievements.

However, Bill Lee had his fair share of devoted fans. During both his tenures with the Boston Red Sox and then Montreal Expos, the left-handed pitcher's quirky behavior and frequent comments on marijuana advocacy had earned him the endearing nickname "Spaceman" and a host of unlikely celebrity admirers. With Warren, the admiration was mutual. Both men excelled within their chosen fields, but a similar sense of deep-seated individualism had worked to make each a dark horse, or maverick, within those fields.

Like Warren's own reputation as the hard-partying "excitable boy," Lee had made headlines for similar offbeat and controversial behavior.

In the spring of 1978, he became a household name of dubious distinction after admitting he used marijuana regularly and had been for over a decade. The notorious interview resulted in a $250 fine and a widely publicized scolding from Major League Baseball commissioner Bowie Kuhn. In response, Lee clarified that he didn't actually *smoke* pot—he preferred to sprinkle it on his pancakes.

If ever a public statement would draw the amused attention of Warren Zevon, Bill Lee's revelation was it. When Lee went on to declare his love of Warren's music, claiming that *Excitable Boy* had become a staple soundtrack throughout the Red Sox clubhouse, the flattered singer-songwriter made it a point to seek out his baseball doppelgänger.

While the Expos were in Los Angeles for a face-off against the Dodgers—and Crystal was still in Ireland—Warren was able to get Lee himself on the phone, expressing his own admiration for the ballplayer and extending an invitation to his rental off Sunset Boulevard. "Don't bother comin' down to the game," Lee had told him. "It's family night, you won't be able to handle it." Instead, Lee hiked to Warren's house, a case of imported beer under his arm.

Before the famed pitcher even arrived, aide-de-camp George Gruel was apprehensive about the effects such a visit could mean for Warren's then fragile sobriety. Gruel remembered, "For Warren, it was the old, 'I'll just have one, George. You watch me.'"

Warren later confessed the depths of his self-denial during that period, explaining to Paul Nelson: "I said, 'Now look, George, we don't necessarily have to buy *all* this stuff that the hospital tells us. I've been taking drugs since I was *born*. Let's consider that alcohol may be just another drug experience that I had. So, let's see if I can drink moderately.'"

Warren continued, "So there was this one occasion—especially unfortunate since I think it left a bad impression on Bill Lee—when George said, 'Okay. You can have a drink when he gets here. Don't drink anything all day, and I'll let you have a drink then.'"

Gruel recalled, "It was three days of debauchery."

During the next seventy-two hours, Gruel and Lee "drank a bunch of Dos Equis and Warren swilled vodka." Warren proudly presented Lee with seven demos for the upcoming *Bad Luck Streak* sessions, including the tentatively titled "The Ballad of Bill Lee." Both inebriated *and* touched by the gesture, Lee proceeded to teach Warren and Gruel the countless card games he'd learned for needed amusement while on the road or between innings—those monotonous stretches when "ball-players are supposed to sit around and nod at simple things."

After three days of drinking, mastering Lee's preferred game of "Liar's Poker," and signing one of Warren's beloved bass guitars, the Expos champ staggered out—but not before Warren exchanged the autograph for one more gift: the collected works of T. S. Eliot.

"[Warren] was quite a fan," Lee later remembered of the day, noting that he had been impressed with Warren's demos, especially his own personal ballad. "I liked 'em. They had a lot of classical feeling." Of Warren himself, Lee added, "He burns hard, man. He lives up in the Hollywood Hills; he'd just as soon not live there, but they want him to be alone and write. I suggested he put nothing out for a long time."

With the deadlines for *Bad Luck Streak* still looming at that point, Warren was under too much pressure to put Lee's advice to use. He compromised with a brief sabbatical, however: according to Paul Nelson, Bill Lee's visit unintentionally set off the binge that drove Warren into Pinecrest for the second time. As Warren later recalled, "A couple of days later, George said, 'You don't control the amount you drink. You didn't stop yesterday. You didn't stop today. When are you going to stop?' I had a bottle and a half of Wild Turkey left. I said, 'When that's gone.'"

The demo version of "Bill Lee" Warren played for its eponymous subject was not far removed from the final studio cut. In another first, Warren performed the brief track—which tersely clocked in at just over the one-minute mark—in a near solo setting, playing both piano and the clever harmonica phrases that symbolically substituted Lee's notorious off-the-cuff witticisms. Aside from Warren, visiting Eagles alumni Glenn Frey's soft harmonies are the only other sound on the track, making for an intimate ballad with an appropriately bluesy send-off. Leading into the track was Warren's second and final classical portion, "Interlude No. 2," presenting Bill Lee's story with an almost majestic symphonic commencement. But with humorous observations—which easily could have been made by either Lee or Warren himself—"If you don't, they'll screw you / If you do, they'll screw you, too"—the classical shadings only added a layer of sonic maturity to the otherwise darkly sarcastic lullaby.

In terms of a baseball motif, Warren's portrait of Lee certainly was not "Casey at the Bat," or any other traditional representation of

America's Pastime. With only the most fleeting mention of the sport itself, the song's true subject became Lee himself: a character study weighing the burden of individualism and the stigma of displaying an outspoken progressive attitude. In the post-Watergate era, Lee's rebelliousness, while actively excelling within one of the country's most wholesome and enduring symbols of its own identity, resonated with his generation. The baseball commissioner was the principal and Lee was the class clown who had been sent to his office. Warren could relate. And in the same way that Jackson Browne's romanticism provided a wistful voice to the spirit of disillusioned idealism felt by the maturing flower children, so Lee spoke as the snarkiest and most angst-ridden alter ego of that same spirit. Warren could relate to that, as well. Like Warren, Lee was another Offender, with a capital "O."

During Warren's intervention, Paul Nelson had admitted his own concerns that Warren could come to a tragic end, not unlike the protagonist of F. Scott Fitzgerald's classic "The Crack-Up." While autobiographical self-reflection pervades even the most seemingly unrelated material on *Bad Luck Streak,* Warren's playful "Gorilla, You're a Desperado" is as close to directly addressing Nelson's fears as Warren would get—albeit in a very humorous style. Here, the song's narrator visits the Los Angeles Zoo only to switch places with the gorilla of the song's title, providing a list of advice to aid the simian in adjusting to human society. Handing the ape the keys to his BMW and apologizing for the poor state of his apartment, the narrator provides sad updates on the gorilla's progress: following a divorce, our beloved ape suffered an apparent midlife crisis, taking up racquetball, jogging, seeing a therapist, and moving into a bachelor pad at the luxurious L'Ermitage hotel in Beverly Hills.

Presumably, our human narrator remains quite comfortable in his cage at the zoo; his animal counterpart, on the other hand, grows accustomed to life wearing a "platinum chain" of materialism and leisure for which he had traded his own primal nature. Ironically, Warren would flip the symbolic images of a humanized simian trading his freedom for the soft comforts of bourgeoisie living in exchange for a worthless trinket in another of his later songs: the second of two homages to Elvis Presley, "Porcelain Monkey." There, Warren and co-writer Jorge Calderón worked together on a stinging commentary of fame—"from the glitter to the gloom"—by way of the many worthless antiques and unnecessary luxuries the King had amassed during his twilight years within Graceland.

By the time the album's recording sessions were winding down, Warren and actress Kim Lankford had become a solid couple. For months, she had been dividing her time between the long hours on set for her hit television series *Knots Landing* and keeping Warren company at the Sound Factory. One episode had required exterior shots at the LA Zoo and, between takes, Lankford dropped a few coins into a souvenir "Vac-u-form" arcade machine, purchasing Warren a miniature statue of an angry gorilla. When she presented the gift to him later that night, Warren found the gesture so amusing he gave it a place of honor atop his Yamaha grand piano. Not to be outdone, George Gruel soldered custom spectacles for the toy, completing the gorilla's full "Warren look"—and inspiring the song's opening line. It also inspired the trio's daytrip to the zoo soon after. There, Warren saw that the real-life monkey cages had been adorned with a brass plaque created by none other than Hollywood legend Lee Marvin, another of Warren's favorites. In rather cheeky fashion, the actor had made the generous donation in his ex-wife's name, further adding to Warren's playful gorilla song narrative.

The up-tempo, near-calypso vibe of "Gorilla, You're a Desperado" was further enhanced by the all-star guest appearances that accompanied the standing core of Warren on synthesizer, Marotta and Sklar. Aside from J. D. Souther and Jackson Browne's guest harmonies—and Browne's memorable slide guitar work—the song holds the distinction of marking the fourth appearance by an Eagles member on the album. As Don Felder, Glenn Frey, and Joe Walsh had all contributed to previous songs, so Don Henley now came aboard to provide backup vocals to a loving parody of his own song, "Desperado."

Warren later remembered what a good sport Henley had been, willingly replicating the refrain of his own 1973 hit. "To their credit," he said, "when the Eagles came in to sing backup, they asked me if I wanted them to make fun of themselves; I said, "No, no, just sing like you do.'"

According to George Gruel, in many ways, the Eagles' participation—particularly Henley's playful cameo—was like a reaffirmation of Warren's reputation among his peers. "He had amazing musicians playing on his records because he was so respected as a songwriter," remembered Gruel. "How many times have Don Henley and Glenn Frey sung backgrounds on someone else's song? And on Warren's 'Gorilla, You're a Desperado,' they actually sing the word 'desperado' just like they did on their [own song]."

Bringing the pace back down following the gorilla's adventures, Warren followed the track with his first songwriting collaboration with longtime friend and musician-cum-legendary-producer T Bone Burnett. "Bed of Coals" was a soft piano-based ballad—played with the tone of a gospel hymn, the song was compositionally reminiscent of the spiritual weariness Warren had previously expressed in "Mohammed's Radio." Here, he again avoided the direct references to his own ongoing personal turmoil yet offered his most vulnerable observation: "I'm too old to die young, and too young to die now." The striking declaration spoke volumes of Warren's own concerns and regrets regarding the addictions that had slowly driven so many of his loved ones away.

Warren's self-revelation also related to the growing number of personal heroes and musical influences he had watched living fast, dying young, and leaving behind the proverbial attractive corpse. When David Letterman humorously observed that Warren's intake of "a couple of quarts of vodka a day" demonstrated "the resiliency of the human system," Warren couldn't argue; on that theme, he followed up with Letterman many years later, memorably adding, "I got to be Jim Morrison a lot longer than he did." The veiled form of survivors' guilt echoed in "Bed of Coals" surely struck a chord with many of his rock-and-roll peers: the hard-partying bad boys who, by now, were well past the age of thirty—many of whom were well represented in the roster of all-star cameos throughout the entire album. On the recording, Warren's consistent lineup was joined by J. D. Souther on supportive vocals and Ben Keith who, in his only album appearance, filled in for David Lindley with soulful, appropriately twangy pedal steel guitar.

It is perhaps with Warren's own rebelliousness in mind that *Bad Luck Streak in Dancing School* closes with a rousing celebration of that very same youthful spirit—the one that directly inspired both his romantic restlessness and romanticized recklessness. The joyous perspective with which Warren unabashedly presents irresponsible wanderlust in "Wild Age" worked as ironic bookend for *Bad Luck Streak,* contradicting the desperate mantra of its opening title track—"I swear to God I'll change"—with the wide-eyed stubbornness of its own promise: "Well they tried so hard to hold him / Heaven knows how hard they tried / But he's made up his mind / he's the restless kind."

On the recording, the romantic "bad boy" declaration is made even more sincere as, coupled with David Lindley's guest lead guitar, both Glenn Frey and Don Henley joined Warren as his backup vocals—a harmony of generational voices singing a pact to remain young, and reckless, at heart.

∽

The momentum of *Excitable Boy* had, for better or worse, solidified Warren's persona as the mischievous intellectual, the two-fisted troubadour who drank like Hemingway, wrote like Raymond Chandler, and could rock like Bowie. He would take the stage in a three-piece Armani suit, yet be shirtless and soaked by the final encore. The design and marketing for the highly anticipated *Bad Luck Streak in Dancing School* would reflect each of his signature eccentricities—guaranteed by the return of Jimmy Wachtel.

For the album cover, Wachtel's conception played perfectly into Warren's original intention to push for a music video of the title song: like the two Elektra/Asylum releases before it, Warren is decked in an expensive suit, now surrounded by a bevy of young ballerinas in various poses of stretching and warm-up exercises. As desired, the iconic final image succinctly hit the most important elements in representing the facets of its complex artist, especially his humor: a literal translation of the album's title, taking place in a genuine dancing academy, and with Warren the centerpiece, à la Sean Connery as 007 surrounded by beautiful women in the classic movie posters. Adhering to Warren's mandatory ironic twist, the "bad luck streak" is seen in the women's indifference to his presence.

Wachtel had arranged for the photo shoot to take place in the early morning at a willing Pasadena ballet school. The exhausted look on Warren's face in the final images were not the product of method acting, as George Gruel later remembered: "Warren and I had been up all night, not certain why, we just were. Jimmy Wachtel did a wonderful job . . . the dancers were fantastic. It was a fun time, too." As a professional photographer himself, Gruel used many of the photo opportunities to take his own shots, many of which proved strong enough in quality to be used in later tour marketing and merchandise. He later recalled how fortunate he'd been to be surrounded by like-minded creative types who let him grab the best candid shots of Warren behind the scenes. During the cover shoot for *Bad Luck Streak,* Gruel captured nearly as many iconic moments as Wachtel, furthering their own mutual admiration. "While Jimmy was shooting, I was too," remembered Gruel. "Some photographers freak when another photographer is shadowing them on their shoot, not Jimmy. He's a true gentleman and artist."

Wachtel's greatest attributes were truly put to the test, however, when it came to the album's *back* cover. Like the famed inner sleeve for *Excitable Boy,* which featured Crystal's "Willy on the Plate" still life of a .44 Magnum atop a home-cooked meal, firearms would be the motif. In the two years since that album, Warren had upgraded his arsenal: the Smith & Wesson had been swapped for an Uzi. It wasn't so much the gun itself that caused controversy, but rather the ballet pointe shoes surrounded by used shell casings beneath the submachine gun.

For the dramatic photo arrangement, Wachtel had to rent the gun, along with the hourly services of a mandatory weapons expert. For all the trouble to design and execute the shot, more trouble came in the form of advocacy groups unhappy with the image's violent inference. As Wachtel later remembered, "This women's group got up in arms that it was saying we were going to mow down these ballerinas with a gun. And I had to go to Asylum Records, to Joe Smith's office, to defend the album cover to some lesbian women's group."

One addition to the album's back cover had no basis in humor or satire, but rather a small and heartfelt message to a mentor. In the bottom left-hand corner, Warren had penned: "For Ken Millar—*il miglior fabbro,*" calling to mind T. S. Eliot's own dedication to mentor Ezra Pound in *The Waste Land,* which in turn had referenced Dante's *Purgatorio.* The literal translation offered the Italian master's definition of a troubadour as "the greatest craftsman of the mouth tongue."

∽

Bad Luck Streak in Dancing School was released on February 15, 1980. The label planned for three singles, two less than Warren's previous album: "A Certain Girl" / "Empty-Handed Heart," the playfully linked "Gorilla, You're a Desperado" / "Jungle Work," and the very deliberate "Jeannie Needs a Shooter" / "Interlude No. 2" / "Bill Lee."

With "A Certain Girl" as the album's flagship single, Elektra/ Asylum had selected the only song not penned by Warren himself, making for the second instance in a row where the label's commercially minded strategy undermined his primary stature as a songwriter. Additionally, with "Jeannie Needs a Shooter" chosen as the third single, A&R heavily played on the song's collaboration with Bruce Springsteen, using the larger superstar's mass appeal to draw attention.

It was with the latter's release that Warren had been able to enact a sly revenge, taking a cue from Paul McCartney's notorious advice to *Abbey Road* assistant engineer Alan Parsons: the seasoned Beatle had once urged the aspiring young rocker to register his songs' introductions and preludes as autonomous copyrighted compositions, doubling all future residuals. The Cute One's words of wisdom paid off handsomely when Parsons's own 1982 release, "Eye in the Sky," became a minor hit—but its B-side, the instrumental prelude "Sirius," became a staple of television commercials, movies, and especially major sporting events for decades. Following suit, Warren insisted the flip side of "Jeannie Needs a Shooter" not only include "Bill Lee," but its extended classical segue, "Interlude No. 2"—releasing it as a "double B-side," or the increasingly popular "maxi-single," featuring two separate compositions attributed solely to Warren.

As with *Excitable Boy,* Warren's latest release had its fair share of both champions and detractors. While the polarity in opinion usually stemmed from critics' appreciation—and comprehension—of Warren's unique brand of humor, this time around, most reviews noted the artist's heavier new style. With significantly harder-edged rock tracks spread out among ballads, tearjerkers, and two classical pieces, many also found the album uneven, especially when compared to Warren's last two albums.

"On the back cover of his latest album, *Bad Luck Streak,* Zevon's trusty gat is thrown down alongside a pair of ballet slippers, spent bullets strewn about the floor," noted *Washington Post* critic Boo Browning. "It's only the first indication that something uncharacteristic is happening here."

Browning continued, "Zevon has been through a transitional period of late, including a divorce and a drying-out, and these songs supposedly represent a catharsis. What he's actually wound up doing is trading his usual rapid-fire lyrics and straight-to-the-gut subject matter for a skin-deep commitment to change . . . Instead of the rhythmic surprises or the dissonant tension he has used to maximum effect in the past, Zevon serves up music that sounds familiar, if not downright redundant."

The assessment concluded with, perhaps, the worst affirmation Warren's fragile semi-sobriety needed: "There's little we can learn from innocence, and though this album is hardly a wasted effort, Zevon is ultimately more enlightening when he is an excitable boy."

Robert Christgau was slightly more forgiving for Warren's shifts in topical and sonic tones, but, like other self-declared admirers, stressed his confusion over the changes. "I don't know why the title tune's the title tune," he wrote, "except maybe to contextualize the classical interludes he composed all by himself . . . though the brucellosis is a nice touch. In fact, just about every song boasts a good line or three."

"As a kid, Zevon obviously devoured horror comics, cowboy flicks and *The Untouchables*," observed *People* magazine in its overtly playful review. "Nothing else would account for his uniquely baleful brand of dirge-rock and a singing style as ominous as twin six-shooters. Zevon's fans will find this album a macho-morbid match for his previous two . . . Sometimes Zevon misses—on the meaningless title cut and on a clumsy tribute to wacko baseball pitcher Bill Lee, for example."

Like Christgau, other critics directed some of their harshest words toward the album's title cut, despite its earliest consideration as a potential single. Not surprisingly, "Gorilla, You're a Desperado" came out as a front-runner as one of the album's most popular tracks, with many comparing the tongue-in-cheek autobiographical fable as a spiritual follow-up to "Werewolves of London." As *People* added, "The gorilla winds up in Transactional Analysis while Zevon remains at the monkey house. The image ideally suits his chest-thumping virtuosity."

But there was something about Warren's enigmatic, ever-shifting persona that consistently brought out the most meditative writing and literary aspirations in the crew at *Rolling Stone*. Soon enough, staff writer Paul Nelson would be beginning the long and difficult process of persuading the magazine to run an epic, unadulterated, and unflinching profile on Warren's battle with alcoholism—a labor of love monster of a manuscript that would take the journalist over a year to complete, and ultimately bring about his literary demise. In his place, another of Warren's friends, Jay Cocks, took to the plate and penned an extended review of *Bad Luck Streak,* offering a critical assessment so in-depth it would be assumed to end any debate regarding the album's merits.

"*Bad Luck Streak* could be Zevon's best album," Cocks wrote. "Certainly, it's the best-sounding record he's ever done, with supple guitar work by David Lindley and drumming by Rick Marotta that gives no quarter. There are various instrumental guest appearances—by Jackson Browne and Joe Walsh most strikingly—and string arrangements by Warren Zevon that show, as clearly as anything ever has, the results of his adolescent pilgrimages up behind the Whisky a Go-Go to visit Igor Stravinsky."

Cocks's lovingly written track-by-track analysis read more like a full-on defense of the album's overall execution than a mere review—and a glowing one at that. Like Nelson, Cocks heavily benefited from knowing Warren in real life, recognizing the autobiographical scars within even the most seemingly unrelated tracks that his fellow critics wouldn't spy. For certain readers, Cocks's intimate knowledge of the stories behind the songs, however, made his words of praise cut to the bone—as was the case in "Empty-Handed Heart," the track that he zealously heralded as the album's "core" and "centerpiece."

Of the song's heartbreaking lyrics—which Warren had written specifically for Crystal at the very turbulent end of their marriage—Cocks wrote: "You hear the pity and the vast anger just beneath the surface. These are weapons, not memories: the past used as a blunt instrument. The descant [provided by Linda Ronstadt] moves way past teary counterpoint and becomes a woman's act of desperation. Even at this short distance, 'Empty-Handed Heart' sounds like a classic, one of Zevon's finest numbers, and one of his most direct."

Crystal knew full well the song's intimate message was directed toward her. Before the studio sessions for the album had even begun, and despite the finality of their latest separation, Warren had sent a demo of the track to her on their anniversary along with a note: "Old Girl, ain't we had some times?" When the album was finally released, Crystal recognized among its track listing her personal letter of goodbye. When she later read Jay Cocks's review in *Rolling Stone,* she disagreed with the critic's interpretation of "Empty-Handed Heart" so vehemently, only Paul Nelson could talk her out of sending the magazine's editor, Ben Fong-Torres, an angry letter. Even after nearly a year apart, the wounds remained fresh.

In a more general defense, Cocks ended with his own summation of Warren's new work, stating, *"Bad Luck Streak* is a hard-fought record. That's what makes Warren Zevon hard-boiled, like Ross Macdonald, Raymond Chandler and Dashiell Hammett. Not the posture or the gunplay or the scars. It's the willingness to peel the scar tissue, to stand without it and go for more, that makes these men tough. And makes them great. All of them."

∞

Warren had met Kim Lankford midway through recording *Bad Luck Streak.* She was longtime friends with Fred Walecki, the owner of Westwood Musical Instruments, which Warren frequented regularly for new gear. The striking blonde immediately caught his eye and, although she was then dating mutual friend Doug Haywood, Warren persuaded her into having dinner with him at his Los Angeles home. She later recalled, "I didn't accept, but I did say I'd come over and make him dinner. He was so nervous he ate all the appetizers and couldn't touch the swordfish." Out to impress, Warren had worn his finest ribbed cashmere sweater, à la Steve McQueen, which the younger woman found appropriately "dapper."

As the two later told *People* magazine in a joint interview, within three months of meeting, Lankford "knew it was 'something serious.' Warren knew 'a little sooner. It was a slow building for her, a lot of frustration for me.'"

It wasn't long before they were inseparable. As the recording of *Bad Luck Streak* had coincided with the disintegration of Warren's marriage, Lankford was soon the consistent studio presence that Crystal had been.

In many ways, Warren's relationship with Lankford benefited from the chronology of his creative process. The immeasurable pressures of writing enough new material to fill an album had long been his greatest enemy; as George Gruel observed, it was in the studio, enacting the synergy of quality musicians around him, that "the magic happened." With a daily studio regimen providing Warren with both a creative outlet and a somewhat stable routine, he was as close to achieving a healthy mindset as a functioning alcoholic could muster. In meeting the beautiful twenty-four-year-old television starlet, Warren approached the third major romantic commitment of his life, and although he had not always been faithful within his marriage to Crystal, it was his first attempt at monogamy in half a decade.

He was admittedly drawn to both Lankford's youth and the health-conscious fitness and diet regimens that fueled her endless energy. She not only played guitar and was a passionate equestrian, but also studied martial arts with Chuck Norris's brother, Aaron, and inspired Warren's new interests in karate and ballet. In return, he gave her his own personal crash courses in books, classical music, and interpreting art.

"When Kim and I first met," he told Paul Nelson, "I felt almost like a virgin because I wasn't used to being sober around women. We talk for days and days. We were both determined not to jump into a symbiotic relationship, and we don't try to be like each other. I no longer feel that a woman is supposed to be a reflection of my attitudes, or vice versa." He added that Kim reminded him, more than anyone else, of Clint Eastwood. Later, he playfully punctuated that observation by changing his answering-machine message to the famed ".44 Magnum" monologue from *Dirty Harry*.

"Much later, I told [Warren] that if he wanted a divorce, he should file for it," Crystal later admitted to Paul Nelson, "because, if it were up to me, I wanted to try to make the marriage work. I would have chosen to separate for a while and get our acts together, but I didn't think Warren could exist without someone for that long."

Yet even in his new perspective on relationships, there were the inevitable self-delusions of Warren's unconquered addictions. Warren had allowed his glamorous new love affair with a younger, vivacious woman to inspire his own feelings of renewed youth, but in the era of his recent bachelorhood, his substance consumption had evolved; if he had to cut back on the booze, then substituting harder drugs would have to suffice. For an addict, the unspoken benefit of a new relationship is that the other person is unaware how truly dire things had once been; they also can't possibly know how bad things can still get. By the time Lankford was moved in with Warren, cocaine had been added into the mix. Soon, painkillers and, for what Warren would insist had been "a brief flirtation and not a tragic love affair," heroin.

At the beginning of their relationship, Lankford was largely unaware of Warren's habits. With his dirty laundry having been thoroughly aired throughout the news media, there was no reason for her to doubt his sincerity about being clean and relatively sober. While she admitted that her own lifestyle was "much more on the tame side" when compared to the public persona, his charm and intelligence won her over. If Warren insisted that he could handle the occasional drink and joint for the sake of his writing, who was she to question the older and established artist?

As their relationship deepened, both Warren and Lankford grew weary of the rental on Sunset Boulevard; he bitterly described it to Paul Nelson as a "stupid, pretentious, screenwriter's idea of a screenwriter's idea of a screenwriter's house." Instead, the couple found a new house further removed from downtown Hollywood that once belonged to Maureen O'Hara in Nichols Canyon. It could even accommodate Warren's ever-growing collection of instruments and gear—which now included both a Yamaha grand piano and a Yamaha upright, a Roland synthesizer, a portable keyboard he used for composing on the road, a Martin acoustic guitar, a Gibson SG, a Les Paul, a Fender Broadcaster given to him by David Marks, a four-track cassette recorder, a micro-cassette recorder, mixers, amps, microphones, and hundreds of wires.

Warren and Lankford, along with George Gruel, moved into the house on Zorada Drive just before the tour for *Bad Luck Streak* was about to begin. All three would be taking to the road together, and the new home promised that some form of domestic stability awaited Warren upon his return.

Just as the production of the album had been a direct product of the drastic changes in Warren's personal life, so the tour would include various new practices and protocols to mark his "new" era of balanced sobriety. As he had dryly said to David Landau when convincing his old friend to pick up a guitar and join him on the road, "David, I'd like you to meet Warren Zevon. You've never met him before, you know."

As far as his playful "reintroduction" to Landau, Warren would be making numerous such new introductions before the tour's kickoff: in another major shake-up of the status quo, he had mandated an entirely new band lineup for the tour. With Jackson Browne, David Lindley, Rick Marotta, Leland Sklar, and Waddy Wachtel all booked for their own respective gigs and tours, and the members of the Eagles busy *being* the Eagles, a new touring band had become a necessity.

Not since the early 1970s had Warren been obligated to hold auditions, and only then as the paid bandleader for the Everly Brothers. That experience, however, had led directly to his integral introduction to Waddy Wachtel, so there was a hopeful prospect in actively seeking some new talent. In a surprise outcome, Warren selected a rock band from Colorado, composed of excellent, though relatively inexperienced, younger musicians.

Despite their band name, Boulder had originally formed in Florida in 1972, beginning as a seven-member ensemble including five vocalists. The group's lineup had evolved during its three-year odyssey of colleges and bars throughout the United States, finally taking root in the Colorado city that gave their latest incarnation its name. There, they built their own garage studio, as drummer Marty Stinger later recalled: "One of our roadies was a carpenter, and we went all out with hammer and nails and plasterboard." Their professional-grade demos attracted the attention of Warren's own label, Elektra/Asylum, in 1978, and their debut album even featured a ferocious rock cover of Warren's "Join Me in LA."

It had taken one perfect stab at Chuck Berry's "Johnny B. Goode" for Warren to hire them on the spot. Their full lineup now included David Landau on lead guitars, Bob Harris on synthesizer, Roberto Pinon on bass, Marty Stinger, Zeke Zirngiebel on various guitars—and Warren himself. With four backup vocalists behind him, two lead guitarists, and—for the first time—an additional keyboard player, Warren was geared to become completely liberated and electrified before his audience. Like his tours before it—and much to the amusement of his traveling cohorts—he concocted this album's promotional bookings with two alternate, but equally apropos aliases: the All Hell Is Breaking Loose Jungle Tour, and The Dog Ate the Part We Didn't Like Tour, the latter lovingly cribbed from friend Thomas McGuane's bestselling novel *Panama*. Aside from a few warm-up shows during the first few weeks of April, and a triumphant grand finale back in Los Angeles, the band was slated to travel the country for just over three months. As had been the case with *Excitable Boy,* the tour's official launch was set on the East Coast: New York City's famed 3,400-seat Palladium.

Through both the turmoil and the successes that had defined the last decade of his life, Warren hadn't had many opportunities to keep in contact with much of his extended family. When his mother and grandmother had come to one of his shows during the *Excitable Boy* tour, it had been years since he'd last seen them; in his condition on that particular night, he didn't remember their attendance anyway. Many of his father's brothers, the original band of Zivotovsky boys, had remained in New York.

By 1980, his cousin Sandford had moved back to New York with his own family and looked at Warren's Palladium performance as a great way to introduce his two young sons to their famous rock-star cousin.

For the sold-out April 12 kickoff show, Warren and company pulled out all the stops, as his younger cousin, Lawrence Zevon, fondly remembers: "[Warren] was really popular at the time and the show was well attended by celebrities . . . I remember walking up some stairs backstage, when I came face-to-face with Gilda Radner, who might have been a little tipsy! She explained and demonstrated out-of-the-blue how the backstage passes, cloth decals, were damaging the finish on her leather coat. The concert was amazing and backstage, everyone was dancing—even my father and Gilda danced together."

Lawrence added, "After the show, Warren was carried offstage and whisked away—a sweaty rock star being ushered somewhere other than with his family. I mention that because every show I went to after this, especially when I was in college in the late eighties, I would spend hours with Warren backstage. He seemed to crave family and asked a lot of questions about everyone in the family . . . Maybe he enjoyed the distraction of being with family while on the road."

Despite the overwhelming success that the Palladium show had seemingly been for all in attendance, fans and critics were two different crowds to be pleased. Although tickets were selling, and Warren's new brand of over-the-top physicality got the crowd to its feet, his earliest critical admirers were growing confused by the artist's evolving persona. Not everyone was accepting of a rendition of "Jungle Work" that required pyrotechnics, a light show, and a state-of-the-art special effects device that simulated sounds of gunfire throughout the concert hall. Nor did all warm to Warren's numerous other gimmicks, such as road manager and aide-de-camp George Gruel bringing Warren out on stage in handcuffs, or the camouflage attire that accompanied his physical gymnastics during his "Jungle Work" circus.

As critic for *The New York Times* Robert Palmer admitted only after the tour's conclusion, he was not alone in shaking his head, wondering to where the pulpish troubadour of "song noir" had vanished. "He spent half his Palladium show running around the stage as though he was practicing for the marathon," Palmer wrote. "He crouched and jumped and shouted and raised a clenched fist and finally ripped off his shirt. Frankly, he made an embarrassing spectacle of himself . . . Several critics gathered in a neighborhood bar after the show. 'I sure am glad I didn't have to review that,' said one of them as he sighed after downing a stiff drink. 'Maybe it wouldn't have been so bad,' another suggested, 'if we'd just listened to it and hadn't had to watch it, too.'"

Ever the defender, Paul Nelson proudly offered his own take, writing, "Onstage at the Palladium, he's in fantastic form and gives such a kinetic, physical performance that some critics take him to task for exhibitionism. To me, these charges are small-minded and ridiculous. This is the first tour on which he's been in shape and sober enough to move. There's a celebration going on up there, and Zevon is trying hard to make up for all those drunken debacles in the past. Once you understand that, it's very touching."

What was undeniable, however, was the chemistry between Warren and his touring band. Although a seemingly unlikely match, the younger members of Boulder brought out a hard edge to Warren's rock abilities; in turn, the skilled though unseasoned tour-mates erupted with sonic enthusiasm before the largest crowds they had ever seen. In effect, everyone had brought their A game—a far cry from the disastrous spiral of the *Excitable Boy* tour. Now at every stop along the current tour, Warren made a very specific point of indicating his gratitude for his team, taking a back seat during "Join Me in LA" to allow the band to give the audience the hard-rock version of their debut album. At every show, he called George Gruel his "best friend" when dragging him out onstage to dance, bellowing, "Come on out here, George, or I'll kill ya!"

When it came to David Landau and his guitar acumen, Warren's extensive vocabulary ran toward the Joycean, calling the seasoned pro "industrious, illustrious, well-renowned, iridescent, phosphorescent, luminescent, indescribable, ineffable, ever-mercurial, unquenchable, irresistible, irrepressible"—and, a "jaguar." As for the critics' harsh words regarding his onstage antics, Warren had no bones about expressing his views during the nightly self-introduction: *"I'm Warren Zevon—I sing as good as I can and I dance as well as I want!"*

In due time, that anonymous critic yearning to hear Warren's electrified performance would get his wish. Warren planned to close his fourteen-week road show by recording the live rock-and-roll album to end all rock-and-roll albums—one that Paul Nelson would later claim was, aside from Neil Young's *Live Rust,* "the best live rock & roll LP" he'd ever heard.

CHAPTER SIX

(1980–1983)

AFTER THREE MONTHS OF SHOWS IN OVER THIRTY CITIES, THE band and crew were given a few weeks' respite before the tour's grandiose official conclusion at the Roxy in downtown Los Angeles. The Roxy was booked as an exclusive five-night engagement for the middle of August, making Warren available to attend Ariel's fourth birthday party. Even prior to the tour, Warren hadn't seen much of his children. Over the years, he would attempt to compensate for his absence by bestowing expensive and elaborate gifts on his family, especially his children Jordan and Ariel—much as William "Stumpy" Zevon had done in giving Warren a piano, a Corvette, and wads of cash.

Warren took over the tradition with Ariel's birthday that year, buying her a brand-new swing set—the assembly of which employed as many cameo appearances as one of his albums. For hours, Jackson Browne, Greg Ladanyi, and Crystal's father assisted as a hapless Warren attempted to put it together. Ultimately, George Gruel stepped in with Crystal's father, who was growing irritated with his *still*-son-in-law's behavior. "We finally got it together and tweaked all of the nuts and bolts, and it was the hit of the party," Gruel later remembered. "All's well that ends well."

Crystal and her family, however, were not nearly as cavalier regarding how Warren had conducted himself, especially toward his young daughter. Clifford Brelsford later recounted how that day had been the closest he'd ever come to punching Warren out in front of a crowd—not discounting the Christmas when Warren had brought the Brelsfords a bottle of top-shelf scotch, only to single-handedly down it alone by the end of the night. Although accidental, Warren had knocked Ariel down as she raced to hug him during the swing set debacle. With the birthday girl in tears, Crystal told Warren it would be best if he'd explain to Ariel that he wouldn't be living there anymore. Afterward, he gathered all his leftover items from the Montecito house and threw them into paper bags. He told Crystal that he and Kim would take Ariel out the following day for a birthday lunch. She agreed, but, recognizing that he was drinking again, was not surprised when he arrived three hours late.

∞

Had *Bad Luck Streak in Dancing School* met sales and critical expectations, the decision to release a live album might not have occurred so early within Warren's Elektra/Asylum tenure. But by the first week of April—after seven weeks of release—it only had peaked at Number 20 on the *Billboard* chart. While that was a vast improvement over his 1976 debut's placement at 189, the new album's final tally was a noticeable twelve-spot drop from *Excitable Boy*. And out of its three singles, only the non-Warren-written "A Certain Girl" had charted at all, placing on *Billboard*'s 200 at a mediocre Number 57. Amid the consistently conflicted critical reception—and without a breakout hit like "Werewolves of London"—further evidence would be needed to prove Warren's popularity and, more importantly, his staying power.

Causing all hell to break loose back in Los Angeles seemed like a perfect homecoming. As New York City had consistently been picked as the starting point for Warren's previous tours, the five-night engagement at the Roxy in West Hollywood was billed as the grand finale of his US tour. For a truly definitive representation of the *Bad Luck Streak* tour, the entire lineup of Boulder returned for the hotly anticipated residency, alongside David Landau on lead guitars. When Warren announced that the concerts were to be professionally recorded for a live album release, there was cautious excitement; while being part of a major rock album came as a pleasant bonus to the younger members of the band, Landau later admitted having heard rumors that the album was more of a contractual obligation, with Elektra/Asylum weighing their options regarding Warren's future with the label. As Landau said later, "It was exciting to do, but I also got a sense that Warren's success was on a downswing." His suspicions were deepened by Elektra/Asylum's plans to have the live album rushed out by the end of 1980, curiously releasing two of Warren's mandatory projects within the same year.

Whether or not Warren was aware he'd been treading on thin ice within the industry, he approached the prospect of a live album with even more optimism than *Bad Luck Streak* itself. With the studio album, Warren had wrestled with the burdens of writer's block and his rapidly disintegrating marriage; now, he would be crafting an album primarily made up of prewritten material. He'd be able to emphasize his wild energy and stage persona. Rather than negatively interpret Elektra/Asylum's plans for the album's quick turnaround as their putting a shelf life on his contract, Warren viewed the live recording as the crown jewel of the tour—a proper representation of this era in his career in all its maniacal majesty. With Warren fueled by a combination of painkillers and steroids that helped keep his alcohol intake tempered, Jackson Browne knowingly labeled it his "karate-on-speed period."

The engagement ran from August 17 through the 21, and each night included a varied form of the same set list, culling from fan favorites and crowd-pleasers that had electrified audiences throughout the tour. For the occasion, Warren broke down and wrote two new songs, making the release something other than a live "best of" compilation: "The Sin," a hard-edged track in the self-deprecating vein of "Bad Luck Streak in Dancing School," and "Stand in the Fire," a thunderous commencement anthem penned just for the opening of the show. Appropriately summoning up the rock-and-roll spectacle Warren envisioned, the song not only lent its title to the promotional materials for the Roxy shows, but for the eventual album itself.

Warren later compared to Paul Nelson the experience of playing the Roxy to returning home in triumph, candidly admitting, "Let's just say that it was like rescuing a little boy who had fallen through the ice. Rescuing him while the whole world was watching."

∞

For *Stand in the Fire,* Warren cherry-picked ten of his best-known radio hits, a few of his personal favorites, and some of the hardest rockers off *Bad Luck Streak.* As had become a practice on both his studio albums and in live performance, there was one cover song; rather than performing the flagship single "A Certain Girl," Warren opted for two favorites from his youth, performing a medley of "Gunslinger" and "Bo Diddley," both hit oldies by the R&B artist. David Landau was on hand to record and mix the final selections, and Jimmy Wachtel returned for the promotional photos and graphic design—all adding to the polish and consistency of the live album within Warren's string of releases.

As a stand-alone album released within the same time frame of *Bad Luck Streak,* the live recording served as its spiritual companion piece, making a perfect balance of the cerebral and the kinetic, with each re-cord emphasizing a different side of Warren's mystique. Released on December 26, 1980, *Stand in the Fire* spent a disappointing ten weeks on the *Billboard* chart, peaking at Number 80 on February 14, 1981. Although live albums were never regarded as the sure-fire bestsellers of even the most popular artists, the sixty-spot drop within only half a year of *Bad Luck Streak* left the ambiguous notions of a market oversat-urated with Warren, or a public that still didn't know him well enough to rush out for either release.

As had been expected due to the largely positive reviews of his tour, *Stand in the Fire* earned some of the finest reviews Warren had received since his 1976 debut. Still, some familiar critics remained tainted by the residue of the polarizing *Bad Luck Streak*. "The three best songs are all from *Excitable Boy,*" wrote consistent critical frenemy Robert Christ-gau in *The Village Voice,* "and only one of the two new originals stands the fire, but any Zevon album that bypasses 'Hasten Down the Wind' and 'Accidentally Like a Martyr' is the one I'll play when I need my fix."

While claiming that Warren seemed to be enjoying "his ongoing public exorcism," Boo Browning of the *Washington Post* also noted that he had "rediscovered the art of turning his scathing wit on him-self, a quality conspicuously absent from *Bad Luck Streak in Dancing School*." Browning added, "It's as though someone or something grabs Zevon by the collar and jostles that stuff right out of him—not just the music, either, but all that crushing optimism and Pollyanna pessimism, all that life-affirming blood and gore, all that alliteration and onomato-poeia, too. And never has Zevon been all shook up like he is on *Stand in the Fire,* his latest, live album."

Popular late-night host David Letterman later concurred with Paul Nelson's early assessment, calling *Stand in the Fire* the greatest live rock album he'd ever heard.

Although the tour was a success, it had only covered the United States. It was acknowledged that Warren had a solid international following, and with *Stand in the Fire* available as a form of "teaser" for those potential audiences, a European leg of the tour was in the works. *Stand in the Fire* had powerfully captured on vinyl the experience of the *Bad Luck Streak in Dancing School* tour, and with the live album in record stores, Warren was temporarily free of pressing deadlines and obligations—and happy to be settling into his new home with Kim Lankford.

As for the triumphant climax of a tour during which all hell had broken loose, Warren had the best memento he could have asked for:

"After the *Bad Luck Streak in Dancing School* tour in 1980, we had a lot of T-shirts left over," George Gruel remembered. "Warren and I decided to donate them to a mental hospital. We got a photo sent to us of quite a few of the patients wearing the shirts. On the shirt was an Uzi laying on top of ballet shoes, similar to the back of the album. It made quite a photo."

Stand in the Fire had been released the final week of the year, making for the disadvantage of missing the holiday season—yet allowing Warren a suitable "release" for the start of 1981. Warren began the year reveling in the curated balance of mild-mannered literary rock star before plans for any European dates were booked, sharing with Lankford their own form of casual domesticity.

Paul Nelson, still in the throes of his own battle with *Rolling Stone* regarding his massive, always-in-progress opus on Warren's addiction and "recovery," had remained a constant friend throughout this period. He viewed Warren's new relationship and outlook on life with a hopeful optimism. "I fly to LA in October," he later wrote. "Zevon and Lankford have moved into a new house, this one not cursed with red bathtubs."

Warren had viewed the Zorada house as the summation of his ongoing road to sobriety and redemption; with his fresh start embodied in his "controlled" use of substances, fitness regimen, and increasingly serious relationship with a young starlet, Warren had taken Nelson's old advice to heart: this time, he *was* going to enjoy it all.

During his trip to Los Angeles, Nelson had planned yet another of his famed surprises for his old friend. Under the guise of a simple visit to Warren and Lankford's home, Nelson was actually in town for an exclusive interview with mutual hero Clint Eastwood—and had invited the movie legend and his then girlfriend, Sondra Locke, to the Zorada house. Nelson wrote, "Eastwood remembers Warren from three years ago ('He did everything but drink vodka from a silver boot then') and is delighted at the change."

One of the more glamorous aspects of Warren's new life was his status as one-half of a celebrity "power couple." Thanks to both his own current star power and Lankford's substantial industry recognition, Warren's social circle widely expanded past the superstar musicians who were already some of his closest friends. Hollywood stars and members of the literati could now all be counted among his regular visitors and companions. During their last visit to New York, Nelson and Jay Cocks had orchestrated for the couple an intimate dinner in the Manhattan home of Martin Scorsese. Awestruck by one of his cinematic heroes, Warren was humbled to learn that his music had, apparently, helped the famed director get through his recent divorce from Isabella Rossellini. In return, Warren had dedicated *Stand in the Fire* "For Marty."

Many of Lankford's *Knots Landing* castmates would stop by the Zorada house on a regular basis, sometimes socially, or often to run lines for that week's script. Paul Nelson had been present during a jovial visit by Lankford's co-star, Jim Houghton. But while that night had ended with clever conversation and card tricks, a separate visit by dashing leading man Michael O'Hare ended in blood. Upon discovering O'Hare's amorous intentions for Lankford, Warren drunkenly proclaimed his own intention to spit on the young actor's mother's grave. It was only a matter of time before Warren had mouthed off to the wrong person, and O'Hare was it. After chasing Warren into the backyard with a hatchet, the actor tried to drown him in the decorative koi pond. Once George Gruel and Aaron Norris were able to get O'Hare subdued, the actor got in a single vicious punch, sending one of Warren's teeth flying.

Not all of Warren's dinner parties ended in fisticuffs. In fact, some friends suspected his brazen, ego-driven arrogance was being worn as a misguided badge of honor. Famed novelist Thomas McGuane was one recent acquaintance who, as a writer, could sympathize with Warren's outwardly conflicted nature. McGuane, too, held near-impossible standards for his own work, citing a mantra that echoed Warren's own creative philosophy: "Find a way to avoid trivializing the serious stuff without undermining the comedy of it."

Aside from penning bestselling novels, among them the critically praised *Panama*, the Montana-based McGuane also practiced a stoic form of "genius for living well," according to McGuane's neighbor, fellow writer William Kittredge. In recent years, Hollywood had beckoned McGuane to try his hand at screenwriting. The forty-year-old wordsmith had experienced moderate success with *The Missouri Breaks,* starring Marlon Brando and Jack Nicholson, and had just completed his script-doctoring for *Tom Horn,* a star-vehicle for Steve McQueen. McGuane's former reputation for drinking and "some drugs," plus two divorces, had once earned him a nickname of his own, "Captain Berserko."

Predictably, Warren was drawn to it all. As had been the case with Expos pitcher Bill "Spaceman" Lee, he now deliberately sought out McGuane to make a formal introduction. The novelist was staying at Warren's notorious old haunt, the Chateau Marmont, while working on *Tom Horn,* making it easy for Warren to track him down. Over the phone, the two hit it off right away. Lankford recalled, "Warren really respected and loved Tom . . . [He] was in town and staying at the Chateau Marmont—the worst of worst places. We had him come and stay at our house."

After expressing a mutual appreciation for each other's work, Warren and McGuane decided to take a stab at writing a song together. In the past, Warren had only acquiesced to collaborating with trusted fellow musicians; in now working with McGuane, he began a lifelong practice of soliciting authors he admired to partake in his creative process. "Warren was pretty enthusiastic about writers," McGuane later recalled, "and I think writing was what interested him, in a way, more than anything else he did."

McGuane had also fought tooth and nail for an emotional stability that Warren still strove to achieve, and their creative styles reflected some core differences. The author later described their dynamic over those three days as similar to "passing ships," adding, "I'd be up doing things in the day and [Warren would] be sleeping. . . . I was very fond of Warren, but we really didn't have the world's greatest comfort level because he was so intense . . . But that was his style, everything dialed up to ten."

Despite their conflicted schedules, Warren and McGuane had a busy three days. Despite the partying, the two were able to complete a song together, something Warren could toy with until the next grueling round of album preparation. The two stayed in contact and the new comradeship affected McGuane enough to be mentioned in an interview that soon followed. "McGuane was in Hollywood recently to write rock-and-roll music with his friend Warren Zevon, whom he considers a fine musician, as well as a fine songwriter," wrote Jim Fergus of *Rocky Mountain Magazine*. "Although the life of rock-and-roll artists seems to recall the dark sinkholes of *Panama* days, McGuane now has the overview of a man who has been there and memorized the way back. He and Zevon, who is renowned for excesses of his own, have performed small, mutual rescue missions for each other; they are both fond of Ernest Hemingway's admonition to F. Scott Fitzgerald: 'Of course you're a rummy . . . most good writers are. But good writers always come back. Always.'"

Months later, McGuane reciprocated Warren's hospitality by hosting a dinner in his honor at his Montana home. Warren flew in from Los Angeles with another new friend, mystery author Jim Crumley. The two got stoned in the airliner's bathroom and had drinks at the local Livingston Bar and Grill with fellow writers Michael Koepf and McGuane's neighbor, William Kittredge, before heading up the valley to McGuane's vast property.

McGuane had invited a number of esteemed guests; Warren spent the memorable night partying with poet Richard Brautigan and actor Jeff Bridges. By the time Peter Fonda arrived, McGuane steered him toward the more sober guests in the kitchen, telling him, "There's some people out there who're having trouble speaking English."

Characteristic of both Warren and McGuane, their song, "The Overdraft," was a hard-driven near-rockabilly composition with biting lyrics and an outlaw narrator—a balance that McGuane also felt suited Warren himself. "To me, Warren is a very enigmatic character," he later recalled. "He had his life in rock and roll, and he idealized some of his grimmer aspects. At the same time, part of his mind was given over to high culture. High art. Serious literature. Classical music. It was an anomalous combination of traits, which was one of the things that was so interesting about him."

∞

By midyear, it was decided that Warren would head off to Europe. But despite having two albums to push for promotion, Elektra/Asylum had already begun cutting their costs toward artists that failed to meet profit expectations. In a curious move Warren would be hitting only a small number of specific European venues, and it would be without the support of a band. But that was only the start of the bizarre compromises.

In later years, Warren would hone his one-man gigs into tour de force performances of varied instruments and genres, with everything from his songbook recontextualized as intricate solo pieces. He was aware ingenuity had been the product of necessity, his tour budgets ever-shrinking.

In this first instance, he wouldn't even be *playing* in concert—nor singing. After negotiations with the label, it was strangely arranged for Warren to appear on various European variety shows, *lip-synching* a cycle of three preselected hits. Following the raucous glory of the All Hell Is Breaking Loose Jungle Tour, pantomiming in front of a nonspeaking studio audience made no sense. "After *Stand in the Fire* there was the 1981 tour where [Elektra/Asylum] just sent me and Warren," George Gruel remembered. "I had a two-track tape of three songs under my arm and we did every European version of *American Bandstand*."

Confused by the label's strategy, and usually doped up on painkillers, Warren nonetheless planned to make the most out of the trip, particularly the rare opportunities for in-store appearances and gobbling up an entire continent's worth of "local color" to aid in the writing of his next album. As road manager, George Gruel worked with Claude Knobs and George Steel from Asylum European A&R in booking as many major cities attainable, at least guaranteeing Warren the star treatment when greeting his foreign fans. "He did a lot of interviews and radio-talk in whatever city we were in," remembered Gruel. "Secluded and as secretive as he could be at times, he enjoyed the hell out of meeting people."

This brief tour, though so strangely structured compared to the heavy-rock albums being promoted, at least provided Warren with a much-needed change of scenery and the semi-solace of a road journey sans an entire band and crew. Using the dubious experience of his *American Bandstand* European adventure for as much raw material as he could draw, Warren cleverly circumvented his old formidable foe, writer's block. By the time they had adventured through Paris, Rome, Germany, and Belgium, he had enough material for the next album— although, according to Gruel, Warren's idea of research was more akin to method acting. "That's where Warren gathered the information for *The Envoy*," Gruel remembered. "We were in Belgium, and he's upstairs in the casino thinking he's James Bond with his zillion-dollar suits on. It was a movie [to him], basically."

Gruel later offered another telling recollection, one that called for Warren to keep a memento of the affair. "One night when we were in Hamburg in some fancy hotel, Warren got all dressed and James Bond–like and went upstairs to the casino . . . [He] ended up with a not-so-good-looking hooker and her bulldog." When later designing *The Envoy* graphics with Jimmy Wachtel, Warren insisted a purple ten-mark casino chip from that night be added to the back cover, hidden among the collage of various intrigue-themed items.

Publicly, Warren had no compunction in citing his favorite secret agent's influence over the concept album and its title song, playfully admitting to David Letterman, "[*The Envoy*] originated with a natural desire, I think on my part, to play James Bond at some point in my career. I've kind of built everything towards that."

It was apparent that Warren envisioned the next album to be more of a singular, cohesive piece than *Bad Luck Streak* had been. Using Ian Fleming's 007 merely as a thematic reference, Warren was creatively returning to Graham Greene's literary territory. While *Bad Luck Streak* had included plenty of action and gore, it had noticeably lacked the foreign intrigue of a "Roland the Headless Thompson Gunner." If critics were to accuse the album of being uneven or scattered, it could be chalked up to the frazzled circumstances in his personal life throughout its conception. Now, Warren planned to address that criticism directly, crafting a solid stand-alone that attained continuity in both quality and theme. In effect, a new novel.

Warren later told *Rolling Stone* he saw the new album as a challenge to himself—a test as to "whether he can pull off art, as well as life, straight." As an ever-evolving artist, Warren opted to draw from the strongest suits of *Bad Luck Streak,* while bringing back full-force the narrative lyricism and signature humor the critics vocally craved. For the writing, Warren had already begun shaping the wealth of material his international excursion had afforded; for the proper balance of sonic quality that his new, refined work would require, he turned to an old friend.

⌘

"They started planning *The Envoy* without me, then Warren called me and asked if I wanted to play on some things," Waddy Wachtel recalled. "I went, 'Yeah, okay,' and I went down, and things still needed arranging— it was a fucking mess. [*Bad Luck Streak*] had been a bit of a commercial failure and, to me, a sonic mistake. And at the end of the night, Warren and Rick came over to me and said, 'Would you want to just come in and co-produce this record?' I told them, 'Now you're talking.' But, like I said, Jackson had warned me about this."

Recording for *The Envoy* began soon after Warren returned from Europe. Aside from the few songs he'd completed before the trip, he had been able to pump out the ones inspired by the journey—the first time such a frenzied burst of creative energy had struck in nearly a decade. With a number of strong songs ready to go, the booth occupied by Wachtel and David Landau, and a varied assortment of incredible session players forming the core ensemble, *The Envoy* sessions began with an enthusiasm lacking from the frantic beginnings of Warren's last studio endeavor.

Although he didn't name his inspiration directly within the lyrics, Warren was very forthcoming in identifying the real-life "envoy" of his mysterious and theatrical title track: the legendary career shuttle diplomat Philip Habib, only recently promoted by President Reagan on special assignment to the Middle East to act as intermediary throughout the escalating US incursion in Lebanon. Prior to his unofficial appointment, Habib had gained worldwide recognition deescalating conflicts between Israel and Syria, then averting an Israel–PLO war in 1981. Warren had followed the ongoing political dramas in the newspapers, fascinated with the vague discretion that Habib's unclassified title entailed. He explained to *Rolling Stone*'s Mikal Gilmore how the mystique around the top secret position had sparked his imagination, morphing into a "kind of workmanlike, self-disciplined version of a James Bond–style agent. I like him because he has a will, because he's a problem-solving kind of guy, and because I need his kind of control."

As a contribution to the album itself, "The Envoy" not only provided the title, but the type of action-and-suspense tale that Warren's fans had come to expect. But unlike the ghostly mercenary Roland or the hell-bent Learjet SWAT team of "Jungle Work," Warren was quick to point out his latest heroic protagonist was "a peacemaker." And while he admired Habib's diplomatic diligence, he admitted to Judith Miller of *The New York Times,* "I wasn't really disappointed that he didn't win the Nobel Peace Prize because, despite his efforts, nothing's really solved out there."

Of the noticeable thematic shift away from cannibal sociopaths digging up dead prom dates and monsters mutilating little old ladies, Warren later said, "I think I'm beginning to defuse that central undeniable violent theme I pursued for so long."

Following the album's release the next year, every interview included the inevitable question of the song's origin. Warren always made it a point of mentioning that he hadn't a clue if Habib himself was pleased with the rock-and-roll homage—he hadn't heard from the famed diplomat at all. "Mr. Zevon says that he has never met his hero, and doubts he would have much time to write letters," *The New York Times* reported. "'But,'" [Warren] added wistfully, "'I'll keep checking my mailbox, hoping for that note on State Department stationery.'" When that didn't work, he offered a nightly update to every audience throughout the tour, sadly reporting that Habib had yet to say anything. But it didn't bother him. He told David Letterman and his millions of viewers, as he had also written a song about Elvis and hadn't heard from him either.

Soon after, Warren's note on State Department stationery arrived in the mail.

∞

The Envoy's recording sessions began toward the end of 1981 at Record One in Los Angeles. As co-producer, Wachtel had become very familiar with the studio space over the last few years, only recently completing some work there on Linda Ronstadt's *Mad Love* for producer Peter Asher. He now brought along some familiar faces from those studio dates, many of whom had previously appeared on Warren's albums. With the exception of Jackson Browne, *The Envoy* soon became an enthusiastic reunion of key players responsible for Warren's highest-quality recordings. As had been the practice for both *Excitable Boy* and *Bad Luck Streak in Dancing School*, a semi-regular lineup of core players was assembled, give or take rotations with guest musicians as the sessions went on.

Having Wachtel back in the producer's chair also meant having his invaluable lead guitar throughout the album, as well as a few turns on backup vocals. David Landau came hot off the *Bad Luck Streak in Dancing School* tour to contribute a rhythm guitar style that was creatively utilized mostly as a secondary lead; on tracks where Warren came in for more guitar work, *The Envoy* held incredible moments of all three guitars within the same song—a virtuosic feat that could have been poorly executed in the hands of a less skilled production and engineering team. The full crew—consisting of Wachtel and David Landau, along with engineers Jamie Ledner and Wayne Tadouye—also integrated more creative overdubbing than had been present in Warren's other work, providing areas for the artist to perform up to three instruments in a single track. It would prove particularly useful considering the ample amount of synthesizer portions the album contained.

Warren's generous use of the synthesizer—four songs out of a nine-song album—was not without recent precedent within the world of rock and roll. At the same time he was in the studio with *The Envoy*, English prog rockers Queen were in Munich recording *Hot Space*, their first album to rely almost entirely on synthesizers. Opting for a commercially minded, dance-pop sound that deliberately excluded lead guitarist Brian May's signature licks proved controversial among Queen fans, to say the least. It bombed. Worse yet, the synth-heavy flop was eventually released only two months before *The Envoy*'s own US street date.

But there the comparisons could end. With the reteaming of Warren and Wachtel, the use of synth was appropriately counterbalanced with the even more generous use of heavy lead guitars and, of course, piano. And with his composer's hat firmly upon his head, Warren's integration of the synths smartly played upon the instrument's atmospheric qualities, enhancing the cinematic themes of the intrigue throughout the album.

But synthesizers or not, *The Envoy* was rock and roll.

The title track, Warren's gung-*homage* to Philip Habib, opened the album with a grand epic movie quality, reminiscent of the James Bond films he aimed to evoke. Had Warren ever been asked to compose a 007 theme, it could be safely assumed "The Envoy" would pose a fair and suitable template.

For the session date, the crew aimed for big sound, with Wachtel and David Landau jointly accompanying Warren on his own guitar, piano, and yes, synthesizer, and Leland Sklar returned to provide bass with the team. But if there was any member of the lineup uniquely catered to play along the balanced sound of traditional instrumentation and studio tech wizardry, it was drummer Jeff Porcaro. More than a widely renowned session man, Porcaro had by this point successfully launched his own band, Toto; within the next year, Toto would not only have its longest string of mainstream hits, but Porcaro would be scouted to make crucial contributions on the Quincy Jones–produced Michael Jackson blockbuster *Thriller*. To round out the lush rock sound of "The Envoy," Don Henley visited for additional backup vocals.

Warren's collaboration with Thomas McGuane, "The Overdraft," had been the first song written for the album, dating back to their infamous three-day drinking and brainstorming session the previous year. Despite the fact that Warren later claimed honky-tonk rocker Jerry Lee Lewis "didn't interest" him, here, a classic rockabilly thump rolls through—providing the album with its first true taste of fast-paced rock and roll. "The Overdraft" was appropriately arranged with a bare-bones quintet, sans synth, and benefited from a visit from Lindsey Buckingham, giving additional vocals.

A humorous tale of a self-deprecating cuckold on vacation, "The Hula Hula Boys" had been one of the last songs Warren penned for the album. In an effort to reconnect with his now thirteen-year-old son, he had planned a trip for them, along with George Gruel, upon their return from Europe. The three headed to Hawaii, but as Gruel remembered, it didn't turn out to be "much of a father-son bonding experience." Warren's painkiller usage had reached its peak. During interviews, journalists began to take note that the Nichols Canyon house was "conspicuously" dry of alcohol—but few outside of Gruel and Lankford knew of Warren's growing dependencies on drugs and prescription pills. As an adult, Jordan Zevon recalled that he had spent most of the Hawaiian trip off playing alone, only retrospectively aware how thin his father had been at that time, or how his physical appearance was just as akin to heavy cocaine use as it was the painkillers.

Although the vacation had been intended as a way for the two to spend quality time together, Lankford's absence also stemmed from her work commitments—and a growing intolerance for Warren's behavior. With this in mind, he had begun writing a bittersweet song of a lover jilted for various strangers throughout his own honeymoon—parking lot attendants and an obese native by the hotel swimming pool among them. And while the emotions behind the song were autobiographical, Warren veiled his own instability with Lankford by emphasizing the song's humor, the narrative's suggestive scenarios playing like a Blake Edward's sex romp fused with *South Pacific*. Warren was particularly proud of the song's most memorable middle section, the lines directly cribbed from a Polynesian phrase book Jordan had bought for him as a gift.

"The chorus," he later explained, "*'Ha'ina i' a mai ana ka puana,'* is an idiom which means 'Sing the chorus,' or, 'Get to the point.' No one could pronounce the Hawaiian but my son, Jordan . . . So Waddy and I had him sing all the background parts."

The recording of "The Hula Hula Boys" marked the studio debut of Jordan Zevon, who was joined by some of his dad's most esteemed cohorts during his session initiation. Aside from the album's strong core lineup, Jeff Porcaro worked double duty on percussion, adding Tahitian log drums and *puili* sticks to his arsenal for more Polynesian authenticity; Jim Horn provided the wistful recorder lines between verses, adding a soft air of melancholy to the swaying ballad. Warren himself played the only appearance of an electric piano on the album.

"Jesus Mentioned" was one of the two most haunting tracks on the album, both of which offered ruminations on the subject of death. Unlike Warren's well-known comedic morbidity, neither "Jesus Mentioned" or "Charlie's Medicine" offered much to laugh about. While the former song offered Warren's own unique eulogy for Elvis Presley, the latter was based on the violent murder of Warren's drug dealer, the eponymous "Charlie." As George Gruel later recalled, he had been a young fan in his midtwenties who happened to work at the Hollywood Boulevard pharmacy where Warren would get his legitimate pills. "So it ended up that we'd go over to Charlie's house on Fairfax [Avenue],"

Gruel said. "He lived with his mom in this apartment, and he would sell Warren bags of these pink downers."

On the final trip to Charlie's house, Gruel was stopped at the door by the young man's mother, informing them he had been killed. "He was blown away out in the street in front of their apartment," Gruel remembered. "Warren went to Charlie's funeral. He went by himself. He said, 'I'm going alone. I just want to do this.' That's where the line in the song, 'I came to finish paying my bill,' came from."

The song would also hold a later resonance when, only a few months prior to the album's release, Warren's old friend John Belushi died tragically at the age of thirty-three. Belushi had acted as emcee for Warren's New York City debut at the Bottom Line in 1976, formally introducing him to the world. On that occasion, Belushi had dropped so much acid before taking the stage, he was incoherent during Warren's introduction. Remaining both a fan and friend, Belushi had been spotted wrestling with Tom Waits in the Roxy's men's room by Jimmy Wachtel during Warren's triumphant shows for *Stand in the Fire*. Worse yet, it was reported that the comedian had fatally overdosed on a particularly potent combination of cocaine and heroin known as a speedball—at the Chateau Marmont.

"Charlie's Medicine" was the final song written for the album. Initially, Warren hadn't intended to use his dealer's murder as the subject for a song—especially one that held such revealing references to his own substance use. But when the original cut of the album clocked in way under the half-hour mark, producer Wachtel, for the second time, had to demand another track. Wachtel recalled, "We got to a point where we were a song short. I couldn't believe it happened again, and I said, 'I need another song for this. We need another tune.' I hated doing it again, but remember, this was a time when we would only get paid if a certain amount of music was on either side of an LP . . . So, I went away again, maybe a week, and he wrote 'Charlie's Medicine'—and it was just so astounding."

Although Warren did not directly address the celebrity death in interviews, his newfound lease on life became consistent topics when promoting the album. Adamant that he was a changed man, Warren's explanations regarding *The Envoy*'s origins fluctuated between his own "secret agent" fantasy and a deep, introspective accountability for the mistakes of his past. Seemingly unrelated, Warren emphasized the apparent associations between being a "man of action," like Philip Habib or James Bond, and the realization that the "action" in question is merely a sense of personal responsibility and focus. He told *Rolling Stone,* "If there's a pervading idea that comes from *The Envoy,* it's the idea of problem-solving, or sorting out your choices and applying a bit more control to how you make them." He later elaborated to *The New York Times,* "What I didn't realize is that my audience never took all the chaos and conflict all that seriously. They never wanted me to be that self-detonating shaman figure, living on the edge. They knew a writer isn't obliged to live out all his dark fantasies, but I didn't know that."

Warren had written "Jesus Mentioned" in Memphis on the last tour. Seeing the near-sacred pilgrimage destination that Graceland had become to Elvis Presley fans in the wake of his death had inspired him to contemplate the larger aspects and sacrifices of fame. Through his mournful lyrics, Warren presented Presley as a symbolic vessel for the broader scope of aging, mortality, and—in Presley's case—legacy.

Like his later song for Presley nearly two decades later, "Porcelain Monkey," Warren here revealed his own reflections on fame as both a blessing and a curse. In an example of some of his most metaphysical and spiritual imagery, he gently blurs the poetic narrative into a Presley-as-Messiah/martyr archetype—walking on the water "with his pills."

As Mikal Gilmore had observed in *Rolling Stone,* it appeared as though the excitable boy had grown up.

For the session recording, an intimate, simplified arrangement made the track a gorgeous centerpiece to the album. Warren performed vocals only as a gentle duet with Wachtel on acoustic guitar. For "Charlie's Medicine," however, Warren amped it up full throttle, beginning with a particularly haunting guitar twang he personally performed on his twelve-string, leading straight into the rock-and-roll doom of Wachtel's thunderous lead over the synth fusion. For the session date, the team shook things up, bringing in, straight from Jackson Browne's band, Bob Glaub on bass. Wachtel and old friend Rick Marotta had worked on numerous projects in between their previous collaborations with Warren—including a band of their own, Ronin, in 1980. Now, Marotta returned on drums, completing the heaviness needed for one of Warren's darkest rock tracks.

Following the solemnness of his homily for Presley, Warren ended the first side with one of the two most optimistic songs on the album.

As with much of the more romantic shadings on *The Envoy*, "Let Nothing Come Between You" was wholly inspired by Kim Lankford—or at least inspired by an old friend's first impressions upon meeting her. At the time, Warren and Lankford had been seriously discussing marriage and, as he later remembered, "I was engaged to a wonderful woman, about whom Jackson Browne had once observed, 'She's good around the eyes.'" Later, *The New York Times* critic Robert Palmer would state that the tune was "the sweetest thing" on the album, largely benefiting from the "bittersweet edge" it displayed, more akin to a soul ballad. It was also the only song selected by Elektra/Asylum to be released as a single.

The session for the upbeat love tune found the core ensemble returning, with Jorge Calderón visiting for harmony vocals that Warren later said "gave the song a great life," and Jeff Porcaro's regular bandmate and fellow Toto founder Steve Lukather filled in for David Landau on guitar.

The Envoy's second side opened with a signature Warren rock anthem that would go on to be a consummate staple in rousing his largest crowds. "Ain't That Pretty at All" was one of the mean, smart-alecky hard rockers that worked to remind listeners that maybe Warren hadn't grown up all that much after all. Directly inspired by his absurd jaunt through Europe with George Gruel, the song's title became a humorous catchphrase between the friends at stops along the tour. Throughout the hard track, on which old friend LeRoy Marinell had stepped in to provide some additional colorful punch lines, Warren angrily lists the major sites of the world he's seen, leaving him unimpressed and jaded. At the Louvre in Paris, he cries his intentions to get a running start and hurl himself against the wall—curiously comparing even the most elegant of cultural experiences to undergoing a root canal. It was as though his brazen inner ego had been held prisoner within his matured, peaceful, and domesticated id—that voice of relative reason that had revealed *The Envoy*'s most introspective and pensive moments. The wild ego had been awakened, leaving Warren wailing for blood.

During the sessions, Warren's bloodcurdling howls of rebellion were matched with his guitars and synth. It was completely appropriate that the track welcomed back so many faces from Warren's three previous projects: J. D. Souther stopped by to add to the whoops and hollers; old friend and co-writer LeRoy Marinell was on hand for additional guitars; and for the first time since his contributions to *Excitable Boy* in 1978, Danny "Kootch" Kortchmar arrived, blending his own heavy guitar work with David Landau's stinging licks. Stepping in on drums and percussion, Bread alumni Mike Botts and Steve Forman added to the energetic anthem. For "Ain't That Pretty at All," the all-encompassing electric sound stood out, especially as the only song that found Wachtel poring over the engineering controls in lieu of playing along on the track. More than one critic likened the ferocious track to the then burgeoning Los Angeles punk scene.

"Looking for the Next Best Thing" was probably the most commercially acceptable and uplifting track on the album—not to mention the most accessible for critics who viewed deconstruction as their bread and butter. Its knowing and joyous acceptance of life's obstacles had many convinced Warren was addressing his own approaching middle age and his blissful relationship with Kim Lankford, although he was quick to indicate his minor participation in the song's writing. "LeRoy [Marinell], Kenny Edwards, and I wrote this one," he later commented. "In a rare outburst of social organization, I was inviting various musician friends over for songwriting evenings in a big, gruesome house I'd rented in Nichols Canyon."

Even so, the song's overall theme of a fruitless lifelong quest to find true love, then finally settling on "the next best thing" as a form of a defeatist, yet mature, lesson learned, seemed awfully autobiographical to many critics and listeners. And who else could lyrically liken such a romantic crusade to those of Don Quixote, while perfectly rhyming Ponce de León's "cruise" with Sinbad's seven-voyage "ruse"? In the meticulous eyes of many critics, the intelligence behind the song's humor gave much of its true authorship away.

Warren's previous albums had all ended on rousing high notes, rock anthems whose respective fade-outs could be interpreted as the singer's own spirit of never-ending youth and rebellion. "Lawyers, Guns and Money," for example, drifted off with Waddy Wachtel's seething guitar leading its listener down a path of raucousness along with Warren as a hedonistic pied piper. Likewise, on *Bad Luck Streak in Dancing School,* the cinematic fade-out of "Wild Age"—further enhanced by the symbolic harmonies of maturing rock bad boys Glenn Frey and Don Henley—offered all the bittersweet melancholy of watching your closest buddies drive off into the sunset following a long weekend of boyish adventures. But it was with the latest closer, "Never Too Late for Love," that Warren ended an album with a heartfelt, gentle ballad for the first time since the revelatory "Desperadoes Under the Eaves," off his 1976 self-titled release—and drew comparisons to other recent albums that likewise seemed to "celebrate domesticity," Lou Reed's *The Blue Mask* and John Lennon's final collaboration with wife Yoko Ono, *Double Fantasy*, among them.

In light of Warren's ongoing public romance with Kim Lankford, most critics were quick to read between even the most seemingly un-related of his lines. This track, however, made it easy for them. He ex-plained to Robert Palmer of *The New York Times:* "When I started writing songs for the album, I knew I had a lot of emotions available to tap . . . But I also felt that if I happened to stumble on something pos-itive, like the lyric I wrote for one of the love songs on the new album, 'It's Never Too Late for Love,' that maybe I could sing with a certain amount of credibility."

He added, "The experience I've been having lately is love, so that's what I've been writing about. But love can be terrifying."

Every element of *The Envoy* spoke of Warren's relationship with Kim Lankford, including its iconic cover. Aiming for the "James Bond" mystique of Warren's vision, Jimmy Wachtel and George Gruel had gathered a full studio's worth of extras—mostly made up of Lankford's *Knots Landing* co-stars—for an ambitious photo shoot at Burbank Air-port. With Warren centered against the Warner Bros. jet, dressed dap-per in his 007-inspired suit and with trench coat slung over his arm, he looks every bit the proper man of action. On the back cover, he had written his dedication simply, "For Kim."

Unfortunately, the innocence and anxiousness of newfound love wasn't exactly the kind of terror Warren's listeners had come to ex-pect. While critics pulled no punches in their conflicted assessment of his new work, fans merely ignored it. *The Envoy* was released on July 16, 1982, and spent a total of thirteen weeks on the *Billboard* chart, peaking at a disappointing Number 93 by mid-September. "Let Noth-ing Come Between You" / "The Hula Hula Boys" had been issued as the only US single, peaking at a noticeably low Number 23. It was only on the chart for just over a month before falling off completely. The label may have had more success had they issued singles matching the promo editions sent to radio stations and media outlets. Along with PR materials, *The Envoy*'s title track had been sided with "Looking for the Next Best Thing," guaranteeing those songs would be in rotation, while having no effect on the charts.

"We were really crushed by how it was received," Wachtel remembered. "We had worked really hard with that album and were particularly proud of it when we were done . . . I think we got like a four-star review in *Rolling Stone* saying it was the best thing [Warren] had ever done—and then it just didn't sell."

In his highest praise since *Excitable Boy*, Robert Christgau of *The Village Voice* joined the many critics pleased with Warren's mature offerings. "It's a wise, charming, newly written going-to-the-chapel number that I would have sworn was lifted from some half-forgotten girl group," he wrote. "If 'Never Too Late for Love' and 'Looking for the Next Best Thing' announce that this overexcitable boy has finally learned to compromise, 'Let Nothing Come Between You' is his promise not to take moderation too far."

Craig Zeller of *Cream,* however, was merciless in his words, claiming Warren to be one of the music scene's most "critically overrated troubled troubadours," adding, " 'Member those in-print cartwheel raves his debut garnered? Ever listen to the damn thing? A very dull dry run, easily as somnambulistic as the worst (best?) of Jackson Browne."

"[Warren's] lyrics have all the trademark macho bluster and dark humor—about international terrorism, Wild West outlaws, B-movie monsters and what-all," wrote Davin Seay in *People* magazine. "But also as plain as the piano he pounds is what may be the real Warren Zevon: introspective, solemn, maybe even nervous."

"Asylum Records really should get rid of Warren Zevon," Sandy Robertson of *Sounds* quipped. "He's so good he shows just how dire everybody else on the label really is." Big words, considering the label then counted Jackson Browne, the Eagles, Queen, Linda Ronstadt, and Carly Simon among their bestselling artists.

Warren's initial signing with Elektra/Asylum—being listed within their ranks was a badge of honor around the Los Angeles scene—earned him a certain amount of recognition before his first label release. Founder David Geffen's idealistic intentions had always been in providing a creative vanguard for artists he deemed just off the radar of the mainstream, but much had changed within the music industry since his 1975 departure. One entity in particular was quickly shaping every facet of how American youth was discovering new music and the hottest trends—and its name was MTV.

The revolutionary cable network, running all-day music video programming, had instant viewership among America's teens—and had launched only nine months prior to *The Envoy*'s release. Warren had rightly predicted the inevitable importance of the music video format and had unsuccessfully pushed Elektra/Asylum for a promo video to accompany *Bad Luck Streak in Dancing School*. By the time *The Envoy* hit the market, however, his demographic was largely past the age of MTV's cultural influence. Nonetheless, the channel soon provided the perfect outlet to mark this era in Warren's career—the peak of his popularity and the hardest he ever rocked.

A tour had been booked for the later part of 1982, curiously constructed as both an extension of *Bad Luck Streak in Dancing School*'s well-received hard-rocking spectacle—which was supposed to have officially ended in a blaze of glory with the Roxy's five-night residency—and as a promotional tour for *The Envoy*. After the arduous journey that had been 1980's All Hell Is Breaking Loose Jungle Tour (aka The Dog Ate the Part We Didn't Like Tour) all across the United States, this trip would be shortened and tightened. Over the course of one month, Warren would embark on a whirlwind tour that hit thirty stops in fifteen states, and included in-store appearances and a tv performance.

Toward the end of September, Warren, George Gruel, and a new band of backup musicians hit the road for 1982's To the Finland Station Tour. After a few warm-up gigs at the Metro Club in Boston and around Connecticut and upstate New York, Warren had his major launch at the Ritz in New York City.

The night before the large kickoff show, he was booked for his first major late-night television appearance as the musical guest on NBC's popular *Late Night with David Letterman*. A self-professed Zevon fan, Letterman was as curious to meet the singer as Warren was anxious to nail the appearance. At the time, Letterman's edgy follow-up to the late-night staple *The Tonight Show with Johnny Carson* was only in its first season, but the youthful and irreverent host drew both iconoclastic guests and a hip, youthful viewership. When Warren took to the *Late Night* stage on September 27, 1982, Letterman had only been on the air for half a year. Warren would share the bill with conservative political commentator and editor of the *National Review* William F. Buckley Jr. George Gruel recalled Warren's awkward pre-taping greenroom encounter with the famed journalist: "[Buckley] . . . proceeded to ramble on and on, about how many times he's had his picture taken, which segued into something about sailing and his new book."

Once Warren was onstage, Letterman's own line of questioning ran the gamut, everything from the truth behind reports of Warren rubbing a pot roast on his chest in real life to his well-known intervention for substance abuse. Sandwiched between two musical numbers— "Excitable Boy," at Letterman's backstage request, and an appropriately rocking rendition of "The Overdraft"—the playful yet revealing interview set a warm precedent between Warren and the host. Humorously pointing out that the high-profile example for intervention therapy had already been set with the widely publicized scandals surrounding the New York Yankees' heavy-drinking manager Billy Martin, Warren opened up about his alcoholism to Letterman with candor and self-deprecating, biting humor.

With chemistry and a natural camaraderie, the two hit it off, both on- and offscreen. The appearance marked the first of many for Warren on Letterman's show, as well as the beginning of a twenty-year friendship.

Warren's kickoff show was only a night away. "When he first performed in New York six years ago," Stephen Holden in *The New York Times* wrote, "Warren Zevon wasn't so much a rock-and-roller as a singer-songwriter with a feisty, cynical edge. He seemed like a performer capable of exploding into something quite different, though one wasn't sure just what . . . Now it turns out that Mr. Zevon is a rock-and-roller to the bone."

As a commencement show for a tour that had never really ended, Warren's appearance at the Ritz was both a critical success and an audience draw. Although he had been unable to retain the members of Boulder for this second tour leg, a fresh crop of young musicians with similar hard-edged sensibilities rose to the challenge. Guitarist Randy Brown, drummer Joe Daniels, bassist Larry Larson, and lead guitarist John Wood had been successfully added to Warren's To the Finland Station Tour back in Los Angeles. Critics were pleased with the seamlessness with which the new band took over from Warren's former ensemble. Holden added, "Driven by hard, lean arrangements, featuring two guitars and keyboard, these and other songs assumed a furious, compelling irony . . . Mr. Zevon's droll, rusty-voiced delivery tinged everything with sarcasm."

The Envoy meant to represent the new leaf Warren had turned through his apparent sobriety and a new, optimistic outlook on life. Audiences, however, had grown accustomed to the physical pyrotechnics and unadulterated rock and roll his concerts delivered. As an amalgam of both the new album's artistic themes, and the brazen fury of *Bad Luck Streak in Dancing School*, this new tour had to satisfactorily strike the right balance of both. As Stephen Holden concluded following the Ritz kickoff, "Mr. Zevon, who began as a relatively sedate performer, has developed a charismatic grace that included such acrobatic feats as leaping double-splits. On Tuesday, the acrobatics were very much connected to Mr. Zevon's songs, many of which celebrate the spirit of anarchic, boyish adventure."

The New York Times' affectionate review couldn't have run on a better morning. That night, Warren and crew were headed to Passaic, New Jersey, preparing to give their first-ever live televised performance via MTV's new concert series. For his *Late Night with David Letterman* appearance, Warren had performed his two songs with the program's house ensemble, Paul Shaffer and the World's Most Dangerous Band. MTV was slated to be the glorious debut of Warren's new official lineup.

While MTV's increasing popularity would soon have wide-ranging influence over trends in the very music and pop culture they broadcast, as an evolving junior network, executives were still open to experimenting with programming and content. Overall, *Bad Luck Streak in Dancing School*'s tour had received better write-ups than the album itself, making it the ideal rock-and-roll circus for a live television event. MTV's all-music dictum could provide the perfect venue for bringing the energy and excitement of *Stand in the Fire* into every American household with a cable-box.

Only a few months before, MTV had launched what would later be regarded as one of the most successful advertising campaigns in television history: "I Want My MTV!" provided a brilliant means of getting nationwide cable providers to offer the network—and inadvertently introduced a new idiom into mainstream pop culture. As reported in *The New York Times*, by its one-year anniversary, the network added 145,000 subscribers throughout New York alone, thanks largely to its generation-defining slogan.

The network's viewership was at its highest peak on October 1, 1982, when Warren went live. George Gruel, appropriately attired in his own "Excitable Guy" T-shirt, brought a hand-cuffed, leather-jacketed Warren out onstage to thunderous applause. "Rock and roll," Gruel shouted, commencing a raucous night on par with the best of *Bad Luck Streak in Dancing School*'s tours. "They say that everything that dies will come back—and if that's true, I hope I come back as Suzanne Somers," Warren quipped just before the dynamic show's encore. "No, just kidding—but in case I don't, I'd like to thank everyone for a great time—*and have a great life!*"

He closed with "I'll Sleep When I'm Dead."

The band was back home in Los Angeles the first week of November. That same week, Warren's whirlwind media blitz continued with a lengthy profile in *People* magazine. It was an unlikely periodical for the now "former" excitable boy, but such mainstream attention had become normal as one half of a celebrity power couple. *People*'s feature piece was as much about Kim Lankford's career as Warren's music and sobriety—but nowhere else provided a better place to play up the "domestic bliss" angle of *The Envoy*.

"By rights," he told *People,* "I shouldn't be here—I was on a straight Jim Morrison course. I know I owe a lot to God and even more to the friends He has blessed me with. So many people have been so supportive, and Kim has been the most supportive of all." In the same article, the couple mentioned their "aim to wed, someday, on the Montana ranch of their novelist friend, Tom McGuane."

By the time the issue ran, however, things between them had drastically changed. Despite Warren's public professions to have achieved a level of sobriety almost akin to enlightenment, nothing could have been further from the truth. While he had managed to cut back drastically on his drinking, even going so far as to show off his soft drinks and cups of coffee to interviewers as proof, he had substituted numerous narcotics in its place. He'd been smoking marijuana from such a young age, it barely registered as a slip of sobriety by his logic, while cocaine and prescription painkillers and downers had slowly become addictions. Lankford later recalled returning home to find Warren and a few unfamiliar friends—among them the drug dealer and later inspiration behind "Charlie's Medicine." Much to her horror, the group was sitting around shooting heroin.

As things began to turn turbulent between Warren and Lankford, they made the decision to move once again, this time to a three-level house in the more tranquil Laurel Canyon. Unlike the Nichols Canyon house, this one was in Lankford's name—a fact that did not, however, prevent Warren from shooting holes in the floor. Meanwhile George Gruel had moved into a place in the Palms area of Los Angeles, none too upset to be leaving the Zorada house or, as he later called it, "the House of Drama." With the touring finally finished and no immediate future album plans indicated by the record label, the group expected 1982 to end with some rest and relaxation. Warren even acknowledged that his dependency was growing worse, seeking to temper off of the urges through an acupuncturist recommended by Jackson Browne. He booked an appointment just prior to a much-needed Hawaiian vacation with Lankford. The therapy worked, only too well, leading Warren into an instant state of intense withdrawal. Lankford was helpless as Warren suffered a seizure at the airport.

"Kim was freaking out, the usual drama," Gruel remembered, "so I picked her up and put her in a baggage rack and said, 'Shut up and sit down.' She was no help. I called the paramedics, and [Warren] ended up in the hospital for a day, and he got mad at Jackson for it. He thought he was trying to kill him when, of course, he was trying to help him."

The incident was one too many for Lankford. Afterward, their relationship grew more strained; she was exasperated by his apathy toward her own career. She had been notified that her character was soon to be written out of *Knots Landing*, coinciding with the unexpected announcement that Warren was expected to head back out on tour. Amid the growing contention between the two, she refused to go with him on the trip.

"He was getting stoned and drinking, and I just didn't want to be a part of it anymore," Lankford remembered. "I didn't want to go home again until he was gone. I had to leave my own house when he should have left." Warren disappeared, avoiding Lankford's ongoing demands that he come and pick up his things. When that didn't work, she called the record label and threatened to have all of Warren's belongings donated to Goodwill if Warren didn't respond. He didn't. But his business manager sent around a crew to collect everything.

"As for the romance," Warren later admitted, "everything ended wretchedly."

Lankford's excommunication of Warren—or more accurately, *his* of *her*—represented the final nail in a coffin he had long been carving himself. With very few exceptions, he had spent the last few years severing ties with almost every intimate friend or relative who had helped during his intervention. In March of the previous year, *Rolling Stone* had finally run Paul Nelson's epic profile on Warren's battles with alcohol and addiction, granting Warren his one and only appearance on the magazine's cover. Nelson's own internal battle with publisher Jann Wenner over the piece had not only ended Nelson's career at *Rolling Stone*, but ultimately drained his passion for writing. He was rarely published again. Worse yet, Warren didn't seem to care; the two hadn't spoken in almost a year. And wouldn't again.

In his impassioned and bitter appeals at *Rolling Stone*, Nelson had defended Warren's sobriety and insisted on the cultural significance of his music, almost to the degree that his own integrity as an impartial journalist began to come into question. It finally ran after the manuscript had been forcibly taken from Nelson and whittled down by a third. The editors also tacked on their own title, "The Crack-Up and Resurrection of Warren Zevon," which, while suitable, was another dig at Nelson's helplessness. When Warren's extreme relapses into booze and drugs began to circulate around the music industry, Jann Wenner's earlier insistence that Warren Zevon would never again appear in his magazine became editorial dogma.

As time passed, Wenner's stern mandate would only have two exceptions; Warren would appear in *Rolling Stone* twice more in his lifetime, both under very different circumstances.

Even on paper, Warren's Live At Least Tour read like a desperate move.

Initially, there hadn't been definite plans for another tour at all. Playing off the positive reviews that the *Bad Luck Streak in Dancing School* tour had garnered, Elektra/Asylum was now grasping at straws.

Warren, for his part, had also learned the major burden in being part of a celebrity power couple: the inevitable breakup can either rack up as much press as the glamorous courtship, or get lost in the shuffle of finding the next hot topic that will sell ink. In less than six months, Warren's album had flopped and Lankford was off one of prime-time television's hottest dramas. The promises and pontifications that Warren had drilled into interviews throughout his promotional tour all now seemed utterly invalid. Critics and editors took notice. And while Warren still had his share of devoted fans, in the face of a rapidly changing music industry, the MTV generation was already clamoring for newer, trendier acts.

It was only to recoup their losses over *The Envoy* that the label even considered sending Warren out on tour again. This time around, bare bones wouldn't even do the circumstances justice: no band, no bus, no large venues. No television. Everything Warren was expected to need for his performances would have to fit into a rented station wagon. Compared to the triumphant homecoming of *Stand in the Fire*, the only thing that seemed to be missing was a hat to be passed among the audience for loose change.

In a fog of drugs, alcohol, and denial, Warren nonetheless prepared to start the new year on the road. He would be alone—save for George Gruel, the one friend he hadn't yet tossed aside. Paul Nelson was gone; Crystal had opted for a new life abroad, taking now six-year-old Ariel to Paris; Warren remained convinced Jackson Browne had attempted to sabotage his health via acupuncture. And Kim Lankford had moved on—but only after Warren had vanished first.

The last matter was of little concern to Warren, or so he behaved; he already had another lady in waiting.

The Live At Least Tour kicked off the second day of 1983 at the Park West Club in Chicago. It was the first time since *The Envoy*'s absurd lip-synching tour that Warren took to a stage alone. This time, however, he got to play all the instruments—and he didn't have to share the spotlight. "Reaganomics isn't the only reason I'm on this solo tour,"

he told an audience in upstate New York. "Once a folk singer, always a folk singer!"

In private, Warren offered a different reason for his need to disappear. "When you're a moving target," he said, winking over his glasses, "they can't hit ya."

Part Two
HEAVY METAL FOLK

CHAPTER SEVEN

(1983)

IN 1976, ANITA GEVINSON WAS A YOUNG WAITRESS WORKING full time at a fish market in Philadelphia the first time she met Warren Zevon.

On a night in mid-June of that year, she and a girlfriend from the market headed to nearby Bryn Mawr, planning to hang out at the Main Point, a legendary music venue and coffeehouse. Known for its intimate setting and trendy vibe, the tiny venue had developed a reputation among the hipper performers as an obscure yet popular spot. Over the last decade, such countercultural icons as Captain Beefheart, Leonard Cohen, Leon Redbone, and Tom Waits had all played surprise gigs there; likewise, some of Warren's old gang, including Jackson Browne and Linda Ronstadt, had used the venue to host sold-out acoustic sets. During Warren's first tour for Elektra/Asylum, it had been wisely selected as a moderately sized place to accommodate his "song noir" styled debut. "I feel great," he told the crowd, "and here we are after our triumphant engagement at McDonald's in Libya."

Two years before its studio recording and release, Warren even unveiled a ferocious version of "Werewolves of London" to a very enthusiastic and amused audience. "I've heard some out on the west coast," he opened, lightly tapping the signature piano riff. "I've heard there's a bizarre cult of werewolves in Bryn Mawr. . . . I guess you know how to howl, when the moon is full? *Well, the moon is always full! Ah-hoooooo!*"

The audience was putty in his hands—especially Gevinson, who not only had a passion for rock and roll but, admittedly, for "the boys in the band"; Daryl Hall and Billy Squire could be listed among her future beaus. So, it came as no shock to the club owners when Gevinson stayed for Warren's second set, then talked her way backstage. She and Warren chatted and flirted, but he was quick to mention his pregnant wife back home.

"Warren told me that he was married right away," Gevinson remembered. "I think when people are out on the road, the last thing that they are looking for is to meet someone they want to, necessarily, keep in their lives. But, for some reason, that's what happened. He ended up being in my life for the next seven years."

Following their first encounter, Warren was immediately racked with guilt. He drank himself into a stupor before boarding his return flight home and was still inebriated when Crystal came to pick him up from LAX. That night, he confessed to her his numerous infidelities while on tour. She later recalled, "He assured me over and over again that he had told each woman, before he slept with her, that he was in love with his wife and would never leave his marriage. I wanted so desperately to believe that we could make it, but deep down I knew this was the beginning of the end."

By *Excitable Boy*'s production two years later, Gevinson had started her professional career as a radio DJ in her native Philadelphia and was quickly developing a loyal following. It wasn't long before Warren reached out to Gevinson again, this time during the debauchery of his pseudo-bachelorhood days recording *Excitable Boy*. He had kept tabs on her and knew to reach her at her new post at WMMR in Philly. "I flew into Boston to meet him at least one more time after our first meeting," she later recalled. "I guess I did it to find out if my feelings were as real as they felt. He picked me up as we went to see Toots and the Maytals, and he danced with them in this crazy suit that he wore. I just thought that he was this amazing, fun guy that I just couldn't stay away from."

That had been two years ago. Gevinson was now coming to the West Coast for an upcoming wedding and the two arranged to meet. During her extended stay, their relationship became unspoken knowledge among Warren's friends and fellow musicians, and she was present during some of his *Excitable Boy* sessions. "I visited him when he was living in Sunset Towers on Sunset Boulevard," Gevinson recalled.

"He was recording his *Excitable Boy* album and I hadn't seen him in a while. One of the first things he said to me was, 'You have to meet Uncle Waddy.' He had to go to the studio the next day, so I went with him and as soon as we got into the parking lot, I went crazy when I saw guys unloading a truck with Jackson Browne."

Gevinson sat in the studio during Warren's vocal tracks for "Accidentally Like a Martyr," after which she got her first glimpse at the secret his friends seemed to keep hidden. She recalled, "Jackson seemed astounded that Warren was driving. See, I didn't know his reputation behind the wheel, and it was kind of like this unspoken thing not to let Warren drive. I knew then that it was a matter of, 'Nobody wants to tell you what's really going on.'" Amid the glitz and glamour of living in Warren's rock-and-roll world, Gevinson was caught off guard by the actual depth of his alcohol intake. "I guess I was a little naïve about how much drinking he was doing, but I had never met anyone like him, and I just thought that was all part of the life," she said.

Admittedly, she "didn't see the early warning signs of how deep the alcohol addiction was," but many presented themselves during that one week. "[Warren] would drink mixed drinks during the day," she remembered. "He always liked vodka, and he might add a little orange juice. I was so enamored that I didn't see how bad off he was."

Warren and Crystal eventually reconciled but he attempted to keep in touch with Gevinson. She recalled, "Warren called me from Hawaii when he wrote 'Lawyers, Guns and Money' and he was there with Burt Stein, and he played it for me over the phone. I said, 'Shit, Warren, they're never going to play that!' And he just goes, 'Oh, they're *going* to play it.'"

Like many of the women who had fallen victim to Warren's charm, Gevinson was admittedly a sucker for simply listening to him. She recalled, "His voice on the phone was always amazing. It would just stop you in your tracks when he would say, 'This is Warren.'" According to Gevinson, Warren's ongoing self-consciousness about his singing voice never wavered, however. "There wasn't anything about it that he loved," she said. "Just look at his friends, the Henleys and the Jackson Brownes. He always wanted to be able to make those little tweaks to have the crossover appeal into superstardom like those guys."

Excitable Boy was greeted by an equally excited public. He reached out to Gevinson just before the promotional tour was set to begin.

"I got a phone call from him soon after and he invited me to stay with him and Crystal," she remembered. "This was the end of the era of 'free love,' and everything, and still kind of into those lifestyles—so I really didn't know what he was getting at. I was flattered, but that something—that was just out of my world, you know."

It was during that tour Warren reached the peak of his sales and popularity—just as it had been during this stop in Philadelphia that the Zevons were triumphantly treated to limos, swanky hotels, caviar, and champagne. And their next encounter with Gevinson.

He was sure that Gevinson would be in attendance for his May 7 appearance at the Academy of Music. When he was proved correct, he used his good-luck streak to give Crystal an indecent proposal. "In the exhilaration over Warren's sudden star status, he asked me to do something I could never have imagined I would agree to," Crystal later wrote. "He thought we should take Quaaludes and invite her back to our hotel suite after the show . . . take the drugs and have our little orgy." But she did agree, at least to give it a try. It didn't get far, however, before the three of them heard newborn Ariel crying in the next room. Immediately regretting her decision, Crystal ran off to rock her baby daughter back to sleep. Gevinson remembered, "It was obvious that [Crystal] wasn't into this."

Although she reveled in the world of rock and roll, Gevinson had never allowed herself to lean toward the dubious distinction of "groupie," or the more generous "road wife." A free-spirited young professional with all the frills that being a local celebrity in Philly afforded, Gevinson admitted to shying away from any form of monogamy. While long-smitten with Warren *the rock star,* she had never intended to play house with Warren *the man.* "Kim [Lankford] had had enough of his bullshit," Gevinson claimed. "Frankly, I would have preferred that she stay in the picture. My attitude was, 'Let her play mommy; we'll play house on the side.' It's always better to be the girlfriend than the wife, especially in 'Warren World.'"

She added, "I don't know if I had a higher tolerance for Warren's behavior, but I knew that I'd been around enough rock stars to understand the dynamic—it's their world and you're just in it. I'm not judgmental, but with Warren, I always knew from the beginning what I was in for. I never felt the women in his other relationships knew what to expect. And with Warren, I don't throw the word 'genius' around easily, but I know now that they each have that one demon that they fight, the one that tries to keep them from their talent."

Her career in Philadelphia was on an upswing. Through Gevinson's new job at WYSP, it was commonplace for daily commuters to drive past billboards of her in full, sultry pin-up mode. Successful and independent, she was completely unprepared for the weary and beaten version of that man who showed up at her Rittenhouse Square doorstep in 1983. "I knew the difference between the public Warren Zevon and the private Warren Zevon before I even signed on for the Girl Friday duty," she recalled. "I hadn't heard from him in two years, but then things began to cool between him and his girlfriend [Kim Lankford]. . . . She refused to go out on the road with him, so when he was coming to the East Coast, he called. A lot." He left her eighteen messages to ensure she knew he was on the way. Wasting no time, Warren was already booked for a January 27 performance at Penn State when he decided to fly into Philadelphia three days early to meet her. Throughout his Live At Least Tour, Gevinson accompanied him on the road as much as her radio schedule allowed. "Things were chaotic at the station and I thought going out on tour would be, finally, our chance, of sorts," she recalled. "I mean, I had known him for about six years already, but never single."

The Live At Least Tour crisscrossed throughout New England, upstate New York, and Philadelphia. If a gig was three hundred miles or less, they'd rent a station wagon and drive.

In the middle of February, one stop in particular boosted Warren's spirits, allowing him to see a lifelong dream fulfilled: playing a true solo recital. George Gruel remembered, "Warren was beaming when he played the [Philadelphia] Academy of Music. It was a real concert hall and it thrilled him, to no end, to realize that he was playing his music where so many great symphonic performances had taken place."

With what enthusiasm he could muster, Warren used the solo format to rework much of his known songbook. For the first time, he began to rearrange older fan favorites and create new, complex arrangements for the material usually dependent upon a full backup band. It was a healthy exercise for Warren, whose songwriting had hit a drought—although out of necessity, the tinkering with known arrangements for the versatility of unpredictable tour circumstances would become a skill Warren mastered to an exact science.

Critics took note of the innovative solo approach Warren was bringing to his signature rock-and-roll material. Following a sold-out February 28 show at the Bottom Line in New York, Ron Powers of the Associated Press reported, "Performing solo, [Warren] says, gives him the freedom to perform his songs as he originally wrote them—without the key changes and compromises that come with band arrangements. . . . At his club engagement, he alternates between six- and 12-string guitar. The only other instrument on the stage is a grand piano."

Warren's creative explanations for the tour were only half true, yet he was able to slip back into the folk figure of his youth effortlessly. "This is something I've talked about and wanted to do for years," he told Powers in the same article. "I'm always surprised at songwriters who won't admit they wanted to be Bob Dylan. I certainly did.

"There are some things I just can't do with a band," Warren added. "I have a way of playing guitar that appalls guitarists. I finger and just kind of clod-hop away, but it produces chords I like, voicings I like."

The solo tour also brought out some new, folkish touches to songs Warren had written in other genres. He paid homage to Bob Dylan in his reworkings of "Hasten Down the Wind" and "Play It All Night Long," for which he now played piano or acoustic guitar concurrently with a harmonica. For the first time, he also sang the Spanish verses to "Veracruz," softly and eloquently, having to replicate Jorge Calderón's unmistakable harmonies on the album's original cut. Returning to the Roxy in Los Angeles, once host to the single greatest-reviewed concert of his career, Warren quipped of his now lone appearance, "[*The Los Angeles Times* critic] Robert Hilburn called my band the 'best band in Los Angeles.' I guess that was the kiss of death!" While the audience continued to laugh, he introduced the esteemed members of his "Stand in the Fire" ensemble, all in attendance in support of Warren's solo endeavor, despite the fact that budgetary reasons had prevented them from taking the stage.

After the third song, Warren made one final shout of honor. "I'd like to dedicate this set, if I may, to a man who stood by me through a pretty arduous process growing up," he said, "and that is my son,

Jordan Zevon." Now thirteen years old, Jordan was in attendance, and received his own round of thunderous applause. The young drummer had already started his first garage band and, like his father, would get more of that applause in the future.

There were times, however, where new additions to old songs took on much darker forms. George Gruel's assertions about Warren holding a misguided grudge against Jackson Browne became evident in his new, improvised verse to "Werewolves of London." Warren had once paid loving homage to his friend on *Stand in the Fire* by alternating the famous lyrics, "I saw Jackson Browne walking slow down the avenue. . . . You know his heart is perfect!"

Three years later, Warren hissed in its place, "Jackson's going over to Gary Gilmore's house, he's just trying to get along. . . . Old Gary's going to teach him *The Executioner's Song!*"

While Norman Mailer references were nothing new to Warren's onstage banter, the same could not be said for siccing an infamous mass murderer on the godfather of your daughter.

Throughout the press tour for *The Envoy*, Warren had emphasized the fresh start his romance with Kim Lankford had provided to him, going so far as to call her his "salvation." Things had changed by the first month of 1983. Both in his frail condition and depressed over the true nature of the tour's scaled-down circumstances, an air of sadness pervaded much of Warren's banter. His humor took on a tone so self-deprecating, it bordered on character self-assassination. Audiences noticed his vocal cords strained, tired, and sometimes unable to reach the higher notes. He also nervously covered the countless false starts and flubs with sly jokes or a cheap shot at the equipment he was playing.

To interviewers, Warren saved face for the sparseness of the solo tour by emphasizing both his solo classical roots and longstanding self-image as a folk singer. Before an audience, however, he jokingly blamed his "massive fucking ego" for wanting the spotlight all to himself. Sometimes, however, the combination of pills and booze would allow for a slip in the curtain and an awkward vulnerability would silence the room. At one of the first stops in the Live At Least Tour—and only days before flying to Gevinson—Warren had hinted at his well-publicized breakup with Kim Lankford, taking on a noticeably melancholic tone before performing "Hasten Down the Wind."

"One nice thing about being a songwriter, is that you can go back over the years and look at a particularly melancholy kind of tune that reflects a period of your life that you otherwise would have preferred to forget," he told an audience at the Old Waldorf in San Francisco. "You kinda sing it over the years by rote because people expect it. But you never know, one day along comes fate and another terrible trauma happens and the song is singularly appropriate again."

He added, "I got my health and with this kind of cycle I might just keep going around every decade."

For the first few months, Warren would meet up with Gevinson at different concert dates all across the country. Elektra/Asylum may have booked the tour to recoup losses over *The Envoy*, but they at least provided the type of accommodations for which Warren had become accustomed. "At first, we lived pretty large in four-star hotels, and it was all fun, fun, fun," Anita Gevinson remembered. "There were good times—hanging in the 'girlfriend box' at the Roxy on the Sunset Strip with Springsteen, drinks with Marty [Scorsese] in the Village while watching Warren perform."

Like all women in Warren's life before her, Gevinson soon learned that the "Chivas and roses" that represented the early days with him never lasted. A committed relationship with Warren seemed to follow a recurring arc: a blissful beginning, slowly fading in luster once the reality of his tortured mind revealed itself; finally, there would be little left but the torture. The depth of his instability was already a sad suspicion Gevinson had carried throughout the seven years they'd known each other. As a casual, part-time companion, however, she'd never had to clean up his messes. "I knew what it was like to live with him," Gevinson later recalled. "I had seen firsthand how he treated his former wife, Crystal—seen him drunk and in his bathrobe, waving a pistol around like a turkey leg."

She had also taken note of the main reason downers and sleeping pills had so largely replaced alcohol as his primary addiction: he wasn't tempted to drink when he was asleep. "He would time things out so that he would sleep up until showtime," she claimed. This provided him with "a window of relative sobriety" during which he could perform.

Gevinson was already apprehensive at the thought of living with Warren by the time he brought it up. "I realize now that for him, Philadelphia was a place he could go where none of his friends could watch him the way they did back in LA," she remembered. "They had staged interventions, there was shouting and shoving, people got pushed up against the wall . . . And like all addicts, he'd become adept at hiding his disease from anyone who might care. But that act had been wearing thin with his closest buddies in LA—Jackson Browne and others—and people were starting to give up on him. . . . He was no longer a functional alcoholic. He was just an alcoholic."

Against her better instincts, she allowed Warren to move into her place at Le Chateau, which overlooked Rittenhouse Square. He immediately set up camp in her back room, which she later dubbed his "tree fort," bringing whatever instruments and recording equipment he had on the road, as he no longer had a place of his own in which to stash it all. He also had his own bathroom, which meant he could seclude himself for as long as he wished with complete privacy. Although it was her own apartment, Gevinson took the warning signs to steer clear of Warren's private space, but only once entered "his" bathroom, only to discover the vodka bottles hidden under the sink. "My life with Warren started out as Bonnie and Clyde," she later recalled, "and by the end it turned into *Who's Afraid of Virginia Woolf?* . . . I covered for him because I loved him. I never told anyone how bad it got."

The US leg of Live At Least was set to end in the last week of April, and as far as anyone knew, there were no plans for further bookings— or another album. Lost in his own world, Warren ignored the writing on the wall.

∞

By effectively removing himself from Los Angeles—and everyone there— Warren hadn't been privy to the internal rumblings within Elektra/ Asylum. In only a few years' time, MTV had successfully changed the way audiences found new music, as well as the music they demanded. As one of many record labels feeling the sting of a rapidly changing industry, new leadership had been instilled at Warren's label, and heads were about to roll.

The previous year, Joe Smith resigned from his post as head of Elektra/Asylum, paving the way for Warner Bros. talent executive Bob Krasnow to take over and clean house. Within the first six months of assuming the new position, Krasnow fired two-thirds of the label's employees and moved its headquarters to New York. He also cut the company's talent roster of over 150 artists by a whopping 90 percent. Those artists who had previously proven themselves as tried-and-true hitmakers for the label were none too happy with Krasnow's unapologetic explanations to the press, defending his strategy to stock up on younger talent. "Some people play so as not to fail," Krasnow told *Billboard*. "There's no way to win doing that. If Elektra is to succeed, we will have to gamble heavily on contemporary talent." When Krasnow's plan brought the company back as a hit factory to be reckoned with, his later comments were a tad more smug. "I went through the roster with a hacksaw," he later told *The Los Angeles Times*. "It didn't take a rocket scientist to figure out they needed to get rid of most of those acts and start over."

Warren's various personal and career debacles had blindsided him to his fellow artists' own frustrations. While still with the Eagles, Glenn Frey and Don Henley had been two of Elektra/Asylum's highest-selling artists. Feeling a lack of support for their respective solo debuts, both had taken to the media to express their anger and confusion. "[Elektra/Asylum] started signing all kinds of acts, from Tony Orlando & Dawn to Pink Lady," Henley claimed. "I looked at the roster in the late seventies and there were like 80 or 90 acts, and I think I recognized about five of them—and, of course, we [the Eagles] were paying for all that."

When it came to the new leadership's role in the company's shifts, Henley pulled no punches, adding, "[Krasnow] made some comments to the press about 'all the old dinosaurs we have on the label,' and it really pissed me and Glenn off." When the label passed on demos for Frey's next album, *The Allnighter,* he brought it to Warner Bros. and scored his biggest solo hit with them. Likewise, Henley was more than happy to sign with old friend David Geffen's new label, presenting him with *Building the Perfect Beast* as his label debut. Like Frey, the label switch marked Henley's first solo bestseller. But Henley was far from finished. In February 1983, he and manager Irving Azoff took Krasnow to court, claiming that the CEO was in "breach of promise" in allocating the necessary funds to get Henley's first solo endeavor off the ground. According to Azoff, Krasnow had agreed to underwrite over $33,000 that Henley had to put up himself for his previous album's promotion—and was refusing to pay up. "The deeper significance of the suit involves the sudden deterioration of relations between the new Elektra regime and Azoff," reported *The Los Angeles Times,* "who represents several of the label's most potent artists, including Henley, Joe Walsh, Glenn Frey and Warren Zevon."

When yet another Eagle alumni and Azoff client, Joe Walsh, followed suit and signed with Warner Bros., it triggered what would become long-standing animosity between the Elektra/Asylum executive and Azoff's clients. *The Los Angeles Times* picked up on it, claiming Walsh's move was "apparently just the latest installment in the Hatfield-and-McCoys-style family feud between Walsh's Front Line Management company and newly appointed Elektra chairman Bob Krasnow." Front Line Management, of course, was owned and operated by Irving Azoff.

The feud would have lasting effects on all involved. Later, Krasnow would go on to become co-founder—along with, among others, *Rolling Stone* publisher Jann Wenner—of the Rock and Roll Hall of Fame, for which the Eagles would only be inducted as a group, never as singular artists, and Warren completely ignored.

Of the old Southern California "mellow mafia," only Jackson Browne and Linda Ronstadt remained signed with Elektra/Asylum.

Warren knew none of the drama back home. After the Live At Least Tour, no one knew where he was or how to reach him. From her new home in the Parisian neighborhood of Belleville, Crystal had attempted to reach Warren numerous times—both because six-year-old Ariel's only intimacy with her father was clutching an album cover of his, and also because he was countless months behind on child support. When calling friends had led to nothing, as did calling Elektra/Asylum, she taped a voice message from Ariel and sent it to him, via the record label. Although Crystal didn't expect a response, Warren got Ariel's message in the mail. Gevinson later recalled, "Warren hit 'stop,' popped the tape out, and padded to the back bedroom in his bathrobe. I could hear him playing it over and over all night."

Soon after, Crystal received a postcard in the mail. "He wrote to 'Old Girl' and said something about sitting on the square in Philadelphia drinking coffee and thinking about what should have been," she later recalled. "No return address, no mention of [Gevinson] or that he was actually living there."

Only days later, Warren headed back to Rittenhouse Square once again and picked up the latest *Rolling Stone*, a magazine that, according to Gevinson, was capable of enraging him should he find any favorable reviews garnered by old friends in Los Angeles.

Despite the magazine's ongoing coverage of the massive shifts within the music industry, Warren had either been too apathetic or too lethargic—or most likely, a combination of both—to suspect he would be directly affected by his own record label's new leadership and restructuring agenda. Had he read about Glenn Frey and Don Henley's recent career lows, he may not have cared—but he might have noticed his name documented as a fellow "potent" client on Irving Azoff's roster within the industry trade magazines.

Returning from the newsstand and thumbing through the May 27 issue, however, he immediately spotted a heading in the "Random Notes." It read, "Zevon Dropped by Asylum," and followed with a short blurb explaining the decision as a result of Elektra/Asylum's ongoing rebranding campaign. Of the 150 artists dropped by the label, *Rolling Stone* had singled out Warren for the focus of his misfortune and, in that, Jann Wenner had broken his own mandate, allowing Warren's name to once again make headlines in his magazine. It wouldn't happen again for nineteen years.

"[*Rolling Stone*] had it in this little box, as if it were an obituary," Warren later said.

"He went to pieces," remembered Gevinson. "It was devastating for him, especially the way it was handled. He became deeply, deeply troubled." Clutching the magazine, Warren stormed to the back room. He didn't appear again for three days.

It had been eight years since he had penned "Desperadoes Under the Eaves." Now, in the back room overlooking Rittenhouse Square, the air conditioner hummed again, louder than before.

∽

"I got to where I wasn't doing as good a job of bookkeeping as I should have, and that was a sign that something was going awry," George

Gruel recalled. "There was nothing going on. There wasn't another album planned. Nothing was lined up to go back in the studio."

Gruel remembered that, although he didn't remember an official end to the friendship, with Warren drifting on the other side of the country, things between them sadly just "fizzled out."

Years later when compiling his own heartfelt memoir of photographs and memories, Gruel found among his boxes a small sticker—the spare individual labels that came with blank cassette tapes. On the road, Warren used to write on any available blank surface if inspiration struck and pen had to meet paper. On this, he had written his own epiphanic mantra for the secret to songwriting:

> *start songs—remember: a*
> *Title becomes a chorus becomes a verse becomes a line*

But above it, Warren had scrawled the philosophy behind the mantra:

> *keep going regardless.*

"I remember being in the living room, while he'd be working on one of his classical symphonies at the seven-foot Yamaha grand," Gruel later remembered. "Many were the times that I'd lay flat on my back, on the carpet, with a fat one, directly under the piano's soundboard. . . . I would quickly be transported to a special place. We had a wonderful ride."

Without a record contract, Warren's only means of income would come from touring—at least until the possibly of a new contract elsewhere sprung up. All former Eagles members who had gone solo were now thriving on rival labels. At one time, Tom Waits had been the epitome of David Geffen's original Elektra/Asylum vision, but by 1983, the iconoclastic hipster poet had also had enough of the label's new direction; he had wisely signed up with the smaller, independent Island label, which allowed him to self-produce his *Swordfishtrombones* passion project with complete autonomy. Had he been in better physical and mental condition, it would have been an ideal scenario for Warren to likewise attempt. But with the knowledge that he was back to square one, he couldn't even summon the focus to write.

However meager, Warren did have one final chip in his favor. Front Line Management was yet to drop him as a client. He could appeal to them for performance bookings and, when mentally ready, demo funding. Gevinson recalled, "Despite Warren's shaky fortunes in the States, European promoters were hungry for a tour."

Having a European fan base was a good safety net, yet if it ever came down to the direst of circumstances, a self-funded tour of the United States would be far cheaper. Still, without any recording contract, performing live was now more of a personal responsibility than a promotional strategy. "[Warren] never really made a lot of money and he never really cared that much—until those times when you really needed money," Gevinson claimed. "Even though he knew he wasn't around for them that much, he was guilty when he couldn't send money home for his two children. I didn't realize that touring was important to him both for the money and as an escape, until I went out on the road with him. I think it just becomes easier than living in the real world."

Heading to Europe provided the perfect means of getting even further away from his problems, while also paying off some of the credit card debt accumulated by the end of Live At Least. This time, however, Warren would not only be performing solo—he'd be traveling without George Gruel, or any road manager, for that matter. In his weakened condition, Gevinson was left to pull her Girl Friday duty upon their touchdown at Heathrow Airport in London, where Warren was booked for dates throughout May and June.

The tour itself met with mixed results. While Warren did maintain a small yet solid international following, over half of the gigs had been appearances within larger music festivals, giving two major disadvantages: many of his international fans wouldn't necessarily shell out the larger admission price for a full festival, nor would the festival-goers be certain to embrace his folk-infused solo set when so many energetic, younger rock bands filled the same bill. Despondent over his career low and, with no back room in which to take solace, openly drinking and popping pills in front of Gevinson, Warren seemingly had an epiphany regarding his career and priorities. While in London, he reached out to

Crystal in Paris. He explained that he would be traveling Europe with Gevinson for the summer and wanted to pick Ariel up from her summer camp in Chamonix at the tour's conclusion, hopefully to bring her back to Philadelphia for an extended visit. He wanted to reconnect with his daughter and her upcoming birthday seemed a good time. "Warren acted as if I was aware of everything that had been going on in his life," Crystal later wrote, "and the implication was that he had totally straightened himself out, and he lived this wholesome life, far removed from LA and rock and roll."

Crystal continued, "He put his girlfriend on the phone, and she swore he was sober and that this would be a good experience. I wanted Ariel to know her father, so against my better instincts, I agreed."

Admittedly, Gevinson knew Warren hadn't given up his drinking or pills but noticed a steep decline in his demeanor once the Elektra/Asylum news hit. But just prior to their flight to London, Warren had begun to write new songs. It was the first time since his move to Philadelphia, and with his daughter's pending visit, Gevinson saw an opportunity for Warren to come out of his fog. "We were both really excited about Ariel coming to stay with us," she later said. "He started writing. He even got his drinking under control again."

Only days before their flight, Gevinson claimed "something strange happened." In anticipation of their European excursion, she had opted to get a fashionable, short hairstyle at the salon on her building's ground floor. Warren "went berserk" when he saw it, locking himself in his back room to brood and drink. When Gevinson saw the windows of the salon smashed the following morning, she suspected the worst, but kept it to herself.

Even with Ariel's pending visit, Warren's condition wavered throughout the European shows. It came to a head at what should have been the meager tour's crowning achievement—a spur-of-the-moment slot at the Open Air Festival in Werchter, Belgium, on July 3 that saw him swooped into the festival grounds on helicopter. Most were there to see the show's headliner: Irish rock trailblazers U2, who were on the third leg of their massively successful *War* tour. A few flubs and flat chords during "Lawyers, Guns and Money" didn't help. Gevinson, waiting in the wings, had the closest view of all. "Warren won over the crowd but all he could see when he was onstage was a guy giving him the finger and a kid waving the white U2 flag, and he fell off the wagon again," she recalled, adding that things only worsened before the tour's end. "In Ireland, Warren tried bravely to get through his shows, but he was too fucked up from pills and drink . . . he ended every show in Ireland by offering a refund to anyone who didn't like the concert. That's about where his self-esteem was. Giving it away for free."

Gevinson claims it was around that time that Warren, in a rage, confessed to having smashed all the windows in her salon back home. At the admission, she admits to being shocked, appalled, and "a little flattered." The topic never came up again.

When they arrived to pick up Ariel at her camp in Chamonix, Warren did his best to put on a brave face. Hidden behind the scraggly beard and gaunt cheekbones—and after nearly three years without seeing each other—she barely recognized him anyway. To impress his little girl, he persuaded Gevinson to let him drive to the airport for their return flight home. Pulling out of the parking spot, he ran over Ariel's suitcase.

According to Gevinson, Warren's erratic sleeping habits kept him awake all night and sleeping throughout the day. When coupled with his drinking and pills, his condition throughout Ariel's visit was distant at best. When Crystal telephoned from France to check in, Gevinson would answer, worried that the shakiness in Warren's voice would give him away. When he grabbed the phone from her and threatened to keep Ariel, Crystal could hear that he'd been drinking, then cut short her own trip in the French countryside to immediately fly to Philadelphia. When she arrived at the Le Chateau apartment, Ariel answered the door, holding back tears. "When she saw me, she broke down sobbing," Crystal later recalled. "She clung to me like I was her last lifeline." Gevinson was at work and Warren was asleep.

Crystal took Ariel out for lunch and a much-needed sense of normalcy, then had to wake Warren to let them back inside. She couldn't believe what had become of the man she used to know. "He was in bad shape, shaking and disoriented," she remembered. "He wanted to know what I was doing there. I said I was taking Ariel, and that I'd talked to his girlfriend. He followed us to Ariel's room and watched while we started stuffing her belongings into bags as quickly as we could."

Over the phone, Gevinson had invited Crystal to stay with them as their guest for as long as she wished, but now, having seen Warren, she couldn't get far enough away. If Gevinson had mentioned her pending visit, Warren either didn't know or more likely couldn't remember. But he had been thinking of Crystal, and of Ariel, throughout the loneliest period of his life. When they were almost done packing, Crystal turned around to find that Warren had done his best to wash up and change out of his bathrobe. "He said we needed to talk, and he insisted that we leave Ariel there and take a walk in the park," she recalled. Trusting that this was a rare moment of clarity for Warren, she humored him and went along to Rittenhouse Square. Once seated together on the park bench, however, she claimed his demeanor instantly changed. Angrily accusing her of "blindsiding" with a visit he wasn't prepared for, Warren did not believe that Gevinson had extended the invitation. According to Crystal, when he attempted to get physical, "in front of mothers with strollers and the park police," she rushed to get Ariel and didn't look back.

She later said that the experience provided her own moment of clarity. "I realized how, with all I had been through with this man," she later said, "I had actually sent my child into harm's way."

Gevinson remembered that during Ariel's visit, she had her own concerns for the girl's safety alone in the apartment, given Warren's condition. He had already called her while she was live on the air, frantically asking for directions to the toaster. She'd had to play "Jukebox Hero" for thousands of Philadelphians in order to explain how the appliance worked to him over the phone, mainly because she didn't want her apartment burned to the ground. With that in mind, she had brought Ariel to work with her at WYSP's studios a few times, knowing it was a safer environment.

She recalled that the seven-year-old would sit and draw while Gevinson took to the airwaves, and one doodle in particular had given her pause, reminding her of the old adage that animals can instinctively sense a coming storm. "One day Ariel drew me a picture in crayon," she said. "It was of Le Chateau, a tall building with a big waving tree and a little girl inside. And it was raining. What makes a little girl draw pictures of the sky raining on our home?"

In anticipation of Ariel's visit, Warren had made his first play for some form of sobriety in over two years. It hadn't taken, but he was writing again—and had even started a sketch inspired by a visit from friend J. D. Souther; the news in *Rolling Stone* had prompted the lyrics and title, "Trouble Waiting to Happen." As Gevinson remembered, "Warren had a little keyboard, a little eight-track machine, and a few acoustic guitars . . . I remember he would write and rewrite and rewrite. He would sit with headphones on at the electronic keyboard and pore over each song. He had started a song called 'Piano Fighter' and worked on it endlessly."

Music wasn't the only thing on Warren's mind. There was also the "quiet, normal life" that he had dreamed of for so long. He'd attained it more than once throughout his life and lost its solace and stability each time. After Crystal's visit, he didn't contact anyone for a long time. Like both his daughter and his son, Crystal had been in Warren's mind during his frequent strolls in Rittenhouse Square, but her disastrous trip to Philadelphia negated any chance, however small, of a reconciliation. And when would she ever allow Ariel to visit again?

What he hadn't told either his ex-wife or his young daughter was that he had already asked Gevinson to be his wife. She'd been on the road with him prior to the European tour and, while at a stop in Denver, he'd proposed mid-coitus following a gig. She'd responded with, as she recalled, "a breathless 'yes,'" but was already having second thoughts by the time a bunch of groupies came knocking on their hotel door. "Honey," Warren had said, turning back to her lying in bed, "these girls came up here to tell me how great the show was . . . I don't know how they found me." Only a few hours after their engagement, the couple was arguing. "It's the job, it's what I do," he had told her. "You should be glad they find me so attractive."

"What fucking ever, Warren," she had said. The honeymoon was already over.

After their return from Europe, and Warren's abortive attempts to reconnect with Ariel and Crystal, engagement presents started to arrive in the mail. Realizing she needed to "put the brakes" on their pending nuptials, yet somehow do it without shattering Warren's already fragile state, Gevinson's initial apprehension turned into full-on paranoia. "I'd said 'yes' to him for all the wrong reasons," she later claimed, "for my parents, my girlfriends, and for revenge—to prove wrong every guy who didn't consider me marriage material." Desperately seeking advice, she began meeting with her parents in WYSP's parking lot—one of her only places of respite from Warren. She recalled, "It was sort of like meeting Deep Throat in *All the President's Men*. I told them I couldn't go through with it."

Finally, Gevinson reached her breaking point. Following another argument, she threw on her fur coat and stormed across the square in the rain to the Warwick Hotel. When she returned in the morning, Warren's things were already packed. "He was sitting on his suitcases with his overcoat on," she later recalled. "He was going into rehab, he said, and they would be calling me in a few days."

"Don't tell 'em anything they want to know," he said, winking, then walked out the door.

∞

During his time in Philadelphia, Warren got to know many of Gevinson's friends and fellow radio personalities. Kevin Dunn, a longtime producer at WMMR who worked there during her tenure with the station, remembered something very distinct about the Warren Zevon he met in 1983. "Every year, we would do the Morning Zoo in Atlantic City for a week, and Warren came with us twice," he recalled. "He couldn't go near a casino because his father was a heavy gambler. He had to stay away from bars. He would basically sit in his room and smoke.

"It's like Warren lived his life in a house of mirrors of things he had to avoid in the second half of his life."

∞

Years later, Warren was asked what had kept him in Philadelphia for so long. "I bet J. D. [Souther] that if the 76ers beat the Lakers in '83, I'd stay for another year," he'd said. "I've never been a good gambler."

CHAPTER EIGHT

(1984–1987)

WARREN WAS NEVER ONE TO STAY IN CONTACT WITH HIS FAM-
ily, at least not until his final decision to get clean and sober, once and
for all. It had been hard enough for his own children to reach him during
his self-imposed Philadelphia exile; for the extended members of the
Zevon clan, their relationship to Warren had been little more than brief
exchanges following one his shows.

Warren's youngest cousin, Lawrence, hadn't seen his superstar big
cousin since their backstage adventures at the Palladium in 1976. Now
thirteen years old, Lawrence barely recognized the bearded, exhausted
figure beside his father. He watched as Dr. Sandford Zevon assisted his
own younger cousin into the living room. "Warren had shown up unannounced at my parents' house," Lawrence remembered. "He had a
Nike bag in one hand and a guitar case in the other. The Nike bag, he
said, was given to him by Aaron Norris, Chuck's brother, with whom
he practiced karate. The guitar was from one of the Beach Boys, I believe, and I think Warren marred it with a key when he was drinking
and regretted it."

Warren had called Sandford's New York office days earlier. Not only
was it the first time they'd spoken since 1976, but it was the first time
Warren had ever actually asked anyone for help. "He said that he was a
mess, that he thought he was dying," Sandford remembered. "I told him
to take the train to Rye and I'd pick him up at the station. He was one of

the last people off the train and I couldn't believe my eyes. . . . He was unshaven and shaky, and looked terrible."

Sandford's sons, Lawrence and his older brother Paul, were excited at their famous cousin's surprise visit. As Lawrence remembered, however, the boys recognized right away that he was visiting for serious personal reasons. "Before he went to speak with my folks, he gave [Paul] and I a studio cut of Bruce Springsteen's *Born in the U.S.A.*," he recalled. "Warren talked with my parents in their family room for hours, and there were a lot of emotions shared . . . we heard it through the walls."

At that time, Sandford's wife, Madeline, was a social worker for the National Council on Alcoholism—leaving Sandford puzzled as to why his cousin hadn't reached out to them before. After making a few calls, they were able to get Warren accepted into a substance abuse program at St. Mary's Hospital in Minnesota. Far from the serene landscapes and warm sunshine of Santa Barbara, this facility's mandates entailed a harsher, more intense detoxification—which in turn required a massive amount of dedication and painful perseverance. Warren swore he was ready. "My father and brother dropped Warren at the airport," Lawrence recalled. "It was apparently an emotional departure and a linty of narcotics made their way from his pockets to a paper bag my dad used to collect them, and then deposited them into the trash at the airport."

As Sandford remembered, "We took him to LaGuardia. He handed me his Darvon and other stuff he was using. That was the beginning of his path to sobriety."

∽

In just over two years, Warren had lost everything dear to him. After the catastrophic visit with Crystal and Ariel, he knew he wasn't ready to face that closest of inner circles—his children and their mothers. But Sandford and his family had provided what he needed the most, even at its briefest: the quiet, normal life.

Warren's family, so far removed by distance and time, had given him a semblance of normalcy, understanding, and unconditional assistance. In the end, that sense of family had won out. He wasn't kicking and screaming when he entered St. Mary's—not the way he had at Pinecrest, clutching Crystal's hand.

He instead began 1984 motivated by two incentives, both of which would have seemed unimaginable less than a year ago. With Gevinson, he hoped to at last settle down with a woman perfectly suited for him: a woman who had seen him at his worst yet hadn't judged—or found herself broken in its destructive wake. Another rock-and-roll animal like himself. He had brought along a photo of her to help keep him strong.

Warren was also slowly recognizing the sincerity and ambition in the new manager apparently assigned to him at Front Line Management. The young man claimed to want nothing more than to provide Warren with a much-deserved comeback. And so far, Andrew Slater hadn't let him down. Over the last few weeks, demos had already been professionally recorded and ready to be shopped, and a few small gigs around Athens, Georgia, had gone incredibly well. The few new songs Warren unveiled seemed to resonate with the college crowd—and even the band that Slater had put together was better than he'd expected.

In fact, Slater wasn't nearly the novice Warren had assumed. By the time the energetic twenty-five-year-old executive called Anita Gevinson's place at the end of 1983, he already had a number of major projects under his belt. Having befriended future co-founder of R.E.M. Peter Buck while classmates at Emory University in Georgia, Slater became active in the local music scene, beginning a career path writing rock reviews for the school newspaper and culminating with his new role as senior publicist for Irving Azoff. As one of his very first assignments with Front Line, Slater was coordinating videos and acted as a liaison between the agency and Warren's old pal Don Henley, with whom Slater had spent hours in the studio during production of *Building the Perfect Beast*. He later told *The Los Angeles Times,* "I went into the studio every night and I was fascinated by everything. I saw how Don worked, what he did with the drums and the overdubs. He was the consummate record maker."

There was one other thing about the promising young manager and producer: he loved the music of Warren Zevon.

Slater had expressed his enthusiasm at one of his earliest meetings with Front Line in which their client roster was up for review. As Slater later recalled, when someone claimed that Warren was "$180,000 in debt to the IRS, he has no record deal, he's moved to Philadelphia, and he doesn't want to work," and announced plans to cut Warren from the agency's list, Slater had unceremoniously defended his favorite artist, citing Warren as "the best artist" they represented.

"He was a tremendous fan," remembered Gevinson, whom Warren had urged to screen calls. For weeks, he had ignored Slater's messages. Finally, Gevinson had persuaded him to at least hear what the young manager had to say. "When Andy called and had all these ideas and mentioned the members of R.E.M., I knew all about their local popularity," Gevinson recalled. "I thought it was an amazing opportunity. I thought it would be the healthiest thing for [Warren], really."

Although he couldn't promise a record deal right away, Slater assured Warren that he would find an amazing band for a few solid preliminary gigs, followed by some high-quality demos that he was positive would attract a new label. Eventually, both Slater's enthusiasm and logical strategy won over Warren's hardened skepticism—or at least softened it a bit. In the hopes of a "home-team advantage," Slater had called old friend Peter Buck and arranged for the members of R.E.M.—sans lead singer Michael Stipe, who was taking a hiatus from touring—to back Warren up for a few shows around their old stomping ground of Athens, Georgia. Gevinson recalled, "Andy went to school in Georgia, so he was very familiar with the music scene up there," although Warren remained apprehensive. That changed following a few electrically charged gigs at the 40 Watt Club toward the end of February. "I think Warren felt it was like he had been set up on a blind date," Gevinson said. "When they were out playing early gigs together, he would call and laugh and say, 'It's freezing,' and 'These guys are so young—we had to drive around to find a drum kit!' But I knew he loved it."

At that point, Warren and Slater had never met in person. On the night of the gig, Warren eyed Slater suspiciously, not quite sure who he was, but certain he was some form of industry executive. Slater later recalled, "At this point, I'm standing in the corner of the dressing room and Mike Mills, the bass player from R.E.M., comes to me and says, 'Andy Slater, back in Georgia, oh my God, isn't that great?' Warren's sitting about five feet from me, and he comes over, he puts both his hands on my shoulders, and he goes, 'You're Andy Slater!' he had no idea who I was. So that was my first meeting with Warren."

However, Anita Gevinson quickly recognized the growing admiration that Warren had for young Slater. "He really sensed that Andy was going to be 'the one,'" she said, "the one person who would recognize what he had left to offer. I think it took awhile, but Andy finally convinced him."

Even if Warren didn't admit it, playing with the younger musicians had brought out much of his former self, the stage presence that had been so magnetic while performing alongside the boys from Boulder. But Warren also allowed that persona to spiral out of control while offstage. The trick would be to harness it, to take control of it himself. And for that, there was only one cure: non-negotiable and total sobriety.

It was right after the successful Athens gigs that Warren made his desperate call to his cousin Sandford.

It was with genuine determination that Warren flew to Minnesota—and he needed it. Unlike the then experimental intervention therapy that had so prominently distinguished Warren's first attempt at sobriety, the St. Mary's program offered the latest in modern trends: the group therapy session. But with Warren's determination came the incentive of Andrew Slater's faith in him, and his renewed faith in himself. The few new songs that he'd unveiled during the Georgia shows had really won over the young crowd, and he even had a few more ideas in the bag. Being back in rehab offered Warren plenty of inspiration for new material, and he was chomping at the bit for an opportunity to record; and sobriety meant focus.

Warren told as much to Gevinson when she arrived at the Minnesota hospital. She instantly found the facility's atmosphere to be "dreary and institutional," noting the beds all covered in plastic and "the smell of sickness everywhere." Gevinson's photo hung above Warren's own plastic-lined mattress.

As his fiancée, she was expected to be more than a mere participant in Warren's recovery—she was expected to be his moral anchor and pillar of strength. The idea made her shudder. "At that point, I really wasn't equipped emotionally to accept that he could come back to Philly and we could move on with our lives," Gevinson later admitted. "I knew he was shocked when I told him that, but I had already been through so much . . . I just didn't believe that I could live in a world where this would be my main focus. It wasn't that I didn't want to do it, I just felt that at that point, I couldn't do it."

What had hit Warren hardest was that Gevinson had shared these fears during a mandatory group therapy session. She later recalled, "I had always had my own misgivings about interventions and rehab places, and I felt that the person who came out on the other side may be healthier, but there was something missing. I felt it led to the beginning of an entirely different person, and I didn't know if that was a good thing or a bad one. I probably shouldn't have told Warren that, but he got very angry when I did."

In proposing to Gevinson, Warren had sought to complete the trifecta of stability that would define his ever-elusive quiet, normal life: a shot at career redemption through Andrew Slater's ongoing campaign to enact his comeback; a bright future without drugs or alcohol; the strength of his family to keep him focused. Gevinson factored into all three. He hadn't expected to lose that final piece of the puzzle. He ran out of the therapy session and back to his room. Gevinson followed and, when she sat down on his bed, he reached under his pillow to reveal that he had brought with him one of her T-shirts. She recalled, "My heart was breaking . . . I told him I just didn't think it was going to work and he shouldn't come back to Philly. But I remember thinking that if I left Warren there, he wouldn't die on my watch." He asked her leave. On her way out, Gevinson was asked to stop at the counselor's office. They needed to know who should now be listed as Warren's contact in case of an emergency.

"Call Jackson Browne," she said.

❧

In order to pull together as many successful gigs and the demo recordings, Slater had to use every trick in the book. Warren was not only a genuine hero of his, but Front Line viewed this as Slater's first true client—meaning, there was no room for error. After contacting as many A&R representatives as his Rolodex held, Michael Austin at Warner Bros. agreed to invest $5,000 for four high-quality studio cuts of Warren's new material. At the time, Warner Bros. was home to numerous Elektra/Asylum expatriates, including former Eagles Glenn Frey and Joe Walsh, making Warren a logical fit to the label's expanding roster of *established* talent. "I called up Peter [Buck] and I said, 'Warren's up in Philadelphia, and if I send him to Atlanta, could you guys back him up and get a demo made?'" Slater later remembered. "Peter said, 'Sure, man, send him down.'"

Like the unexpected chemistry between Warren and the young mavericks from Boulder in 1980—and the musicians who had composed his makeshift lineup on *Stand in the Fire* two years later—Slater's buddies from R.E.M. brought the very best, youthful energy to Warren's new work. At the 40 Watt Club, the three younger musicians seemed to enjoy playing "Werewolves of London" more than he did—and had really fired up his early debuts of "Boom Boom Mancini" and "Trouble Waiting to Happen" for the club's crowd.

The group had originally formed in Athens in 1980 and had, at that point, released two studio albums on the Universal offshoot, I.R.S. Records. Those releases had garnered critical acclaim, but very little sales—something to which Warren could deeply relate. Then at a crossroads regarding the direction of the band, lead singer Michael Stipe had taken an extended hiatus from the band, leaving drummer Bill Berry, bassist Mike Mills, and guitarist Peter Buck available for a fun side project. For the Athens dates, the loose ensemble had billed themselves as the "hindu love gods"—the first time Warren had been an official member of a band since his folk duo lyme and cybelle in the mid-1960s, as well as the last time he'd used all stylistically lowercase letters for its name. Once the chemistry between the four had been properly established, it made it that much easier to work together for Warren's new demos.

That summer, the band entered the studio. They were joined by a fellow pianist from the Athens-based bands Oh-OK and Time Toy, Bryan Cook. The quintet laid down Warren's four semi-polished originals, "Boom Boom Mancini," "Detox Mansion," "Reconsider Me," and "Trouble Waiting to Happen"—all of which had proven audience favorites throughout the Athens club dates. Additionally, they took the studio time to record fun covers of old blues favorites, since those had made up the bulk of their 40 Watt Club performances. For the recording, they picked an obscure 1968 tune by Australian rockers the Easybeats, "Good Times."

Due to R.E.M.'s growing popularity, I.R.S. later coupled the track with "Narrator," a Bill Berry original, and eventually released it under the hindu love gods as "Gonna Have a Good Time Tonight." Noticeably, the label didn't merely mistitle the song; they'd also forgotten

Warren's name among the credits. By then, Slater was already shopping Warren's demos around Los Angeles.

∽

Following his discharge from St. Mary's in Minnesota, Warren was picked up from LAX by Jackson Browne and his new girlfriend, Hollywood actor Daryl Hannah. Before leaving the terminal, Warren walked to the payphone and left a message on Anita Gevinson's answering machine. "I just wanted you to know that Daryl said when I smile, I remind her of Ryan O'Neal," he said. "Goodbye."

Browne then drove Warren to the Oakwood Garden apartment that he and Slater had found for him. Gevinson knew of the complex, which apparently had a steady clientele of newly single bachelor bad boys on the emotional rebound; as Gevinson claimed, it was a place where "all the rock stars wind up" after their divorces. Warren later deemed it "Cat Piss Manor," furnished in "early hotel room."

But even in a somewhat meager living situation, Warren's quiet return to Los Angeles had behind it the momentum of his circulating demos, plus a newfound popularity among the smaller performance venues. For most of the following year, Warren remained on tour, sometimes alone, sometimes with Slater-assigned road manager Ron Moss. While scaled-down solo gigs were about as far removed from the champagne and caviar of his glorious *Excitable Boy* days, Warren was slowly realizing that he still had a loyal following, regardless of its size and demographic. The acoustic solo recontextualizations of his older hits went over well with the *real* fans among the crowd, and the brief string of shows with R.E.M.—or rather, their hindu love gods incarnation—had proven that he *could* attract younger listeners under the right circumstances.

There was also the pragmatic bonus that smaller, intimate gigs provided great venues for testing out new material, as his preliminary shows had helped shape the final versions of his latest songs prior to their demo recordings. With that practice put in place, Warren toured endlessly throughout 1985 and 1986, refining both the songs that would make up his new album—whenever the hell that would be—and his own unique methods of solo performance. Throughout 1984, Warren had been slowly integrating new work into his set lists. Audiences were privy to the earliest debuts of the tracks that would compose his next

William "Stumpy" Zevon. Throughout his career in organized crime, Warren's father's specialties included running numbers and fencing losers' collateral valuables for underground poker parlors. Arrested many times but never incarcerated, his son inherited Stumpy's natural abilities for smooth talking—and his temper.

(Photo courtesy of the Federal Bureau of Investigation)

(Facing page) Warren on a smoke break outside the Roxy, home to what many critics and fans regard as his greatest live performance, 1981's *Stand in the Fire*.

(Right) In full "Song Noir" mode, circa 1978.

(© 2018 George Gruel. Courtesy of the private collection of George Gruel)

Warren at his Yamaha grand piano in the Zorada house that he shared with actress Kim Lankford and road manager George Gruel. Gruel recalled laying under the piano, smoking a joint, and listening to Warren lose himself in his long-in-progress symphony.

(© 2018 George Gruel. Courtesy of the private collection of George Gruel)

For 1980's "Bad Luck Streak in Dancing School," Warren initially wanted a music video with a roomful of ballerinas to match the song. The record label didn't go for it, but his idea was worked into the 1980 album's cover.

(© 2018 George Gruel. Courtesy of the private collection of George Gruel)

During his turbulent time in Philadelphia, Warren slowly began to mold his new "heavy metal folk" persona, circa 1984.

(© 2018 George Gruel. Courtesy of the private collection of George Gruel)

(*Left*) Warren's hand-written sheet music for "Accidentally Like a Martyr."

(*Below*) For the single release of 1978's "Werewolves of London," Elektra/Asylum had fun with promotional materials. A few lucky fans were able to snag genuine silver bullets, the only known force powerful enough to stop a rampaging werewolf running amok in Los Angeles.

(*© 2018 George Gruel. Courtesy of the private collection of George Gruel*)

During the 1960s, former Beach Boys guitarist David Marks became a close friend and early mentor to Warren. Aside from acting as his personal escort around the sex, drugs, and rock and roll of the downtown LA scene, Marks introduced Warren to psychedelic rock, British blues, and, ultimately, the Everly Brothers.

(Top) Warren and Julia Mueller dated for over two years; she was the last of his fiancées. Seen here in 1992.

(Bottom) Unless he was snapping the photo himself, Warren was selective over who would grab a surprise candid. Julia Mueller made the cut. Circa 1992.

(From the private collection of Julia McNeal)

Stills from Warren's music video for "Searching for a Heart," 1991.

(From the private collection of Julia McNeal)

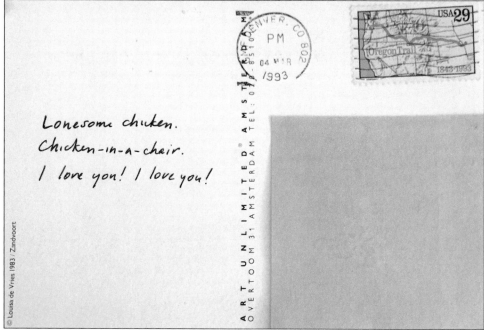

Lonesome chicken.
Chicken-in-a-chair.
I love you! I love you!

Warren liked to call Julia Mueller his "chicken," and on the occasions she wasn't on the road with him he'd find the strangest postcards with her "spiritual animal" in various compromised positions.

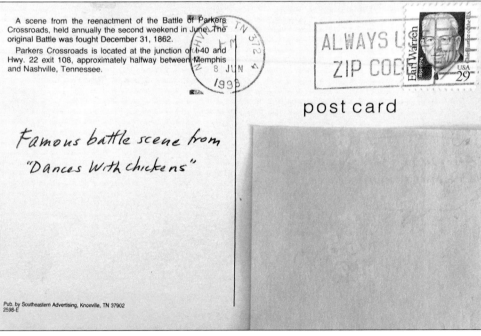

A scene from the reenactment of the Battle of Parkers Crossroads, held annually the second weekend in June. The original Battle was fought December 31, 1862.

Parkers Crossroads is located at the junction of I-40 and Hwy. 22 exit 108, approximately halfway between Memphis and Nashville, Tennessee.

post card

Famous battle scene from "Dances With Chickens"

Pub. by Southeastern Advertising, Knoxville, TN 37902
2598-E

(From the private collection of Julia McNeal)

In the late 1990s, Ryan Rayston became like the sister Warren never had. Seen here after a disastrous trip to the movies that soon found the two trapped in a broken elevator for hours, Rayston was one of the only intimate friends who could talk Warren down from a panic attack.

Even amid a massive migraine, Warren could strike a pose to get Rayston laughing.

(From the private collection of Ryan Rayston)

"If you looked up the word 'autonomy' in the dictionary, it would be a picture of me wearing a fishing cap." Circa 1997.

Warren with friend and neighbor Billy Bob Thornton— seen here during sessions for Warren's final album, *The Wind*, in 2002.

(From the private collection of Ryan Rayston)

Warren initially met country star and actor Dwight Yoakam through mutual friend Billy Bob Thornton. Seen here during the 2003 session for *The Wind*, Yoakam not only appeared on a few of Warren's later albums but also gave him a role in his independent western drama *South of Heaven, West of Hell*.

(From the private collection of Ryan Rayston)

(Top) Warren and his younger cousin during a visit on the *Mr. Bad Example* tour.

(Left) Whenever Warren was in real trouble he would reach out to his cousin, Dr. Sandford Zevon.

(From the private collection of Lawrence B. Zevon and Family)

Wind and Percussion Section

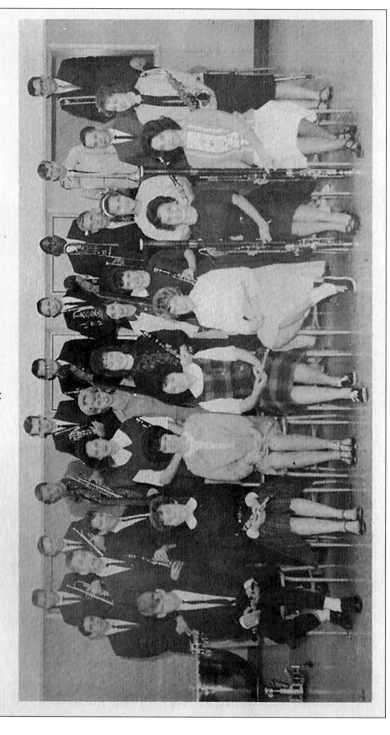

Warren's scowl is unmistakable in the first row, bottom left.
Fairfax High School band club, "Wind & Percussion Section," 1964.

(From the private collection of Lawrence B. Zevon and Family)

album, and some unorthodox arrangements that would be reworked by the eventual studio dates. For the hard-edged rockers that had obviously been written with a full band in mind, Warren attacked his acoustic six- and twelve-strings à la Pete Townshend, humorously informing the audience of the musical classification by which he now described his new style—"heavy metal folk."

In September, he played the Stone in San Francisco—solo, but with an invigorated energy that had been severely lacking in his performances the previous year. The audience took note, with the playful banter hitting as many right notes as the songs themselves. Gone was the self-loathing Warren who had offered refunds in Ireland; in his place, a smart-alecky curmudgeon who offered self-deprecating jokes laced with world-weary wisdom, all while rocking out without the need of a backup band.

"Let's just say it's inappropriate for me to be an excitable boy at my age," he told *The Chicago Tribune.* "But after what I consider a long, disheartening creative drought, I have a lot of new material. My manager and I have decided that since I'm touring and enjoy it, it gives us a base to hold back and jump in later."

Warren was proud of the new songs he had in the bag, should a record label finally agree to a deal. He'd been performing "Boom Boom Mancini" ever since picking up the guitar again, and "Trouble Waiting to Happen" had received a huge response from the college crowds at the 40 Watt Club—thanks in no small part to the well-known sins of his past. And while that song openly referenced *Rolling Stone*'s 1983 notice of his Elektra/Asylum termination, he had written it with J. D. Souther only days following the real events. At that point, Warren hadn't yet made the determination to get clean and sober, nor contacted his cousin Sandford. It was only fitting to now write a song that directly addressed his latest stint in rehab, both as a pseudo-sequel to the events of "Trouble Waiting to Happen," and a social commentary on rehab itself becoming the latest celebrity trend. He hinted as much during his San Francisco performance, dedicating "Carmelita" to his "friends at 'detox mansion.'"

Only months later, the joke became a title—which in turn became a chorus, then a verse, and then a line—and finally, a tremendous fan favorite.

"There are a few places in the country where people can go 'the morning after,'" Warren quipped when unveiling the new sketch at

Rockefeller's in Houston, Texas. "You know, even after maybe twenty or thirty years of those. Well, we got one out in California that my friend Jorge calls 'Detox Mansion.' And Calderón is wont to remind me, when I'm hefting a Coca-Cola, 'You're drinking soda, Warren, because you don't want to go back to 'Detox Mansion.'" He then launched into the song in its earliest incarnation, incorporating a fingerpicked, rolling bass line and vocal drop at the chorus, both elements paying clear homage to Johnny Cash's "Folsom Prison Blues."

No one could know the later, final version of "Detox Mansion" would go on to become one of Warren's best-known songs; its earliest listeners simply found the autobiographical country tune amusing. When he took the song into the studio later with the backing of an all-star lineup of musicians, however, the country and western flair would be traded for a pure hard-rock sound—and a concert staple.

Warren performed yet another new song he'd been tinkering with, "The Factory." In its earliest form, it was a hard anthem of a blue-collar union man with the same acoustic ferociousness of "Trouble Waiting to Happen," but added a nostalgic 1960s twang to the near-rockabilly beat. "This song's about seven weeks old," he told the audience, "but this riff's about twenty-five years old. Duane won't miss it!" The audience laughed at Warren's reference to famed surf-rock pioneer Duane Eddy, but the song owed more to Warren's own frequent cover of Eddie Cochran's "Summertime Blues."

At his Rockefeller's gig in Houston, Warren had also played the new song of which he was most proud—his message to Crystal, the one that had to be completed and perfected before he dared even approach her following the events in Philadelphia. The words had to be just right and had to express the emotions he'd felt overlooking Rittenhouse Square, words he could not find in his daze of pills and alcohol. Those words were ready now. But when Warren introduced "Reconsider Me" to his audience, he simply told them he'd written it with Don Henley.

When tuning up his twelve-string before "Boom Boom Mancini" during the same set, Warren had quickly tossed out the signature melody of "Backs Turned Looking Down the Path." It was one of his first love songs for Crystal, written just prior to their 1975 idyllic jaunt to Spain—and he hadn't played it live in almost a decade. The audience didn't seem to notice.

By coincidence, Warren and Crystal had both moved back to Los Angeles at the same time. As he settled in at Oakwood Garden Apartments, she and Ariel had taken a condo in Burbank. She recalled that very soon after, he had called to say that "he was sober and that Philadelphia had all been a huge mistake." Apprehensive as ever, Crystal granted Warren a visit with her and Ariel for that Easter weekend. He came over the night before a planned daytrip to Knott's Berry Farm, guitar case in hand, visually eager to play Crystal her new love song. But while the lovelorn Warren serenaded his former wife with the now finished "Reconsider Me," all she could notice was his cavalier behavior toward their eight-year-old daughter. "There was a moment when we both thought it might work out between us again," Crystal later wrote, recalling that Ariel had been waiting to proudly show her father a glowing report card from school and drawing she had made, only to meet his indifference. "Ariel was crushed," Crystal added, "and Warren was totally oblivious. That overshadowed what used to allow me to forgive anything. I offered him some platitudes but not what he was looking for." Crystal noted that when Warren arrived for their Knott's Berry Farm excursion the following day, he was two hours late—and had been drinking.

One of the biggest benefits to come from Warren's association with Andrew Slater was the young maverick's PR savvy. Despite still not having a record deal by the last few months of 1985, Warren's ongoing live appearances—and even his quest for a new label to call home—made frequent press. "[Warren's] streak and recording contract with Elektra-Asylum ended with the uneven efforts of *The Envoy*," wrote Justin Mitchell in a Scripps Howard News Service report, later run in *The Chicago Tribune*. "Zevon filled the gaps with tours, but no new product. However, last year Zevon mentioned that a recording contract was possible and noted that he had been working with members of R.E.M. . . . The record label negotiations continue and Zevon said he would like to have a new album out by the end of the year."

In a glowing review following Warren's June appearance at the Bottom Line, *The New York Times'* Stephen Holden took note of his newfound creativity and patience. "Throughout his set, the interplay between two very different musical worlds underscored the running theme of his songs: civilized and destructive impulses at war . . . The best of Mr. Zevon's new songs, 'The Factory,' used the vocabulary of Bruce Springsteen to evoke the same struggle . . . In recent years, Mr. Zevon has gone begging for a record contract. 'The Factory' alone ought to win him one."

The reviews were not only positive, but critics in major publications were once again paying attention. Here, Slater's influence in pushing for better-known, moderately sized venues—such as Warren's successful stint at the Bottom Line—all contributed to the growing buzz of a potential comeback. But with a record deal still nowhere in sight, those consistent, well-received live shows became crucial to keep that buzz going. Slater left nothing to chance and sought out a semi-permanent road manager to oversee Warren's upcoming spring tour of the East Coast. The gig stipulated one unique element: as an out-of-pocket, bare-bones tour, the candidate would be alone with—i.e., responsible for—Warren for the entire trip.

He eventually persuaded Duncan Aldrich to take the position. Affectionately known by his closest friends as "Dr. Babyhead," Aldrich was already a seasoned road manager within the jazz world. He also moonlighted as a studio musician and engineer, giving him the well-balanced experience of both the road and the music. Aside from some early negotiations regarding pay, Aldrich's major apprehension stemmed from Slater's apparent reluctance to introduce the new road manager to Warren until the day of the trip. "I was aware of Warren's work, but I wasn't so much of a fan back then," Aldrich later recalled. "In fact, I only met him after I kept telling [Andrew] Slater that I should meet him before we went off on tour. And he told me, 'Don't worry about it—he's in rehab . . . '"

Aldrich was relieved when things seemed to go off without a hitch, he and Warren engrossed in conversation throughout the five-hour flight to Rochester, New York, where Warren was booked for one of the first shows of the tour. By the very next night, however, Warren's dissatisfaction over the venue and conditions immediately brought about their first argument. Aldrich later recalled, "I lectured him, 'As far as I'm concerned, you're among the luckiest people in the world to be doing this kind of work . . . You could be working in a factory." Instinctively, Aldrich had used the strongest method of reaching Warren, previously recognized by only his closest friends. Like Jackson Browne and Paul Nelson before him, Aldrich had used sheer logic to stump Warren's ego in its path. "From that point on," he added, "I guess he took on a respect for me that I guess I'd had to learn through that little exchange."

Warren was fascinated by Aldrich's knowledge of digital recording equipment and soon, the endless hours on the road became crash courses in the latest studio trends. Although he'd told reporters that he'd "tinkered" too long with *The Envoy,* deep down Warren had a lifelong curiosity for unorthodox instrumentation. From the "fuzzbox" qualities of his psychedelic sound collages with David Marks to the classically tinged synthesizer hybrids of *The Envoy,* Warren viewed sounds like an artist's palate. He told *The Chicago Tribune* that he'd recently "succumbed to the romance of technology," and that his sixteen-year-old son Jordan was advising him on which computer he should purchase.

Slater saw the warning signs of Warren's sobriety lapsing early on in his return to Los Angeles. It had started with Warren's visits to Slater's downtown office, uncharacteristically smoking a large cigar. It wasn't difficult to surmise he'd been using the smoke to mask the scent of alcohol on his breath. And, Slater wondered, what other incentive would lead Warren to throw knives at the wall, leaving the interior of his Oakwood Garden apartment riddled with unsightly holes? He later recalled, "[Warren] was constantly writing, but there were all sorts of shenanigans that were going on there . . . It became clear to me that he was going to have to get sober if he was going to be able to work."

Aware that Slater had the six-week East Coast tour lined up for the end of April, Warren unceremoniously asked to be escorted back to rehab; he wanted this round of sobriety to stick, and everyone to know it. Proud of his client and friend, Slater not only agreed, but headed out at Warren's request to pick up a "cheeseburger for the condemned man." As Slater recalled, when he got back, Warren had already knocked back two beers and was gulping his third as though he were "going to the chair," recognizing that it was just Warren's way of saying, "'You know what, fuck you, I'm going to have my last beer.'" And although this particular rehab stint had been his own idea, once Warren and Slater walked in, he immediately regretted his decision. "He kicked and screamed," according to Slater. "Within forty-eight hours, he was in rehab, only he didn't last too long." However, as a necessary element to his bid for lasting sobriety, Warren began attending Alcoholics Anonymous meetings. As was the case with most new members, his initial attempts were met with mixed success and lapses were frequent—and when Warren crashed, he crashed hard; but he had come too far to fall back into the depths of the last few years. It helped that, in an effort to ensure the intimate nature of the sponsor-sponsoree relationship remained on a relatable level, A.A. had paired Warren with a well-known character actor and musician named Stefan Arngrim. A former child actor who had spent his life battling a fair share of inner demons, when Arngrim spoke, Warren listened.

Coupled with the unbridled faith of Andrew Slater, Warren stood fast. When he had caught up with old friend Don Henley, now a thriving solo artist, Henley had advised him to continue to walk the narrow path; he didn't want "to rake leaves." Warren couldn't agree more, and began to take his twelve-step work seriously. He'd even quit smoking.

Over the next few months, Warren made every attempt to negate the bad luck that had plagued the previous decade of his life. Although a potential reconciliation with Crystal had been, as she recalled, "a disaster," he made it a point to remain some form of presence in Ariel's life. Likewise, he had contacted first-love and Jordan's mother, Marilyn Livingston, to arrange a long overdue family dinner before taking his son for a trip to Fresno to visit his own mother and grandmother—Warren's first return visit in nearly a decade.

Warren marked March 19, 1986. Almost three years to the day of *Rolling Stone*'s devastating Electra/Asylum termination blurb, it was now his first official day of complete sobriety.

He didn't have another drink for seventeen years.

Warren had just completed writing a song entitled "Bad Karma" when his own karma began to drastically improve.

Four years earlier, he had dedicated *Stand in the Fire,* regarded by many music critics to be Warren's crowning achievement, to friend Martin Scorsese. Following his own glorious heyday with 1980's *Raging Bull,* the young director had been through his own recent career slump. He too was now gearing up for a comeback of sorts, filming the long-awaited sequel to the 1961 classic *The Hustler,* with returning leading man Paul Newman and rising superstar Tom Cruise. Returning Warren's earlier heartfelt dedication, the director was eager to use "Werewolves of London" in a crucial scene within the new film. It was only fair; Warren had once reveled in a critic's description of him as "the Travis Bickle of rock and roll," drawing a comparison between him and *Taxi Driver*'s angriest of angry young men. When the soundtrack to *The Color of Money* was released in conjunction with the hit film, Warren found himself on a bestselling release that also included old and new material by Eric Clapton, Don Henley, B.B. King, and Robert Palmer. Thanks to the exposure, a new generation of college students was howling; thanks to the film itself, Warren was forever linked to an iconic cinematic scene—and one frequently reenacted in pool halls with working jukeboxes.

Just as Warren had hoisted a final beer as a "fuck you" before entering rehab, so Elektra/Asylum found a reason to put out their first Warren Zevon release in three years. In anticipation of Scorsese's "Werewolves" usage, his former label cobbled together a compilation of best-known songs from his tenure there. It was another effort to clean house of the label's former roster, lock, stock, and barrel. In the case of former labelmate Tom Waits, Elektra/Asylum had already put out not one but two "best of" albums before he even jumped ship. A year later, they released a third, *The Asylum Years,* including almost identical material.

When his former label contacted him for a title of his collected songbook, Warren submitted a phrase of personal, intimate meaning— the line from author Wallace Stevens to which he clung like an elusive dream: *A Quiet Normal Life* was released on October 24, 1986—two weeks after *The Color of Money.*

But being back on the *Billboard* charts on two separate albums for the same song had its benefits: Warren's earlier work was being positively reassessed in major media outlets, all while Andrew Slater continued to shop his new demos. "Unlike so many songpoets, Zevon's a real writer," wrote Robert Christgau in *The Village Voice.* "Because he inhabits his tricksters, blackguards, and flat-out psychotics rather than reconstituting variations on a formula, he tops his boy Ross Macdonald any day. . . . Thompson gunner, mercenary, NSC operative, werewolf, easy lay, he puts his head on the tracks for penance, and when the train doesn't come gets up and hurls himself against the wall of the Louvre museum. Really now, could Ross Macdonald imagine such a thing?"

While emphasizing Warren's longstanding reputation for mischief, *Billboard* nonetheless put it succinctly: "Greatest hits package from the City of Angels' No. 1 bad boy. Exposure of 'Werewolves of London' via the 'Color of Money' soundtrack could spur interest."

It did, almost instantly. Slater later recalled that based on the strength of the dual releases, especially the mainstream attraction of the hit film, his next meeting finally yielded the results they'd been hoping for. "I was able to convince my friend Jeff Ayeroff, who was starting Virgin Records with Jordan Harris, to sign Warren as one of their first artists based on the demo of 'Reconsider Me' and the activity with [*The Color of Money*]." Ever the publicist, Slater not only admitted that the song was a personal favorite of his, but knew the title's apparent double meaning would resonate with listeners with fond memories of Warren's younger, wilder persona. The poignancy of the title and the heartbreaking emotions of Warren's lyrics attracted other admirers, as well; although it wouldn't be released for years, Stevie Nicks recorded her own emotional cover before the ink had even dried on Warren's Virgin contract. It was apparent to many that Warren Zevon the songwriter was back in good form.

Warren, however, was immediately concerned about what effects sobriety would have on his creative process. During even the most focused and professional of sessions, Warren's albums had been made in the safe haven of a studio where everyone drank, smoke, popped, or snorted without batting an eye. Half a decade later—and with a can of Coca-Cola on the engineering console—Warren feared he wouldn't be able to create a new album without so much as smoking pot.

Before he could even address his own internal concerns, Slater's enthusiastic PR blitz went into full effect. Within a month of *A Quiet Normal Life*'s release, unintentionally bringing Warren back to the "New Release" wall of record chains and into the purview of a younger generation of listeners, the November 22 issue of *Billboard* ran the announcement they'd both been waiting for: "First sightings to reactivated U.S. Virgin Records are Warren Zevon and Steve Winwood."

Upon the same page, *Billboard* reported Virgin's intention to test their new marketing concept, the CD single, throughout England, providing Genesis fans with twenty-four minutes of new music for three dollars. Elektra/Asylum's greatest hits compendium of Warren's songs had been his first appearance on compact disc—the digital medium slowly phasing out the LP as consumers' preferred means of hearing new music. With Virgin's energetic and competitive approach to marketing, Warren was slated to be given the rock-star-of-the-1980s treatment. It was a brave new world. "I've got songs to play for you, I've got some new songs to play for you," he told a crowd in Texas. "I got my Miami Vice haircut—and I'm all set to party like it's 1999!"

∞

It was inadvertently through Slater's aggressive PR campaign that Warren met the woman who would become his next love and inspiration— and at of all places, the one publication sure not to give him the press Virgin sought: Jann Wenner's *Rolling Stone*.

Merle Ginsberg later remembered, "Andy Slater called me up and said, 'Warren Zevon's having a comeback. He's gone through rehab and he's got this great new album and he's such a genius.' I didn't know that much about Warren Zevon, so I bought all his records and as I listened, I realized this was really fascinating." Then in her early twenties, Ginsberg was unaware of Warren's not-so-illustrious years. Curiosity led her to the *Rolling Stone* archives, where she read the full chronicle of Warren's dirty life and times. When she got to the 1981 Paul Nelson masterpiece that had doomed its author, "The Crack-Up and Resurrection of Warren Zevon," she was certain Slater had given her more than a solid lead; to her, Warren was "a fucking wild man" and represented "what rock stars used to be." She immediately began work on a profile of her own. From the *Rolling Stone* office in New York, she called Warren in the hopes of booking an interview, but admittedly was under his spell before even meeting. "Nobody intimidated me much, but I was very intimidated by Warren," she later recalled. "His voice went right through me—this gravelly, masculine voice." He suggested they meet during her next visit to the West Coast, which she had already planned for coverage of the Grammy Awards a few weeks later.

Despite being over a decade younger than Warren, Ginsberg was quickly taken by his boyish charm when he picked her up at the Sunset Marquis. When he awkwardly told her he wasn't allowed inside because of past behavior, she remembered the *Rolling Stone* files she'd devoured and wasn't quite certain if he was joking. Fully aware that she was on a date with a tried-and-true rock star, Ginsberg was nervous enough to want a drink to loosen up; also aware of Warren's past, she purposely broached the subject. He took her back to his Oakwood Garden apartment, which she found uncharacteristically modest for a perceived music legend; more so, she was surprised to find that Warren seemed equally nervous. "I definitely did not think this guy was going to seduce me," she later recalled. "He was so quiet and shy. . . . Of course, I thought he was unbelievably quirky and shy. He was nervous, and I was dying to tell him because I was so nervous." Playing the good host, Warren insisted that she have a glass of wine, even if he couldn't. She was again surprised to find that he seemed to have no problem smoking pot with her—although Andrew Slater had warned her ahead of time to keep *all* substances away from him. After the two began to get intimate on Warren's bed, Ginsberg noticed his words slurred and his drowsiness deepening. When he finally passed out, she leaned over his side of the bed to find a large, empty vodka bottle. He'd apparently polished it off by quickly sneaking off to the bedroom all night. Two days later, Ginsberg was poolside at the hotel when she spied a large, expensive arrangement of flowers being delivered somewhere inside the hotel. When she returned to her room, she found that they had been from Warren, along with a note. "When I meet you again, it will be like the first time," he wrote. "If you want to. I'm so, so sorry."

Still very much under his spell, the two cautiously began to date. With Ginsberg still working at *Rolling Stone*'s New York headquarters, they attempted to start things slow.

In the meantime, Warren entered the studio for the first time in five years.

Although the word "comeback" was never officially attached to the promotion of *Sentimental Hygiene*, every element of its production and promotion rang of a full-fledged return to form for Warren Zevon. In Slater, Warren had truly met the right manager at the most-needed time in his career—a young fan with a marketing and publicity background who also knew his way around the studio, and intimately knew the latest industry trends. Not since Jackson Browne's all-encompassing efforts during the mid-1970s had any one individual pulled so many tricks just to get public awareness aimed in Warren's direction.

When it came time for the actual recording sessions for *Sentimental Hygiene,* Slater's push for the highest-quality everything carried over into the studio. With Slater's insistence on Warren's long-term bankability, and both Jeff Ayeroff and Jordan Harris in his corner, Virgin had no issue in allocating $225,000 for the album's budget. Warren was, after all, the first artist to have joined the fledging label's roster, and therefore benefited enormously from their proactive attempt to stake a claim within the American market. It was also decided that the album would be given the largest "star treatment," with six total singles slated for US release—the largest number Warren had ever been granted, even during his peak at Elektra/Asylum.

Seasoned producer and engineer Niko Bolas was not only good friends with Slater but was also a devoted fan of Warren's before he was even approached to co-produce the new project. "Warren is the reason I became an engineer," Bolas warmly recalled. "I first met him in 1979 when he was doing *Bad Luck Streak in Dancing School,* and I worked on part of that record as an assistant—but, *Excitable Boy* was the album that convinced me that this was what I wanted to do for a living, to be an engineer and mixer and producer." While working as a young assistant and "runner" on Warren's third Elektra/Asylum release, Bolas had worked under Greg Ladanyi, and had impressed Waddy Wachtel during the sessions for "A Certain Girl." When that production had ended, the three became friends and, as Bolas recalled, he "fell into that camp."

From the very beginning of the sessions, Bolas saw a new focus in Warren's studio approach, although the talent had never wavered. "Warren was just good," Bolas recalled. "He was good before and he was good after. What probably changed significantly was his personal life and his spiritual life. But in terms of his musical life, the only thing that was really different now was that he was a lot more responsible. He'd show up on time and was prepared, and maybe it didn't take as long to get things done. But, I mean, except for work habits, sobriety doesn't affect your muse. You're either talented or you're not."

The countless hours on the road with Duncan Aldrich truly proved their worth once Warren and company set up camp in Record One studios in January 1987. Much had changed in the way of professional recording since Warren had set foot in a studio and, thanks to the generosity of Virgin, every new toy was at Warren's disposal. "If it was new, Warren would tinker with it," according to Bolas. "He was the first guy to have a Steinberger guitar—one of those all–carbon fiber deals. And he was hanging around a lot with Duncan, and Duncan was always bringing in cool, weird shit." As both a now trusted friend and unofficial modern technology tutor, Aldrich was elevated to an engineering role at Record One.

Additionally, Slater had guaranteed that the album would carry on the Zevon tradition of hosting a "who's who" of guest musicians in addition to a rotating core ensemble. By the time the album was completed in time for its summer release, old friends Jorge Calderón, Don Henley, David Lindley, Leland Sklar, Waddy Wachtel, and Neil Young would be joined by the next generation of rock superstars: the Red Hot Chili Peppers' Flea, the Stray Cats' Brian Setzer, and R.E.M.'s Michael Stipe are listed among Warren's everything-but-the-kitchen-sink Virgin debut.

"Slater was calling everybody in and then using stuff that I thought was kind of dismal," Aldrich later claimed, describing the full experience as a "producer war," with the threat of Warren being left to his own devices. In Warren's view, Jackson Browne and Waddy Wachtel had been needed to produce his work largely due to the self-inflicted limitations brought on by years of drugs and drink. He was sober now, and focused. As had always previously been the case, Warren truly wanted complete creative control, but now made a compromise in taking on an assistant while he pushed his own creative agendas, track by track. And thus far, there was only one person who wouldn't say "no" to him about pretty much anything. At his insistence, Slater was given a role as co-producer for the album. Only later, claimed Slater, did he realize the offer had been a ploy for a "fall guy" should the shit hit the fan. He later recalled, "I thought, I've never made a record, I'd been in the studios, and I was a guitar player, but gee, I'm a manager." Warren insisted that his inexperience wouldn't be an issue. "Hey man, it's easy," he'd told Slater. "You'll book the studio time and come down and help me."

Niko Bolas later recalled that "most of the collaboration and artistic exchange happened between Andy and Warren. Not a lot of people know that, and certainly not enough people give Andy enough credit . . . And Warren was there to make a record with people. He knew what he was good at, and he let you be good at what you were good at. Somewhere between those two things overlapping, you make something brilliant."

In hoping to maintain control in yet another new role, Slater chose the most logical musicians he could think of to compose Warren's core studio group—his friends from R.E.M. In the three years since Peter Buck had gotten his bandmates to back Warren in his earliest comeback shows in Athens, Georgia, their band's following had steadily grown and were now on the brink of superstardom. But as loyal friends to Slater—and having enjoyed their brief collaboration with Warren— Buck, Bill Berry, and Mike Mills agreed to play the roles of session cats; lead singer Michael Stipe would contribute harmony vocals during the "Bad Karma" sessions, making R.E.M. the only other band besides the Eagles to have made a full appearance on one of Warren's albums.

"The real secret impetus behind *Sentimental Hygiene,* and the driving force, was Andy Slater," said Niko Bolas. "Andy was a huge Warren fan and a brilliant manager, and those two things connected when he started managing Warren. He wanted to jump-start him creatively and jump-start a record—so he brilliantly got R.E.M. to be the backup band. They were huge fans of Warren's, too, and they jumped at the opportunity."

The album's title song had been written on the road. To Warren's amusement, there seemed to be as many questions surrounding the ambiguous meaning of the title as there were accolades for the song itself. He seemed to approve of Chauncey Mabe's interpretation in Fort Lauderdale's *Sun-Sentinel,* in which the reporter stated that the album's title track was "the one that captures the essence of a dying decade," while applauding the lyrics' "cunning directness," which found Warren "lampooning" the baby boomer generation's loss of social freedoms in the AIDS era. "That's one way the song could be interpreted," Warren had acquiesced. "Everybody has an idea of what it means. I've felt vindicated in avoiding the question. The more you explain the lyrics of a song, the less meaning they actually have." He did, however, later tell an interviewer in Chicago that one fan had summed up the meaning of "Sentimental Hygiene" satisfactorily enough when attempting to explain it to her four-year-old son: "It's about keeping your feelings clean." Pleased with the interpretation, Warren had added that he personally tried to keep his own thoughts "clean enough to eat off of." He later admitted, "['Sentimental Hygiene'] is one of those titles that just come to mind unbidden; I emerge from a momentary daze of congratulating myself." But he kept his true inspiration to himself.

Sharing the same title as the album itself, "Sentimental Hygiene" was chosen as the flagship single, followed closely by both "Boom Boom Mancini" and "Reconsider Me," the latter of which benefited from a major radio push, thanks to its romantic marketability and its apparent allusion to Warren as a comeback kid.

While R.E.M.'s Bill Berry, Peter Buck, and Mike Mills were the true core of all the *Sentimental Hygiene* sessions, both Warren and co-producer Andrew Slater made ample use of their options to swap out players, hoping for the best possible "fit" track by track. Warren explained, "I write each song individually and each one calls for individual musicians . . . You sit around and [ask] who can we get to play a Neil Young solo, and then you realize there's a good chance you can get Neil himself."

Duncan Aldrich recalled those first few sessions. "With Warren, he wrote the songs, and he knew when it would sound right," Aldrich said. "The people that were brought in were brought in because of what they could add to a track without too much, or really any, direction—like Neil Young, who's a genius in his own right."

It had been the exact case with "Sentimental Hygiene." After running through the song "for a couple of weeks" and still not entirely satisfied with the song's direction, old friends Jorge Calderón and Waddy Wachtel visited for a much-needed "Gentleman Boys" reunion, with the duo contributing bass and acoustic guitars, respectively. For the first time in many years, Warren was in a position to add yet another major cameo to the track. Slater later recalled, "Neil Young was working in the room across the hall from us. . . . Niko went down the hall to ask him to play. Warren and I were sitting in the control room, and Neil sets up his big red pedal board, and he's got his black Les Paul, and we turn the track up in the control room. . . . [Neil] did three passes, and after the first pass, Warren leans over and says, 'This is like Woodstock, man.'"

Warren told of the experience to John Milward of the *Philadelphia Inquirer*, "[Neil Young] arrived with his Les Paul, which he calls 'Old

Black,' and ran it through these foot pedals that were half high-tech and half Tinkertoys. Then, he started wailing just like he does in concert."

When Young was finished with his solo, he turned to both men. "I think you guys got it there," he said. "You can cut something out of that."

Warren turned to Slater. "Yeah, Andy, you edit something," he said.

Following the session, Warren began collecting guitar pedals.

Warren's new status as Virgin's debut artist made the push for a large-budget music video not only possible, but in the face of the MTV generation, a marketing necessity. "Sentimental Hygiene" would be his first since "Werewolves of London" in 1978—and this time, the budget allowed for more than Jorge Calderón running around in a latex wolf mask. The ambitious video to match *Sentimental Hygiene*'s title song was stylishly filmed in black-and-white to match Herb Ritts's iconic album cover photograph; the three-minute short itself was characterized by Fellini-esque imagery of Warren existentially surrounded by the melancholy rolling tide of California's waves and sand at winter's dusk. Warren coolly wears a long black overcoat, pant legs rolled as he stands alone, shin-deep in the water, almost as if waiting for the miraculous powers of Jesus or Elvis to allow him to walk upon the water, as in his song "Jesus Mentioned." The video, which was added to MTV's normal rotation, also drew unintentional comparisons to Don Henley's blockbuster music video for "Boys of Summer," shot in almost identical gray-scale, cinema verité style, with common themes of advancing age and confusion in facing a new, unfamiliar landscape brought on by youth's end.

Beginning with "Boom Boom Mancini," the final grouping of *Sentimental Hygiene*'s track listing deliberately ran with five consecutive songs that Warren and company had already run through years earlier in their demos. With "Boom Boom Mancini," Warren knowingly entered the proverbial ring with literary luminaries Ernest Hemingway and Norman Mailer—not to mention pragmatic musical heroes Bob Dylan and Miles Davis—in using boxing as the ultimate existential analogy. As their literary descendant, he had every right to rise to the challenge; an avid boxing fan, his own father, William "Stumpy" Zevon, had earned his nickname throughout a rough-and-tumble adolescence in the ring himself. And the true story of Ray "Boom Boom" Mancini not only fascinated the ardent pulp fiction connoisseur within Warren but had symbolic parallels with Warren's own life during his "lost weekend" in Philadelphia. Mancini, as the song accurately portrayed, was a tough kid from Youngstown, Ohio, who had pursued a career as a lightweight contender. On November 13, 1982, twenty-one-year-old Mancini had been pitted against South Korean challenger Duk Koo Kim; the fight ended in Mancini's favor after a TKO in the fourteenth round, but Kim lapsed into a coma from which he would never awaken. The international fight's widely publicized death in the ring led to massive changes in the boxing industry and had lasting emotional effects on many of the figures involved: Kim's mother, racked with grief, committed suicide in February of that year; the bout's referee, Richard Green, likewise took his own life in July. For Ray Mancini, being the reigning champion hadn't been worth the guilt of killing a man in front of the entire world. He disappeared from public eye for nearly half a year before quietly working his way back up through the ranks; in January 1984, he was set for a major comeback fight against former champion Bobby "The Schoolboy" Chacon.

Bottomed out in Philadelphia, Warren was watching the fight with bated breath. He was rooting for Mancini, someone he viewed as a similarly conflicted figure—another "man's man" whose personal demons and self-doubt had been given the full treatment of publicly enacted microscopic scrutiny. Mancini's overtly human portrayal in the media had worked to shape the public's perception of him into one of an iconoclastic, atypical sports figure: a blend of the savage and the philosophical—Warren's bread and butter. In effect, the Bill Lee of boxing.

Warren had written the song while watching the fight on HBO in real time. Anita Gevinson remembered, "I was working a telethon that night and I called home to remind Warren to tape the fight for us to watch together, since we both were excited to see the outcome. He kept saying to me, 'Well, hurry on home, hurry on home.' I told him I'd be as fast as I could . . . When I got home hours later, he was sitting on the couch with his guitar. The song was already completely done by the time I walked in." Overjoyed to see Warren finally writing again, Gevinson let it go that he'd watched the fight without her. Even before meeting Slater and embarking on the small, tight Georgia gigs that resulted in his major comeback, Warren was performing "Boom Boom Mancini" as early as the first few months of 1985. He playfully fibbed to his audience that Mancini had retired after it had taken him "two years to write it."

For the definitive, final studio cut, "Boom Boom Mancini" became, arguably, the album's hardest rock track—benefiting tremendously from the stripped-down nature of the production itself. Of the ten tracks making up *Sentimental Hygiene,* it is the only session that included no outside guests or cameos; Warren alone with R.E.M., particularly the added reverb to Bill Berry's already thunderous drums, brought out the needed primal tone not present in Warren's style since 1980's "Jungle Work."

A point of contention to Warren during the recordings of nearly every one of his albums was his teams' reluctance to allow him lead guitar duties. While he was largely associated with the piano, throughout his career Warren proudly reminded many interviewers that he'd been playing guitar for nearly the same number of years—and had made his first major breaks in the music industry *as* a guitar player. Even his respective producers had always urged him to showcase the same virtuosic keyboard skills that had impressed Igor Stravinsky so long ago. Most of the time, even Warren couldn't be persuaded. Andrew Slater vividly remembered Warren's insistence that he get "tipped" accordingly if he was going to be expected to play the piano by request.

"I know you love playing lead guitar, but you're a piano player," Slater had said to him during production. "I know you wrote the song on guitar, but it needs a piano part for rhythmic and musical foundation for the chord structure."

"Well, I'm not playing piano," Warren said.

"What do I have to do to get you to just try it on the piano?" Slater asked.

"You got cash?"

"Yes."

"You got two hundred dollars?"

Slater checked his wallet and nodded.

Warren said, "You put two hundred dollars in cash on the piano, I'll go play it."

Even during future solo performances, Warren never let "Boom Boom Mancini" slip from his repertoire. "My father was a boxer, so

I've always liked the fights," he later claimed. "Ray [Mancini] got in touch with me after the album was released to tell me [he] liked the tune, and we became friends." The track was released as the album's second single. Critics cited Warren's piano coda at the song's end as a highlight of the album. In later years, he would look back on that famous solo, but remain adamant that his guitar parts were just as crucial to the song's final sound. "For some curious reason, Duncan and I spent all night doubling that piano part with guitar," Warren later recalled. "And I don't know why but I think it's worth noting. So, I have, in fact, never played a piano solo, but it was also a guitar solo."

He had also been performing "The Factory" for close to two years, his live solo arrangement taking on a truly Bob Dylan–influenced folk feel with the newly established use of harmonica. While the song's narrative voice as that of American blue-collar workingman earned instant comparisons to the usual themes within the music of Bruce Springsteen, critics often overlooked the influence that Warren's 1984 solo tours had on the shifts within his own thematic content. His Elektra/Asylum work had always been described as representative of "California rock and roll," largely due to both the Los Angeles musicians appearing on the tracks, and the overwhelming sense of Southern California's sun-kissed presence in even the most seemingly unrelated and macabre of Warren's songs. Songs like "The Factory" proved that the peripheral vision of his writer's eyes hadn't overlooked the steel mills, rundown farms, and dilapidated industries that crossed his path throughout his bare-bones tour along the East Coast. Unlike the fevered Los Angeles crowds at the Roxy who had howled along with Warren, and just as loudly, the men and women who inspired the frustrations depicted in "The Factory" were the ones who directly related to them. It was only fitting that for his first social commentary song in years, the maestro of the form made his one and only guest appearance on one of Warren's albums. Three days after his fortieth birthday, Warren arrived at the studio late to discover the ultimate belated present. "I came in one day," he later recalled, "and the receptionist said, 'Mr. Dylan is waiting.' I thought it was a joke, but there he was, and he came up and said, 'I like your songs.' What could I say but, 'I like your songs, too.'"

It was a tremendous understatement on Warren's behalf. While a number of writers, composers, and fellow musicians had found their way into Warren's seemingly endless cache of influences and reference points for his own work, Bob Dylan was the only figure with which he spoke of with near reverence: to David Letterman, Warren had once credited Dylan for "inventing" his own profession of singer-songwriter. Former wife Crystal later confirmed Dylan truly was the greatest inspiration for Warren's own self-image as a singular performer; his surprise visit to Record One held all the personal and emotional weight of Ken Millar's mercy visit in 1978.

"I went in the control room, and we started playing [Dylan] the songs we were doing," Slater remembered, noting that this was also his first encounter with Dylan's young son, Jakob. As their acting manager a decade later, Slater would help bring Jakob's band, the Wallflowers, to international superstardom. Now however, he immediately began strategizing a possible Bob Dylan cameo for Warren's album. He knew some of Dylan's representation and considered that the legendary songwriter would be more likely to agree if his vocals weren't necessarily required. He recalled, "I said, 'Can you get Bob to come down and play harmonica on this one song?' . . . Some days later, Dylan came down and played on 'The Factory,' did three passes. He was Warren's hero."

The inclusion of Dylan's spirited harmonica breaks proved a perfect nod to the socially conscience songs that had inspired Warren—and his entire generation—during the 1960s. His wailing harp offered not only a cultural blessing by the workingman's great musical champion but also fit perfectly into a song that had been specifically composed to include the instrument—a rarity for one of Warren's edgier rock songs.

"Trouble Waiting to Happen" was the very first song written for the album, having been a cathartic exercise immediately following the devastating notice of his termination at Elektra/Asylum. J. D. Souther was visiting Warren in Philadelphia that fateful weekend and attempted to cheer up his old friend by pushing him to vent his anger through writing. In effect, as Warren's direct answer to *Rolling Stone*'s "obituary" for him, "Trouble Waiting to Happen" marked the next phase of his career. Coupled with "Detox Mansion," "Trouble Waiting to Happen" was also the most overtly autobiographical song on an album that many critics initially regarded as quite the opposite. Warren's signature self-deprecating humor, now safely returned to its recognizably biting best, kept those critics at bay. Don Henley stopped in for the session, adding to the lush harmony vocals, as well as rockabilly guitarist Brian Setzer from the Stray Cats, who provided the mean, distinctive lead.

The sessions for "Reconsider Me" took place toward the midpoint of the album's production, in time for a major single release. By the time Warren laid down the track, which had been for Crystal all along, its arrangement had been meticulously refined through numerous live solo performances. Stevie Nicks had already recorded her version, and Warren's initial demos with R.E.M. had made "Reconsider Me" a prominent selling point to record labels. That original lineup did not return for the studio cut, however, and Slater compensated with an all-star ensemble. Mike Campbell, best known for his ongoing work with Tom Petty and the Heartbreakers, took lead guitar, while Waddy Wachtel visited to play the warm, acoustic rhythm; seasoned session bassist Tony Levin came in, as did additional keyboardist Jai Winding, which allowed Warren to focus on his ballad vocals. According to Slater, he had been haunted by the heartbreaking tune ever since Warren had first played it for him. "I was so moved by 'Reconsider Me' that I was obsessed about getting Warren a deal—based on that song," he later remembered. "When I couldn't get anybody interested, I wanted to get somebody to cover that song because it just struck a chord in me that has not been rung too many times since."

If *Sentimental Hygiene* was a deliberate push in introducing Warren to a new generation of fans, "Detox Mansion" was the song that his original listeners—those critics and baby boomers who still held fond memories of the energetic heyday of Los Angeles's most notorious rock troubadour—were surely waiting for. With Warren's cunning humor back in full force, he gives a tongue-in-cheek account of his times in and out of rehabilitation, taking on the exaggerated role of a burned-out rock star detoxing at a luxurious rehab clinic. Among his fellow "guests" are Liza Minnelli and Liz Taylor and, much as "Gorilla, You're a Desperado" had parodied the propensities of the "Me Generation" for racquetball and therapeutic analysis, so the spoiled celebs at "Detox Mansion" pat themselves on the back for doing their laundry between rounds of golf. While some critics didn't approve of his teasing attitude toward the dark trend of celebrity substance abuse, indoctrinated Zevonites applauded the return of their favorite rock-and-roll social commentator. Warren later claimed that the earliest version of the tune had sounded like Johnny Cash's "I Walk the Line," while the earliest performances found him also incorporating Cash's signature thumbed-guitar bass line, coupled with a melodic mimicry of Cash's famous baritone drop in in the verses of "Folsom Prison Blues."

"It wouldn't be a Warren Zevon album if it wasn't likely to stir up trouble with someone somewhere down the line," wrote Chris Willman in *The Los Angeles Times*. "The new 'Sentimental Hygiene' is the acclaimed singer/songwriter's first album in five years, and one of the incendiary record's most prominent satires is a sizzling ditty called 'Detox Mansion,' which pokes sharp-pointed fun at the celebrity withdrawal syndrome and those who would check into the well-appointed Betty Ford Center rushing to tell their victory stories on *Entertainment Tonight*." In *The Village Voice*, Robert Christgau added, "'Detox Mansion' sends up every pampered substance abuser turned therapy addict in Tinseltown."

As the man who had inspired the song's title, it was only right that Jorge Calderón come down to the studio to sing alongside Warren. As Warren later recalled, David Lindley overdubbed "many layers of lap steel guitar parts, one of which he referred to with great seriousness as 'The Wibble-Wobble.'" Lindley's almighty "Wibble-Wobble" was in fact a *baglama*—or bowed *saz*—an obscure Turkish lute not usually associated with rock-and-roll albums. The track was released as the fourth single off *Sentimental Hygiene,* and to many older listeners who remembered Warren's ongoing, very public struggle with addiction, the song became synonymous with his comeback and welcome return to their musical landscape.

The next track utilized a similar oblong, plucked instrument, as Warren incorporated session sitar player Darius Degher into his final arrangement of "Bad Karma," perhaps the most R.E.M.-influenced of the album's sessions and the album's fifth single. Lyrically, Warren had here penned another humorous "woe is me" fable in the recognizable vein of "Poor Poor Pitiful Me," but now from a weathered and world-weary narrative voice, and from a man ready to chalk his misfortune up to a spiritual level. R.E.M.'s lead singer, Michael Stipe, laid down harmony vocals, giving "Bad Karma" the good fortune of having that band's entire lineup present, giving Warren's "mild reincarnation spoof" the appropriate balance and palatable pop leanings. The same could be said of "Even a Dog Can Shake Hands," the biting pseudo-sequel to "Detox Mansion," in which our antihero narrator is apparently back home in Los Angeles, trying to get by in a house on Mulholland while every possible person already has their hands out for a financial piece of his comeback; as stated, even his beloved canine seemed to have his own agenda these days. He later described the song as his version of the Byrds' 1967 satirical pop hit "So You Wanna Be a Rock 'n' Roll Star." Of his Beatles-influenced incorporation of the Indian sitar, Warren later offered, "It seemed like an agreeable gag."

Although unintentional, as a companion piece to "Detox Mansion," Warren had come full circle with a short, semi-autobiographical narrative, updating all the themes and humor of F. Scott Fitzgerald's later Pat Hobby stories, swapping an aging screenwriter's various misadventures through a haze of functional alcoholism for the similar challenges facing a 1980s rock star cashing in on his much-hyped sobriety. "Those looking for Zevon to release a highly personal, confessional saga of his struggles after five years' absence may be disappointed by the lack of overt autobiography in *Sentimental Hygiene,*" wrote *The Los Angeles Times,* overlooking Warren's veiled roman à clef within the rock and roll. And nearly a decade after radios across the world had blared the soon familiar sound of Warren's primal howl, he now made sure to bark appropriately for the hard anthem's fade-out.

As close to home as the humorous rock track's subject material seems, it had actually been an equal-parts collaboration between Warren and the three R.E.M. members who'd made up his core band. While Warren may have had years of playing the Hollywood celebrity game under his belt, Berry, Buck, and Mills's stars would only rise over the next decade; their additions to this critical assessment of the music industry was only a harbinger as they slowly became one of the quintessential bands of the next decade.

"Reconsider Me" had become the unofficial theme song of *Sentimental Hygiene*'s release, even more so than the title track or the immediately popular "Detox Mansion." With "Reconsider Me," Warren had crossed over into the most popular of radio-friendly 1980s genres, the power ballad. But even within the confines of his new, self-described "heavy metal folk" status, he composed a genuine ballad to help round out the album. Upon their earliest meetings, Virgin executive Jeff Ayeroff had made it a point to emphasize Warren's potential romantic appeal in the album's marketing. Notoriously self-conscious about his vocal work, Warren leapt at the chance to record a proper ballad. With "The Heartache," he returned to terrain similar to "Hasten Down the Wind" and enlisted some old friends: bassist Leland Sklar, Waddy Wachtel on guitars, and Jennifer Warnes for harmony vocals. As far as his instructions to the members of R.E.M. on the delicacy needed to address the gentle tune, he advised them, "You gotta pick this thing like pussy," mimicking his own father's similar advice.

With the reunion feel of its guest appearances and an arrangement reminiscent of Warren's 1970s work, had *Sentimental Hygiene* been made during his Elektra/Asylum tenure, "The Heartache" could have potentially served as a traditional Zevon closer. Marking a distinct departure from that era, Warren's Virgin debut concluded with his first foray into overtly commercial dance trends with "Leave My Monkey Alone"—an electronically fused, funk hybrid. Featuring prominent cameo appearances by Parliament funkmaster George Clinton and flamboyant Red Hot Chili Peppers bass virtuoso Flea, the song ushered in Warren's first use of computer programming via drum machines and sound effects—in this case, the calls of chimpanzees.

When the song was selected as the sixth and final single off the album, Warren was given the full 1980s treatment: a ten-minute dance remix was added, in the hopes of it working its way into the Los Angeles club circuit. The colorful music video, featuring Warren dancing alongside George Clinton bizarrely juxtaposed against public domain footage of political violence in Africa, was choreographed by singer and dancer Paula Abdul, only one year away from her own string of mainstream hits. But, as was always the case with Warren, even in the most commercial of circumstances, his subject matter was unorthodox, to say the least. *The Los Angeles Times* accurately described it as "a dance number that touches on the violent conflict between the colonialists and Mau Mau in 1950s Africa"; the song also gave Warren homework for the first time since "Veracruz." As he later recalled, "It took some research to find the Swahili part of that song. . . . And as far back as 'Frank and Jesse James,' I've tried to make sure that the facts [that] are presented as facts in a song are historically accurate. Which takes some of the burden of being poetic off me, too, when I'm getting things out of history books."

Niko Bolas remembered of the sessions, "Warren knew what he was doing, always. His professionalism was always the same during that album—it wouldn't matter if we were doing demos, or if it was a real record, or live at the Grammys—he only knew one way, which was all the way. To me, that was what made him a genius."

∞

Critics and longtime fans were quick to note the apparent shifts in Warren's persona and songwriting. Unlike the unrepentant alcoholic who had once asked his wife to have press releases issued to alert the world of his rehab stints, during the promotional tour for *Sentimental Hygiene,* Warren deliberately steered all interviews away from the subject of his checkered past. "Although he wrote and sings about addiction and rehabilitation, Zevon will not discuss his own battles," the *Sun-Sentinel*'s Chauncey Mabe wrote, "at least not with reporters."

"I don't have much to say about alcoholism," Warren had responded. "'Detox Mansion' is about people who go through it and become oracles just because of their celebrity. It's clear that I don't drink or do drugs, and I will talk about it to people individually. But it's much too serious a topic for me to be quoted on."

Warren had uttered similar sentiments to the *Philadelphia Inquirer,* apparently regretful for the extreme candor with which he had once revealed himself to Paul Nelson. "[Now] I don't even use mouthwash," he told John Milward, "but I've also decided that talking about it publicly is no longer helpful to me. Whatever my intentions were back then—to save the world, I suppose—no longer apply. Certainly my sobriety is important to me, but it's a personal matter now."

Many critics wouldn't let him off the hook so easily, however. "Wait a minute," wrote *The Los Angeles Times*' Chris Willman. "Wasn't it Zevon who was publicly detailing his battles with alcoholism years ago? And didn't he have a few problems before he finally climbed on the wagon not all that long ago? Where does he get off giving those who are 'raking leaves with Liza' and 'cleanin' up the yard with Liz' a hard time?"

To that, Warren had retorted, "Well, I figured I was giving myself a hard time first and foremost."

But those critics had also noted that in a relatively short amount of time, Warren's well-known, long-term classical ambitions had seemed to shift, as well. Earlier in the day of Bob Dylan's harmonica session for "The Factory," Warren had proudly played some of an in-progress symphonic work entitled "Prelude" for Virgin executive Jeff Ayeroff.

Ayeroff had responded, "Don't give up your day job."

Five months later, the *Philadelphia Inquirer* said of Warren, "He no longer pretends that a symphonic work is just around the corner." When Steve Tarson of the *Sun-Sentinel* inquired about his "long-awaited symphony," Warren had offered, "When there's time, I'll try to write something a little more realistic."

∽

The *Sentimental Hygiene* tour kicked off the first week of September 1987, less than a month after the album's release. Virgin had opted to release all six of Warren's individual singles in the weeks building to *Sentimental Hygiene*'s August 29 street date. By the time he made his triumphant return to *Late Night with David Letterman* in mid-July, the studio audience was already familiar with his night's performance piece, "Boom Boom Mancini." Once seated across Letterman's desk, the two had no problems getting their warm camaraderie going again. Following a glowing review of *Sentimental Hygiene*, Letterman was quick to ask what Warren had been up to for five years. "Touring salad bars," Warren had quipped to the host's amusement. "I'd be putting my amp next to the Thousand Island, going, 'Don't get any croutons in the electric piano!' But," he added, "I was going to tell you I was breeding pit bulls."

Letterman had been particularly surprised by Warren's turn at lead guitar during the "Boom Boom Mancini" performance, prompting Warren to proudly relay how he'd gotten $200 out of Andrew Slater for the album recording's final piano solo. In his recollection, however, Warren added that Slater had first tried to write him a check—which just wouldn't do. "I need cash, man," he recalled telling the young producer.

"Didn't you feel guilty?" Letterman asked, grinning.

"For about five seconds," Warren said, smirking.

∽

Having the members of R.E.M. had its pluses and its minuses. While the album had benefited greatly from the youthful and stellar playing of Bill Berry, Peter Buck, and Mike Mills, their own superstardom kept the band's dance card pretty full. For the *Late Night* appearance, Warren performed his latest single with Letterman's esteemed house band.

But a full-scale world tour was imminent, leaving him and Slater the crucial task of recruiting a tight, steady road band. They were able to get star founding members of Little Feat, Kenny Gradney on bass and Richie Hayward on drums, joined by seasoned lead guitarist Greg Beck and multi-instrumentalist Karen Childs, now primarily handling keyboards, to allow for Warren's starring lead guitar turns.

"Mr. Zevon has suffered from alcoholism, but at the Beacon he was in full control and strong in voice," reported *The New York Times*' Jon Pareles. "While he slighted his best album, *The Envoy,* his set mixed a few good new songs with tough-minded old ones . . . The set showed the geopolitical savvy of Mr. Zevon's older songs, and he updated lyrics on the spot, landing 'Roland the Headless Thompson Gunner' in TriBeCa and singing about Judge Robert H. Bork in 'Mohammed's Radio.' The concert wasn't a comeback, but a return from hibernation, lean and mean."

Critics took note that Warren still seemed to enjoy performing his older, better-known material, both to take full advantage of once again having a large, quality band, and also for the energetic recognition that the songs received from tried-and-true fans in attendance. "Zevon worked the crowd at the Front Row Theatre in Highland Heights like a carnival barker, dusting off his unique, terror-laden pop repertoire," wrote Carlo Wolff of *The Akron Beacon Journal.* "His trademark baritone sounded fine, and he played vigorous piano and guitar . . . Though his band performed little from his new *Sentimental Hygiene* album, it stormed through material from his best record, *Excitable Boy.* Surprisingly, he also delivered a hard, funny version of Prince's 'Raspberry Beret.'"

Critics also took note of the political edge present in his stage banter. "These are terrible times," Warren had said to his New York audience at the Beacon Theater, "and I shouldn't be joking about them." That didn't prevent him from suggesting that the NFL players then striking be sent "to third-world countries where we don't belong," as his biting cue for the band to launch into "Jungle Work." Only a few weeks later at the Landmark Theater in Syracuse, he returned to the theme. "People sometimes ask me why I write disturbing songs like that," he quipped to the amused audience. "I tell them I never found rock and roll particularly disturbing . . . Reading the newspaper? Now that disturbs me. Acts of war in the Persian Gulf? I find that kinda disturbing. All those earthquakes back home, those are disturbing . . . But then again, there's the most terrifying of all—the NFL strike."

At any given time in his life, Warren was in the middle of reading upward of five books during the same period; he admittedly used current events and the daily newspaper headlines as fodder for his writing and took advantage of his touring schedule to scout each visited city for local museums, art galleries, and concert halls. But he had always steered clear of politics. Crystal recalled that Warren had only taken part in 1978's "Save the Whales" concert campaigns because Jackson Browne had urged him to join him for the brief tour. Likewise, Anita Gevinson recalled Warren's panic when an interviewer had begun asking his views on international affairs. "He was funny politically, unless he was fascinated by the topic," she said. "I remember being in a hotel suite with him and he was being interviewed and I was still in bed in the adjoining room. They had asked him some topical thing and he burst in and asked me, 'Am I for the Sandinistas or the Contras? Which one is Jackson for, again?'"

After coping with disintegrating tour budgets for over half a decade, the one for *Sentimental Hygiene* was easily the most extravagant of Warren's career. Having grown accustomed to rearranging and modulating his old songbook for the necessity—and having also acted as his own road manager of sorts during the Philadelphia years—the end of 1987 found Warren in a lap of luxury unimaginable following the Elektra/Asylum termination. Many of the stops throughout the tour included a few days of press opportunities and rounds of interviews with local major outlets; in New York, Virgin had put Warren up in a suite at the Helmsley Palace, which John Milward noted made Warren appear "somewhat self-conscious about his sumptuous surroundings."

Clad in black jeans, a black T-shirt, black sneakers, and a fully cultivated sandy beard, Warren had walked to the window before commenting on Milward's observation. "At these rates," he finally said, facing the New York City street below, "they let you jump if you choose."

During the interview, Milward also took note of the eclectic hodge-podge scattered around Warren's sitting room: coffee, Silk Cut cigarettes—he was smoking again—and a stack of well-thumbed books, including the 1969 compendium of world poetry, a poetry compendium called *Technicians of the Sacred,* a mystery novel by Jonathan Valin, and both David Schiff's biography of American atonal classical composer Elliott Carter and a separate book of Carter's original sheet music. Warren shared his preference for reading along with the score when listening to classical works on his new headphones. He also had just purchased the books during that New York visit; bookstores within walking distance of the hotel was the first order of business in every city he visited—once he had cleared the room of any and all "unlucky" objects and omens.

Warren's odd behavior had a cause. It was a by-product of his diligence in remaining sober, but only flickers had shown themselves throughout his years of drinking and drugs. Years earlier, Warren had enlisted his father's help in getting him out of the military draft. Crystal later recalled that Warren couldn't bear to look at posters for Army recruitment following his disingenuous play at dodging service in Vietnam, and now girlfriend Merle Ginsberg was witness to seemingly stranger behavioral ticks. At first curiously charming, she noticed that his entire wardrobe now exclusively contained gray items of clothing—a symbolic ritual that harkened back to his banishment of the color green following his departure from lyme and cybelle in 1967. "He was truly the most superstitious person I have ever met," Ginsberg later recalled how his behavior shifted toward changing color preferences. "He wore gray cashmere sweaters from Ralph Lauren, gray jeans, which were never easy to find, gray knickers, gray Calvin Klein underwear, gray Calvin Klein T-shirts, he had a gray Corvette and all his furniture was gray. He wouldn't even touch black."

Old friend Jimmy Wachtel later recalled a memorable sight in Warren's home in "Cat Piss Manor," having taken a peek inside his sock drawer. "He had a drawer of socks that were all the same socks," Wachtel claimed. "He had like forty pair of gray socks all balled up in this drawer, and I thought it was one of the greatest art pieces I'd ever seen." He also theorized on the nature of Warren's unspoken obsession with the color itself, recalling, "Warren was hung up on the color gray, which for me is like not white and not black, it's gray. It's like walking down on a tightrope . . . you're not here, you're not there."

Even Warren's new brand of Silk Cut cigarettes came with its own set of dogmatic practices. Later in the tour, Warren's new road manager, Stuart Ross, quickly caught on to the demands that the syndrome seemingly dictated. "[Warren] told me Silk Cuts were hard to get in the places we were going," Ross later recalled, "so he said, 'I need you to get me three or four cartons of these cigarettes.' Then he said, they can't have the C-word on the warning."

"What?" Ross had asked, confused by the request.

"Look," Warren told him, "I don't care what they talk about on the warning, but it can't have the C-word."

Before the tour launched, Ross found a tobacco shop in Beverly Hills apparently unfazed by the strange requests of their patrons. When he stipulated that "cancer" couldn't be present on the warning disclaimers of the packs within, they didn't "bat an eye." Low birth weight wasn't an issue, but the "C" word was unacceptable.

Although no one in Warren's life was completely certain when or how his obsessive-compulsive disorder began, it became overtly pronounced to friends and colleagues soon after his release from Minnesota's Detox Mansion. Andrew Slater recalled Warren asking him in the studio how often he washed his hands throughout the day. When Slater estimated about two or three, Warren had asked, "You don't ever wash 'em like thirty, huh?"

"He had the whole thing about stepping on lines in the street," Slater recalled. "He told me that whenever he heard the word 'cancer' in a day, anything he had bought, shoes, food, anything, he'd have to return everything, or get rid of it."

Gevinson recalled that Warren's OCD seemed to manifest when things were at their lowest points, both his career and personal life. And when he was distancing himself from alcohol or drugs, the concept of luck became his focused nemesis. "He thought anything bad that happened was just bad luck," she later recalled. "Any time something would work against him or roadblock an idea or project, he would go, 'Now look!' or 'More bad luck!' He would mutter and repeat his little mantra in the apartment, 'Nothing's bad luck, is it?' but not to anyone in particular."

In the past, Warren had often used his touring schedule as a way to visit with friends and family; his longest gap in keeping in touch had been during his stint in Philadelphia, which, aside from his condition at that point, had also yielded no performances he'd wanted them to see. Now riding the wave of the largest and highest-budgeted tour of his entire career, he was proud to connect with his cousins in New York, returning to them in glory.

"During my college years, [Warren] mainly toured alone, although I saw him perform in Providence with some of the Eagles," his cousin Lawrence recalled. "That was a cool show because none of the people I met in school believed that Warren was my cousin and, suffice it to say, this convinced them—especially when they waited for me to reappear from backstage to catch a ride back to campus." Lawrence recalled that most of his best visits with his famous big cousin was when Warren would be passing through with Duncan Aldrich, beginning with their New York stops during the *Sentimental Hygiene* tour. "Duncan was very cool and always remembered me and my brothers," he said, "and without so much as asking, he made sure we got to spend time with Warren . . . After [*Late Night with David Letterman*], my brothers and I wanted to hang out with Warren, who was sober at this time, and my brother Dan convinced him to take a walk with us to his bar, Crossroads, on Seventy-Seventh and Second Avenue. It was a cold fall night and I think Warren was frozen when we got there, but he was game to show us how to make a 'great drink.' In the end, it was just a Diet Coke and a slice of orange—so much for the mystique!"

On the few occasions that Warren was able to carve out time for his younger family members, the generosity that he always bestowed on his own children in lieu of being physically present trickled down. As a child who been bounced around between the homes of both divorced parents, Warren seemed to revel in becoming the cool older-brother figure for his cousin Sandford's sons. "I also want to convey how generous Warren was," Lawrence said. "He loved Hammacher Schlemmer and our gifts were these cool things like, for example, a snow-cone machine—totally random, but so cool. Once after a show when I was in college, Warren mentioned his next stop was playing St. Lawrence. I said, 'Oh man, I'd like a shirt,' since I wanted my first name as its logo. A week later, I had every conceivable item from the school bookstore—shorts, hats, T-shirts, a sweatshirt, everything.

"Most of my time with Warren was backstage at clubs, and when the conversation moved away from family and usually to random topics like Francis Bacon and intellectual talk, I struggled to keep up with him," Lawrence fondly remembered. "Warren was incredibly bright and witty and sometimes it could be intimidating, frankly, because I think he assumed I was at his intelligence level—and I'm sure not many were."

∽

Even amid the positive reviews, both Virgin executives and Warren himself began to notice that audience numbers dipped as the two-month-long, fifty-city tour rolled on. By the first week of October, the second half of the *Sentimental Hygiene* tour was downgraded to smaller venues, finding Warren playing sold-out club dates as opposed to semifilled arenas. Still, the insinuation made by the budget cuts depressed him. When the numbers for *Sentimental Hygiene* rolled in just prior to the European leg of the tour toward the end of the year, their results sparked no more enthusiasm. Releasing the six singles within a short amount of time prior to the full album's release hadn't quite backfired, but it resolved much of the mystery behind Warren's "comeback" before the push that was needed to catapult *Sentimental Hygiene* to blockbuster status. Songs like "Boom Boom Mancini" and "Reconsider Me" had been on the radio and available as stand-alone singles for nearly a month before their parent album hit the street. The album's title track fared best of the bunch, remaining on the *Billboard* charts for nine weeks, and reaching its peak at Number 9 by the first week of June. Enthusiasm waned by the time "Detox Mansion" was released at the beginning of August, spending a mere three weeks on the chart and only reaching a peak 44 position. When the album itself came out two weeks after that, the buzz had already dimmed. *Sentimental Hygiene* spent a reasonable eighteen weeks on the *Billboard* chart, but terrified Virgin executives with its meager spot at Number 63—not the numbers the record label had been expecting when Warren, Slater, and company had gone way over their original budget, ballooning to the $1 million Virgin had no choice but to cover.

Playing a near-identical touring strategy Elektra/Asylum had used in recouping their losses for 1982's *The Envoy,* when Warren returned from Europe in July 1988, he was already booked for another around the United States—a solo tour.

CHAPTER NINE

(1988–1990)

WARREN HAD VERY LITTLE PREVENTING HIM FROM EMBARK-
ing on a European trip for as long as the label dictated. After a little over two years together, his relationship with Merle Ginsberg had
come to what she later described as an "ugly" end. The first few months
had coincided with three consecutive lapses in Warren's sobriety, all of
which had required Slater to escort him back to rehab.

On tour, he'd been able to stay as strong as possible, even amid the
stress of returning to the stage after so many years away. The small-
time gigs he'd suffered through at the end of 1983 were like a boxer's
rise to a title shot through a series of human punching bags. That disastrous European festival circuit, his drunken offering of refunds to
dissatisfied attendees in Cork, Ireland—experiences like palookas in
comparison to a heavyweight challenge like New York City's Beacon
Theater. But that pressure hadn't broken him—*The New York Times*
had praised the show, and his focus. Even the constant temptation of
watching younger musicians drinking and smoking pot on tour, as annoying a spectacle as it was, didn't wear him down. "He could never
be around alcohol," Merle Ginsberg later recalled. "If he saw a liquor
bottle, he'd have a meltdown." But that mental willpower manifested
elsewhere, as Warren's OCD habits deepened and expanded, as did his
temper. Noting that Warren was "always in a dark mood," she recalled
one incident when they were grocery shopping and she'd inadvertently

selected a carton of milk that wasn't "lucky" enough to his satisfaction. "I'd come back with the milk," she said, "and he'd say, 'That's not lucky. You didn't get a lucky one.'"

Like many within Warren's close circle of friends, Ginsberg initially wrote off the odd habits and mood swings as just Warren being a typical creative type—a brooding rock star, with all the spoiled demands and behavior ticks that came with it. Only after they had been dating monogamously for a number of months—and Ginsberg had been privy to more than a few of Warren's tumbles off the wagon—did she realize the correlation between his drinking and his obsessive superstitions. Those in turn had also started influencing his eating and cleaning habits, which Ginsberg found "disgusting." She didn't know what to make of his explaining a love of fruit flies being the reason he wouldn't take out the accumulating trash. When he told her that he had begun to name them, she couldn't be sure whether he'd been joking. "But," she recalled, "he was fastidious about himself. And his laundry. He was fanatical about how his laundry was done. He loved art and beautiful things, but he lived in squalor."

It was a dynamic that Warren's friends had long noted: even in his ongoing pursuit of the seemingly unattainable "quiet, normal life," there was a part of him that needed a timeshare in the seedier part of town. For every cottage in Los Feliz, there was a room at the Hollywood Hawaiian he couldn't cover; for every single-family home in Montecito, there was a mink-lined sniper's nest at the Chateau Marmont, down the hall from a willing groupie.

Warren had first asked Ginsberg to move to Los Angeles indefinitely before the *Sentimental Hygiene* sessions were underway. Since his return to Los Angeles, Warren had made a genuine attempt at his recovery, never missing his A.A. meetings and instilling its positive influence in his personal life. Within a month of becoming Virgin's first US client, he had successfully completed the fourth step of A.A.'s twelve-step program. Having proudly made the required "searching and moral inventory" of himself, Warren had set the list aflame and watched as his sponsor advised him to welcome the smoke's aroma as the smell of victory. Although Warren had been warned by multiple advisors from A.A. about the risks of attempting a serious romantic relationship so soon in his recovery, his long-distance love affair with Ginsberg seemed stable enough to continue its path. Serenading her over the phone was one thing, but what good was having a beautiful, younger girlfriend if she wasn't around to attend concerts and PR events with him? With a certain amount of misgivings, but excited nonetheless, Ginsberg put in the machinations to leave *Rolling Stone* and find some form of journalistic employment in Los Angeles.

As Ginsberg later recalled, by the time she up and left New York, there was very little love lost between her and the editors of *Rolling Stone*. Many of her fellow writers began to treat her differently now that she had crossed the unspoken, sacred line of becoming personally involved with one of her interview subjects; Paul Nelson had made the same mistake years earlier, inadvertently making himself a major player in the epic saga of Warren's 1978 downward spiral. Now, *Rolling Stone*'s new corporate atmosphere had almost no tolerance for a writer who had no issues in dating the stars they were supposed to cover objectively. She later recalled, "Suddenly, I was a rock star's girlfriend and my coworkers started to hate me for that."

The mood at *Rolling Stone* had shifted almost immediately after her feature article pitch to publisher Jann Wenner. Having read all of Paul Nelson's extensive coverage of Warren's past, Ginsberg was excited at the prospect of penning a new work on his newfound sobriety and apparent return to superstardom. She was shocked at Wenner's response, and vividly remembered the heated exchange that took place in the publisher's office when she told him of Warren's new sobriety and comeback status. "He's not sober," Wenner said. "I've known him for years and it ain't happening. We are not running that bullshit." Wenner put his feelings succinctly, adding that to him, Warren was merely "the greatest at fucking up."

Ginsberg hadn't been completely deterred by Wenner's words. Although the interview with Warren that she'd prepared for publication never ran, her fascination with him continued past the confines of the journalistic assignment. They continued to date as the *Sentimental Hygiene* sessions rolled on, until finally she was able to solidify a job in Los Angeles with the new basic-cable entertainment network, the E! channel. As soon as Ginsberg shared the good news, however, his nerves immediately took over. "I told him I was going to move there, thinking that's all he wanted in the world," she later recalled. "But, he was freaked out . . . He said, 'What are you going to do? Where are you going to live?' I thought, don't you want me to be with you? The minute I was going to give everything up to be with him, it freaked him out."

Ginsberg had already walked from *Rolling Stone* and her start date at E! was imminent, making her relocation to Los Angeles a done deal. In balancing his focus between the studio work for *Sentimental Hygiene* and proactively walking the tight line of maintained sobriety, Warren soon became a higher-maintenance boyfriend than the younger journalist had bargained for. She later recalled that their relationship soon became for her "a full-time job," with all the chores, habits, and unconditional acceptance of his behavioral quirks thrown into the mix. "He expected me to go to the grocery store with him," Ginsberg recalled. "We'd go to Book Soup and buy a million magazines and books. Then, we'd go to the video store and rent movies he'd already seen."

Ginsberg later realized that Warren not only watched the same films over and over again out of habit, but that all the rituals that were becoming his creature comforts were part of the larger scope of his aggressive alcoholism suppression. She added, "I realized that this is the behavior of someone who is disturbed and depressed, but he was in recovery, and my idea was that this was the life of someone in recovery. As he got sober over the next year, he was working on his album. The happiest I ever saw Warren was when he was in the recording studio. He came alive and he was a different person."

As part of Ginsberg's new position with the fledging entertainment network, her assignments shifted from covering the music industry to the movie industry. Initially excited at the boost she was able to give her career with the move to Los Angeles, Ginsberg recalled the disappointment over Warren's lack of enthusiasm regarding just about everything—including the swanky events and movie premieres her new job entailed. "He never wanted to go out in public," she later recalled. "He felt like people were staring at him. He hated most movies. I started dragging him a little bit because he was utterly miserable."

Warren returned from the *Sentimental Hygiene* European leg at the end of February, just in time to celebrate his second anniversary of sobriety. He had successfully reached the eleventh and twelfth steps—advanced-level spiritual maxims urging the alcoholic to use prayer and meditation in their struggle for inner strength. He reread them obsessively before their final phone call. "The conversation was very short," Ginsberg remembered. "He said, 'My sponsor says I've been drunk and married, drunk and alone, and sober and with you. But I've never been sober and alone, and I think it would be a good thing for me to be sober and alone for a while.'" Ginsberg recalled leaving the conversation with a "very different" view than Warren, as she had assumed it would be a temporary breather in the relationship, yet "Warren thought we were breaking up."

∞

By 1988's Sick 'Em Dogs on Me Tour, critics were beginning to refer to Warren as a "cult favorite." While accurate, those were not exactly the words Virgin executives were hoping to hear about the recipient of an unprecedented—and costly—PR push to win him mainstream appeal. He was contracted at Virgin for two albums, meaning much was riding on *Sentimental Hygiene*'s follow-up.

Fortunately for Warren, he wasn't pressed for new material. Sobriety and travel had provided inspiration enough to fuel his writing. As the new songs came together, it was apparent that for the second time in his career, the resulting product would be an ambitious concept album. Just as his goofy 1981 *American Bandstand* European lip-synch tour with George Gruel had inspired the international-intrigue themes of *The Envoy*, so Warren's new interests in digital technology and cyberpunk literature attracted him to the science-fiction genre.

Despite conflicting critical opinion, *Sentimental Hygiene* had been densely autobiographical; songs like "Detox Mansion," "Trouble Waiting to Happen," and "Reconsider Me" had all come from such a personal place within Warren, they could have been poetic journal entries. And any debate regarding the true meaning of "sentimental hygiene" need only consider the sixth step of Warren's new twelve-step code of sobriety: he was indeed ready to have a higher power remove his defects of character, and to ask Him to remove his shortcomings. He prayed the third-step prayer over and over like a mantra, begging for a release from the bondage of self. He prayed for the cleansing of a soul riddled with filth from years of rock-and-roll debauchery.

Warren's follow-up would find him coming to grips with strange, new external surroundings. After devouring William Gibson's 1984 science-fiction masterpiece *Neuromancer* while on the road, and "woozy from reading the Thomas Pynchon canon in one sitting," he had decided a nightmarish dystopia would be tellingly appropriate for expressing those observations. His debut on Virgin had been deeply autobiograph-ical: an honest expression of his struggle to attain lasting sobriety; the new album would explore the urban nightmare only those now sober eyes could see.

"I wanted to make this one like a really good novel," he later told *The Chicago Tribune*. "For good or ill, it was going to be a concept album. Which meant that three-quarters of the way through, I couldn't write a song about 11th Century Indian architecture because I felt like it." Upon his return from Japan in July 1988, Warren put his full fo-cus into the production of his "2010 sci-fi project," soon to be entitled *Transverse City*.

∞

This time around, Virgin refused to hand over nearly as generous a bud-get as they'd done for *Sentimental Hygiene*. The bulk of the recording took place at Red Zone studios in Burbank, but with the option of more digital technology in the arrangement and editing processes, War-ren was able to use the scaled-down experience to his advantage.

With his unique expertise of the modern engineering equipment be-ing used, Duncan Aldrich was promoted to a place beside Warren and Andrew Slater as a fellow producer. "It was odd for me because I came off of working with people like Chick Corea," Aldrich recalled. "I was originally looking down on rock [music] after working with musicians with such amazing chops, versus working within a music that could be considered much more primitive—you know, great musicians, but in a much more primitive style. So, there was a period of adjustment, but I admired Warren and the musicians that I had been working with."

Aldrich later recalled *Transverse City* as the instance when Warren's elevated creative control reached its most expansive. "I was trying to make the thing as good as possible and keep it in a budget, which I was [doing]," Aldrich later said. "Then, Slater would come along and hire all these people, and he ended up not paying me more for a bunch of it, and that ended up ripping the seam between Warren and myself, even though I knew he had nothing to do with it."

While Virgin hadn't exactly left the trio high and dry, the slashed budget was meager in comparison to the inflated financial backing of *Sentimental Hygiene*. As the label saw it, handing over less funding for *Transverse City* wasn't punishment for going over the previous budget;

those bailout funds had been more like an advance on the new album—and as Virgin saw it, Warren, Slater, and Aldrich had already spent it. As far as what was left over for *Transverse City,* the three producers would just have to get creative.

Much to Aldrich's dismay, even working within the confines of their budgetary limitations, Slater insisted on enlisting the usual suspects of high-profile guest appearances—something Aldrich didn't feel was necessary, and stated so. Ultimately, compromises would be plotted to make a few of the most prestigious cameos happen, thanks in no small part to Aldrich and Warren's innovative use of digital computer-editing—a first for such a rock-and-roll album. By 1989, high-quality digital audio workstations and digital multitrack systems were slowly becoming the industry standard, and with Aldrich's guidance, Warren was ahead of the curve. As *The Chicago Tribune* later reported, "With the aid of Duncan Aldrich, Zevon learned the musical capabilities of a Macintosh computer and created the glistening orchestrations."

The use of new digital technology worked to keep costs lower, while some of the guest appearances, such as David Gilmour's and Neil Young's, were recorded off-site and sent back for editing. Given the dystopian, postapocalyptic tone of the album, the technological fail-safes throughout the production seemed entirely appropriate.

Throughout the Sic 'Em Dogs on Me Tour, Warren had tested the waters on a few of the new songs. Knowing ahead of time that their final versions would be heavily produced in line with the sonic scope of the album he was planning, Warren first introduced songs like "Networking" and "Splendid Isolation" acoustically. Audiences were somewhat confounded by the maudlin, dystopian tone of some songs' earliest forms. When he played the Park West in November, *Chicago Tribune* critic David Silverman wrote of his appreciation for the older fare, yet noted audience disapproval of Warren's new work. "There is little doubt that Zevon knew what his audience was hoping for," wrote Silverman. "He delivered these favorites willingly, with a smile and a wink. Then it was time for some untitled songs, new cuts from a yet-to-be-released album, *Transverse City*. It was a collection of sordid ballads, probably due for reworking in the studio, judging from a lukewarm audience response."

By the time Warren got down to Red Zone studios, each song had been refined enough to accommodate the many layers of overdubs and special effects he had in mind for his cinematic song cycle. From the opening sounds of *Transverse City*'s title track, listeners were transported into the nightmarish landscape of Warren's design: the audible electric current summoning computer-programmed arpeggios like an electronic overture, his narration soon rhyming a list of dark imagery like ominous signposts—equal parts futuristic technological advancements and poverty-stricken tenements. More Ridley Scott's bleak neon iridescence of *Blade Runner* than William Gibson's *Neuromancer, Transverse City*'s immediate sense of angered culture shock and crippling paranoia made it all Warren.

Unlike with his previous albums, *Transverse City*'s tightened budget had necessitated much of its overdubbing; with *The Envoy,* producer and lead guitarist Waddy Wachtel had likewise experimented with layering, but for dramatic effect. With Virgin now pushing a quicker turnaround time and hurried promotional tour, Warren, Aldrich, and Slater had to work with the respective schedules of the album's many esteemed guests. Coupled with the few instances of those guests sending in their prerecorded parts, this also meant that some of *Transverse City*'s songs sat in periods of limbo, awaiting different parts to be edited in later—the first time Warren had been given the task of assembling individual tracks piecemeal, and over extended periods of weeks. It was largely due to both the modern digital technology that the team had at their disposal—and Aldrich's and Slater's pragmatic use of it—that the frazzled production came together.

Although the album's title track had been written even earlier than preproduction, in order to secure Jerry Garcia's wailing lead guitar sections of both "Transverse City" and, later, on "They Moved the Moon," the sessions were pushed to mid-June. Warren and Slater had to drive to San Rafael to Garcia's home, aka the Hog Farm, in order to lay down his leads. As was common practice—and more practical with *Transverse City* than ever before—Warren utilized a rotating lineup of session players but was able to secure two mainly consistent solid players for the bulk of the sporadic studio dates: old friend Bob Glaub on bass, and Little Feat's Richie Hayward, who had brought his thundering drum and percussion skills to 1987's *Sentimental Hygiene* tour.

As part of the overarching thematic links between the songs of *Transverse City,* for the first time on any of his albums, Warren opted to "bleed" the tracks into each other, rather than cut each song into individual tracks; the experimental practice wasn't as noticeable on the radio edits or single releases, but the album's overt cinematic tone runs through each track like a daisy chain. For the title track, Warren and Aldrich were able to tinker in postproduction to cross-fade the electric current sound effects seamlessly into the dark tonality of "Run Straight Down"—the second consecutive song emphasizing Warren's inner sense of paranoia amid his strange new landscape. The product itself was a point of pride to the team, as they had been able to secure one of their highest-profile guest appearances on the track: Pink Floyd's legendary lead guitarist David Gilmour. However, due to both budgetary constraints and Gilmour's own hectic schedule, it was arranged for the twenty-four-track tape of his prerecorded lead parts be sent over to Red Zone straight from London. Warren was particularly pleased to find that the audio samples had been sent directly from Abbey Road.

To Warren, "Run Straight Down" epitomized the themes of *Transverse City* even more so than the album's title song. He later recalled, "This track, with several simultaneous vocal lines including a list of carcinogens in the environment I got from [nonprofit organization] the Sierra Club, suggests the dense texture I was striving to create when I ran out of Virgin's money."

For over two years, critics and interviewers had taken note of a distinct coyness in Warren's demeanor when two specific topics would be approached: while in the past, he was not only open about his struggles with addiction, he seemed to wear those battles as badges of honor, proving publicly his priorities were on straight; following his "comeback" signing with Virgin, his candor on the subject rescinded completely. Likewise, he had stopped all mentions of his ongoing frustrations in making time to complete his symphonic works. Once his greatest motivation and ultimate passion project, when the subject of his classic aspirations were broached, Warren now steered the conversations toward his own working knowledge of music theory itself, and how he was adapting those ideas to his rock-and-roll material. Duncan Aldrich's fascination with computer programming and digital editing had unlocked a world of musical options to Warren, who slowly saw the potential for the full creative autonomy the technology could provide. While not nearly as publicly vocal about those interests anymore, Warren nonetheless continued to monitor his contemporaries within the classical music community with as much fervor as his rock-and-roll peers. They were dual interests that would never fade away, even behind the closed doors of Cat Piss Manor—and even when his creative vision seemed to stump even his most ardent advocates.

In the end, Warren would be penning almost all of the album's material without a co-writer—but not for lack of trying. Once one of his closest collaborators, Jorge Calderón's role within Warren's creative process had lessened since the Virgin comeback. He later admitted the primary reason was Warren's overtly personal approach to *Transverse City* and the uncompromising ways in which he was tackling that latest project. He recalled a surprise visit from Warren while bedridden at home with chicken pox. "At the end of the eighties, Warren was obsessed with cyberpunk music," Calderón later recalled. "He gives me a copy of *New Cyber Punk* magazine and says he wants me to get into the theme of his next album. It's a big deal when you get chicken pox at forty, so maybe I didn't get excited enough or something, but I didn't have anything to do with *Transverse City*."

Consistent attendance of A.A. meetings had worked in surrounding Warren with positive influences, a distinct counterbalance to the seedier elements of Los Angeles that he had actively sought out in his youth. Of the lasting friends he made during those meetings was well-known character actor Michael Ironside, who embodied the kind of rough-and-tumble "man's man" that Warren most admired. Ironside recalled his major misstep in offering honest feedback the first time Warren played for him some of the in-progress tracks from *Transverse City*. "There was one song about pollutants and stuff," Ironside later remembered. "I went into the studio one night and just read the list of chemicals in the background when they were mixing it . . . I only listened to it once, and I just didn't get it. I thought it was very overproduced, and it's a lot like a film where it gets so overproduced that what it's about gets lost."

Despite accusations that *Transverse City*'s themes were too fatalistic—some critics considered the album's tone morbidly dark, even for Warren—it was primarily the album's first three tracks that addressed the dystopian themes and pointed paranoia. Linked together, "Transverse City," "Run Straight Down," and finally "The Long Arm of the Law" formed their own thematic trilogy—a three-act cyberpunk tale including all the true elements of a literary dystopia: a futuristic society where technological advances, and the power they yield, are concentrated in the hands of an omnipresent government; economics are polarized between the rich and powerful and the impoverished residents of urban slums; the powerful display an apparent indifference to the dying environment; and finally, digital references, computer-speak, and science-fiction lingo abound. This wasn't the "Song Noir" of Jackson Browne's astute 1976 description. Warren had evolved. This was "Song *Neo* Noir."

Just as stylized electrical currents reminiscent of a Tesla coil bled "Transverse City" seamlessly into the opening of its following track, so the dramatic sounds of urban dissonance bridged "Run Straight Down" into its succeeding track, "The Long Arm of the Law." Here, Warren used the sound effects integration at his disposal to its fullest extent, adding police sirens and search helicopters, crafting the album's most cinematic moment.

As Warren later recalled, he had written the song in the back of his tour bus, presumably with the intention of incorporating the ambitious studio effects for the final version. Like much of the material on *Transverse City,* he rarely performed the song during later tours, mainly due to the material's overall dependency on not only a backing band, but oodles of additional effects.

For the elaborate studio edit, Warren again benefited enormously from Duncan Aldrich's background; not only an expert in the modern equipment that characterized *Transverse City*'s unique sound, the engineer had also spent years working sessions and touring gigs for some of jazz's biggest names. With Warren largely preoccupied with using the new album as a showcase for his guitar acumen, Aldrich reached out to an old friend, jazz fusion pianist Chick Corea, and was able to nail one of the album's most unlikely and highest-profile guests.

None of the first three songs on *Transverse City* would make it to Warren's performance repertoire past the album's promotional tour. On those occasions throughout 1990, the three thematically linked tracks were always played consecutively and with no break in between— solidifying Warren's unspoken intention of making "Transverse City," "Run Straight Down," and "The Long Arm of the Law" a stand-alone cyberpunk rock performance piece. When later asked about the material's thematic thread, Warren joked that the songs had been deliberately sequenced for "maximum depressive effect." He added, "Hey, if the Cure can do it, why not us?"

With "Turbulence," Warren returned to the somewhat playful, hard-edged tunes loaded with geopolitical humor and topical references that had so inspired *The Envoy* six years earlier. As tuned in to current events as ever, Warren aimed his biting and cynical eye toward the then new "glasnost" foreign policy, seeing the United States and the Soviet Union make their first attempts at civil diplomacy in decades. Most notably, the song required Warren to brush up on his language skills—he had penned a full verse in Russian and was gung ho about performing it as authentically as possible. And just like the Polynesian non sequitur of "The Hula Hula Boys," he had been able to cobble just enough humor into the translation. Ultimately, he was able to call for his mommy in near-perfect Russian.

"They Moved the Moon" was one of the bleakest and most intro-spective set of lyrics Warren had ever penned. Brief in its verses and with his slow, reverberated baritone, it wouldn't have been out of place on a spoken-word album. On the surface, words used to describe an ended love affair find its narrator questioning whether or not he is visible to her, or anyone, at all. As Warren had been writing the song during the earliest days of his sobriety and with an apparent spiritual influence, he matched the pensive nature of the song with a sparse studio arrange-ment. Recorded in mid-April, Warren used Jerry Garcia's lead parts from the June visit to the Hog Farm, then overdubbed the famed bassist of Jefferson Airplane and Hot Tuna, Jack Casady, into the moody mix. With Warren's turn on ambient synths, cut with Garcia's periodic ex-clamations of lead guitar riffs, "They Moved the Moon" remained one of the moodiest pieces he'd ever composed.

Confidence had been restored to Warren's ego in the period between *Sentimental Hygiene* and its follow-up, at least in the studio; much of the emotions hidden beneath the science-fiction exterior of the new album were as autobiographically charged as its predecessor. When luminaries such as Bob Dylan and Neil Young had stopped into the studio—first as social calls, then both for collaboration—Warren was assured his work was taken seriously by two fellow writers he'd always admired. In the case of Young, Warren had loved relaying stories of their Record One encounters to friends and interviewers. He jumped at the chance to get Young involved once again—and this encounter would prove even more memorable.

Due to Young's own touring schedule, his guitar parts would have to be recorded at his home in the Santa Cruz Mountains. To Warren, Young's participation was worth the trip. Toward the end of May, he and Slater flew to San Francisco, then drove south the rest of the way to Young's place in Redwood City; Warren had insisted ahead of time that the rented Cadillac be gray in color. From there, they followed Niko Bolas's directions to the sprawling rural property that Young lovingly named Broken Arrow Ranch, seeing firsthand the veritable petting zoo that surrounded the rock legend's home. Warren later recalled that "dogs, ducks, cows, horses, goats, a cat, [and] peacocks" all came up to the Cadillac to "stare at" the visiting city folk. Deep inside the rural facade, however, Young's personal playroom was a state-of-the-art recording studio. *AudioTechnology* journalist Andy Stewart later wrote his memories of the near-mythical studio, where Young enforced a strict no-photography policy. "The interior of the studio looks like a classic California bungalow retreat cabin like the ones you see in old movies," Stewart wrote. "There are pictures, paintings and memorabilia everywhere ... There's nothing about the place that feels remotely like a commercial studio. Redwood is, in fact, the ultimate home studio plonked in the middle of a forest surrounded by hundreds of acres of silence, a silence broken only when Neil plugs in 'Old Black' in the next room. Soundproof, this building most certainly isn't."

Even up until that point, Young hadn't heard any of the completed cuts from *Transverse City,* so Warren and Slater brought along a few new demos. Young opted to add a ferocious lead guitar overdub to "Gridlock"—although Warren sensed he "wasn't that into it"—and harmony vocals on his personal favorite, "Splendid Isolation."

He wouldn't allow Warren and Slater to leave Broken Arrow Ranch before proudly showing them his prized train set.

Before *Transverse City* was released on October 1, 1989, Warren had been through two difficult breakups. Facets of his previous relationship with Merle Ginsberg had worked their way into the album's lovelorn ballads, yet the song he'd written specifically for her, "Angel Dressed in Black," remained unfinished. Throughout the writing and production of *Transverse City,* his primary muse was a young woman he'd met soon upon returning from the European leg of the *Sentimental Hygiene* tour. Continuing his trend of deliberately surrounding himself with "positive influences" that would best relate to his ongoing battle to remain sober, Warren was immediately drawn to Annette Aguilar the first time he had seen her at his regular A.A. meeting in April 1988.

"We were both in twelve-step programs and I had seen him at some of the meetings in Beverly Hills," the now Annette Aguilar-Ramos later recalled. "I think we probably had around the same amount of time living with sobriety and we were both pretty hardcore 'meeting junkies'—meaning we both went every single day. I was not familiar with his work as an artist at all, but I found him quirky and interesting and awkwardly funny."

It took encouraging words from a mutual A.A. friend, "John," to convince Aguilar-Ramos that despite the rock-and-roll facade, Warren's boorish behavior was merely a boyish nervousness. Like a high school student passing a note in class, Warren convinced John to give him the pretty brunette's number. She later recalled the message left on her answering machine: "Hello, this is Warren Zevon," he said. "I'm not going to ask you out on your answering machine, so you'll have to call me back."

Aguilar-Ramos was instantly flattered by the playful message, especially coming from someone who "embodied the reclusive rock star." She remembered, "When he was onstage, he was so electric and 'out there,' but in his personal life, he was quiet. He had this sense of boundaries that was really good, I thought." As a fellow recovering alcoholic, Aguilar-Ramos was uniquely accepting of Warren's constant fear of being around alcohol or other temptations. Looking to impress her, Warren planned their first date at the Ivy; when she immediately agreed to a second outing, he invited her back to his apartment. "He was naturally romantic," she recalled. "He served grape juice for us in wine glasses and serenaded me with his music." When Aguilar-Ramos admitted she didn't know his work, Warren grabbed his acoustic guitar and played for her "Desperadoes Under the Eaves" and "Hasten Down the Wind." She told him they were beautiful, but they still weren't familiar. He then played her "Werewolves of London." She recalled, "I didn't realize how funny it was until later, but he made sure to play that one for me last."

Only a few weeks later, Warren pulled out all the stops for their third date: he took her to a Bruce Springsteen concert, giving his old Asbury Park buddy a heads-up beforehand. Aguilar-Ramos was awestruck to find herself sitting backstage and chatting with Springsteen, still casually reclining in a bathrobe following the electrified performance. But more memorable to Aguilar-Ramos was Warren's shy approach toward her during the drive back. "On the way home, Warren's like, 'Do you want to go steady?'" she remembered. "I'm like, 'Heck, yeah!'" Admittedly, Warren shared her enthusiasm; he had found a new love who knew virtually nothing of his old self—but understood everything he now was.

She also found his new "homebody" personal habits compatible with her own, citing the most basic creature comforts shared as a couple making their eventual relationship "the most magical time" of her life.

Warren had Aguilar-Ramos in mind when he began writing *Transverse City*'s title track by the same name—the "Pollyanna" addressed throughout the song was his nickname for her, inspired by the sunny disposition he claimed she never lost. Their eventual breakup, however, was the inspiration for the album's most heartfelt and most haunting tracks. As had been a pattern in all of Warren's romantic relationships— or any relationship—he was drawn to the person who most embodied his own current persona; Aguilar-Ramos had been the ideal soul mate for the Warren she knew at the time. Where his A.A.-mandated code of sobriety affected every element of his new life, Aguilar-Ramos had already been there; she even sympathized with the deepening OCD habits that others found so strange. "I loved massaging his hands because he had that 'wash-his-hands-one-hundred-times-a-day syndrome," she recalled. "His hands would bleed and crack, so I would massage them with good moisturizer at night."

Despite any normal relationship woes that the couple faced, or the personal quirks that came with being in Warren's innermost circle, Aguilar-Ramos was forgiving and understanding, largely driven by the mystique of his creative process. "I actually was fascinated enough to ask him about it directly one time," she recalled. "He told me that he 'dreamed the notes,' maybe five notes, or seven, or a whole sequence of notes. And I said to him, 'Well, do you hear the notes?' and he said, 'No, I *see* the notes, and then I put them together and rearrange them in front of me. Then, I lay down the tracks, and then the last thing I do is hear them.' To me, that was his mathematical, analytical, scientific mind. He was always writing down notes, and I knew he was a classically trained musician, and that's when I could really see it. He was, truly, a refined composer."

Along with the solid foundation that A.A. had instilled over the course of his three years of sobriety, Warren's relationship with Aguilar-Ramos had given him a confidence that carried over into his once-again assertive behavior in the studio. In the past, Warren had eventually considered marriage within each of his relationships; his quest for the quiet, normal life never truly wavered, although the definition of "normal" seemed to be in a constant state of negotiation. Three years of proactive sobriety, on top of mounting stresses in the studio regarding *Transverse City*'s marketing potential and his place at Virgin, had made even the dubious squalor of Cat Piss Manor seem suitable enough. At that time and at that place, it was a rare instance when marriage would only upset the delicate status quo that was holding him together.

The subject finally came up in July. She later recalled, "We broke up because I started getting itchy in my later twenties to find a relationship that was consistent. It probably broke his heart when we first broke up."

More than she knew. For Warren, Aguilar-Ramos had represented a balance of understanding and acceptance that he knew would be hard to replicate. She had stood by him and had seen him through the roughest moments of early sober living. Her departure had turned the stability of his earth—so dependent on consistency and the comfort of habit—completely upside down.

Within weeks of his breakup with Aguilar-Ramos, Warren had completed writing "They Moved the Moon," "Nobody's in Love This Year," and "Searching for a Heart," ultimately deciding to hold the final song for future use. He did, however, take full advantage of the studio setup to quickly add a lush arrangement of "Nobody's in Love This Year" as *Transverse City*'s closing track.

Here again, Duncan Aldrich's contacts within the jazz world proved useful. With Bob Glaub and Richie Hayward returning alongside Waddy Wachtel on lead guitar, Mike Campbell on mandolin, and a visiting J. D. Souther for harmony vocals, jazz horn player Mark Isham came down at Aldrich's behest to add a soulful flugelhorn to the ballad. It proved to be a major contact for Warren, as Isham also worked composing scores for film and television.

Following the recording session, Isham approached Warren about contributing some music to a new film he had been working on, one that required a jazzy, throwback torch number. Playing to the retro, film noir tone of the movie, Isham had selected a 1941 tune from the Great

American songbook, "You Don't Know What Love Is," made popular by, among others, Billie Holiday, Chet Baker, and Tony Bennett. It wasn't exactly Warren's normal fare—he admitted later to not knowing much of the genre. "I'm not a big jazz fan," he claimed. "I missed jazz, kind of. And by the time I came to it in life, it was too intimidating to enjoy thoroughly." However, Isham had convinced Warren to step out of his comfort zone and record his own unique spin on the famous standard. Warren recalled his curiosity about the song, initially asking Isham, "Who wrote it?" "I don't know," Isham had said, but, "Bird did it—Trane did it." Even though he was a novice to the world of jazz, those artists, along with Miles Davis and Chick Corea, were among the few jazz artists that Warren spoke of with genuine admiration.

As Isham was a fellow Virgin Records artist, it was effortless for Warren to add both his cover of "You Don't Know What Love Is" and soon, the completed version of "Searching for a Heart" to the soundtrack of Alan Rudolph's romantic noir drama *Love at Large*. Upon its release in March of the following year, the movie tanked at the box office—but Warren saw the potential in dividing his time between songwriting and composing incidental music for other media.

Warren walked away from the production of *Transverse City* having completed the ultimate crash course in independent production and new recording technologies. He may not have offered much in the way of updates when asked about his long-percolating incomplete classical symphony, but Warren was already planning his own home studio, one that would provide complete autonomy and perhaps the opportunity for more personal projects. During their time together, Annette Aguilar-Ramos had noted Warren's interest in utilizing the digital technology at his disposal to potentially, and finally, complete his classical symphonic works. "When he finally got his Mac [computer], he saw possibilities to record the works he hadn't been able to afford before," she recalled. "It was like, those multiple levels of his audio tracks were the multiple levels of his thinking and his creativity. That was really it for him—to be able to work on what he wanted to work on."

∽

As suspected by all involved, *Transverse City* immediately polarized both fans and critics upon its release in early October. "With his eye on the fate of the earth, from malls and gridlock to entropy and deorbiting heavenly bodies, Zevon succumbs to the temptations of art-rock," wrote Robert Christgau in *The Village Voice*. "This beats country-rock, at least as he defines it, and given his formal training it was decent of him to wait until his material demanded *sci-fi key-bs*—arpeggios and ostinatos and swirling soundtracks . . . 'Splendid Isolation,' about solipsism as a life choice, 'Turbulence,' about perestroika and Afghanistan, and 'Run Straight Down,' about the fate of the earth on the 11 o'clock news, are exactly as grim as they ought to be." *The Philadelphia Inquirer* also singled out two of Christgau's favorites, stating, "New songs, such as 'Turbulence' and 'Splendid Isolation,' displayed Zevon's knack for driving pop that is both witty and melodic."

The long leash that Virgin had given Warren, Aldrich, and Slater hadn't been in the name of trust or gracious autonomy; all three had sensed the label's growing concerns over Warren's bankability. Tensions had grown throughout the production, with the stop-and-start piecemeal assembly of most of the songs proving to be both a blessing and a curse. On the positive side, Warren and Aldrich had been able to mix and master certain completed track elements as they went along, which meant the album was set for presentation almost immediately following the final sessions in mid-June. However, Virgin was more anxious than excited in getting a reasonable return on their investment; they opted to send Warren out on tour right after the holiday season.

In what would later be perceived as a final grasp at earning back the fortune sunk in staking their first American client, the label agreed to not only an extensive tour of the United States, but also an extended tour throughout the Australian continent—a first for Warren, and admittedly, a lifelong dream. Due to the rapid turnaround of *Transverse City*'s release and its promotional Millennium Paranoia Tour, many of his best critical write-ups weighed the content of the experimental rock album with the lavish stage performance meant to match it in cyberpunk tone and futuristic style. Following his February performance at the Beacon Theater, Stephen Holden of *The New York Times* observed, "'Transverse City,' the title song of Warren Zevon's newest album, is a futuristic nightmare in which the grimmer trends of the present are the only realities in a world that has deteriorated into a living hell . . . The song is only one in a gallery of grim scenarios in which Mr. Zevon expresses a generalized disgust and despair in his characteristically punchy style. What is missing from most of the new songs is the sardonic sense of humor that has given his best work an antic zing."

After a few warm-up shows on the East Coast, the Millennium Paranoia Tour officially kicked off in February 1990. Warren's practice of scouting younger, though seasoned, musicians from small indie bands had paid off well in the past, making that the best strategy for the hardened, dark rock of *Transverse City*'s live performances. With Duncan Aldrich and Andrew Slater's help, a solid touring band was ready for the February launch: bassist Jennifer Condos had just come off tour with Fleetwood Mac, while drummer Ian Wallace was not only a founding member of King Crimson, but had long collaborated with all Warren's old pals, including Karla Bonoff, Jackson Browne, Don Henley, Bob Dylan, and was a prominent member in David Lindley's own band, El Rayo-X. Of guitarist Frank Simms, Warren told his audience, "Perhaps every lead guitarist, or every heavy-metal guitarist, is a frustrated nuclear physicist—but our lead guitarist isn't frustrated. He's our expert in wave mechanics, card tricks, and everything in between."

The live performances of *Transverse City*'s dark, electronica influences left critics as polarized as the album itself. "Last night, the relatively obscure quartet Zevon formed for his tour caught a groove and carved out a powerful identity of its own," wrote Scott Brodeur of *The Philadelphia Inquirer,* who added that the lineup "slipped into wild improvisation frenzies and back into a cohesive unit without showing a seam." He added, "Led by Zevon's computer-driven synthesizer, the combo delivered a sonic version of 'Roland the Headless Thompson Gunner,' and noted that other highlights had included, "a tough version of 'Sentimental Hygiene' and a raucous cover of 'A Certain Girl,' which brought the appreciative crowd to its feet."

Following their in-depth interview before his appearance at the Beacon Theater, *The New York Times'* Stephen Holden was nonetheless impressed with Warren's February 10 show. "At the concert on Saturday," Holden wrote, "the singer faithfully but without much enthusiasm delivered 'Poor Poor Pitiful Me' and 'Roland the Headless Thompson Gunner' . . . Both the band's lean, chugging arrangements and Mr. Zevon's performance suggested a concerted attempt to emulate the folk-rock primitivism of Neil Young and Crazy Horse. And on two of the new album's songs, the Neil Young–style ballad 'Splendid

Isolation,' and the post-Orwellian fantasy 'Long Arm of the Law,' the music began to catch fire."

Holden added, "In several of Mr. Zevon's dissonant keyboard solos and in some electronic effects, one also sensed a more esoteric musical side of the singer's personality struggling for expression." Holden wasn't the only critic noting a disconnect on Warren's behalf. But while *The New York Times* critic had interpreted it as a limitation in creative expression, others sensed a lack of intimacy between Warren and his audience. "Rarely does [Warren] give the impression that he's reaching into his own depths for his material, so there's an emotional distance to much of his work," claimed Jim Washburn in *The Los Angeles Times*, writing that Warren's March appearance at the Coach House had "made that distance even greater."

There was one other possible cause for the perceived distance left unsuggested by critics. Many were unaccustomed to seeing Warren sober. Gone were the days when he gleefully stood in the fire, infusing himself with quarts of vodka and a multitude of drugs just for the courage to face the screaming crowd—to proudly be unleashed from handcuffs and howl before them. During his first attempts at sobriety, Warren had dosed himself with pills in order to sleep through a day's worth of temptation, purposely awaking just before showtime. By 1990, his once fragile sobriety had strengthened enough to rule out that option—but how was one to be a rock-and-roll animal when living the lifestyle was no longer possible? The mixed response to his attempts in recapturing the same youthful, "throw myself against the wall" rock-and-roll band experience indicated a need to somehow reconnect with his audience. Virgin had funded his most ambitious and creative concept project, also to mixed response; he would need to reconnect with his listeners, too. Like he had once joked to David Landau, "I'm Warren Zevon," he'd said, smiling. "You've never met him before."

CHAPTER TEN

(1990–1995)

"ALL MY SONGS ARE REALLY ABOUT FEAR," WARREN HAD TOLD *The Chicago Tribune*—largely in response to the polarized opinions of *Transverse City*.

But controversy was nothing new. Even in his earliest press, while critics lauded his songwriting abilities, they had also consistently noted the recurring themes of violence, blood, gore, and an apparent glorification of general mayhem within the lyrics. Yet when Warren tried to reveal his tender side, there was always another round of critics ready to nail him for deliberate sentimentality; Robert Christgau had long criticized what he perceived as a saccharine sweetness to "Hasten Down the Wind," and never let Warren forget it; he still brought it up in reviews written over a decade later. Likewise, opinions surrounding 1982's *The Envoy* wavered between those hailing it as Warren's masterpiece and others the self-indulgent vanity project that cost him a record contract—and nearly killed him.

As *Transverse City* had fulfilled Warren's contract, Virgin had its own pragmatic way of determining the album's success: letting the numbers do the talking. Of its two singles, "Run Straight Down" and "Splendid Isolation," only the first had made it to the *Billboard* charts, peaking at Number 30 at the end of November. "Splendid Isolation," despite becoming one of Warren's most beloved fan favorites, hadn't charted at all. Worse yet, neither had the album itself—the first such commercial failure since 1969's *Wanted Dead or Alive*. But there was a substantial difference when it came to *Transverse City*. Here, Warren had been truly creatively invested in the project, from conception to release and promotional performance. Its all-encompassing foray into cyberpunk had been personal to him creatively, and he had fought tooth and nail to defend the genre's importance to the album; likewise, the album's themes of paranoia and heartbreak were personal to him on every other level. Warren later admitted, "When I looked for more material, I asked myself, 'What is symptomatic of living in society?'" But the public had largely ignored his observations.

Critics who had noted Warren's apparent "distance" during the Millennium Paranoia Tour weren't privy to another probable cause, one he'd kept to himself throughout the album's promotion: Virgin had dropped him before he'd even headed out on the road.

Initially viewing the success of *Transverse City* as a means of re-upping his contract, having the prior knowledge that such a deal was already off the table created for Warren a number of new pressures: he'd still have to be on his best behavior throughout the promotional tour, and he'd still have to give a dynamic show throughout the entire run—no longer for the good of Virgin, but now in the hopes of attracting yet another new label.

Adding insult to injury, the Millennium Paranoia Tour still required several press dates—for which Warren had to stay silent regarding his relationship with the very label footing the bill. He kept his tempered frustrations in check, even when his termination became public knowledge following the tour. "I liked them," Warren later told *The Chicago Tribune* of his former employers at Virgin. "I liked them very much. And I think that there's an unfortunate tendency we artists have—when a record doesn't sell big—to say that it's got to have been their fault. But I think there may have been a little confusion there. I think that as much as I liked them, they looked around at each other one afternoon, like maybe an hour-and-a-half after I signed the contract, and said, 'Who is this guy?' Perhaps one of them said, 'I think he's like Jackson Browne with novelty hits.' But I didn't turn out to be Steve Winwood."

∞

The hammer had fallen at the end of January. Warren and the production team saw the writing on the wall when Virgin pulled the plug on funding during *Transverse City*'s final stages. Determined to see the project through, however, Warren ignored the red flags.

Andrew Slater couldn't afford to ignore them. As both co-producer on the album and as the manager who'd signed Warren in the first place, Slater had just as much to lose. He quickly assembled a contingency plan. Over three years earlier, the camaraderie between Warren and the members of R.E.M. had not only yielded some of the strongest tracks on *Sentimental Hygiene,* but when that album had wrapped before schedule, the quartet had celebrated with a raucous jam session. Reminiscent of the long, freestyle psychedelic blues jams he'd savored with David Marks decades earlier, Warren joined Bill Berry, Peter Buck, and Mike Mills for a night filled with covers of Bo Diddley, Robert Johnson, and Muddy Waters, and—at least for the younger musicians—plenty of celebratory booze. The band wailed through hard-edged, modernized covers of blue classics "Crosscut Saw," "Mannish Boy," "Wang Dang Doodle," and—at Slater's playful suggestion—Prince's recent funk-rock hit "Raspberry Beret." According to Warren, the sessions also yielded covers of Eddy Arnold's 1959 country hit "Tennessee Stud" and another Ernie K-Doe hit, 1961's "Mother-In-Law"—although he admitted to losing track of the master recordings.

Slater still had the recordings, and by 1990, R.E.M. was quickly becoming one of the biggest bands in the United States. Now facing the problematic challenge of having to find Warren yet another record label, he viewed the old master tapes as a bargaining chip in both his and Warren's favors. Slater's former mentor, Irving Azoff, had recently taken a back seat at Front Line Management and was in the early stages of forming his own independent music label as a joint venture with Warner Bros. As Azoff had a longstanding history with both Warren and Slater, it only made sense to bring him the R.E.M. collaboration before anyone else. Unfortunately, both Warren and the members of R.E.M later claimed none of them knew about the negotiations taking place. When Slater successfully sold the recordings to Azoff's newly named Giant Records—entitling the one-shot *hindu love gods* after the clandestine name the group had used around Athens, Georgia, in 1984 and billing the release as a "supergroup" of sorts—none of the principal players were pleased. To R.E.M., half a decade after collaborating with Warren as a favor to Slater, the dog had finally learned to shake hands.

"I think it's really great but unfortunately, there's a whole side to it that's very black and ugly," Bill Berry later claimed of the deal. "Basically, we were exploited. We love Warren and don't regret doing it at all, but his management and record company kept begging us to support it with publicity and a tour or something. But we can't just drop what we're doing. It was just one fun drunken night long ago."

Likely, Warren retained his innocence—and slight annoyance. "I didn't have anything to do with the packaging or anything," he later claimed. "[R.E.M.] think I'm exploiting them, and I think they resent [that], but it has nothing to do with any of us. I told my manager, 'This is yours. I don't want to see it, I don't want to argue about it, I don't want to hear about it. Whatever you want, whatever you're gonna do, it's up to you.'" He added, "Well, we ultimately would have preferred it not come out at all, I think. It sold for like a dollar."

Although losing favor with the guys from R.E.M. was something that had upset Warren personally, he had a fundamental problem with albums rubber-stamped with his name. *The Chicago Tribune* noted, "Zevon, who has a reputation for perfectionism in the studio, needed to make some mental adjustments before feeling comfortable with the idea of releasing a jam session done one afternoon a few years ago for fun." Zevon elaborated: "At first it was a little troubling to me, the idea of putting out performances that hadn't been and really couldn't be polished up. Because I spend a lot of time polishing. Maybe a lot of wasted time, some of it useful time. I assume that's why we all learned studio techniques all our lives."

Regardless of the artists' ambivalence toward the *hindu love gods* release, the R.E.M. connection—and the surrounding controversy regarding their resistance to it—brought Warren higher *Billboard* chart numbers than his final album for Virgin. Within two months of its release, the album peaked at 168, while its only single, "Raspberry Beret," hit Number 26 on the newly formed "Alternative" chart—peanuts to R.E.M. at the time, but just the moderate boost needed to attain its true goal. Within the year, *Billboard* reported, "Warren Zevon will make his Giant solo debut in October with *Mr. Bad Example*."

He had started talking up the next album almost a full year before any official announcement had time to run. With *hindu love gods* newly on the shelves, Warren told *The Chicago Tribune* in December, "My old friend Waddy Wachtel is going to produce the next record, and we're going to start in February. . . . It's Irving Azoff's label. He's managed me for a number of years, and I'm still associated with what was his management firm. So it's not straying far. Irving knows what to expect and what not to expect from me, which may not always have been the case with other labels."

∞

There was nearly a five-month gap between Warren's return from his final tour for Virgin in May and the scaled-back folk tour that Giant would be backing toward the end of October. When he'd referred to Azoff's Front Line in the past tense to *The Chicago Tribune,* his insinuation was only the tip of the drama that had built up between him and Slater during the final weeks of *Transverse City.* The behind-closed-doors deal that had resulted in both the *hindu love gods* release and the public rift with R.E.M. had been the final straw. While Slater's valid attempts to make Warren a superstar had fallen short of Virgin's expectations, other members within the music industry had taken notice of the young manager's ambition. He later recalled that concurrent with *Transverse City,* he was "working with Lenny Kravitz, the Beastie Boys, and Don Henley," while co-producing Warren's album. "Despite the success, it was a terrible time," Slater later told *The Los Angeles Times.* "How can you feel good about yourself when you don't take care of things? I couldn't find the right combination of things, chemicals and alcohol, to make me feel comfortable with myself. . . . I started missing occasional meetings because I'd wake up late or have a hangover. When I felt bad, I wanted to feel good. When I felt good, I wanted to feel better. It just kind of took me out of reality."

It had started simple enough, as Slater was young and a whole new world of Hollywood success had opened to him quickly. He later recalled, "I was always unhappy, and I realized my own disease was progressing. I was trying to get sober, which triggered me going into treatment. . . . When I went into rehab, Warren was finally in good financial shape, sober, had a healthy touring base, and was about to release a new record." Slater admitted that he and Azoff now had "a difficult relationship," and in the best interests of Warren's Giant deal, he didn't want to "alienate the president of his new record company." Azoff replaced Slater as Warren's manager with old friend and fellow producer Peter Asher. It devastated Slater, who was still in rehab when he heard the news directly from Warren. He later recalled, "[Warren] says, 'Look, Andy, I just got off the phone with Irving. He said that if I fire you and make a change in management, he'll really work my record and I'll get better promotion and marketing.'" According to Slater, Warren claimed that at forty-four years old, it could be his "last chance."

"I had loaned money to him and made it my life's mission to get him back in the record business when he was drunk and living in Philadelphia," Slater later said. "I had taken him to rehab three times, and he was a member of the fellowship of Alcoholics Anonymous. His life was going pretty well. Then, when I had a problem, he wasn't there."

For Warren, his now four years of sobriety had been an uphill struggle. Since returning to Los Angeles in 1985, he had made it a point to surround himself solely with positive influences—a major challenge while being part of the music industry and LA scene, and he had continued to attend A.A. meetings throughout the entire production of *Sentimental Hygiene*. However, many were unaware of the personal obstacles being thrown at him during the making of its follow-up. Since Warren's move back from Philadelphia, Crystal and Ariel had both returned from Paris, then returned *to* Paris—then, finally back to the US again. With so many gaps between their visits, Warren was unaware of the pressures his ex-wife had long felt as a single mother, or the drinking problems she herself had slowly developed.

Warren was clean, sober, and in a healthy relationship with Annette Aguilar-Ramos in May 1988, when he received the unlikeliest of phone calls from Crystal. "I said, 'Warren, I think I'm an alcoholic,'" she later recalled. "He said, 'Crystal, that's wonderful.' I didn't think there was anything wonderful about it at the time, but he was right." Warren immediately called his own sponsor, Stefan Arngrim, who was able to put Crystal in contact with a local A.A. chapter. "When I got home, Warren and Ariel were there," she remembered. "Then he held me for a long time." He left her to tell Ariel about the night's A.A. meeting, and the decision she had made to seek help. "She begged me not to go," Crystal recalled. "She said, 'I don't want two parents who are alcoholics.'"

Although it would take time to work his way back into the good graces of his long-neglected children, Warren's aiding Crystal in her own sobriety marked the beginning of a deepened, platonic relationship between them. In addressing her own addiction, Crystal had come face to face with the demons that had plagued Warren throughout their marriage. It was only when Ariel had informed her mother of the corporal punishment she'd been doling out during alcohol-infused blackouts that Crystal recognized a desperate need for help. The incident was all too familiar to her. Warren had been calling to check on her for weeks following her start at A.A., and when the topic finally came up, she was surprised by the narrowness of his apologies, as he left out so many incidents that had remained darkly memorable to her. She recalled that he had "made amends for the time he'd given me a black eye before he left for Japan [in 1978]," but was confused that Warren "only referred to that incident."

Crystal explained the realization that soon came to her: "I understood that Warren had been in a blackout every time he'd gotten violent with me. He never knew half the things he'd done. . . . I carried around resentments over that stuff for years—and Warren never even knew what he'd done." In the weeks that followed, Warren called Crystal twice a day to see how she was handling her sobriety, constantly reminding her of his personal favorite of all the Alcoholic Anonymous prayers, the one he constantly repeated like a mantra: "Relieve me of the bondage of self."

Crystal wasn't the only one Warren reached out to help. Longtime friend and collaborator Niko Bolas had gone through his own personal struggles; when he needed help, he knew who to call. "[Warren] was one of my first sponsors when I went into my own twelve-step program," Bolas later remembered. "I'm in the same program, and he was a pretty important guy in my life . . . He was awesome, and I don't give a shit who you tell."

Using all the focus and energy sobriety brought to his forties, Warren attempted to spread that sentiment around. Virgin may not have found him all that awesome, but as he prepared yet another transition to another record label, Warren continued to wipe the slate clean both inside the studio and out. By the time Crystal and Ariel moved to Ashland, Oregon, at the end of 1989, he hadn't been able to connect with his now rebellious teenage daughter, but the proper amends had been made with her mother. Even before her move, Crystal had noticed his efforts. "For the first time, Warren filled in for me," she later recalled. "He took Ariel to Alateen meetings and flute lessons; he dropped in just to hang out with her. He was doing the same thing as

Jordan, but for some reason, he always saw them separately, which is a shame, but he was learning how to relate to his children, and that's what mattered."

It wasn't only with his children and their mothers to whom Warren reached out. He'd always had checkered relationships with both of his parents, yet as their advancing years were coinciding with his sober ones, he turned his attention to both. Annette Aguilar-Ramos recalled that Warren was always "worried about his mother and his grandmother," although he had been reluctant to introduce them to her. "He never thought they were a part of his life, and when he had to be the son, Warren shied away from that," she recalled. "He bought flowers, gave people things, but when it came down to caring for another human being to the fullest extent, he put all that energy into his art and music."

Crystal did note, however, that Warren had worked to "amend his uneasy relationship" with his father, William, who was now in his mid-eighties and living in a small apartment in Gardena near his old gambling dens. Despite poor health and having outlived all his gangster buddies, William Zevon still acted as a "pawnbroker," collecting the jewelry and valuables from losers at the table who couldn't pay up. As a still-devoted former daughter-in-law, Crystal had stayed in touch with the elder Zevon throughout the years and, upon one of her periodic visits, noticed his deteriorating health. Weighing only eighty-nine pounds and bleeding from "every orifice," William hadn't taken care of himself in years. She took him to a local hospital for tests, which kept him under observation for weeks. Warren and Crystal spent time reconnecting in the hospital cafeteria, while Warren did the same with his father once they were alone. He thanked his old man for always being there for him and asked advice about his relationship with Jordan. He even worked on a song inspired by the massive traffic congestion from Los Angeles to Pasadena; "Gridlock" became one of *Transverse City*'s hardest-rocking tracks.

Warren later told A.A. sponsor Stefan Arngrim he felt like a weight had been lifted. As a testament to his hardened resolve, throughout the entire productions of both his Virgin albums, Warren had been able to check each obstacle at the studio door—and had never once tumbled from the wagon. Which was why Warren deemed it unforgivable when he discovered his sponsor was using heroin. Aguilar-Ramos later remembered, "When [Warren] confronted him, his sponsor admitted using, and that really disillusioned Warren . . . it created a distrust in him for people. Then, when it turned out that his manager was doing drugs as well, it was too much. He stopped going to A.A. meetings right after we broke up."

∞

Sending Warren out on tour during the second half of 1990 was the logical means for Giant to raise awareness of his signing, as well as hyping their own label launch only months before. At the time, however, he had no specific album to promote, save for the now notorious *hindu love gods* release that R.E.M. certainly wasn't going to promote. The over-the-top 1980s superstar approach hadn't worked for Virgin in marketing him, but Irving Azoff remained adamant that Giant's carefully curated independent roster would be the proper home for an artist of Warren's caliber. "In a way, it reminds me of what happened with Tom Petty on *Full Moon Fever*," Azoff told *Billboard*. "[Warren] has made a singer-songwriter album. You can actually hear and understand his lyrics."

Likewise, Giant sought to emphasize that version of Warren while on tour. In anticipation of a more traditional folk-rock debut, his first promotional tour would be a unique hybrid representing each facet of his career crossroads: billed as the Warren Zevon Acoustic Trio, the small, folkish band performed his usual fan favorites, as well as new songs he was refining for the Giant debut. With a heavy leaning toward traditional blues covers, the trio threw in a few of the *hindu love gods* material that none of the original musicians had wanted to promote live. For the two-month tour, Warren was joined by singer-songwriter Gurf Morlix and Dan Dugmore, lead guitarist for Linda Ronstadt and James Taylor's previous few touring bands—and whose "plugged-in" tendencies urged Warren to playfully rename the group "the Patrician Home Boys."

In the intimate, all-guitar acoustic setting, Warren won over the club crowds and earned far better reviews than with his expensive 1989 space opera. With both the smaller, club-oriented tour and a new, working-man's folk-rocker persona well established, critics were noting Warren's genre versatility in a positive light. For the first time in years, he was playing to an age-appropriate crowd, often to a warmer welcome. The trio's eclectic song choices were also a draw. Warren told *The Los Angeles Times*, "There's no setlist or anything; we just do it and see what happens." He cited a recent show in Seattle where old friend Joe Walsh happened to be in the audience; the former Eagle promptly ran up and grabbed a guitar, much to the audience's enthusiastic approval. The quartet jammed on a true "heavy-metal folk" version of "Ain't That Pretty at All." Admittedly, Warren was having a blast playing with his fellow guitarists. "Tonight, we're in San Francisco," he said. "Maybe we can do that song for four hours, if you know what I mean."

On the last day of the year, the trio was booked for a gig in Fort Lauderdale. There, Warren gave his final interview for 1990. "I started as a classical composer and then became a folk singer," he told the *Sun-Sentinel*. "For me, a hit would be a fluke. But I don't see why I can't keep playing anyway."

Warren had started dating media personality Eleanor Mondale soon after she'd interviewed him in February for WLOL-FM in Minneapolis while he was promoting a three-night residency at the downtown club 1st Avenue. Family and friends had noticed Warren's bragging rights about dating the high-profile daughter of a former US vice president. The rambunctious young journalist was known for her quirky, and often scandalous, behavior both on and off camera. With conflicting schedules, their relationship had only lasted a few months.

Yet, even while on tour, Warren had stayed in touch with Annette Aguilar-Ramos, the two even meeting up during the periods when both were single. However, any hopes for a reconciliation were dashed by Warren's apparent cavalier attitude toward monogamy. She recalled that following their breakup in 1989, the "little bad boy became a real bad boy," enjoying his life on the road, and the various freedoms that came with it. "I kept trying to regain what we had had in the beginning of our relationship—that monogamous, committed relationship," she later said. "But, Warren had tasted the other side and liked it."

Production on *Mr. Bad Example* began just after the start of the year. For the sessions, producer Waddy Wachtel booked Dodge City in Glendale, and the Sound Factory in Los Angeles—home to the production of *Excitable Boy* thirteen years earlier. Many of Warren's oldest and strongest collaborators made their respective returns this time around, giving the album the feel of both a fresh start and a reunion of like minds. With Wachtel at the production helm, he was free to hop in for any lead guitar, background guitar, or vocal harmonies as needed; likewise, bassist Bob Glaub, master of all stringed instruments David Lindley, and Toto founding percussionist Jeff Porcaro all made up the recurring core lineup. Most exciting to Warren, however, was that his son Jordan would, for the first time, be on board in the studio full time. At the time, nineteen-year-old Jordan had advanced as a drummer and had already played successful gigs at his father's old stomping grounds, the Roxy and Whisky A Go-Go. "Who is this guy, Jordan?" John Hughes of the *Sun-Sentinel* jokingly asked, prompting Warren's proud reply, "He's the greatest person I know."

Both in and out of the studio, Warren's life had been a whirlwind since leaving Virgin records. In accordance with the twelfth and final step in the Alcoholics Anonymous dictum that had helped him restructure his postoblivion life, Warren had attempted to make amends with his entire family. But he also spent that period chain-smoking through romantic relationships, each one of which helped fuel the album's emotional resonance with new material just in time for *Mr. Bad Example*.

With very few exceptions, all the songs Warren brought in to the Sound Factory had been inspired by an archetypical amalgam of the women recently in and out of his life: he had still been with Annette Aguilar-Ramos during the album's earliest stages and their breakup had led to his penning "Searching for a Heart" only one day later; likewise, his newly invigorated friendship with Crystal, the brief affair with Eleanor Mondale, the periodic phone calls to Anita Gevinson—nothing came of them, but he took a shot—and a fresh relationship with actress Julia Mueller had provided a veritable menagerie of muses.

Before he had given it a proper title, Warren had referred to the album's opening track as simply "the hate song," before settling on the more listener-friendly, though no less bitter, "Finishing Touches." Lyrically, the hard-driven opener seemed to speak for every cuckolded, frustrated, and disillusioned male who'd ever been two-timed by the woman he loved. Incredibly cathartic and one-sided by nature, the angry anthem benefited from appropriately aggressive lead work of Wachtel, whose bluesy riff opened both the track and the album, evoking the start of "Johnny Strikes Up the Band."

Even amid the charging rock of the album's overall tone, Warren worked in two of the most beautiful love ballads he'd penned in years—both of which would remain in his live repertoire far past the release's promotion. In later years, he claimed that "Suzie Lightning" was the best song he felt he'd ever done, and the song included some of his most welcomed characteristics. More or less a power ballad, Warren cited a Bartok postcard sent to him by Bob Glaub from an excursion to Budapest as inspiring the globe-trotting references in the love tune, while buddy Ray "Boom Boom" Mancini was then filming a miniseries in Yugoslavia. The aforementioned "Suzie" in question was a name cribbed from a B-movie Warren had caught on cable in his hotel room; he'd simply loved the name. As for the emotions behind the song, only later did he admit the real-life "Suzie" was "a composite of women who'd recently made [him] unhappy—and vice versa."

Jorge Calderón had always remained Warren's friend, but their collaborative songwriting relationship took a long hiatus in the years following Warren's 1983 purgatorial stint in Philadelphia. Calderón had been admittedly confused by his friend's later experimentations into the science-fiction genre and largely assumed Warren had gone off into his own artistic direction without need of any more help. But with the pressures of debuting with yet another new record company, Warren was apt to continue their always beneficial brainstorming sessions. He later recalled of the session that yielded their deliberately self-indulgent polka, "One evening, Jorge and I drank too much Turkish coffee, we were seeing Kirlian auras." Calderón recalled the memorable night, too: "['Mr. Bad Example'] had too many lyrics—on purpose . . . We used to go to Noura Café. Warren went at least once a day, and they had Turkish coffee. We would have the chicken plate, and then he would order a humongous thing of Turkish coffee . . . but man, we would sit there and drink cup after cup—we were so high, it was almost psychedelic." The two returned to Warren's apartment, still "laughing like kids," when they sat down to write the song. But penning the notorious adventures of the self-aggrandizing, world-weary playboy narrator of the song was too goofy for the old friends to take seriously. Calderón added, "But, we were falling down on the floor laughing . . . I'd complete his line, he'd complete my line. Just laughing . . . " With its "verse after verse" composition and no bridge, the song quickly became a fan favorite, always ensuring a huge rise out of Warren's audience in live performance—mainly due to the virtuosity required to recite the entire laundry list of misdeeds. It also provided him with a new nickname to match the new era of his career: throughout his later tours, "Mr. Bad Example himself" became a very appropriate introduction.

The sessions for *Mr. Bad Example* not only brought back familiar faces—David Lindley's fiddle on the Southern Confederate anthem "Renegade," and his assortment of lap steel guitar, *sez,* and *cumbus* on "Quite Early One Morning" were welcome returns—but new faces also arrived to add to the overall folk-rock, country flair. Dwight Yoakam came down as a mutual friend of Warren's neighbor, actor and musician Billy Bob Thornton, inspiring one of the most overtly Western tracks, "Heartache Spoken Here," on which he joined Jordan for the lush harmonies. "Things to Do in Denver When You're Dead" had been the very first of the songs written. As co-writers, both Waddy Wachtel and LeRoy Marinell work their way into the lyrics as characters encountered through the doomed journey.

Throughout the album's promotion, critics took note of the seamlessness with which Warren was able to slip into the more mature folk-rock genre, inquiring of his influences—or if it was merely a new creative leaning in contrast to the ambitious spectacles that had surrounded his two Virgin albums. According to Warren, much of that influence could be traced back to his work with the Everly Brothers during the early 1970s. "At *that* time, I was exposed to country music," he said. But many of his personal favorites among his peers had veered into similar directions.

While he long cited Bob Dylan's *John Wesley Harding* and Bruce Springsteen's *Nebraska* as two albums he found to be true, individual artistic statements, they were both heavily grounded in early American country tradition. Likewise, the solo works of Neil Young, J. D. Souther, and later turns by friend and early mentor Jackson Browne all demonstrated where many of the former "bad boys" of California rock and roll were headed: back to the dusty roots of the music itself. And much like the quiet yet steady fanfare that Warren's acoustic trio had received in the months building up to *Mr. Bad Example*'s recording sessions, Warren's own fan demographic was keen for the earthy rock sounds. Not only had the intimate, acoustic atmosphere truly emphasized his lyrics and left ample room for jamming, but it had aided in his needed connection with the audience itself. And acoustic touring was significantly cheaper.

The lessons learned from the foray into country and folk recording would have lasting effects on the composition and arrangements of Warren's future works.

The album closed with a love song that could most accurately demonstrate the overall tone and genre in which Warren, now forty-five years old, was comfortably working. "Searching for a Heart" had been written nearly two years earlier, immediately following his first breakup with Aguilar-Ramos. It was soon after, during the sessions for "Nobody's in Love This Year" for *Transverse City*, that jazz horn player Mark Isham had courted Warren for contributing to a movie soundtrack he'd been assembling. As a multi-instrumentalist, Isham not only made a living with high-quality session work, he also scored for television and film, and was in the middle of a project for filmmaker Alan Rudolph. The film, *Love at Large,* was an adult-driven neo-noir suspense love story set in Los Angeles; in a word, it was almost all of Warren's musical themes on the big screen. Warren had already completed writing "Searching for a Heart" by the end of *Transverse City*'s postproduction stage but held it over for a later album. When he played it for Isham, however, the composer immediately wanted it for the film and put Warren in touch with the director. Warren later recalled, "Alan told me he'd use anything I wrote, and he said Neil [Young] had written a song for his last movie—'He took the script home and wrote it that night!' I said, 'Did it have a bridge?'" Baby boomer auteur Lawrence Kasdan loved the track so much he also used it in his new film, *Grand Canyon,* a spiritual sequel to his earlier hit *The Big Chill*.

"I liked both films," Warren later claimed. "They both stiffed."

Unfortunately, even amid glowing critical reviews, so did *Mr. Bad Example.* Neither single hit the charts, nor the album. Not only had many original members of Warren's winning 1970's lineup returned for the Giant debut, but even Jimmy Wachtel came on board for the album's design: a deliberate juxtaposition of Warren from his *Excitable Boy* days, now ponytailed, older, dragging a cigarette in gritty black-and-white; the unspoken companion to the 1978 bestseller. With the amount of star power, focus, and working well within the confines of a meager budget, the team was shocked at the public response—especially when reviewers largely considered the album to be Warren's true return to form. "Warren Zevon tried being a nice guy on his last few records, going the whole sensitive, confessional, emotional nine yards," wrote Chris Heim of *The Chicago Tribune*, "and a fat lot of good it did him. So now he's gone back to what he knows best with *Mr. Bad Example*. . . . Zevon's latest . . . serves up another round of stories about adventurers, soldiers of fortune and other losers at life and love in songs like the title track, the ironic 'Model Citizen,' 'Renegade' and (in the same humorous vein as his 'Werewolves of London' or 'Poor Poor Pitiful Me') 'Things to Do in Denver When You're Dead.'"

The Los Angeles Times' Richard Cromelin was equally laudatory of the album. "Warren Zevon might finally be outgrowing the 'Excitable Boy' epithet that's been applied to him since his 1978 album of that ti-tle," he wrote, "but even sober and mature, he remains a loose cannon in the Eagles-Linda-Jackson axis of L.A. pop, the rowdiest guest in Hotel California. . . . On Zevon's latest album, a man stomps a dying relationship into oblivion. The title character swindles his way around the world and revels in his treachery. A crack addict sinks deeper into anxiety. A 'model citizen' approaches the breaking point in suburbia. In 'Quite Early One Morning,' they finally drop the big one . . . [the album] recalls the tradition of Zevon's defining works—scathing, sa-tirical works."

Warren told Roger Catlin of *The Hartford Courant* that the songs for the album had come quickly and that, coupled with the familiar col-laborators who surrounded him, the work went smoother than it had in the past. Compared to the epic struggles that had defined the postpro-duction of *Transverse City,* he claimed that that project had been "an elaborate production that was slow and painstaking to make. This one was simple and painless to record."

Even as the first album of Warren's that had bypassed vinyl for a straight-to-CD release, the numbers for *Mr. Bad Example* were the low-est of his mainstream career, which did not go unnoticed by Giant. Al-though they hadn't offered much in the way of a promotional budget, the lack of even a crack in *Billboard* proved a bad omen. The experi-mental Warren Zevon Acoustic Trio had been a considerable success, but that had also been concocted for the good of promoting both *hindu love gods* and the as-yet-recorded *Mr. Bad Example*. Discouraged by the sales figures of the latter album, yet aware it required some form of promotion, the label lapsed into the old strategy of previous labels that didn't know what to do with the conundrum of Warren Zevon: have him tour, get him a solid younger rock band to open and back him—and decide if staking another album was worth the investment.

Critical reviews and audience response had a funny way of not accurately determining Warren's true fan base. With every album, his sales numbers appeared to drop, yet critics had all noted the focus and maturity that his lyricism had reacquired in the half decade since he'd become sober. Even the members of the band that would be touring with him this time out were a bunch of young guns from Canada who proclaimed to be huge fans of his music.

It was a trend that worked in Warren's favor ever since he needed a solid touring band for the promotion of *Bad Luck Streak in Dancing School:* he had scouted for the young band Boulder and things had gone so well that rock-and-roll symbiosis would occur when the full lineup took the stage; likewise, the energy of his work with R.E.M. Now, members of the band Odds were helping grab Warren some of his strongest performance write-ups since *Sentimental Hygiene* had worked the critics up from their apathy years before. "Mr. Bad Example may be Warren Zevon's new nickname," wrote Mike Boehm of *The Los Angeles Times,* "but he didn't live up to it Thursday night at the Coach House . . . Instead, Zevon came off as Mr. Good Influence." According to Boehm, once Warren took the stage, he led the younger rockers "down a path of healthy aggression," adding, "Middle age apparently hasn't mellowed Zevon . . . Maybe hanging out with younger rockers helps."

Or maybe it was that Warren had successfully proven wrong a certain revered French philosopher: "The old begin to complain of the conduct of the young when they themselves are no longer able to set a bad example," wrote La Rochefoucauld.

Like hell. La Rochefoucauld hadn't known Warren Zevon.

∽

Much like his previous experiences with younger musicians out on the road, Warren's apparent curmudgeonly persona only went so far; the band admitted to revering his work and were more than open to all suggestions he offered regarding songwriting and advice from his years on the road. Having learned by example from Don and Phil Everly,

Warren now embodied a Zen-like indifference to the transient nature of his modern troubadour lifestyle. Odds' lead Craig Northey remembered numerous occasions when the *Mr. Bad Example* tour took on a form of an extended crash course in Warren's world. "Well aside from sending us out all over the world in order to find his Mountain Dew, Warren was really quiet unless we prodded him to join us in writing and hanging out," Northey recalled. "[The band] is really a group of lighthearted guys and it didn't take long for us to get him laughing and rolling his eyes."

Northey recalled that there were times during the tour when Warren would take the gaps between shows to offer advice and tips to the younger musicians. "There was a lot of discussion around then regarding [Warren's] outlook on touring, and I guess, his changing audience— his audience, in general," he recalled. "To us, all we saw were full houses and crowds of young fans yelling and screaming and everyone knew, you know, 'Detox Mansion' and his hits, but it seemed harder for him [to] enjoy it the same as we did."

The band always tried fruitlessly to get "the legendary Warren Zevon" to jam and hang out even more. "We'd sit in the back of the bus with our guitars, but if he caught us not working on our stuff—like if we were taking a break or watching a movie on that little TV—he'd come in and be really disappointed in us," Northey remembered. He called me 'Craigy-Weg' and he goes, 'Craigy-Weg, have you all seen this movie before?' And I'd be honest and go, 'Well, yeah, I've seen this already.' And Warren would pause and look at me and go, 'Well, then you should be writing.'"

Warren's influence on the boys' writing extended not only toward their work ethic, but in influence and inspiration, as well. Northey recalled that he celebrated his own birthday while on that tour and was honored to receive a gift, a copy of Joyce Carol Oates's latest release, *The Rise of Life on Earth,* from Warren himself—even if it led to one of his diciest yet most memorable tales from the tour. "After a while, Warren got very comfortable with us and hung out more and we got to discuss his own influences and his writing and reading," Northey recalled. "And Warren was always reading. So, for my birthday, he had given me this Joyce Carol Oates book—and I remember it was a really dark psychological novel about a nurse killing her patients. Well, he gave it to me with a huge recommendation, you know, 'Craigy, you're going to love this, and everything,' and he was right, I loved it. Well, one night I'm still in the bus reading it, and I have like a few pages left, and I missed the beginning of the show. I throw the book down and race out to the stage and, of course, they're all playing—and Warren, wearing his guitar and playing and singing—shoots me the dirtiest look imaginable when I run out."

According to Northey, any anger that Warren felt quickly subsided after the performances once he was able to explain the cause for the tardiness. "Warren comes up to me right after the show and is still annoyed and said, 'Where were you?' I had no other excuse. I said, 'Warren, I have to be honest—that book you gave me blew my mind and I couldn't put it down. I was so into it that I lost track of time. But I finished it!' And Warren just looks at me really quietly and really long and finally goes, 'Well, okay then.'"

The shows themselves seemed to bring out the best in both the band and the audiences. Northey recalled, "I have always loved 'Mohammed's Radio' because it meant we had earned a second encore. [Warren] would save that one for the very last and the audience and band had to earn it . . . The chorus is huge and emotional so the crowd couldn't help but sing along. It was a great way to go out.

"I guess he always knew how to make a grand exit."

Throughout both his acoustic trio tour and now with the full backing of Odds, Warren had been using fluctuating tour budgets and the unpredictable arrangements for additional players as a way of honing his solo capabilities. Both critics and fans noted the enthusiasm with which he jammed with other musicians, particularly the younger ones who got his excitability back, but there was no longer any way of knowing what the next tour would bring. With that in mind, Warren not only waxed philosophical about his work and career but hinted to *The Los Angeles Times* that he was perfectly content to tour on his own. "I guess every year is a kind of a contrast to the [tour] before it," he said. "I had done the rock band with no drummer—in spiritual intent it was like an acoustic trio. The *Transverse City* tour was band and computer. I really don't want to see that screen flickering on a stage for a few years after that tour . . . I found myself touring for a couple of months, even a couple of times a year. I think in that regard it was a very good thing for me. It put me in touch with the reality of what I was doing, and who was listening to it, and what it was like to go out and play, earn a living that way."

⌒

Warren was aware that the low sales of *Mr. Bad Example* would surely equal budget cuts for both touring and his potential follow-up album. The contract with Giant warranted two further releases, but with the surprisingly pitiful sales of this debut, the label was no longer as eager to stake another studio booking—at least not so soon.

Giant had used the 1990 preliminary press announcements for Warren's signing as an excuse to pump up their own launch. His contract was made public only months following Giant's ill-fated attempts to get R.E.M. on board for a cross-promotional tour for *hindu love gods*. But once his debut was on shelves—and not doing all that hot—the attention paid to him by the company became noticeably meager.

Again, with a three-album deal, compromises for the next one would have to be made on both sides—a fact that now applied to Warren's touring plans, as well. Throughout his successful and, apparently, enjoyable tour with the young members of Odds, Warren's one-sided remarks to numerous interviewers had hinted at his acceptance as both a "cult act" and as a professional musician who would, no doubt, be relegated to traveling the road indefinitely to earn a living. He had mentioned as much to Mike Boehm of *The Los Angeles Times,* perhaps already aware that Giant would be sending him out again almost immediately to make up for their losses.

Warren's acceptance was another testament to his six years of sobriety. In 1982, the failure of an ambitious passion project had been a primary factor in the yearlong binge that had nearly killed him; now, he was strong and focused enough to quickly put Giant's backhanded strategy to his own use. He and Duncan Aldrich had worked together so closely using new tech throughout three studio albums and too many gigs for either of them to count. It was the latter task that could provide a solid album.

Aldrich had recently acquired a digital audio tape, or DAT, machine—the latest mobile-engineered tool used for preserving live events. Sony had been refining the small, though expensive, industrial playback device since 1987, and in many ways it was a traveling musician's wet dream. Although generating only one directional track of recorded sound, the cassette-based system was a higher "lossless" quality, making it ideal for inexpensive, studio-quality tracks. Warren hadn't released a live album since 1980's *Stand in the Fire,* the pinnacle of both his mainstream fame and reputation for incredible live sets. Although his sales on Giant had been astronomically low compared to his old Elektra/Asylum numbers, what hadn't changed was the critical acclaim he received from every critic that witnessed his live show.

It only made sense before Warren was once again exiled to the road that he and Aldrich hatch a plan to get Giant's approval for a live album release: if the live performances were going to generate the most buzz about Warren's amazing live sets and new material, then it was time to make that experience available on store shelves. The two made their case and, seeing this as the most inexpensive way to honor Warren's contract and potentially use his mandated tour as a way of doubling potential revenue, Giant agreed.

The massive world tour was set to begin just before the summer of 1992, with the first stop booked for the Carefree Theatre in West Palm Beach, Florida. Warren's new manager at Front Line, Gloria Boyce, told the *Sun-Sentinel*'s John Lannert that Warren "customarily alternates between performing with a band and playing solo," adding that for the current tour, he would be "accompanied by grand piano, guitars and harmonica."

Lannert was well versed in Warren's live performance history, noting, "Zevon faithful will remember that his last live disc, 1977's *Stand in the Fire,* was an onstage masterpiece that he recorded with a backing troupe. Zevon's live release will be coming out barely a year after his latest album . . . Like the half-dozen or so albums before it, the excellent *Mr. Bad Example* became a disc of its word, at least from a commercial standpoint. The album never made a dent on any trade magazine chart."

Warren and Duncan Aldrich set off in "The Lipcutter," as Warren had lovingly dubbed their touring van, at the end of May. Their journey was truly to be one of the longest in Warren's career, starting with a major jaunt across the United States—beginning at the end of May with his West Palm Beach show and ending three months later with a closing performance at the Belly Up in Solana Beach, California—and then a second excursion throughout Europe and Australia for the rest of the year. Warren later recalled, "In the spring of '92, Duncan, guitar technician Roger Bell and I embarked on a world tour with the intention of recording every performance live-to-DAT. After traveling from Helsinki to Woy Woy, I found myself with the hideous task of sorting through ninety-two show tapes."

Warren wasn't exaggerating. After only a brief respite from the self-described "Homeric quest," the team headed off to Modena, Italy, for the Fiesta Dell'Unita. From there, Warren and company hit Norway, Sweden, Finland, and Germany before an extended trek of the Australian continent throughout the month of October. By the time they made it home for Thanksgiving, they actually had nearly a hundred tapes to be sorted through at Red Zone.

"That whole project was really commando," Aldrich recalled. "I put together this whole rig with the DAT machine, then sat next to the house operators in each venue and every show. We had agreed to keep the same set list for the entire tour, more or less, because we knew we'd end up having to listen to each one carefully later. It the end, it was actually ninety-six total versions . . . But it was the man and his music, you can really hear where his voice is in the harmonies, like perfect song-realization, with no edits. It wasn't just, 'this chord, then this chord'—it was a way of really hearing the parts of Warren's compositions."

"If I had to pick a favorite performance of a certain song," Aldrich added, "I think that the 'Werewolves' version that Warren did in London was pretty special. I mean, we knew that we were going to have about a hundred versions of that song to weed through, but he was determined to make the London performance the best. And it really was."

Throughout his career, Warren never shied away from performing "Werewolves of London," despite it being low on his list of favorites to pull out of the songbook; he admitted many times, however, that giving the audience what they wanted and expected was one major facet in being not only an artist, but a true entertainer. But there was also a catharsis of sorts. He later admitted to *The Boston Globe*'s Jim Sullivan, "I suppose on some deep and profound level, the evening would seem incomplete to me without three minutes of howling."

∞

The excursion's saving grace was its creative alternative to working within the confines of a studio setting. For most of Warren's career, he'd had to practically beg just for the opportunity to lay down quality recordings of his work. Since his active fascination with modern digital recording advances began under Duncan Aldrich's guidance in 1987, Warren had all but mastered professional self-production. Since his earliest days as a recording artist, the single most important goal he'd had to work for each time out was the autonomy for complete creative control and, if possible, final approval on song selection, track listing, and overall album design; being a lifelong perfectionist, it went with the territory.

Now, if Giant was going to display signs of apprehension in their backing of him—and was going to demonstrate it with a grueling world tour in lieu of a proper second studio album—he would have no trouble once again using the situation to his advantage.

Throughout his career, Warren had gone to great lengths to avoid being labeled as any one style of performer—or being pigeonholed into any one genre of music. Shedding the skin of "stephen lyme" as the 1960s came to an end, he had played with numerous alternate stage names, going so far as to use them in social circles; Jackson Browne had initially been introduced to "Sandy Zevon," an aspiring songwriter who avoided the color green because "it was bad luck."

When Warren's first few Elektra/Asylum albums had earned him both critical recognition for his songwriting abilities and a dubious reputation for a chaotic personal life dangerously on par with the desperate, outlaw characters of the songs, he responded by leaping from behind the baby grand and sliding to the microphone on his knees, howling and gyrating with such a frenzied lack of inhibition that critics described his live shows as like watching an exorcism. When that spectacle grew tiresome, at least to the majority of the record-buying public, he crafted *The Envoy* as a literary rock album with both political and intimately personal themes. That album had coincided with Warren's very public dog-and-pony show, candidly praising the joys of sobriety, positive thinking, and the comforts of domicile living. A mature album called for a mature artist.

He had now made it to middle age, having survived decades of the same dangerous habits and brazen behavior that had killed younger men—some of them musicians Warren idolized and later, some he had known. While he would later joke about having "lived like Jim Morrison a lot longer than he did," in his younger years, he had touted that mischievous "werewolf about town" persona in the media as a means to enable the alcoholism his fans didn't witness. It was only after achieving sobriety that he'd acknowledged the effects of allowing a public perception to shape his image.

By 1990, for good or ill, he was far more stern in addressing what he was, and what he was not. When interviewers now made the error of addressing the clichés or stereotypes attributed to his work, he would make it a point to offer patient yet glib corrections—usually in a detailed fashion that included as many literary or obscure classical references as he could logically fit into one answer. Likewise, when his earlier classical aspirations would come up, Warren now waved the subject away. In its place, he began substituting the topic of the unfinished symphony with his own philosophical approach to music theory and its place in modern pop music.

"If I was influenced by anything, it was probably when *Revolver* came out," Warren told *The Hartford Courant*. "It was just like the classical composers who would write an opera, then follow it with a little church piece, then do a string quartet, and remain the same composer. And here was an album of songs; the first would be Indian-flavored, the next would be country, then it would be sweet pop, then move to hard rock. And through it all, it would stay intact because they were the same composers." He soon reiterated that same idea to *Goldmine*, claiming *Revolver* was "the album, the only album" that had influenced his concept of what "pop music was supposed to do."

Throughout the tour, Warren made it a point to emphasize its experimental nature to the press and audiences alike, making everyone aware that each stop was another piece in the larger puzzle of his live "concept album." It had already been decided that this new live album would honor Warren's second album with Giant—and would cost far less than they would have to pay for a studio. Instead, Warren would proudly give over a hundred stellar performances—each professionally digitally recorded for an ambitious solo live release of greatest hits, pruned from only the very best from around the world. It was an acceptance that his own career path—as infused with literary ambition and personal integrity as it was—would most likely continue along the workmanlike "nuts and bolts" grind that kept most professional musicians forever on the road.

"Unless someone is a virtuosic singer or instrumentalist," wrote *The Los Angeles Times*, "performing a solo act is a double-edged sword.

It allows for the most intimate glimpse at one's art while exposing compositional and technical warts that a full deck of musicians can conceal . . . During the course of his 100-minute show, in which Zevon played amplified acoustic guitar, grand piano and electronic keyboards, the audience saw plenty of both."

Fuck record labels. All he needed was a tape recorder and a car.

Warren was back from Australia the first week of November, officially wrapping on the near-hundred recordings he and Duncan Aldrich had collected during their half year away from home. The trip's purpose to collect copious amounts of usable recordings for a live greatest hits album, while concurrently maintaining Giant's cash flow through ticket sales, broke from Warren's longstanding traditions in album preparation. Under the normal circumstances of a studio release, the gap between albums would permit him the time to write new material—and he often needed quite a lot of it.

And then there would be the studio sessions themselves, of which Warren had mixed experiences. While still on tour, he had told *The New Zealand Herald*'s Graham Reid, "The way I come to terms with it philosophically is, as long as record companies don't become destructive and I end up horribly in debt or completely compromised in terms of what I can do in a studio, then it's alright." In most instances, however, the end result would find Warren accusing fellow producers of compromising his work, while they—according to Jackson Browne, Waddy Wachtel, and Andrew Slater—needed to find ways to rope him in.

With his second album for Giant, Warren had been given the green light to creatively restructure both the very nature of a "live" album and the means of its recording. There were two specific words that he'd urged all involved to avoid: "greatest hits" and "unplugged." Although the project had been pitched as a collection of Warren's best-known songs—and he had delivered just that—he also chose the live setting to debut four new songs: the slide-guitar-driven "Worrier King," an extended instrumental intro to "Roland the Headless Thompson Gunner" entitled the "Roland Chorale," the recently penned-on-the-road "The Indifference of Heaven," and "Piano Fighter," which Warren had almost dually used for the album's title. As *The Boston Globe* reported, "Last summer, as he was in the early stages of playing concerts being taped for a live album, Warren Zevon decided the album would be called *The Piano Fighter,* also the title of a new tune he was recording for the album. Then, he reconsidered. The forthcoming album's new title: *Learning to Flinch.* It is suggested that Zevon's therapist might have a field day with the switch."

Making an album largely composed of older songs eliminated the pressure of writing an entire album's worth of new material, leaving much of Warren's creative focus on the actual showmanship of each and every gig, enthusiastically aware that every night was being taped for potential inclusion on the final release. "If we record every show," he'd told Reid, "I figured, I'd eventually stop being self-conscious about the fact we're recording."

Even before leaving for the European and Australian legs of the tour, Warren's apartment had been "knee-deep" in the DAT cassettes from the US dates alone. This initially prompted Giant to consider releasing the live album as a double-disc set. Had *Learning to Flinch* been recorded only a few years earlier, the final decision of whittling the recordings down to a single disc would have still filled two LPs; at seventy-five minutes in length, it was by far Warren's longest album. Still, Warren was disappointed at having to cut his acoustic version of "Detox Mansion."

"Armed only with an acoustic guitar and piano, Zevon plows through over an hour of old and new material recorded around the world in the most intimate setting possible," wrote the *Daily Vault*'s Christopher Thelen upon the album's mid-April 1993 release. From the comfort of your living room, you feel like you're watching Zevon in the front row—and you're in for one hell of a show . . . While *Learning to Flinch* may not be a substitute for a greatest hits collection, it's the perfect place for the uneducated like myself to start learning how talented Zevon is . . . Pick this one up—it's an education worth having."

Despite critical enthusiasm for Warren's energetic live release, with a single to be released and very little promotion, it spent a single week on the *Billboard* 200, peaking at Number 198 the first day of May before vanishing completely.

∽

Following their disappointment over both *Mr. Bad Example* and *Learning to Flinch,* there were no immediate plans from Giant for any form of follow-up. Both the near-constant life on the road itself and some of the questionable venues in which he had to perform were slowly beginning to grate on Warren's creative psyche. When he'd officially signed with Giant in early 1991—although, quite unofficially the year before, with *hindu love gods* tossed in as a form of "creative advance" on Warren's end—his label debut had been deliberately structured within Giant's wheelhouse as a traditional, folk-rock studio album. And it had tanked.

Going into *Learning to Flinch,* Warren had made the best out of the sly comeuppance doled out by Giant for stumbling out of the gate— sales-wise, at least. Both critics and audiences had enthusiastically approved of the solo shows that had made up the album, but those were the built-in demographic of his most devoted fans. Attempts by both Virgin and Giant to expand Warren's mainstream appeal beyond the initiated had expensively failed. It mattered to neither that the music he was making was among the most focused of his career. But it mattered to him—as well as the fact that *Learning to Flinch*'s entire road show production had inadvertently been the ultimate crash course in independent production. He and Aldrich had only needed to use Red Zone's facilities for postproduction; they'd made the entire album by themselves.

If Warren could get as far away from the watchful eyes of record executives as Helsinki, while still recording an album, there was no reason why he couldn't do the same at home. When he and Andrew Slater had trekked to Neil Young's mountain home to record his parts for *Sentimental Hygiene,* both had been astounded at the state-of-the-art home studio the rocker kept hidden behind the redwoods. Young had spent years assembling his Broken Arrow studios and kept it as modernized as any professional facility in Los Angeles; he even had a small, hand-picked staff of trusted engineers who assisted in his personal recordings and the studio's daily maintenance.

While Warren couldn't afford an extravagant setup such as Young's— not on an income based largely on touring and residuals—his most recent work wouldn't necessitate nearly as much gear anyway. He knew Young not only used Broken Arrow to produce full albums; the convenience allowed him to produce professional-grade demos and sketches, helping him along in refining new songs. Warren was happy to listen to his homemade playback on his Corvette's stereo—but a modest home studio would allow for as much tinkering or refining as he saw fit.

In April, *Billboard* ran a lengthy feature in their Arts & Music section. "Zevon primarily recorded *Mutineer* at his home digital studio, giving him an independence he had never enjoyed before," Melinda Newman wrote. "And the droll Zevon, who has never been known to use hyperbole, says that freedom has allowed him to make the record 'I've always wanted to make.'"

∽

"When you look up the word 'autonomy' in the dictionary," Warren had told *Billboard*, "there's a picture of me with a fishing cap on."

He could have ended the statement just as accurately without the wardrobe accessory mention, but Warren now wore his beloved pink fishing cap as a badge of honor—as much as he did his aforementioned autonomy. With *Mutineer,* the two were one and the same. He had given the album its title before even penning the ballad that would share its name; the word itself said it all—his long-gestating act of rebellion, the one that had never been an option before digital technology brought the tools of autonomy into his West Hollywood apartment on Kings Road. Here, his decisions would be his own, along with the frustrations. With that in mind, he christened his home setup "Anatomy of a Headache," an apropos reference to the migraines he had begun to suffer during the last leg of the tour, and to his latest fascination with the human brain and the specific areas affected by diverse headaches; he hung a color-coded poster of the annotated cranium above his engineering station.

The songs compiled for *Mutineer* dated back as far as the beginning of 1992. He had started work on "The Indifference of Heaven" after binge reading the works of postmodern English novelist Martin Amis and becoming particularly engrossed with 1991's *Time's Arrow*. Inspired by the writer's distinct and stylish wordplay, Warren penned one his most poetic works. Duncan Aldrich recalled, "I don't know many people, and certainly not many musicians, who were as literate as Warren—sitting with three books on his lap while handing me the TV remote."

Warren had still been with Annette Aguilar-Ramos at the time he started the song. She recalled that when Warren shared the first few verses of his earliest draft, she had remarked, "I'm glad you live in your world and I live in mine." They broke up again soon after and

Warren shelved the song, later completing it with the fresh emotions that his breakup from Julia Mueller had provided—or as Warren later remarked of the song, it was "the first of many depressing songs about my flaxen-tressed fiancée."

∽

When Warren had dropped off the final masters for his original score to Michael Mann's *Drug Wars* in August 1990, his A&R man, Bob Bortnick, had told him of a perfect girl he wanted to set him up with: it was his own wife's best friend, an actress who'd just recently moved to Los Angeles named Julia Mueller. He gave Warren a copy of a film she'd been in, *The Unbelievable Truth,* and said he'd have her call him the next day to see if they hit it off.

"It's funny, I had only heard of Warren because my first boyfriend in college was a huge fan," the now Julia McNeal later recalled. "But because of that, I knew all of his earliest albums really well. But, I knew absolutely nothing of his earlier 'exploits' during that time."

Warren and McNeal had a few rocky first dates, with his apparent quirks taking time to win her over. On their second, he took her to his old fail-safe, the Ivy. She came to accept his frequent acts of oddness once it became clear that she was dealing with a true artist's mentality. She recalled a memorable exchange early in their relationship: "The first time I ever came over to his apartment—I think we were on the way to go shopping, which he loved—I arrived, and he was still getting ready in the bathroom. So, I'm standing there waiting for him, not knowing until later how long he took to wash up meticulously and wash his hands many times before being done, and I noticed his old-fashioned typewriter on the glass coffee table. I looked and there was a half-written song in it."

Growing tired of waiting for Warren to finally make his appearance, McNeal assumed it was safe to take a peek. She recalled the fit he threw upon walking in on her reading the work-in-progress: "Then he came out and I asked, 'Is this autobiographical?' He went absolutely apeshit—like he couldn't contain how upset I think he really was, intruding on an artist's process. Which was right out in the open, mind you. But he kept yelling, 'Who told you to read this? I don't write autobiographical things,' all this stuff, and then stops and just starts hysterically laughing. He thought it was hysterical that I was so honest about looking at it and asking questions. But I learned he didn't necessarily want it known it was autobiographical—and not ask too many questions."

They would eventually be together for over two and a half years, despite his infidelities on the road that he later admitted to her, and a six-month hiatus fueled by his own jealousy. When Warren and Duncan Aldrich returned from the extensive world tour that composed *Learning to Flinch* in November 1992, it was agreed that McNeal would move into Warren's apartment. He hadn't been home for more than two minutes when he'd looked at her. "So, what do you say we get married?" he asked her.

Warren had a few more tours in the following weeks, but with a diligence to remain faithful, he kept his pre- and post-gig activities to bookstores and museums—in Paris, he paid a surprise visit to Ariel— all while sending funny, romantic postcards to McNeal from out-of-the-way spots he and Aldrich had found. They reunited in Hawaii and began to shop for engagement rings. There, Warren told her how remorseful he was that he couldn't afford the expensive ring he felt she deserved and relayed a story about an old friend of his who had to put a faucet washer on his fiancée's finger—neglecting to mention that he had been the one who'd slipped the washer on Crystal so many years ago. They left Hawaii without a ring. McNeal was admittedly unsure of their future together.

"There was a density of artist that was always inside of him and was always present, and it kind of couldn't be messed with—but he did a lot of preparation, both for his work and his image," she recalled. "I would say that *external suggestions* to that would mess with his own, clear image of what he wanted and how he saw himself—his own awareness of presence. But part of that was image, and he could be quite insecure about it."

Warren's insecurities regarding his image and career, and McNeal's own resentment toward the infidelities that were still hard to digest, eventually led to their relationship's end. She later recalled that they broke up due to the jealousy Warren felt toward her major role in an upcoming film, coupled with a remark made toward his recent appearance with David Letterman. It was a remark meant innocently enough but proved the final drop in the "roller coaster" that McNeal felt their relationship had become.

"Warren was going to do Letterman," she recalled. "I'd watched him on the show . . . But I thought he seemed nervous. So, he called the next day and I said he was wonderful, and right away he said, 'What?' I was like, 'No, you looked great. What you said to Letterman was great.' He said, 'What, Julia? I know you don't think it was good.' Finally, I said, 'Okay, you seemed a little nervous . . .' His reaction was, 'Oh my God, how could you say that to me?' . . . He literally cut me off for saying that to him."

McNeal moved out one week before Warren's forty-seventh birthday. He had already been working on "The Indifference of Heaven" at the time, but now added a few new lines. With a third fiancée gone, there was only the sound of the front door closing forever. She had left town and the town burned down.

"The Indifference of Heaven" was not the first instance with which one of Warren's songs had been the product of multiple muses. Not only would the timelines of his writing usually intersect with various relationships, but there were the occasional groupies and one-night stands thrown into the mix while touring. "Warren would complain about being lonely," Aldrich later recalled, "but, unless he meant it, nothing would happen. . . . Merle was there for a while. Then Annette. . . . Julia seemed serious for a while. When [the relationships] were over is when he'd complain that he was lonely and, like magic, these women would appear." He recalled that on one occasion, Warren had seduced an enthusiastic groupie waiting outside a gig. Only later did Aldrich laugh and remind Warren that he'd already slept with the woman during his last tour.

As was the new practice thanks to the convenience of the appropriately named Anatomy of a Headache, Warren was able to stop, start, overdub, remix, and add new layers to every track—meaning that many of the songs for *Mutineer* contained varied recording dates and a postproduction schedule that adhered to Warren's convenience at home, although Duncan Aldrich was on hand for the engineering of master takes and the final mix. For the first time, however, Warren was able to attempt the very "perfectionist" act that had been the biggest rift in his ill-fated collaboration with Kim Fowley in 1969—the playing of any and all instruments himself, and seamlessly layering his numerous instrumental parts into a single track.

"That album was basically recorded at Warren's house," Aldrich explained. "I encouraged him to be himself and not lean on a thousand superstars, especially if we were going to be self-producing it. We brought in people, as needed, and I think Warren liked the one-on-one collaborating, like with Jorge [Calderón] and [author] Carl Hiaasen. I think Warren liked being off the hook sometimes with the lyrics, and liked focusing on his arranging and composition."

Despite the lush sound of a full backing band, Warren had performed and recorded the majority of "The Indifference of Heaven" solo, save for old friend—and Linda Ronstadt's acting manager—Peter Asher, who proved an ideal partner to swing down to Warren's apartment and lay down harmonies. It was a small touch that Warren found particularly amusing, later noting, "That was one of the reasons that it was terrific to get Peter to sing it. Because it was like having an English intellectual singing harmony."

Throughout their crisscrossing of the United States, Warren and Aldrich would often entertain each other by calling out strange road signs and other bizarre artifacts representing the local color of the town they'd be passing through. Sometimes, their little in-jokes would lead to Warren's more playful rock tunes. In the case of "Monkey Wash, Donkey Rinse," Aldrich claimed the odd phrase was a riff on his "impression of an R.E.M. all-access backstage pass," and Warren couldn't get the strange combination of words out of his head. "One of the lines came from a mechanic in South Carolina," Aldrich recalled. They had stopped to service "The Lipcutter" when Warren had spotted the bumper sticker on a car in the lot. "Hell is only half full," it read, immediately giving him his opening line.

In keeping with the playful, humorous take on an apparent celebratory black-tie affair in the Netherworld, Warren invited David Lindley to add a distinct *cittern* to the track; he hung around to add fiddle to another song, "Poisonous Lookalike," which had been inspired by Warren's catching the tail end of a botanical radio program mentioning a flower with the deadly sounding name. The lyrics, however, were another of the many he'd penned for McNeal. The sessions with Lindley were the final recordings completed for *Mutineer* before Warren presented it to Giant for release approval, leaving Warren the time to add Bruce Hornsby's accordion to both "Monkey Wash, Donkey Rinse" and the track that had been with Warren since 1983, "Piano Fighter." He had performed it live throughout the 1992 tour and the song's true debut had been the live version on *Learning to Flinch*. In the new studio take, Warren added numerous keyboard effects to the traditional piano, as well as subdued echo effect, making the studio "remake" more like a ballad.

Of the album's first potential single, the guitar-driven hard rocker "Rottweiler Blues," Warren later playfully credited Carl Hiaasen for the song's gritty crime themes: "In the course of his research for one of his novels, I think he trafficked a little high-end para-military paranoia," he told *The Philadelphia Inquirer*. "I don't know too much about that. But affordable and free-ranging paranoia? That's more my style."

Despite the influence that Warren's recent relationships had had on almost all of *Mutineer*'s songs, the album's only true love ballad was the title track itself—ironically, not penned for any particular woman at all. "I intended this ['Mutineer'] as a gesture of appreciation and affection to my fans," he later claimed, adding, "none of whom bought the record."

Giant released Warren's independently produced *Mutineer* on May 23, 1995. It suffered the same fate of its predecessors, with low sales and mostly good reviews. In any promotion surrounding the album—which included stops with old friend David Letterman as well as *The Jon Stewart Show* in mid-June—Warren focused heavily on the DIY nature of making *Mutineer* and had no problem in continuing to tout the creative freedom that the process allowed. "If I had tried to make this album seven or eight years ago, it would have cost a couple of million dollars," he had told *Billboard*'s Melinda Newman. "Lest I make it sound that making this record was too easy, I want you to know that being responsible for my own budget was harrowing. I allowed myself a 5% breakage fee for my furniture. Maybe throwing a fax machine across the room is a little less controlled than I should be, but I said, 'It's in the budget.'" He later elaborated to *Goldmine*'s Steve Roeser, "*Mutineer* is the first album of mine without a demo stage. Recording at home enables one to eliminate the demo stage, and the presentation stage in the studio."

His article ran in *Billboard* two days before Irving Azoff was featured in a lengthy piece outlining his plans for the future of Giant. Warren noted that his name was nowhere to be found within the article.

∞

With all of his Giant releases, Warren had formed a parallel trilogy to three of his previous albums, all of which represented his passions and persona at the time: Where *Mr. Bad Example* had been created in image alone as a companion piece to *Excitable Boy,* so *Learning to Flinch* and 1980's *Stand in the Fire* had both provided brilliant representations of Warren's stage incarnations in two very different eras of his career. He claimed to have taken the convenience and budget-efficient means of home production to create the album he'd "always wanted to make," with *Mutineer,* while renouncing the overproduction and technical extravagance of *Transverse City.* While polar opposites in regard to genre, tone, style, and production methods, both of those albums nonetheless shared a common bond: they were the only two of Warren's albums that had garnered critical accusations of self-indulgence. To Warren, however, they'd both just been very personal projects.

In the case of *Mutineer,* the personal touch of its authorship reached further than the lyrics and arrangements; as the recordings had all taken place in Warren's own home, it was primarily very close friends who were welcomed to visit and contribute. Two recent friends who made their debut appearances on one of Warren's albums were jazz pianist Michael Wolff and bestselling mystery author Carl Hiaasen.

Wolff had been the music director for *The Arsenio Hall Show* when Warren appeared as the night's musical guest on February 4, 1992. Through the rehearsals, the two discovered a shared love of Norman Mailer and Ross Macdonald. Over time, Wolff gave Warren jazz composition lessons, although Warren admitted that he was not a huge fan of the genre. "I missed jazz, kind of," he later told *Goldmine*. "Michael has shown me a lot of things . . . a wonderful pianist, remarkable." On *Mutineer,* Wolff provided the atmospheric keyboards to "Similar to Rain," but it would be the first of numerous collaborations. Aside from multiple cameos on each other's albums, the two teamed up for an all-star Jack Kerouac memorial album in 1997: *Kicks Joy Darkness* found Warren in company with Eddie Vedder, Johnny Depp, Hunter

S. Thompson, Jim Carroll, Joe Strummer, Patti Smith, and Jeff Buckley in performing the late beat poet's works. Warren recited Kerouac's "Running Through—Chinese Poem Song" over Wolff's tinkling keys.

Warren's friendship with Carl Hiaasen was another story— literally. As a voracious reader whose personal book collection tipped the three thousand mark, Warren's love of pulp and crime fiction had never stopped. Hiaasen was a favorite of his long before 1991's *Native Tongue* featured a lead character with a love of Warren Zevon music. For a mutual fan like Warren, the literary shout-out was as good as canonization. "[R.E.M. guitarist] Peter Buck told me to read [Hiaasen]," Warren later told Marc Weingarten of *The Los Angeles Times*. "By the time I got to *Native Tongue,* I was such a fan I bribed the guy at the bookstore to sell me an advance copy. Then I looked in it and I saw my name on the copyright page."

Just as he had done when major leaguer Bill Lee had publicly mentioned his own love of *Excitable Boy,* Warren opted to formally introduce himself to his high-profile fan, choosing a moment to surprise the author at a signing in Los Angeles. Hiaasen later recalled the shock of looking up to see one of his favorite rock stars waiting for *his* autograph. "At that time, [Warren] had that huge ponytail down the middle of his back, and I almost fell off my chair," Hiaasen said. "I didn't know whether he was there to punch me, or whether he read something he didn't like." Stammering, the author simply said, "I can't believe you actually came."

"I only came for one reason," Warren had said, "and that's to thank you for mentioning my music in your books."

Following the book signing, Warren took Hiaasen to Noura Café for Turkish coffee—which the author skipped—and a ride in his Stingray. It was only weeks after completing *Mr. Bad Example* and Warren popped a demo cassette into the stereo. With their friendship quickly solidified, the two stayed in contact well after Hiaasen returned home to Florida, with Warren bouncing lyrics and song ideas off of him. Within the year, they were full-on collaborators, writing "Seminole Bingo" and "Rottweiler Blues" together.

It had even been during one of their now periodic fishing trips together that Warren had conceived of the title "Mutineer," viewing the project in its earliest stages as his music equivalent to a Hemingway-

esque volume of sea stories and nautical adventures. Hiaasen later recalled, "Warren liked to take pictures of himself. He'd hold the camera
out and take pictures. We were out on the boat fishing, and one of
those shots became the cover of *Mutineer*."

∞

While he was admittedly "cautiously optimistic" each time a new album
of his hit the market, Warren had particularly high hopes for *Mutineer*.
It had included songs he himself regarded as among his very best—
at least in years—and the meticulous approach he'd taken to his first
DIY album had yielded high-quality results. To Warren, *Mutineer* had
been the "personal statement" he'd always wanted to make as a singer-
songwriter—his *John Wesley Harding* or *Nebraska*. If one were to solely
take the advice of critics, the material he'd written and recorded during
his Giant tenure was perhaps his greatest; if one were to go by numbers,
they had been the lowest-selling of his entire thirty-year career.

"At one point, I had the impression that it was selling disastrously,"
he joked to Marc D. Allan of the *Indianapolis Star and News*. "But then
I was informed that everyone with whom I could feel the slightest kinship was also selling fractionally what they were accustomed to selling.
In other words—very, very bad for Mariah Carey, quite well for a folk
singer." But even to the executives at Giant, less than forty thousand
copies would have been low for a folk album. They announced their intention to drop Warren from the label before the end of the year, leaving
him with no other choice than to tour indefinitely. The last time he'd
been relegated to an RV for such a stretch, Warren had been able to write
enough material for his next album, and with his home studio now in
place, there was the option to record another album as soon as he returned. But with no other source of revenue, Warren would be forced
to spend nine months out of 1996 playing gigs just to make ends meet.

He had already started writing the songs that would make up his
next album—whenever that would be.

No one would hear them for five years.

∞

On the occasions that any songs from Warren's Giant three made it to
the airwaves, he now noticed that they no longer played on the familiar

FM rock stations. Even in their meager promotion of *Mutineer*, the label had sent a three-song sampler out for airplay; for the first time, the PR materials were largely focused on National Public Radio as a probable outlet. To his amusement, Warren found that he'd inadvertently made his way into the soft, adult-oriented world of "Adult Contemporary." When he performed "Searching for a Heart" in Boulder, he shared with the audience his own classification for the genre.

"Easy Fucking Listening," he hissed.

Part Three

ADULT CONTEMPORARY

CHAPTER ELEVEN

(1995–2002)

"I FIRST MET WARREN AROUND THE SAME TIME THAT I WAS starting Artemis," remembered Danny Goldberg. "I had been a fan for many years, but I was finally introduced to him by Jackson Browne."

Their introduction hadn't been by accident or a social call. Jackson Browne had seen very little of Warren over the past years, but it had recently been brought to his attention that his old friend was again in a form of dire straits. In 1984, Browne had worked closely with Andrew Slater in getting Warren back home to Los Angeles safe and sound—then had set him up in his old Oakwood Garden apartment. But those had been personal favors, with no connection at all to Warren's career troubles. Browne had fervently stuck to his "no more producing" rule; that was Slater's business now. Even when Waddy Wachtel, LeRoy Marinell, Jorge Calderón, and all of the original "Gentleman Boys" had offered their own contributions to Warren's ongoing work with Virgin, and then Giant, Browne had remained conspicuously absent. It wasn't to say that any resentments were harbored; both Browne and Warren had continued along respective hectic schedules for well over a decade. These days, their paths rarely crossed.

It was at a benefit concert for Jorge Calderón's ailing wife, Yvonne, in May 1995 that Warren and Browne were finally able to properly catch up as the close friends they'd once been. Although Browne kept his composure, he was disturbed to learn of Warren's recent career misfortunes. They had once been driven by alcohol and addiction, but Warren had been clean and sober for a decade. His current woes were quite different than earlier ones that had been almost entirely self-inflicted. The Warren who stood before him at the benefit was stone-cold sober, quiet, focused—older, and even a bit of a charming curmudgeon. They parted ways with the mutual intention of staying in touch.

When Warren handed him a demo cassette of some new songs he'd been wrestling with at his home studio, Anatomy of a Headache, Browne, for the second time in his life, was hell-bent on getting his friend a record deal.

At only forty-nine years old, Danny Goldberg was the epitome of a true rock-and-roll industry veteran. He'd barely been out of his teens when Led Zeppelin hired him as their publicist, then as acting vice president of their Swan Song Records. But for the ambitious Goldberg, attending meditation sessions with Robert Plant wasn't just a perk: the entire experience had led to a career trajectory as Nirvana's manager while president of Gold Mountain Entertainment, chairman of Warner Bros. Records, and president of Atlantic Records.

When Jackson Browne called him up in 1998, Goldberg had just started Artemis Records, his own independent music label. Ironically, his vision of the small, vanguard label mirrored those of David Geffen's toward Elektra/Asylum upon its founding—one of the primary reasons Browne trusted him with Warren's new demos. "I had intended it to be a small indie label from the beginning," Goldberg recalled. "I had really enjoyed working for the major companies and all the fun and the perks that went with it, but I had always preferred working with individual artists, singer-songwriters . . . I was curious about Warren's music when Jackson first called."

Unaware of Browne's favor, Warren was shocked when Goldberg called him up asking for his own copy of the demos. Warren had replied, "I'll have a mime in a top hat deliver it by hand."

Goldberg remembered, "A cassette arrived and it was 'Life'll Kill Ya' and some others that ended up on the album. It seemed like an entire album already, and the songs really, really were great. He'd lost none of his power or mastery of language."

∽

It was true that even after another frustrating five years of apparent anonymity, Warren hadn't lost a step as either an artist or performer.

He had even used the time to refine his already competent production and engineering skills.

However, with the third loss of a record company benefactor, achieving another proved even more difficult than before. He'd largely been relegated to the life of endless touring that, in his youth, he had both glorified and feared. As the next few years passed, and the venues became smaller and lower class, his career status had made him bitter.

Musician Phil Cody witnessed one of Warren's most dramatic outbursts during a show they had been booked to play together at a small brewery. He later recalled Warren's initial disgust upon walking in: "Warren comes in, and he has his leather satchel over his shoulder and it was like a ninety-mile-an-hour fastball. He rips it off his shoulder and hurls it right down the center of the room—three chairs fly, a table goes flying, and he says, 'So this is what my career has come to?'"

Duncan Aldrich had been the sole consistent witness to Warren's growing dissatisfaction with his solo career. The tension and bickering finally came to an abrupt end in December 1996—the finish line of the longest tour Warren had ever undertaken. "Driving around, no matter what he'd look at or what would be happening, he'd just spew discomfort and hate," Aldrich later recalled, "and it was driving me crazy to the point where at the end of the tour, I said, 'This is not a criticism of you at all, but maybe this will help you.' And I gave him *The Book of the Tao* and I said, 'Goodbye' . . . But that was the end. I was with him for twelve years, and I know for a fact that was the longest relationship he had."

Warren had buried his father in Hillside Cemetery in July 1990. William "Stumpy" Zevon had outlived all of his most dangerous friends, making it to the quiet age of eighty-six. "Fuck everybody," had been among his last words. In the spring of 1995, Warren had halted the installation of his home studio to care for his grandmother and mother in Fresno, both of whom had deteriorated rapidly. His grandmother passed in April, his mother in August. He later admitted that he had been moved by the traditional Mormon ceremony, and began to slowly embrace a form of spiritualism that had long eluded him.

But now, in Duncan, Warren had lost his closest friend: a voice of reason and road manager who easily doubled as his collaborative engineering partner. During 1997, Warren opted not to tour at all. He wasn't about to drive himself.

∽

Skipping a year of touring didn't mean Warren had remained completely invisible. As financially strapped as Warren had become by the second half of the decade, his mainstream media visibility was the highest it had been since the most extravagant of his tours in years past. Oddly enough, Warren's frequent forays in front of the camera had nothing to do with any form of album or tour promotion: in five years, he had made cameo appearances on two hit HBO sitcoms, *Dream On* and *The Larry Sanders Show,* and NBC's Brooke Shields vehicle, *Suddenly Susan.* Each time, he'd chewed the scenery as a biting caricature of himself—or at least of the public's perception of him: a sarcastic, world-weary rock star, far too smart for his own good, and in a constant state of amnesia regarding full decades. "You must be the asshole who calls for 'Werewolves of London' at every show," he seethed at *Dream On*'s leading man, Brian Benben, while then being tricked by *The Larry Sanders Show*'s lead, Garry Shandling, into playing the song on the spot before a live studio audience. When asked by *Suddenly Susan*'s Kathy Griffin if Neil Young had played on *Sentimental Hygiene,* his scripted response wasn't far off from his real-life interview banter. "To be honest with you, I don't remember," he quipped. "I was a little medicated during the eighties. To be honest, I'm not sure if *I'm* on that record."

Griffin later recalled that Warren's guest spot was one of the more memorable cameos on the program. "What I remember about his time on *Susan* was that he was one of [the] rare musical icons who was naturally funny," she said. "He might have thought it was an experience worth checking out. I also wondered if this was one of those situations where four other more well-known musicians turned down the gig and we ended up with someone truly great."

His dry growl had been perfect for the appropriately scripted lines, many of which carried the same sardonic humor and self-deprecating candor of his numerous appearances for David Letterman. Over the years, Letterman had been the one late-night host who not only welcomed Warren whenever there was a new album to be pitched but would make requests for him to stop by as a guest just for the fun of it. Over the fifteen years that Warren had consistently sat across from Letterman's two desks—he had relaunched his late-night show on CBS as the *Late Show with David Letterman* in 1993—their banter had taken on a very genuine mutual respect and appreciation. It also helped that Letterman was an actual fan. When longtime musical director Paul Shaffer had to step away from his emcee duties to shoot a cameo for the upcoming *Blues Brothers 2000* comedy, he thought that Warren would be one of the few substitutes that would meet with Letterman's approval. He immediately called Warren. Shaffer later recalled, "All [Warren] said was, 'I have to fly in one day early because it takes me the first day to get rid of my headache.'"

Before flying to New York for the two-week late-night gig, Warren made additional use of the East Coast trip to first visit Carl Hiaasen in Florida. From the author's account, the stress behind Warren's headaches might have already started at that point; as soon as he arrived, CBS had chased him down with requests from Shaffer's band for his sheet music to the songs he was planning for them. He quickly asked Hiaasen if there were any music shops around, or someplace else that might carry blank sheet music. Later, Hiaasen recalled, Warren sat down to write out each intricate part for the songs' scores. "We got some sheet music, and he sat down like I would sit down and write out a grocery list," he said. "He charted, for the whole band, these two songs he was going to do. Every single part—everything. Wrote it in nothing flat and faxed it to Shaffer's office . . . I said to my wife, 'How many rock musicians could do that?'"

When Warren arrived in New York a few days later, he brought with him the original scores that Hiaasen had watched him notate in short-hand. Paul Shaffer recalled, "One of them was the current record by the Spice Girls. He had written it out in full score paper, as an arranger would write out a score, or [a] classical composer would write out a score, for a full orchestra. The synthesizer solo was also transcribed."

The two-week engagement was a successful run for Warren, with Letterman consistently requesting as many of Warren's own songs as the band would play. At one point, both Letterman and the audience were amused at Warren's insistence that he'd already "exhausted" the Warren Zevon Songbook. As Shaffer had recalled, "David loved Warren's music so much it became such that whenever he would do the show, they would play all of his music throughout the evening. I used to call it, in radio parlance, 'All Zevon—all the time.'"

Letterman was particularly taken with Warren's ability to write an original song in the brief length of two commercial breaks. Inspired by "The CBS Mailbag," one his most frequent and popular routines, the host had playfully suggested that Warren pen a new song entitled "Licked by a Stranger." Both men were laughing when the skit rolled on; Letterman wasn't laughing when Warren led the CBS Orchestra in a finished song before the episode's end; he was astounded. "Boy is that good!" the host had yelled. "Genius," Letterman added, nodding.

A consistent run of ten full late-night episodes had been a boost to Warren's public exposure. While he had been making comedic cameos on numerous shows, much of his subsidiary income throughout his misperceived "hiatus" had been through lengthy scoring assignments for television. Martin Scorsese's use of "Werewolves of London" in 1986's *The Color of Money* had been a key factor in his Virgin "comeback" the following year; Warren already knew the potential in getting his existing songs into film. He had been infuriated when an independent crime film was released in 1995 deliberately cribbing one of his most unique song titles. "There's a major movie coming out called *Things to Do in Denver When You're Dead,* for which we are entirely uncompensated and unacknowledged," he had told *Goldmine.* "Poetic, isn't it?"

At one time, future star comedy writer-director Judd Apatow had sought Warren to score a potential film project, going so far as to take him to lunch to discuss the film. Apatow had been a fan of Warren's since working on *The Larry Sanders Show* in 1993. When he told Warren that the new film project was in a temporary state of limbo as he "awaited notes" on the script, Warren had looked directly into his eyes and asked him point-blank, "You take *notes?*" Apatow later recalled, "Here was a real artist. If he wrote a song, he didn't ask for notes! . . . It really changed my philosophy on my own work."

As far back as 1979, Warren had been courted for film work. He had joined George Gruel and J. D. Souther for a private screening of the football drama *North Dallas Forty* on the Paramount lot, and the producers were looking for a theme song. Warren and Souther had joined forces to quickly composes a tune, "Football Takes Its Toll," but the filmmakers ultimately left it out. A decade later, the opportunity presented itself again. During the postproduction on *Transverse City,* industry music supervisor Debbie Gold scouted him for a major three-part miniseries based on the exploits of real-life drug kingpins. The prestigious project was being helmed by Hollywood filmmaker Michael Mann, whose gritty, neo-noir style seemed an ideal fit for Warren's sound.

Warren was intrigued at the prospect of again throwing his hat into that ring. Largely thanks to learning-by-example through old friend and film composer Mark Isham, he was soon pursuing high-profile work scoring film and television, as well, as the exercise paid well and let him flex his creative, instrumental composing muscles. Gold later recalled her surprise at Warren's enthusiasm at the chance to compose elaborate instrumental music, claiming, "It was like a dream for him not to have to write lyrics. Like, Mr. Lyrics had a secret dream to just compose and not have that responsibility of the lyrics that people expected of him."

His dream to be taken seriously as a classical composer wasn't much of a secret; throughout the 1970s, he had made mention of the mysterious symphonic work's progress in nearly every unrelated interview. Although the subject had largely been dropped during his all-encompassing persona shift during the modern rock Virgin years, the digital advances that had been slowly revealed to him during his Giant tenure had brought the ambitious classical opus back into the realm of possibility.

"Enjoy Warren Zevon, rock 'n' roller, while you can," wrote Marc D. Allan in the *Indianapolis Star and News* in March 1996. "Zevon is on tour now, performing a mostly solo rock show. But if he has his way, the next time you see him will be with a symphony orchestra . . . last fall, Zevon wrote a piece of classical music . . . he said he expected to pursue this aspect of his work when his current three-month tour ends." It was the only interview throughout the tour during which Warren revealed any completed orchestral works, but its timing made it Warren's immediate work following the ill-fated *Mutineer*.

"I think the prospects of getting such a thing played are probably pretty good," he had told Allan. "I may be deluding myself, but we know there's an orchestra in every town, much less city, in America." He added, "I think that would make a very persuasive letter accompanying the score and tape, particularly if the program directors of symphony orchestras watch David Letterman, but don't have SoundScan to tell them what *Mutineer* sold."

Although Warren didn't elaborate on his apparent plan to put the cost-efficient touring strategy of *Learning to Flinch* to use for his classical works, by the end of that year, he had already decided to spend 1997 off the road.

During his second five-year stint as a member of the record deal–challenged, he nonetheless wrote and recorded new work all the time at home. When he had been commissioned to write original music for specific networks—such as a 1992 episode of HBO's horror anthology series, *Tales from the Crypt,* or NBC's reboot of *Route 66*—they had provided the needed studio spaces required for Warren to make deadline. Starting with William Shatner's *TekWar*—a cable-based sci-fi series created by the famed actor and author—he had been able to use Anatomy of a Headache to its full advantage.

Warren later recalled both the blessing and curse of working at home. "[Shatner] *is* Captain Kirk, rest assured," he later joked. "He would call me at home and demand to hear the [theme] song in progress, then he'd say, 'We need more guitars! More driving guitars!'"

But that too was part of the beauty in home production: no one had to hear what you were working on until you were ready.

∞

Warren flew to New York at the end of March 1998.

Although Danny Goldberg hadn't stipulated it directly on the phone, all signs pointed to Warren having his first record contract in half a decade. Over those years, he'd learned just enough self-reliance to conduct his consistent touring schedule, while letting his business manager, Bill Harper, book any of the extracurricular activities that might be thrown in his direction, such as the television and movie work both on and off camera. But walking into Café Un Deux Trois on West Forty-Fourth Street in New York, Warren was ready and willing to accept a handshake agreement. Goldberg recalled, "I committed to sign him the very next day. Warren didn't have a manager at the time, so I asked him who his lawyer was so we could get a contract."

"Why do I need a lawyer?" Warren had asked. "Jackson Browne told me to sign with you. I'll sign whatever you give me."

Goldberg knew full well that Ken Anderson had represented Warren for years. He attributed the feigned naïveté as either an example of Warren's innocence when it came to industry business, or "bullshit"— or a sly attempt to flatter his new employer. Anderson negotiated a deal and Warren was budgeted $75,000 to complete and master *Life'll Kill Ya* as his Artemis debut.

One of the primary elements that had drawn Goldberg into staking Warren had been the high quality of the demos themselves. Goldberg recalled, "I tend to work with a lot of artists who just want the marketing, who just want to be packaged; Warren had a real notion of what he wanted, in general, and it made him stand out, I suppose, as an artist."

He had noted that the vocals were so good, there was debate if they'd even need rerecording, and many tracks already sounded as though Warren had been backed by a full band. But while Warren had played the majority of the instruments and run the home-based production, Jorge Calderón was the most frequent visitor to Anatomy of a Headache, and had often added harmonies, bass, percussion, and additional lyrics as needed. As Warren hadn't any record contract while making the demos in his spare time, their individual recordings and production dates were even more sporadic than the numerous overdubbing "field trips" required to complete *Transverse City*.

Now that Warren had finally gotten his hard-earned record contract, Calderón was excited at the prospect of buckling down with his friend once again. He later remembered, "Warren called me one day and said, 'I've got these new songs, but I need a couple more.' He gave me the same rap he always gave me—your sensibility and mine . . . he had a deal with Artemis Records and these guys who produced Courtney Love's band."

It was Danny Goldberg who had put Warren into contact with the two-man production team of Paul Q. Kolderie and Sean Slade, with whom he had "successfully worked on the Lemonheads and the [Mighty] Mighty Bosstones albums." The duo's big claim to fame, at least in Warren's eyes, was their work with Radiohead. "That was all I needed to know," he later claimed.

"I was a monster fan of Warren's and I was very much aware that he hadn't had a new album in years," recalled Sean Slade. "When I finally got to talk with him on the phone, I was more than a little nervous—I mean, outside of maybe Randy Newman, Warren was my songwriting idol. I had to try very hard not to be a total fanboy when we were talking, but finally I said to him, 'Warren, forgive me for sounding like just another fan, but I have to tell you that in college, I had the poster of your debut album on my dorm wall.' And he just goes, 'Yeah, yeah, yeah,' like I'm just saying it—but it was completely true. I had all of his albums and I always thought he was just the coolest artist." Slade knew cool—he and production partner Kolderie held court in their own studio in Cambridge, Massachusetts, where they had already worked with Hole, the Pixies, Radiohead, and Dinosaur Jr. "I knew that he was already talking with other producers," he added. "That was just a normal part of the game. But Paul and I were really impressed with Warren's homemade demos and told him that, emphasizing his self-production. When I told him that the vocals were perhaps strong enough to use as is, I think he kinda responded to that way of thinking."

Likewise, Kolderie was surprised at the high quality of Warren's skills at Anatomy of a Headache, i.e., his home studio in his apartment's upper loft. To the seasoned producer, not having to start from the ground up and focusing on an extended form of postproduction seemed like a worthwhile challenge. "I was like Sean in that I was a big fan of Warren's in my earlier life," Kolderie recalled. "In high school, I loved Warren, Jackson Browne, Linda Ronstadt, the Eagles—that whole scene. And I loved Hunter S. Thompson and *Fear and Loathing in Las Vegas* and that whole Gonzo way of writing and thinking. And I always thought that Warren's work epitomized that way of thinking *in music*. . . . But later, Warren really wowed us with those demos. . . . It was evident from listening to them, that he'd spent a lot of time and a lot of care in their production. When we said to him, 'These may be good to go—you know, we don't have to reinvent the wheel here,' he seemed relieved that a few 'studio pros' were already happy with his work."

According to the producers, Warren had initially recorded his "impressive" vocals using one of his latest toys, a slimmer, modernized piece of mobile sound equipment that was relatively inexpensive—an ADAT machine, which had been introduced to replace the familiar unit Warren and Duncan had originally used during the Learning to Flinch world tour. Astounded, the producers suggested merely remixing those vocals recorded on Warren's kitchen table, under his guidance of course, and bringing musicians in as needed for the rest of the tracks. "We found out later that other producers who were courting the job had offered Warren larger studios and his usual setup of big-name superstar cameos," Slade said. "It was kind of humbling, since he thought our idea was interesting and went with us."

He recalled that the sessions went relatively smoothly from that point on, with Warren's only insistence that no one drink or smoke pot in the studio—he explained that he didn't want to be around it. According to Slade, "He said to us very seriously, but kind of smiling, 'I know you'll do it anyway. Just don't let me see it.'"

Kolderie remembered that Warren didn't even want cigarettes around, but it was an understandable compromise in keeping with his sobriety and focus. But not being in a studio atmosphere for a number of years, there was a compromise on Warren's part, as well, coming down to his overall creative control. "We weren't looking to overload the album with cameos of big names, but part of the project was in fleshing out what was already there," Kolderie recalled. "We brought in a great guitar player and a great friend, Chuck Prophet, but Warren was pretty adamant that he was going to be playing most of the guitar parts himself. He said to me, 'I don't want to fire your friend, but I'm not sure we're going to be using his stuff.'"

Slade recalled that he and Kolderie both got a particular kick out of contributing their own baritone harmonies to "Dirty Little Religion," one of the album's most playful tunes. The only song recorded completely in-house at Cambridge, however, was Warren's second homage to the death of Elvis Presley, the snarky "Porcelain Monkey," for which co-writer Jorge Calderón flew in from Los Angeles to record various parts. "I had said to Warren, 'I love that Elvis song and I think the lyrics are great,'" said Slade, "but I told him that it was kind of close to 'Seminole Bingo' off *Mutineer*. I honestly didn't know how he would respond to the comparison, but I think he was genuinely impressed I was able to quote his worst-selling album! So, we had a good time reworking that one live in the studio."

"Porcelain Monkey" was cut from a similar cloth as Warren's older, playful songs about the danger of celebrity. He and Calderón had one of their usual laugh sessions while composing the song, inspired by the tacky, gauche décor of the late Presley's tourist-attraction estate, Graceland. But while Warren had been genuinely moved almost two decades earlier, mediating on the lonely death of the King of Rock and Roll in the humbling and haunting "Jesus Mentioned," he now directed his keen and sardonic eye on the ultimate symbol of squandered talent: the hideous eponymous sculpture that resided in Presley's velvet-roped-off living room. Not that the topic had any deeper meaning to Warren, as he flatly explained to *Jam! Showbiz* reporter Paul Cantin: "Nothing interests me less than Elvis Presley," he'd said, adding, "We were writing a song, Jorge and I, as we do, sitting on the 'davenport of despair,' the 'divan of doom.' I looked over at his notebook and I noticed his postcard of the TV room [in Graceland]. And I said, 'What's that?' 'That is Elvis' porcelain monkey.' I said, 'Let's go!'"

Warren continued, "We did intensive research, which I found dull and distasteful. I think it is a very sad story, and not an interesting sad story, just a sad story. . . . [But] I wouldn't dream of going to Graceland. It may just be that I have my own priorities, or I am a certain type of snob. But I thought very seriously about going to Glenn Gould's grave . . . "

∞

Life'll Kill Ya was released one day before Warren's fifty-third birthday. The reviews that quickly followed for both the album and the full-backed solo tour couldn't have been a better gift.

"Sometimes the constricting circle of Zevon's spotlight produces strangely stilted music, such as 1995's *Mutineer*," wrote Jon M. Gilbertson in *No Depression*. "About as often, it engenders brilliance along the lines of 1989's sprawling *Transverse City*. With *Life'll Kill Ya*, Zevon seems to acknowledge that he works best satisfying himself, and he does so by assembling 12 thoughtful, often caustically funny, always intimately felt songs."

Many critics picked up on the album's apparent emphasis on aging and, more so, the subject of death. Although optimistic over his newly rejuvenated recording career, Warren's public persona was now one of a genuine world-weariness, and one of cautious skepticism. "I'm old and death is inevitable," he told John Roos of *The Los Angeles Times*. "It makes people uncomfortable, but isn't it as appropriate a subject for me as today's kids singing about being young and angry?" He added, "I've said before that my career is as promising as a Civil War leg wound."

Warren had been only slightly less morbid to Rob O'Connor at the online webzine Launch.com, claiming, "I'd say the hearse is at the curb at this point, both professionally and personally."

∞

The Artemis staff went full force in backing Warren's debut, landing him in-store appearances and interviews with major "Triple A" radio stations. "It stood for 'acoustic, adult, alternative,'" Danny Goldberg recalled. "They were the only stations playing his generation—Jackson [Browne] and Bonnie Raitt . . . It seemed like an ideal fit for Warren."

The sole conflict came when Warren and Goldberg had to select the first single off the album. They had agreed on "I Was in the House When the House Burned Down," the album's folkish opening track. However, a radio edit would be required to eliminate the word "shit" from the song's very first line. For the first time in his career, Warren was faced with a shade of censorship. In 1989, it had been a given that the word "cock" would be bleeped from any airings of his Letterman performance of "Finishing Touches." But for this, they'd need his approval. Goldberg remembered, "Warren went through the motions agonizing over it, and told me he needed to discuss it with Carl Hiaasen and other 'real' writers to determine if he would be sacrificing his writerly integrity by sanctioning a clean radio version before he gave his permission." In the end, Warren agreed.

Out of the gate, *Life'll Kill Ya* earned Warren the best charting numbers he'd had in years. It spent only one week on the *Billboard* 200, peaking at Number 173 in mid-February; low, but still better than any of his releases for Giant. And in this instance, there was a secondary cause for the low charting: for the first time, downloadable internet versions were made available and ranked. For the top internet albums, he had made number 9. It was Warren's first time back in the Top 10 in twenty-one years.

Despite putting in every effort for Warren's "second comeback," Goldberg remained convinced the album should have done better. "But," he recalled, "the record did get Warren back into the market, increased his live audiences, and reconnected him to his core audiences. . . . It drove me crazy that I hadn't been able to figure out how to attain the heights of Bonnie Raitt's latter-day success for Warren."

What success the album did enjoy had a secondary benefit: sales of *Mutineer* nearly doubled.

To promote the album, Warren again went out on a solo tour, only now with the proper road management and accommodations that came with perks of his contract. With stellar new material and a once again renewed vigor for performance, he had refined the one-man spectacle of his *Learning to Flinch* world tour, presenting a matured, folkish set on par with his own description: "grunge classical."

"Mr. Zevon's songs change radically depending on whether they're for guitar or piano," wrote Jon Pareles in *The New York Times*. "His guitar tunes hark back to Appalachian music, often using a dulcimerlike drone and just a handful of circling chords. In two songs, he made the chords a tape loop while he played lead guitar solos. On piano, he uses more elaborate harmonies, by way of Copland and gospel, to back what might be parlor songs for a highly unsavory parlor."

The Philadelphia Inquirer's Jonathan Valania shared Pareles's enthusiasm for both Warren's new material and energetic solo show. "Zevon's voice, that inimitable bleat, was as strong and sure as his guitar work," he wrote. "His acid wit has lost none of its corrosive amusement value . . . Referring to temporary seating that filled the normally standing-room only orchestra pit, Zevon asked the crowd if they had brought their own chairs.

"'Reminds me of a Narcotics Anonymous meeting in Manila,' he said, sounding like a man who would know."

∞

Danny Goldberg may have been disappointed in the overall reception to *Life'll Kill Ya*—at least on Warren's behalf—but the artist himself only wanted to keep the momentum going.

Soon after returning from London at the end of May 2000, he approached Goldberg with a laundry list of ideas for the follow-up, something that he described as a "spiritual album."

Goldberg recalled, "Instead of writing with Jorge Calderón or working with a producer again, Warren wanted to set up a home studio and do everything himself. I figured that since we weren't paying very much for his albums, and since Warren was essentially an auteur, it would be inappropriate to argue." He added, "In retrospect, I probably should have questioned him more seriously about this approach."

The quality of songs on *Life'll Kill Ya* had benefited tremendously from the forced hiatus that Warren had struggled through; ironically, it was during the longest stretches of time, often with the direst of financial and personal woes, that the songs he wrote were the most personal and cerebral. As had been the case with his self-titled Elektra/Asylum debut and then later, with *Sentimental Hygiene,* years of refinement had resulted in the best work. But now in his fifties, Warren didn't have another half decade to let a new cache of material percolate in his mind. While it was true enough that Warren wanted complete control of his next album, it was apparent that help would be needed to write the songs fast enough for turnaround recording and release.

When he explained his conceptual intention for the album to Danny Goldberg, however, Warren played up his creative vision over the pragmatic need for collaboration. As Goldberg recalled, he "had decided to use the literary 'angle' for all it was worth." This entailed inviting nearly every writer friend he had made in the last few years to try their hands at writing some rock songs. He later explained to Marc Weingarten of *The Los Angeles Times,* "A lot of the time it's an awful, unnatural struggle for me to write lyrics. I think of it as a necessary evil. If it gets business-like, I'm unhappy with the results. I have to wait for some kind of inspiration, and that means a lot of extreme frustration, because I'm not being useful."

The writers that Warren had in mind were no strangers to rock and roll. Through his close friendship with Carl Hiaasen, Warren had made the acquaintance of a veritable who's who of bestselling authors, all of whom were also hobbyist musicians. Under the clever banner the Rock Bottom Remainders, *Tuesdays with Morrie* author and columnist Mitch Albom, horror master Stephen King, Pulitzer Prize–winning humorist Dave Barry, and National Book Award finalist Amy Tan periodically got together to form a loose rock band to play charitable events and book fairs. Although the group didn't take themselves all that seriously as professional rockers, the sheer novelty of stellar literary figures jamming to "Satisfaction" for a worthy cause was always a big draw.

"Carl [Hiaasen] had called and told me that Warren was interested in playing with us at a show we had coming up," recalled Dave Barry. "He gave me Warren's number and I called him, and we had a very funny conversation. I don't think I've ever met anybody as accomplished and well-known as Warren who was so determined never to say one remotely positive thing about himself."

Barry admitted that he had been an admirer of Warren's music, particularly his lyrics, since the 1970s. "I was a fan going back to his early stuff," he said, "and I just always thought that it was really intelligent, but they were all just really quirky songs that just killed me. I was surprised when he agreed to play with us—and I was even more surprised when he stuck with us."

During rehearsals for the Miami Book Fair, Warren had connected with the literary types he had so long admired—very much coy to the notion that they were equally excited to have him on board. Barry recalled, "Warren would get lost any time we invited him over, or to rehearsal. He would call multiple times from a phone to double-check the directions. Well, he was over for dinner and my wife and I had a CD player that held, like, a hundred CDs. As we're talking, in the background, Warren heard that his own album had come up. He leapt up while I was talking and changed it. He couldn't stand to have his music on while we were all there."

Mitch Albom met Warren for the first time at a Rock Bottom Remainders rehearsal. He recalled, "[Warren] was already at rehearsal when I got there, and he was playing guitar . . . and he had a little box that had effects on it at his feet, and he kept stepping on these different buttons. It was like looking at a guy stepping on land mines to see if they blew up or not."

At first, Warren and Albom were largely unfamiliar with each other's work, but they connected on a shared love of sports and literature. "I think he was intrigued by the idea of being around a lot of literary types after a lifetime of being around rock-and-roll types," Albom recalled. When the time came for Warren to begin writing material for his second Artemis album, Albom was one of the first writer buddies he had contacted. "We ended up with 'Hit Somebody!' because Warren had said no one really ever wrote a song about hockey. I agreed, and he said, 'Well, let's collaborate.' So, I wrote this song about a hockey goon who hates that it's his job to beat people up and then it's the last game of his life and he has a chance to score his first goal." In the song's lyrics, it is left ambiguous if Buddy, the aforementioned "goon," survives his apparent suicide and gets a shot at personal redemption. Albom recalled, "I think that was the big difference with me and Warren. We talked about the song later, and I hoped, you know, Buddy lived—that he'd scored his one goal. I asked Warren what he thought."

"Well, he dies, of course,'" he said.

Warren was particularly proud of the recording session, as he had been able to get not only Paul Shaffer and the CBS Orchestra to appear on the track, but David Letterman himself came down to add the seminal, "Hit Somebody!" battle cry heard throughout the action-packed anthem. Before entering the studio with the track, however, Warren had chased Albom down to his vacation spot in the islands to notify him that their collaboration would be ready for listening upon his return.

"Wait, you're actually recording that?" Albom had asked, laughing over the hotel room phone.

"Well, of course," Warren said over the line. "What did you think we wrote it for?"

When the Rock Bottom Remainders finally played the Miami Book Fair that year, Dave Barry recalled that Warren was not only willing to play his own songs with the rag-tag group, but was amused at their own nervousness to perform them in front of him. Stephen King was particularly anxious to be singing "Werewolves of London" with the original werewolf himself standing right beside him. According to Barry, it was Warren's own idea. "He said, 'I'll only do it if Stephen King sings it,'" Barry recalled. "He said, 'I'll do the keyboards, but it'll be much funnier if he's the one singing it.' I thought he was also being kinda shy about it."

Barry added, "Warren really fit right in with us, I guess because he was a writer himself, but also because we regarded the [Rock Bottom Remainders] as a joke—and it seemed like nobody really got the joke more than Warren did."

In total, Warren played over a dozen gigs with the Remainders, even accompanying the group on a handful of "mini tours" aimed at raising money for various charities.

"We certainly considered him a member of the band," said Barry. "We invited him to every gig, and he did come to quite a few. . . . I mean, he fit right in—hanging out with us on the [tour] bus—and was just the funniest guy."

Barry added, "Warren didn't come to all of the rehearsals, thank God! It was like, cruel, to have to play in front of him! He certainly didn't need the rehearsal time, especially while we were learning to play his songs.

"I think the biggest problem was that Warren could never find where we were. Like, he would rent a car to meet us wherever, but he would need to run out to buy T-shirts or things like that—his *habits*—and then he would head to my house, say, and I would put him on the phone with my wife, Michelle, since she was so good at giving directions. But then that would lead to a series of phone calls," Barry laughed. "It would be starting with Warren getting lost on the road, and I would just hear Michelle say, 'Okay, wait—*where* are you? Well, what does the road sign say? Okay, now what does the next sign say? Okay, Warren, so you're going the wrong way! Call us back when you've turned around.' Five minutes later, I'd hear her again, 'Okay, now what does *that* sign say?' These were pre-GPS days, and Warren wasn't really a 'direction guy,' so he'd miss a lot of rehearsals. But he was the only one who didn't need them, anyway," he laughed.

Barry added, "Warren was just such a good singer, such a good guitarist—and just so good at, basically, fitting in—plugging in—to whatever had to be done. And I remember that he would simply disappear when the rest of the band could relax later and head to the bar. But he was really the funniest in a group of really funny people—and he got every joke, every reference. He just fit right in."

As Warren continued to assemble a roster of poetic champions to help him with his most literary of concept albums, he not only drew from his friends within the Rock Bottom Remainders, but other authors with whom he had grown close over the past few years.

Warren had already befriended one of his own literary influences years earlier, spending occasional long weekends with Hunter S. Thompson at the writer's "fortified compound" in Aspen, Colorado. In 1996, he and Duncan Aldrich had broken up some of the monotony of the road by visiting Thompson and helping him weed through his thousands upon thousands of personal correspondence, all to be compiled into a future three-volume published collection. Since then, Warren frequently continued to visit his gonzo journalist pal, sometimes for target practice, or to spend an evening of impassioned televised hockey viewing.

Their usual camaraderie was halted in 2001 when Thompson asked for a slightly larger favor. The iconoclastic writer had been on a personal crusade to earn convicted cop-killer Lisl Auman a new trial, in what he deemed "a travesty of justice." Uncharacteristically, Warren had agreed to perform alongside Thompson, actor Benicio del Toro, and Pitkin County Sheriff Bob Braudis at a rally on the foot of the state capitol in Denver. Like Warren's unceremonious public endorsements of Congressman Steve Cohen in 1996 and former professional wrestler Jesse "The Body" Ventura for governor of Minnesota in 1999, it was a rare instance when passionate friends around him provided enough peer pressure to briefly enter the political ring. It didn't happen often and it didn't happen again—although Auman's case was finally tossed out in 2005.

During their brainstorming sessions on Auman's behalf, Warren approached Thompson about working together on a song for his upcoming "literary" concept album. Thompson later wrote of their tea-fueled session, "Warren is a profoundly mysterious man, and I have learned not to argue with him, about hockey or anything else. He is a dangerous drinker, and a whole different person when he's afraid."

And after years of mutually appreciating each other's bodies of work, the two finally collaborated on the moody and appropriately gonzo-driven "You're a Whole Different Person When You're Scared"— not that the collaborative process didn't come with its own set of challenges. As Warren later told *The Los Angeles Times,* "[Thompson] will be utterly responsible if you need him to be. . . . If you show up at his place in Aspen at 2 a.m. with a guitar, ready to write the lyrics, that might not be the night you'll write the song. But by golly, he'll call you on the phone at 9 in the morning six weeks later and start reciting lyrics."

While Warren had to personally ask one of his own idols-turned-friends for a turn at co-writing, he had recently received an enticing letter from an unlikely—and particularly prestigious—fan. Renowned Irish poet Paul Muldoon was already the recipient of both a Guggenheim Fellowship and the T.S. Eliot Prize for his poetic works when he wrote to Warren out of sheer admiration for his rock-and-roll music; Muldoon was a secret rock fanatic and had recently taken up the electric guitar. "Dear Mr. Zevon," the poet had written, "I hope you won't mind my writing to you out of the blue, but I've been an unabashed fan of your work for twenty-five years and thought I'd simply put that on paper." Muldoon had sent along two autographed books of his poetry—unaware that such a gift was an instant way to Warren's heart— and offered them as "tokens of my regard for your achievement."

The two finally met for the first time in person in New York in September 2001, just weeks following the attacks upon the Twin Towers. Among their discussions of art and literature, Warren expressed his own disillusionment over the terrorist acts, and pushed for Muldoon to collaborate with him. They discussed the potential for a long-term musical theater project together—but for now, Warren insisted that Muldoon try his hand at rock-and-roll writing on *My Ride's Here*. Inspired by Warren's faith in him, Muldoon soon registered a music publishing company in his own name for the new lyrics, ordered subscriptions to *Spin* and *Guitar World* magazines, and began to furiously email back and forth with Warren regarding their tunes. Among the playful debates over what instruments would work best for their new songs, "Macgillycuddy's Reeks" and the album's title track, "My Ride's Here," Warren made a point to calm his new friend.

"Rest assured," he wrote Muldoon, "I'd be that much prouder and happier if you co-write everything. I'm quite content playing Keith to your Mick."

Warren acknowledged that many fans and critics would question the necessity of leaning so heavily upon collaboration with literary giants, especially when his own reputation was firmly rooted as a lyricist. "Part of this rather savage criticism I've seen about the album is that people think there is something deeply lazy about collaborating with all these writers," he later commented. "But the simple answer is that I love singing their words."

The majority of *My Ride's Here* was recorded back at Anatomy of a Headache. Over the past few years, Warren had continued to upgrade his home equipment with as many of the latest advances as he could afford. As the original vocal demos for *Life'll Kill Ya* had been made using ADAT, he had sought significant upgrades before starting on the new album. It was while shopping for the much-needed gear that he met Noah Scot Snyder, a young engineer and musician who was fascinated to hear about Warren's major "made at home" rock release. "It was like so many Hollywood connections—I met Warren because we bought gear from the same guy," Snyder later recalled. "At the time, he had been recording to ADAT, which was an industry standard at the time, and I was familiar with it. So, we started casually talking about his equipment and the whole home production arrangement he'd been putting together and how he was learning Pro Tools and things like that."

Working entirely solo at home, Warren wasn't quick to admit his frustrations in installing the much more sophisticated digital editing suites that were now, thankfully, also regarded as an industry standard. "I got the impression that [Warren] was on the verge of really disliking some of the people getting him his equipment and doing the installing," Snyder remembered. "I could see the anger just in his explanation. . . . If Warren didn't like you, he wasn't afraid to let you know that. But the same thing went the other way; if he liked you, he'd make you feel like a work of art. If he met you and he thought you were a putz, he'd treat you as such."

Soon winning Warren over, Snyder was invited to aid in both installation of the new gear and a listen at some of the new demos that Warren had in the works. Talk soon began of collaboration. Snyder recalled, "The first project I did with him was *My Ride's Here*. . . . [Warren] thought I was this hotshot because I was only like twenty-five years old at the time, and he was eager to learn new techniques. He was a very demanding guy, but he made me do a lot. There was a lot of trust and I gained experience very quickly . . . We got very close towards the end."

Even with a sophisticated home setup, there was only so much that Warren could record in the confines of his apartment. For at least two tracks, it was mandatory that the small team move into a professional studio space—if only to accommodate the size of a harmonic ensemble. "Hit Somebody!" had been a true studio date, calling for the full CBS Orchestra. For the closing track of *My Ride's Here,* Warren ended in the grand style of his earliest albums, crafting a haunting ballad with bitter, jealous lyrics and an ambitiously classical string quartet section.

Producer Noah Scot Snyder warmly remembered the recording session for "Genius" as his closest look into Warren's classical influence and abilities. "That song was our only string date together," he recalled. "He wrote each part by himself, and did notation on the computer . . . the violins, the viola, and the cello. But for Warren to not only know the music, but to be able to write out the parts? It was more than a level of understanding, it was a full level of *knowledge*. The music was so easy for him. He used to say to me, 'Once the lyrics are done, the song is done.'"

Despite the amazing roster of literary talent on Warren's most literary of rock albums, Goldberg wasn't as impressed with *My Ride's Here*— although he kept it to himself. "Although I liked several of the songs, the album seemed less focused to me than *Life'll Kill Ya*," he admitted. "The one fully realized song on it, 'Genius,' was a classic Zevon masterpiece, but it was particularly ill suited for radio play, even Triple A, because of the length of time it took to get to the chorus."

Critics had mixed opinions on the album as well, although a few older admirers saw the harder-edge release as an improvement over the folkish country rock that had largely defined *Life'll Kill Ya*.

"*My Ride's Here* makes two crucial improvements on Zevon's honorable 2000 Artemis debut, *Life'll Kill Ya*," wrote Robert Christgau in *Rolling Stone*. "First, it rocks harder (and louder) without stinting on the musicianly colors that have always redeemed his sessionman whomp. Second, it doesn't dwell much on his love life, which, after decades of dysfunction, we have the right to judge a not especially interesting permanent disaster area . . . This reflects the structural strategy of most of these lyrics, which boast input from detective novelist Carl Hiaasen, poet Paul Muldoon, sportswriter Mitch Albom and the right honorable Hunter S. Thompson: Start with a recognizable narrative conceit, Lord Byron's luggage or Jesus at the Marriott, and take it somewhere strange in word or incident."

When it came time to consider a promotional tour for *My Ride's Here,* Warren faced the one conundrum that he'd not anticipated in crafting a lush home production: he'd need a band to replicate them live. That problem proved the first, and only, rift between him and Goldberg. "Warren had done well with the last tour," he remembered. "It was solo and acoustic and the reviews were good. With the next one, he was insistent that he needed an entire band. Artemis couldn't afford that so, he decided not to tour at all. It meant no promotion, and that was really the largest benefit to come out of *Life'll Kill Ya*."

It had become clear to Goldberg that even after two albums together, Warren needed a hands-on manager to prevent him from inadvertently dive-bombing his fourth opportunity for a longstanding relationship with a record label. He was able to get old friend Irving Azoff to take him back on. "It wasn't a hard sell," Goldberg recalled. "He knew Warren was a genius and he knew that both the artists he already worked with and the wealthy baby boomers he did business with admired Zevon." Under Azoff's guidance, Warren's daily business affairs would be handled by Brigette Barr, who knew Warren from her days working with Peter Asher. She recalled that when they were reintroduced, the first thing Warren had done was grab her hand to check for a wedding ring. Her first order of business would be in organizing with Warren upcoming tours to both compensate for the missed opportunity with *My Ride's Here,* and also to continue to make some money while he geared up for another album.

Goldberg recalled that when he next saw Warren for a meeting at the Ivy at the Shore in Santa Monica, it was apparent the next project together would go smoother. "The new songs I'm writing I can perform acoustically," he'd said. Goldberg interpreted this as Warren's regret over his previous decision, even if he wouldn't say it directly. He also knew that Warren had feared the poor sales of his follow-up album would lead to an axe from Artemis's roster.

Warren also regretted that of all the esteemed co-writers who had worked on *My Ride's Here* with him, Jorge Calderón hadn't been among them. As per a usual routine, the two old friends would meet and go to the movies together. On one typical outing soon after Warren's sigh-of-relief meeting with Danny Goldberg, Warren had turned to his old friend and said, "I want to start working on another album right now. Let's do this one together. Let's go back to what we know how to do, and let's do it in my house." The two hugged, both walking off with the agreement that they'd begin work as soon as Warren returned from tour. Barr and Goldberg had found an ideal fit for Warren: a Canadian folk festival with folk-rock and country sensibilities—a perfect fit for his solo acoustic style. It could also act as a refresher for a future solo tour, the one he'd promised Danny Goldberg he'd make work. They'd discuss it when he returned home from Calgary.

                                  ∽

While promoting *Mr. Bad Example* in 1992, Warren had just started opening up to interviewers about his own views on celebrity and the turns that his career had taken. At the time, he had just signed with

Giant Records and, at least on paper, things had looked promising. Richard Cromelin of *The Los Angeles Times* had taken that opportunity to ask Warren if he'd ever felt "intimidated" by either the quality of his older work or the brink of superstardom that he had once circled. As an analogy, Warren had used the career of Norman Mailer, one of his oldest literary heroes—and whose espionage epic, *Harlot's Ghost,* Warren had recently read while on that tour.

"You know, to be really truthful, I suppose you occasionally think that," he admitted to Cromelin. "But then, people always regard writers' earliest work as their best. I mean, nobody's ever gonna say anything but [Mailer's] *The Naked and the Dead* was the guy's best." Warren had paused before adding his final thought to the matter. "There may be a way that writers are taken seriously twice if they're lucky," he said, "at the beginning and the end."

On the same tour, he'd echoed identical sentiments to *Entertainment Weekly*'s Bruce Fretts—only not quite so guarded, or elegant. "If you're lucky, people like something you do early and something you do just before you drop dead," he'd said. "That's as many pats on the back as you should expect."

Part Four

THE LAST TEMPTATION
OF WARREN WILLIAM ZEVON

CHAPTER TWELVE

(2002–2003)

AT THE VERY BEGINNING OF 1997, WHEN WARREN TRULY sought it the most, he'd met the last great love of his life.

In Ryan Rayston—a beautiful young screenwriter and author whom he'd accidentally met at his favorite grocer—he found the ideal female companion who met his every single need, save sexual. He already had that one covered many times over. But Rayston, as he was soon to discover, also suffered from migraines and OCD; she was in a twelve-step program and had her own bouts with creative self-doubt and writer's block. And with no record contract, no more Duncan Aldrich—and some members of the press erroneously using the word "retired" in an infrequent press mention—Warren was in a state of personal and creative limbo when he met his lovely new kindred spirit. At first, Warren's initial response was to leap at the chance for a romantic date. Their very first exchange, however, set the playful tone that would take on a sibling camaraderie and warmth.

"We met casually at a local gourmet supermarket called Chalet Gourmet on Sunset and Fairfax," Rayston later recalled. "We had made eye contact and then just started talking. I knew who he was, and I was familiar with his music—so we made plans and exchanged numbers. But then I had this massive migraine and turned off my phone and had to get in bed right away. I never called him and he left me a vicious message. Instead of letting him get away with it, I called him back and let him have it. 'I had a fucking migraine, Warren!' and he goes, 'Oh. Oh, then you're forgiven.'"

Rayston added, "We had an extremely close friendship. No judgment, no bullshit—although we fought—and a whole lot of love. . . . We both had OCD, and there are things that are simply understood in that ritualized madness that may seem crazy to someone looking in, but to those locked in it, [there's] a transformative freedom just having someone 'get it.'"

There was one particular ritual that Rayston admittedly "got" immediately. She not only lacked judgment in Warren's compulsive mantra but offered the unspoken reply that demanded confirmation. "Nothing's bad luck, is it?" he would ask her.

"No," she always knew to answer.

After Warren returned from Calgary, Canada, in August 2002, Rayston would no longer know the answers to every one of Warren's questions, but she would hear them all—every doubt and fear, and witness every fall.

∽

"My songs are all about fear."

Warren had stated it plainly during his *Transverse City* promotional tour in 1989, later adding "paranoia" into the mix of his recurring themes. Almost a decade and a half later, not much had changed—only the sources of fear and paranoia. It wasn't a specific fear that led Warren to visit a doctor upon his return from Canada; rather, a fear that had kept him away to begin with.

Warren hadn't visited a physician since January 1990. After all the self-inflicted damage to his body that he had survived nearly two decades ago, it had taken the overpowering omens and ever-present specters of his OCD to keep him as far away from the possible bad news a doctor visit could bring. And even then, there was only one medical practitioner he would even consider seeing—his dentist, and only then in an absolute emergency. In the better part of two decades, nothing had seemed important enough to Warren to tempt fate. But in the weeks building up for his trip to Canada in July 2002, he'd made too many excuses for his frequent shortness of breath. When Ariel had taken notice, he'd waved it off as pushing too hard at the gym.

Likewise with Brigette Barr, who saw Warren often enough to have noticed the difficulties he seemed to be having. "I told him that when he came back from Canada, he absolutely had to see a doctor," she remembered. "He said to me, 'I don't go to doctors, I don't believe in doctors. I don't want to know what he has to say.' His biggest fear was that if he went to the doctor, he would get bad news."

No one gave him a harder time than Jorge Calderón, who began nagging Warren to take the matter seriously as far back as July. "Then he went up to Canada to do a few outdoor shows," he remembered, "and he told me the same thing. He called from Canada, and he said, 'I don't know, it must be the altitude' . . . I said, 'Warren you have to go see a cardiologist.'" Calderón explained that a possible obstruction in his arteries could be the cause of his breathing problems. "Oh, no," Warren had said, "it's just stress. I get stressed all the time." Finally, Calderón and wife Yvonne were able to whittle him down enough to agree to call his cousin, Sandford—the only cardiologist he'd trust to speak with. As if Warren couldn't have guessed, his cousin had advised the same thing: he needed to see a doctor right away. On August 25, he acquiesced and visited Dr. Stan Golden, his friend of over twenty years who, incidentally, happened to be Bob Dylan's cousin.

The shortness of breath seemed odd. Warren hadn't touched a cigarette since 1997 and had never lapsed from his sobriety. In recent years, he had stuck, more or less, to a gym routine that included weight lifting and frequent trips to the tanning salon on Sunset Boulevard. Now in his midfifties, up until his breathing issues, Warren had been in the best shape of his life. Having clipped his famous ponytail and slowly developed noticeable muscle mass, he even looked fitter than he had in years. Golden was convinced that, especially with heart troubles on his mother's side of the family, Warren truly needed a good cardiologist; Golden not only recommended one but accompanied Warren there. From the waiting room, he called Calderón. "You're going to be proud of me, Jorge," Warren had said. "Guess where I am? I'm at the cardiologist's office."

Calderón was initially relieved that Warren had buckled down and finally listened to every person in his life that had been concerned. He told Warren to call him when he found out more details. "The next call was several hours later," Calderón recalled. "I was worried because it had been so long, but he called and said, 'It's not so good.' When he told me, I fell to my knees. I couldn't talk. It's like his voice went away, and I couldn't talk."

Warren called Carl Hiaasen from the office, too. "They gave me a glass of water and told me to sit down," Warren told him. "I knew it was bad." He revealed to Hiaasen the doctor's words. It was bad; a bleeding in the lungs had led to further tests, all of which revealed a form of lung cancer. It wouldn't be until more results came through the following day that Warren even learned the aggressive form he had—a rare, particularly aggressive type: mesothelioma. Worse yet, it had spread to his liver. They had been very honest and very blunt—he wasn't expected to make it past three months. Much to Hiaasen's surprise, Warren appeared very level-headed. "This is a lot harder for you than it is for me," he told Hiaasen. "If you had gone to bed as many nights as I did in the old days, knowing that you had taken so much stuff that could kill you, and not knowing if you would wake up, this is not as shocking as you think."

Warren added for clarification, "I've been writing this part for myself for thirty years and I guess I need to play it out."

Even in Warren's closest circle, nearly everyone agreed that this was the time he should be focused on his health and his family. But Warren was adamant to Danny Goldberg that he wanted to use whatever time he had left for productivity, insisting he start an album as soon as possible. He'd recorded albums in less than three months before—what could he put together with the amount of time that the doctors had given him?

"Warren told me that since his children were grown up, his legacy was his music," Goldberg remembered. "His wiseguy intellect had previously resisted formal or sentimental words like 'legacy,' but there was no reason for that now." He also insisted that Artemis issue a press release regarding his disease now, and the plans to continue recording. He'd even informed Goldberg, "I told Brigette we really have to use this. I want her to be the most manipulative, exploitive manager she can be. I want her to milk this for all its worth." It was the same tactic he'd used with his rehab stints: if his fans knew he had a massive goal, it would be harder for him to let them down.

"I told him he should see a therapist," cousin Sandford Zevon remembered. "I thought that that would be the best thing for what he was facing. But Warren said, 'No, no, no—I appreciate it, but this is the therapy I need.' He told me all of the drugs and plans that [the doctors] had presented to him, but he said he wanted to finish the album and leave some kind of financial backing behind for his family." Danny Goldberg had offered to Warren a personal meeting with famed celebrity spiritual guru Deepak Chopra. He'd passed on that, too.

Goldberg and Barr did as Warren had asked, and media picked up the story right away. In accordance with Warren's intuition, every major news outlet that had largely ignored him for years began to flood Artemis with interview requests. He shook his head at the irony, but decided to pick and choose which media figures he would deal with for as long as his disease would allow him. But, as he told Goldberg, the new album had to come first.

However, Warren did make two small exceptions to his now very hectic schedule.

Warren soon heard that Bob Dylan had begun performing "Mutineer" in concert in his honor. He had cracked a smile to Jorge Calderón, telling him, "Maybe this is worth it." When Dylan was booked to perform at the Wiltern theater in Los Angeles, Warren made it a point to attend. Anticipating his arrival, Dylan personally greeted him backstage, offering his own words of regret over the recent news and telling him, "I hope you like what you hear," before meeting the crowd. Without introduction, Dylan and his band then launched into their covers of "Mutineer," "Lawyers, Guns and Money," and "Accidentally Like a Martyr." Warren looked on tearfully as his own hero paid tribute to *him*.

He was soon short of breath and had to leave before the concert's end.

Warren took one final concession before heading back into the studio for his final time. In one of his first interviews after the diagnosis, he'd joked to *Entertainment Weekly* that his true goal was to live long enough to see the next James Bond movie. When the franchise's producers got wind of Warren's comments—especially as he literally faced the battle of his life—they swiftly arranged a private screening of the film series' yet-unreleased latest installment. It was to be the first private screening of an unreleased Bond film since John F. Kennedy had requested a copy of *From Russia with Love* be delivered to the White House days before his fateful flight to Dallas in November 1963. Warren had the movie theater all to himself.

And he particularly loved the movie's title: *Die Another Day*.

∽

Initially, Danny Goldberg and Brigette Barr were confounded as to how they should go about booking studio time or how the project should be presented to the public. At that early stage, it was unpredictable if Warren's health would maintain for the recording of one song, or three; they were admittedly shocked that he had been so stern in making some form of album happen at all. "I didn't know what we would do with the recordings," Goldberg recalled. "We certainly didn't anticipate that he would live long enough to do an entire album. I figured that even if he did one song, we could release it as a bonus track on a 'best of' or something." Goldberg mentioned to Warren Jackson Browne's idea of organizing a tribute album in his honor, featuring different artists performing some of Warren's best-known works. According to Goldberg, Warren had "snarled": "Tell Jackson to make the fucking tribute album after I'm dead. Right now, I want to concentrate on my own new album." It was all Goldberg needed to hear. He allocated $25,000 for Warren's new recordings and booked the first few session dates at Sunset Sound.

After Warren's diagnosis was confirmed, Jorge Calderón was shocked that his friend truly wanted to go ahead with his plans to record. "I tried to tell him that now was the time for him [to] be with his family. . . . Now is the time [to] take care of yourself. If you want to take a trip, or spend your days lying on a beach in Mexico, go for it." But Warren had an answer for that, too. "I've thought about it," he told Calderón, "and what would bring me the best joy would be to do what I love the best, and that is writing songs. I want to do this album—I want to do it like we talked about. So, let's do it."

There was one condition. Warren had stipulated that the public be made aware of his illness, both for his fans' awareness and for his own motivation. The by-product, however, was that he was suddenly receiving calls, emails, and letters from everyone in his past. "He kept telling me that all these people were calling him and coming out of the woodwork from years back," recalled Calderón. "Everyone was getting him on the phone and sobbing. He was getting calls from people he hadn't seen in years, people he'd only met a couple of times. And he wasn't the kind of person who [could] say to them, 'Look, I don't have time for this.'"

If Warren was truly going to make an attempt to complete a full album, as unlikely as everyone secretly believed that possibility to be, he'd need to write quickly and have a core team of studio help assembled even quicker. With Calderón the perfect candidate as chief collaborator, co-songwriter, and co-producer, that only left the need for a solid fellow producer who could helm the primary engineering. Warren immediately called Noah Scot Snyder, whom he hadn't yet informed of his diagnosis, let alone the new album.

"At that point, [Warren] thought he only had a few months to live," Snyder remembered. "He asked me to produce the album with him in the same phone call that he was telling me about the cancer. I was recovering from the news while he's asking me to do the project. I mean, at this point, he was one of my best friends. I admired this man and he mattered to me a lot. So, even if we were just *doing it* for the sake of recording, and no one was ever going to listen to it, it had that meaning to us all."

Carl Hiaasen recalled that for the two months following his diagnosis, Warren threw himself completely into the new album, while "dodging phone calls from acquaintances that he'd long scratched off his list of friends. 'Everybody wants closure,' he complained." David Marks had tried, as had Violet Santangelo. He exchanged a few emails with Duncan Aldrich, had notified Julia, and Annette, and his loves.

One friend who noticed his silence, but later admitted to understanding, was Jackson Browne. Warren had never contacted him. Browne, however, later told *Rolling Stone* that he knew Warren would be working harder than ever to finish his final album, and remained sympathetic. "[But] in order to do what he did, [Warren] had to jettison anything extraneous, to limit himself," Browne said. "He couldn't spend time bidding farewell to the many people that wished they could spend time with him."

Eventually, Browne was able to get Warren on the phone one last time. "He wanted to finish this record. And no matter how much we celebrate the album and the people who came around to do it with him, making a record is real work. He had to retreat into his most personal, essential friendships."

Browne was right. Warren had been forced to halt progress on a number of promising projects when the diagnosis had come. He and Paul Muldoon had collaborated so successfully on their two tracks for

My Ride's Here that they had already laid the groundwork for an ambitious, theatrical stage musical. Tentatively entitled *The Honey War,* Warren and Muldoon had concocted a humorous and biting tale of a dispute over gaming rights to a Native American casino. With a Carl Hiaasen–flavored crime story, Muldoon's signature wordplay, and Warren's "grunge classical" compositions, the stillborn musical was one project that both collaborators were sorry to see fall by the wayside.

Soon after, while on line at Barney's Beanery in West Hollywood, Warren bumped into the famed keyboardist and founding member of the Doors, Ray Manzarek. "I need some lyrics," the legendary rocker had told Warren. "We're putting together a blues album. I need something dark and Raymond Chandler, that dark side of Los Angeles."

Warren made his single exception. "You've come to the right man," he said.

"I know I have, man," said Manzarek. "So, let's see if we can put a song together. Send me the lyrics."

"Well, I'll do what I can, Ray," Warren said. "I'll be dead in six months."

☙❧

Warren made it very clear that it was time to buckle down. Almost as soon as he had been signed to Artemis, Danny Goldberg's overall strategy was to bring him into the most modern and appropriate setting for his demographic—while staying hip. It was a delicate balance, and there was a bit of a challenge in marketing Warren to new listeners. One of Goldberg's first orders of business back in 1999 was contacting VH1 about dedicating an episode of their one-hour weekly documentary series, *Behind the Music,* to Warren's career. The network executive had looked at Goldberg point-blank and asked him, "Want to know why our viewers won't care? Because I don't." In its place, they offered a segment for Warren on their *Where Are They Now?* series, a less serious anthology show that mainly profiled one-hit wonders. Knowing he'd find it indignant, Goldberg didn't even mention the offer to Warren.

Of course, all that had changed once the media had a hook they could cover. For the first time in his career, Warren was able to tell *The New Yorker,* "Too late." Instead, Barr arranged six high-profile interviews: *Rolling Stone, Billboard, People, The New York Times,* and *USA Today*—all selected to reach the largest possible readership.

When Goldberg now reached out to VH1, he got a very different response than he had only two years earlier. With the "death angle" known to the producers, and with an assortment of Warren's high-profile musician friends anticipated for the recording sessions, not only would the network profile Warren's career—they wanted a director in the studio for an in-depth "fly on the wall" documentary of the making of Warren's album. As PR-savvy as ever, Warren not only allowed it—he let the camera crews follow him to the oncologist, to the tailor, and to New York for what would later be deemed a historic night on the *Late Show with David Letterman.*

The sessions for Warren's yet-to-be-titled final album were still well under way, despite the fact that as of his flight to New York, Warren had just made it past the second month of the doctor's initial prediction of only three months. He was well aware of that fact as he and Barr touched down at JFK, and the fact that it would be, in all likelihood, both his final television appearance and his last visit to the city that had launched his mainstream career nearly thirty years earlier. It had been a physical struggle for him to even board the plane. As he later told Danny Goldberg, "I wasn't going to do it, but then I remembered how Sammy Davis Jr. in *Yes I Can* wrote about dancing when he had cancer, so I figured I should make the effort." And both Letterman's people and Artemis appreciated it: Warren was flown first-class and given a penthouse suite at Morgan's on Madison Avenue. He brought with him a small copy of *Duino Elegies* by Rainer Maria Rilke, claiming the German poet wrote "about a universe where everybody's dead except for a brief shining moment when we're not." Along with Boris Pasternak's *Dr. Zhivago* and the Holy Bible, the small book of poetry was one of three books Warren continued to reference for inspiration throughout his battle. He later famously rephrased Arthur Schopenhauer, claiming, "We love to buy books because we believe we're buying the time to read them," although he had read the vast majority of his over three thousand personal book collection.

For his appearance with David Letterman, the host extended an offer that had only been bestowed to one other guest, Vice President Al Gore; on October 30, he would be the show's only guest, amounting to an almost full-hour interview and three songs: "Mutineer," "Genius," and "Roland the Headless Thompson Gunner"—one of Letterman's personal favorites. "He rehearsed each of them with our band, including one that had a string quartet [that he] arranged," music director Paul Shaffer later recalled. "That afternoon, as we rehearsed those three songs, even though I said, 'Warren, just try to mark it and don't blow your voice,' he couldn't help it. It was so much fun playing that afternoon. He was a little more tired in the evening, as anybody would be, but especially somebody as sick like he was. But I remember those rehearsals were amazing."

When Warren was introduced for the live taping, Shaffer and his orchestra blared their own take on "I'll Sleep When I'm Dead," much to Warren's approval. Once he and Letterman were seated, even despite the shared knowledge that this would be the final time, their humor was as genuine and natural as ever, with the same candor and playful glibness that had defined their very first interview in 1982, when Letterman had earned Warren's respect in his approach toward the topic of alcoholism and his well-publicized intervention. "I guess a couple of months ago, we all learned that your life has changed radically, hasn't it?" Letterman now asked. Without missing a step, Warren offered, "You mean you heard about the flu?"

But it was when Letterman asked Warren if his new battle had taught him anything about life and death that the words were uttered that, for many people, epitomized Warren's core philosophy. He shrugged and told Letterman, "Not unless you know you're supposed to enjoy every sandwich." At the episode's conclusion, Letterman warmly thanked Warren and visibly held back tears as he repeated his friend's new quote under the show's end credits. Before he left the Ed Sullivan Theater that night, Warren handed his guitar case to Letterman. It was the very same case he'd had with him many times over the years, containing his Gibson electric-acoustic. "Take care of this for me," he said.

Letterman was not only taken with Warren's gesture, but of the strength he had so clearly displayed on what everyone knew was to be his final public appearance. A few weeks later, Warren's words still haunted his old friend, who admitted to *The New York Times,* "Here's a guy looking down the barrel of the gun . . . And if a guy wanted to indulge himself in great hyperbole in that circumstance, who wouldn't forgive him? But that was perfect, the simplicity of that. If this guy is not a poet, who is?"

That night was also the last time Warren was to see his cousin, Sandford, the man who had solidified his lasting path to sobriety nearly two decades earlier. In recent years, they had not only stayed in touch, but Warren would make frequent visits to the East Coast for the two to play rounds of golf together. Outside the Ed Sullivan Theater, Warren told his cousin to send his love to the boys at home.

"Warren was in great physical shape the last few times I saw him," remembered his younger cousin, Lawrence Zevon. "It just made his illness even more startling. He was sober and exercising and—tying it all together with his touring schedules—visiting art exhibits and all the cultural things he loved. In those last few months, I watched on TV—the Letterman appearance and then on the VH1 special—all these strangers, like the guy who made his suit, get to express their sadness, and all those who actually got to say goodbye. In a way, that frustrated me. I wrote him a long, heartfelt email about how upset I was about his illness and he responded to the effect, 'You take what life deals you.' Despite his bravado, I knew it sucked for him. And us."

Making a major television appearance as an official swan song to public performance killed two birds with one stone; it not only provided a grand finale to Warren's life as a dedicated professional entertainer, but it was also his goodbye to anyone not in his innermost circle, or directly involved with his album. His interviews were done, and so was his much-needed farewell to Letterman—the best friend his music ever had, as Warren liked to remind him.

The world had seen Warren for the last time, still dapper, witty, and undeniably brave. It was the way he wanted to be remembered. No one needed to see the descent he was about to take.

Warren and Jorge Calderón had officially started the recording sessions the second week of September. Luckily, they wouldn't be starting from scratch, as Warren had two songs written and prerecorded from his home studio: "Dirty Life and Times" and "She's Too Good for Me." When they went into Sunset Sound for the final master, the sessions went off to a thundering start with Ry Cooder, Don Henley, Billy Bob Thornton, and Dwight Yoakam creating the backing band's overdubs.

Danny Goldberg remembered his first day visiting the studio. "The song they were working on was 'Dirty Life and Times,'" he said. "[Warren] felt good about the lyric because it wasn't maudlin. I suggested that it might not make a bad album title, which Warren politely appeared to consider, although he wisely jettisoned the idea later on and went with *The Wind*."

The first song that Warren and Calderón wrote for the album, however, was "El Amor de Mi Vida," which was for Annette Aguilar-Ramos; Calderón had to pen the Spanish lyric, which translated to "love of my life." Calderón recalled the first few energetic recordings with the visiting esteemed guests. "The first session we did with live musicians was for 'Numb as a Statue,' which was one of the songs we wrote in a day," he said. "Then we did 'Prison Grove' at Sunset Sound. I remember that being a long day. Warren could sing, but it was apparent he was having problems with stamina."

Warren's physical limitations had slowly begun to show and during the sessions for "Prison Grove," Calderón was not the only musician who noticed. Warren had jokingly called the track his "Robert Redford in prison song," comparing the somber jailhouse tune to the 1980 drama *Brubaker*. Calderón, however, saw the metaphorical lyrics as something significantly deeper, telling Warren, "You know, your body's the prison." Impressed at the self-revelation, Warren later remarked, "[Calderón] knows me better than I know myself."

Ry Cooder had made a surprise visit to Sunset Sound on that night and was instantly taken by Warren's focus and drive. "It's unbelievably sad and unbelievably brave," Cooder later said. "You get that kind of intense focus, and every word and every note is heartfelt. . . . Everything is accentuated and becomes meaningful in an oblique way. There's subtext all over the place. I went in another mental atmosphere for quite some time after that."

If ever there was a gesture that meant the most to Warren, it was Bruce Springsteen's dramatic appearance toward the end of December. When he'd learned of Warren's illness, Springsteen had decided to postpone his own holiday plans to be sure to take part in the new album. Young producer Noah Scot Snyder remembered the session for "Disorder in the House" vividly. "It was like a cosmic event," he said. "There was something so magical about the energy he brought. When he came in, I'm all ready for him to be picky about how he wants to record the guitar, the amp, whatever. Then, all he does is turn the amp all the way up. So, after he plays, he kills the amp." Watching Springsteen destroy the speakers while ripping through an angry lead guitar solo, Warren couldn't keep the grin off his face.

"I've never heard Bruce play like that in my life," Calderón later told Geoff Boucher of *The Los Angeles Times.* "What he brought emotionally into the room, the way he handled himself and gave of himself— well, that to me is a national treasure."

Snyder added, "See, with all those amazing guests on the album, it wasn't unprecedented for [Warren] at all. His albums had always had huge names on them, because they all respected him and I don't think he was intimidated by them, either. I think they all understood each other and worked well together, and that was the point of that album— getting it done and having the best sound."

Following his public announcement, Warren had his fax number rerouted to his management office and began ignoring phone calls and emails from everyone. Again, there were two reasons. While the sessions for *The Wind* were, by all accounts, going as amazing as they could under the sad circumstances, Warren still wanted—and, with the clock ticking, needed—to remain as focused as possible. His focus was there, as was his genuine delight at seeing the likes of Mick Fleetwood, Tom Petty, T Bone Burnett, Mike Campbell, and David Lindley all brushing aside their own schedules to see him and help him see his final artistic vision through to the end. Warren proudly remarked to *The New York Times* that the ambitious, twelve-hour-long November studio sessions were "like, *This is Your Life,* unplanned and unrehearsed."

But what wasn't there was his energy. He'd outlived the initial three-month prediction, but his body was feeling the strain of the cancer spread—and the copious amounts of painkillers that Warren had been taking. His claim to *The New York Times* that work was "the most effective drug there can possibly be" was true; but in order to work, he needed *real* drugs. He confided to Goldberg, "I told my doctors that my [substance abuse] program required me to avoid these drugs, and they said that is not an option." As Goldberg saw it, Warren could now "have his cake and eat it too."

Billy Bob Thornton had bought his home in Beverly Hills from Guns N' Roses lead guitarist Slash, and so his home was fully equipped with what had once been Snakepit Studio. He later recalled that during a session at the home studio, Warren had been mixing a $500 bottle of scotch with the liquid morphine that he carried around in his coat pockets. When Dave Barry visited Los Angeles and took Warren to dinner—another meeting that both friends were aware would be the last time—Barry couldn't help but notice the amount of drugs Warren had on him. As a friend who had been acquired later in life, he had never seen Warren drink, smoke, or do drugs; in fact, none of his Rock Bottom Remainder buddies had ever seen that side of him—the side that had gotten him banned from clubs all over Los Angeles and *Rolling Stone*. But that was a long time ago—wasn't it?

As Barry recalled, Warren was to meet him at his hotel for dinner, camera crew in tow. "That night remains one of the highlights of my life, in a weird kind of way," Barry later recalled. "You don't always get that kind of opportunity with a friend. . . . As I've gotten older, I know that people die, that people you know and people you love will die—and it's so rare when you know it, and you have the chance to talk with them about it and come to a kind of peace about it—if and when you actually can.

"Warren showed up with his video guy at my hotel in LA," Barry said, "and I thought 'This is going to be horrible, it's going to be awful, but I got to get through it because it's for Warren. . . . Luckily, later, when I got back to my hotel room, I was still laughing. He had turned it into one of the funniest dinners I had had in my life! It was like a miracle. It was funny, and yet, it was like, 'Hey, goodbye, I love you.' And it was perfect."

But Barry had also noticed the clinking of tiny bottles in the pockets of Warren's overcoat; on the way to the hotel, Warren had stopped for a fresh supply of liquid morphine, which he set up in a row on their table during the meal. "He brought the bag in to show me how much they'd really loaded him up," Barry said. "[Warren] had kind of joyfully leaped off the wagon that he had been on for so many years. I was certainly not going to criticize him for that. I don't know what I would do." Barry didn't judge, but instead kept his friend laughing hysterically until they parted ways, both saying "I love you" to each other on the way out of the lobby.

Warren was much more open in his deliberate decision to go out in a sanctioned blaze of oblivion with the one person capable of understanding, while also being forthright in her attempts to prevent it. "When Warren found out he was going to die, he said 'Fuck it. I'm going to drink and I'm going to do the Elvis drugs,'" recalled Ryan Rayston. "Not drug-drugs, like cocaine, but the drugs that were prescribed to him, the heavy-duty painkillers . . . he was telling everyone he had the flu, but he was really drunk." She knew from their years as intimate friends that Warren had always had a playful public nonchalance regarding death because he didn't fear it; it was the prolonged process of dying that he feared the most. "It was not a battle he wanted to fight, but he fought it and he wasn't afraid," she recalled. "He had a lot of faith. He believed in God, and he actually started going to church again after September 11, after years of being away from it. . . . We would talk about everything—God and spirituality, women in his life, books, music, Nietzsche, Schopenhauer, and, of course, death."

Although he hadn't attended an A.A. meeting in years, Warren still followed the core mantras and prayers that he had once claimed saved his life. Rayston still attended her own twelve-step meetings and, very concerned for Warren's health, consulted her own sponsor. She was told that there was nothing you could do but pray for someone who had made such a decision—so she did.

Despite Warren's fading condition, and the consistent fogginess from the morphine and pills that he only partially attempted to hide, the team was able to cut nearly all the tracks that they had penned. They'd already scheduled a brief recess from recording during the holiday season, but, as Danny Goldberg recalled, "When the album was almost finished, the session suddenly came to a grinding halt. I was worried that the end was near, but Jordan later explained to me that the problem was that Warren's medical needs for painkillers had trumped his A.A. discipline and left him without the inner compass he had carefully nurtured over two decades."

Jordan had told Goldberg about the oblivion Warren had created for himself at home. He no longer left the apartment, but rather had all groceries, medications, and booze delivered. He had been on a drinking binge for weeks. "When we finally got into his apartment, it was like death had already come," Rayston remembered. "There were bottles and trash everywhere."

Carl Hiaasen recalled that once he'd heard from mutual friends just how bad things had gotten for Warren, he planned to fly to Los Angeles. At the time, Warren wasn't opening the door or answering the phone for anyone. "I was fearing the worst," he said. "Apparently, it was pretty bad, but he told me that the holidays always put him in a depression. It was just multiplied indefinitely by the knowledge that this was going to be his last Christmas and New Year's." Calderón had heard Warren share the same sentiments. "The bravery he had shown, and the humorous way he looked at his illness, really took a turn," he said. "He'd say, 'It's not only Christmas and New Year's—it's my last Christmas and New Year's.' He really went down, I mean really down and depressed . . . He was thinking he was going to die any day." Warren's old OCD also began to rear its head, with the color orange replacing gray as his latest totem; it was his new "good luck" color.

Calderón was also "at the end of his rope just trying to finish the last few songs." Carl Hiaasen advised him to leave a message on Warren's machine saying that if he wasn't going to push himself to sober up and lay down his final vocals, the label would hire fellow musician John Hiatt to finish it in postproduction. "You'll get a call," he told him.

Warren had much greater incentive for pulling himself together one final time. Ariel and Jordan had both visited his apartment for Christmas Eve—and it hadn't gone well. She hadn't seen her father in such a state of lethargy and inebriation since she was a child. Upon learning of his illness, Ariel had moved up the date of her wedding to better Warren's chance of being in attendance. She had been visiting him with regularity up until his joyous leap from the wagon, and told him that, as bad as she wanted to be with him during these last days, she could not do it if this was the version he was going to be. She'd sit in the other room if he was going to sneak scotch into his Mountain Dew can.

After Christmas, Warren locked his door to the outside world for good.

It was only after Jordan staked out his father's house prior to a grocery delivery that he was able to corner him into opening the door. Jordan began keeping a closer eye on his father. Danny Goldberg recalled, "In these final months, there was no one other than Jordan [Warren] could trust. Jordan helped him reduce his drug intake, hired a Jamaican woman to read the Bible to him," and he and Jorge got Warren to do his final vocal on the last song he wrote, "Keep Me in Your Heart."

But there were two others to complete first. Warren had been working on "El Amor de Mi Vida" since before his diagnosis; it was now one of the very last songs he was to record. Calderón had recorded his own Spanish chorus and mixed portions, all during the weeks he'd been awaiting Warren's unlikely return. Warren only needed to sing the song's first two verses to wrap the cut. With his body weakening, but his mind sharper without the booze and far less pills, he had been able to complete his parts. Likewise, he'd been able to muster the strength to nail the dirty blues number, "Rub Me Raw." Calderón was impressed with Warren's ability to "reach all the way down and find a deeper sentiment" in the song and credited it with Warren's own raw emotions coming through. It was, however, the song that everyone was pushing for Warren to make it his own.

In getting him fit and strong enough to complete the album, the ultimate goal had always been for "Keep Me in Your Heart" to be completed by the voice of Warren Zevon. "I said, 'Warren, you have to finish that song,'" Calderón recalled. "'That song is yours. That's a goodbye song.' I told him to keep going, but he was having all kinds of trouble emotionally." But Warren knew how crucial it was for him to finish that song. As "Mutineer" had been a love song for his fans, so "Keep Me in Your Heart" was for his family, friends, fans—and the grandchildren he would never get to know.

Warren's albums had always been more autobiographical than he was willing to admit. Even the most seemingly unrelated, fantastical, goriest fables were deeply rooted in where his heart and mind were at a given point. Likewise, the women of his life also acted as the right muse for the right version of him at that time: he had been his most dominant with Crystal, a dark version of himself that later morphed into a deep friendship, but only once he had become his better self; Anita Gevinson had never judged the darkest side of Warren's behavior, a doomed relationship that inadvertently inspired his need to get on the wagon by himself; Kim Lankford and Merle Ginsberg had reinvigorated him and reminded him of the successful, driven rock star within; Julia had reminded him that a "quiet, normal life" was, indeed, somehow still attainable; Ryan was the spiritual sister he never had; and Annette, well, she was his "El Amor De Mi Vida."

But after a lifetime of muses, it only made sense that Warren's final album, in and of itself, existed for his daughter.

Warren's and Ariel's relationship was the only one that always had been in a shaky state of flux, for nearly her entire life. Now, when it came time to focus all of his creative energies and reach into himself for the greatest amount of personal strength and drive as he could muster during his final battle, Ariel's pregnancy was the incentive to keep him working and breathing. Against the judgment of his friends and colleagues, Warren had deliberately disappeared into the studio, knowing that work would be the only means to keep his wheels turning, and a deliberate PR blitz would—as it always had in the past—guarantee his focus and diligence. But most importantly, in completing *The Wind*, he would reach the finish line of witnessing his daughter give birth to her sons. When he had learned of her pregnancy, it had been the spark to reignite his sobriety. The album—its writing, production, recording, and public announcement—all that effort was in order to bear witness to the most important day in Ariel's life.

The time came for Warren to lay down his vocals for "Keep Me in Your Heart," the only song left to complete. He was at his weakest. Noah Scot Snyder had to devise a way to loop the microphone on a long chord down from Warren's loft, so he could sit comfortably on the couch in order to sing with strained breath and voice. Calderón, Barr, and Ariel watched as he completed three perfect takes then, out of steam, sat back breathless on his "divan of doom."

Where once he had said in interviews that his songs were all about fear and paranoia, Warren had recently changed his tune. Only weeks earlier, the filmmakers from VH1 had spoken to Warren about his legacy and the motivation that was keeping him working. Even now, his feelings were the most optimistic he had shared publicly in years. "I think that writing songs is an act of love," he said. "You write songs because you love the subject, and you want to pass that feeling on."

"Keep Me in Your Heart" was the final song Warren performed. He had smiled as Calderón and Snyder announced the album was wrapped.

∽

On June 11 Ariel gave birth to twin boys: Augustus Warren Zevon-Powell and Maximus Patrick Zevon-Powell. Even in his weakened condition, Warren had still managed to make it to the hospital, having left nothing to chance by renting a hotel room directly across the street from the hospital, as well as retaining a personal driver to wait on standby for

Crystal's call. And he even had a press release issued. "[Warren's] doing alright," his new publicist, Diana Baron, said of his condition. "Listen, when he first started talking about his illness, he was hoping he could make it to see the next James Bond movie. And that was last Christmas. So, every day is a blessing."

As they looked at their grandchildren together, Warren stood at the foot of the hospital bed and took hold of Crystal's hand. "This is where we're supposed to be," he said to her. "Don't you see it, old girl? We made it. We made it to the front porch." Later, he took her aside. "Come on," he told her, "I know where the chapel is in this joint. Let's go thank the Big Guy in the sky."

Even as Warren remained primarily bed-bound, there were other blessings he would witness. *The Wind* was released on August 26, 2003, to universal praise and his best sales in a decade. Danny Goldberg was elated to be able to share the news of the album's success. "*The Wind* SoundScanned forty-eight thousand the first week and debuted at Number 14," he recalled. "The only time an album of his had attained a higher chart position was when *Excitable Boy* had gone to Number 8 twenty-five years ago. We knew in the first week that we had a gold record."

Not only were the sales for *The Wind* the highest Warren had scored in many years, but the critical praise was also unrivaled. While some critics cautiously mentioned the difficulty in assessing the final work of a dying artist still within their mortal coil, much of *The Wind*'s highest accolades objectively compared the work to Warren's strong previous endeavors. Unceremoniously, Warren was most proud that his work had not only come through for himself, but for Danny Goldberg and all of Artemis, as well. "The last thing he said to me was, 'I'm so happy that the belief you had in me is paying off for you.' That was typical. He was very conscious of everybody's role in his life. Very few artists have that kind of responsibility."

Likewise, his VH1 special had been a hit on the network, driving more sales. The night it aired, Warren was in his weakest condition yet. Ryan Rayston had come over, as she had continued to do for weeks. They had planned to watch the documentary's debut together. When she arrived, Warren was in bed and asked her to look under it. She recalled, "I looked under the bed and the bottles of alcohol were gone. He had stopped drinking."

When they locked eyes, Warren told her, "I fought too hard not to go to God sober."

∞

After all the accolades had come in, Warren joked to Crystal about the recognition that had long awaited him. "I better die quick so they'll give me a Grammy nomination. It's a damned hard way to make a living, having to die to get 'em to know you're alive."

∞

Warren called Rayston on September 6, telling her that he had been having breathing issues but still wanted to know if she could bring him soup from Bristol Farms and maybe a tapioca pudding. After they had hung up, her phone immediately rang again. "Yes, Warren?"

"Nothing's bad luck is it?"

"No."

"Nothing's bad luck is it?" he asked again.

"No."

The following day, she was there to make him breakfast and lunch. The fourth can of Coke she found was sufficiently lucky, so he had that with his soup. He also asked if she could call his twelve-step sponsor when he was gone and offer his gratitude. Then, she massaged his hands and feet and rubbed ice on his lips.

Later, Rayston lay in bed with him, under the covers, despite his fear that the act could be "bad luck" for them both. He asked her, as always, if anything was bad luck. She told him, "No." Then twice more. When Warren asked her if she was scared, she knew that he felt the end was imminent.

She held him. "Please stay," he said, and took her hand. When he began to drift off, she quietly went and sat at one of the gray sofas, knowing he liked to fall asleep alone and it wouldn't take him long. She checked on him only a few minutes later and sensed the energy in the room had changed. She checked his pulse and put her mouth to his lips to breath in air.

After she'd made all the necessary calls, Jordan was the first to arrive after the paramedics.

Warren William Zevon was fifty-six years old.

∞

A private memorial service was held for Warren, a small gathering of his closest friends and family.

Jackson Browne spoke to the small crowd of familiar faces. "At some point," he said, "every one of his friends had a falling out with Warren." Amid the laughter, it was easy to look at the faces and remember each time one had been cut off from Warren's life—yet had all now gathered once it had ended.

Jordan scattered his father's ashes over the Pacific Ocean.

∞

Later, Carl Hiaasen remembered something—something that Warren used to do while on tour. When fans would come out of whatever venue he'd just played, sometimes he'd be in the mood to take photos and sign autographs, and sometimes, well, he just wasn't.

Sometimes Warren was keen to get back on the road, or to head into a town he'd visited many, many times before—almost to the point of being an honorary citizen. Finding strange new places was the best, and usually better than some of the gigs.

Sometimes he just wanted some fucking sleep.

Other times, Warren just wanted to keep moving.

For those occasions, Warren had designed a simple business card for his road manager to hand out in lieu of having to spend two hours in a parking lot signing napkins or water-damaged copies of *Excitable Boy*.

For those times, the times that Warren had to leave:

> *Mr. Zevon has gone with the*
> *Great Beaver.*

CHAPTER THIRTEEN

A LEAF IN THE WIND

IT HAD BEEN A CRUEL IRONY THAT WARREN'S GREATEST CRITical appraisements took place after his death.

The Wind earned four nominations at the forty-sixth Grammy Awards—which was four more than Warren had earned while alive: Best Contemporary Folk Album; Best Rock Duet—for the blazing "Disorder in the House" with Bruce Springsteen, which also was nominated for Best Rock Song; and "Keep Me in Your Heart" was nominated for Song of the Year.

As the president of Artemis, Danny Goldberg already had an idea for the show's segment that would usually be slated for a performance by the artist themselves. Instead of getting another performer to fill in for Warren, he worked with Jorge Calderón and Jackson Browne in assembling a choir of Warren's most treasured friends and family. During the Grammy Awards, Browne, Calderón, Ariel, and Jordan were joined by Billy Bob Thornton, musician Tim Schmidt, and Emmylou Harris in singing the harmonies of Warren's original recording of "Keep Me in Your Heart." Above the stage, the large screen displayed the footage of Warren in the studio throughout the recording of *The Wind*. The footage was cribbed from the VH1 documentary and the music video assembled from clips. Upon Warren's passing, the network aired the video every hour, on the hour for a day of remembrance, and the footage of his final visits into the studio would remain a lasting image of his legacy by year's end.

∽

In 2004, Artemis put together the memorial album Warren specifically stipulated was to be made after his death. By that time, Danny Goldberg had sold the company, but he assisted in the earliest stages of the album's conception; Warren had been one of his first Artemis artists and now, with his passing, Goldberg's own participation ended.

Enjoy Every Sandwich was released on October 19, 2004. The album saw a host of Warren's friends and famous admirers alike performing some of his most famous songs: Jackson Browne and Bonnie Raitt performed a blues-based duet of "Poor Poor Pitiful Me," while Waddy Wachtel joined up blockbuster comedian Adam Sandler for a hard-rocking, appropriately goofy version of "Werewolves of London." Warren had ultimately chosen *The Wind*'s title from an existing song he'd prepared with the same name. It had never made the final cut, but it had been a particular favorite of Billy Bob Thornton; on the memorial album, he recorded the official debut of Warren's "The Wind." Live recordings of Bob Dylan's "Mutineer" cover, as well as Bruce Springsteen's impassioned acoustic version of "My Ride's Here" also demonstrated the reach of Warren's influence on some of the music industry's heaviest hitters.

The most heartfelt performance on the memorial album came from Jordan Zevon, who, like Thornton, took the opportunity to debut one of his father's unrecorded works—a bluesy tin-pan alley piano-based ballad, "Studebaker." Now a seasoned singer-songwriter in his own right, Jordan included his father's song on his own debut album, *Insides Out,* in 2008. Continuing to melt his own career while honoring his father's legacy, Jordan continues to produce and record, while also working as a proactive advocate for the Asbestos Disease Awareness Organization and mesothelioma research.

Following his father's death, Jordan combed through his dad's old storage facility on the outskirts of the San Fernando Valley. He had to take time to prioritize: his mother, Marilyn "Tule" Livingston, died from breast cancer on March 3, 2004, leaving him without either parent in the brief span of six months. He tackled his father's storage unit soon after. Among many components of antiquated music equipment and tour paraphernalia, Jordan also discovered enough quality demo tapes and outtakes to assemble a proper collection of his father's "lost" recordings. Carefully packed in one large touring case, he found over one hundred various outtakes and snippets of long-forgotten studio work.

In 2007, *Preludes: Rare and Unreleased Recordings* was distributed by New West Records. The two-disk set, lovingly produced and mastered by Jordan and Danny Goldberg, included some of Warren's earliest solo demos—among them an acoustic version of "Tule's Blues," the first song written for Jordan's mother; the original sheet music remained carefully framed under glass above Jordan's own upright piano at home.

The collection also included nearly every track later rerecorded in the lush, high-budgeted studio provided by Elektra/Asylum for his label release, but here in stripped-down, largely acoustic, and intimate form. As a deluxe set, *Preludes'* second disk was composed of an in-depth interview Warren had given at Austin City Limits Studios for KGSR Radio in December 1999, while he had been touring for *Life'll Kill Ya*— as well as excerpts and family photos from Crystal's own then forthcoming oral history/memoir of Warren's life, *I'll Sleep When I'm Dead*. Published by Ecco Books in 2008, Crystal's work had assembled interviews with many of the musicians, friends, and lovers from Warren's life, arranged in chronological order and maintaining the warts-and-all tone that Warren had once urged her to uphold in such a book.

Likewise, Warren's dear friend and former aide-de-camp, George Gruel, dug through his own trunks of mementos from years on the road, meticulously collecting them into a warm and humorous memoir/ scrapbook, *Lawyers, Guns & Photos: Photographs and Tales of My Adventures with Warren Zevon* through his own Big Gorilla Books in 2012. Along with musings and personal anecdotes from his time as Warren's closest confidante, Gruel's elaborate coffee-table book offered faithful Zevonites scores of never-before-seen photographs that Gruel had taken as road manager, as well as behind-the-curtain glimpses into Warren's creative process. Dedicating his book in memory of "a dear friend and brother," Gruel explained, "We had great fun together through a myriad of adventures, including some that bordered on insanity. Through it all, I had the utmost respect for him and his art. . . . He could be a challenge, but then, who can't be?"

No one could understand those sentiments better than Warren's own daughter, Ariel. Like Jordan, she had opted to preserve her father's legacy in her own ways. While half-brother Jordan would take the reins on the posthumous *Preludes,* Ariel assembled a compilation of their father's gentler and romantic side—the often overlooked persona that was more akin to the dashing and artistic figure she'd once viewed him as during her youth. "In a sense," she wrote in the compilation's accompanying essay, "a father is a daughter's true love." Like her father, Ariel had been a musician all her life, studying flute as a child in Paris and then writing songs throughout her teen years and young adulthood. She released her own debut album, a folk-driven acoustic work laden with biting social commentary, *The Detangler,* in 2018. In May of that year, she truly came into her own while following very closely in her father's footsteps—she opened for her godfather, Jackson Browne, at a gig in Boston.

Warren's memory and legacy left their indelible imprints on nearly every person who had known him, extending from the closest members of his inner circles to the musicians and engineers who regarded themselves as fortunate to have worked alongside him. In the months and years following his death, Warren's literary friends all took to their media outlets to pen heartfelt and honest obits. Soon, new generations of fans also heard the voice of Warren Zevon coming to them through films, television shows, and commercials. "I wrote 'Wanted Dead or Alive' with Warren in 1969," Kim Fowley recalled not long before his passing in 2015, "and it wasn't until forty years later that I put on a show called *Californication* and heard it being used." Indeed, the hit Showtime cable dramedy had benefited tremendously by utilizing numerous Warren Zevon tracks and covers throughout its seven-season run. "What's a five-letter word for 'excitable boy?'" the show's lead character, portrayed by real-life Zevon fan David Duchovny, asks aloud while doing the newspaper's daily crossword puzzle in one of the series' early episodes. "Zevon!" he exclaims, proudly putting pencil to newsprint. Filmmaker Judd Apatow likewise snuck his own form of tribute into his 2009 drama *Funny People,* using "Keep Me in Your Heart" during one of the film's most emotional scenes: as the film's jaded lead character wrestles with denial surrounding his own cancer diagnosis, it is Warren's song that finally breaks him down into tears.

"Serious writers, serious lovers of language, will be discovering [Warren's music] for a long time to come," Jackson Browne later told *Rolling Stone*. "His songs are like short stories—best songs always are. They tell much more about life than books; they communicate so much more than a longer volume would. But it's funny. Here we are, talking at great lengths, to describe something that was the very opposite of that—a guy who could say something in a few words that was immediately understood."

Even amid their checkered working relationship, Jackson and Warren had shared a friendship lasting nearly forty years. More than one of Warren's many significant others had noted that despite any apparent rivalry, he viewed Browne—along with Don Henley, J. D. Souther, and other musicians of the Southern California scene—as "his brothers." As angry as he'd become upon reading a negative review of his work, Warren was often seen losing his temper just as passionately if he witnessed a dear friend becoming the target of a similarly critical poison pen. To Warren, Browne—like Jorge Calderón—was a brother, and one of the rare ones whose opinion was of the highest value. Like Danny Goldberg, Browne started his own independent record label, Inside Recordings, in 1999. Jorge Calderón was one of the first solo artists he signed.

In 2011, Ryan Rayston published her critically acclaimed first novel, *The Quiet Sound of Disappearing*. A thinly veiled memoir of her own painful—and often suspenseful—path to sobriety, the work not only prominently mentioned Warren in its acknowledgments but, as a true testament to their artistic influence toward each other, her book's first-person narration is peppered with small references and turns-of-phrases easily recognized by those familiar with Warren's songbook.

Andrew Slater hit bottom following his days producing Warren at Virgin but had since come a very long way in reestablishing himself within the music industry, with a vengeance. After being fired by Don Henley on June 17, 1991—Slater's thirty-fourth birthday—he began his own path to sobriety and career focus. Having remained friends with Bob Dylan's son, Jakob, ever since their very early encounter during the *Sentimental Hygiene* sessions, he was cautiously hired as the manager of young Dylan's band, the Wallflowers. With a drive and determination unfelt since his days at Front Line, Slater helped bring Dylan's band to superstardom; soon, singer-songwriter Fiona Apple would also be his client, a career trajectory that made him head of Capitol Records only a few years later. He would have a successful future managing the hottest rock and pop acts for decades.

But Slater's career truly began in 1985 when he innocently raised his hand to merely defend the art and legacy of his favorite musical hero.

It is a sentiment to which this author closely relates.

CODA

AS MY FIRST ENDEAVOR INTO BIOGRAPHY, I WAS PERSONALLY divided in regard to career assessment and any form of inadvertent psychoanalysis; I've never found much use for it in the chronicles of other lives I've read. To me, the work—in this case the music and writing—of a given subject should speak for itself. With Warren Zevon, I had to check my own admiration at the door in order to remain both objective and strictly factual: I already knew why *I* was a fan, but it seemed the best method of appeal for new fans and new critical assessments was if I just stuck to the fascinating tales and circumstances behind Warren's songs. But in the course of seven years of research and interviews, the revelations of patterns and psychological "cause and effect" logistics understood only to Warren began to emerge. It was soon apparent that Warren's life and music were too entwined to be assessed separately: his art was too autobiographical.

One of Warren's own literary heroes, Norman Mailer, once advised fellow writers to avoid crafting a lead character that was smarter than oneself; it would only lead to confusion and mental gymnastics when facing the creative task of deciding their actions. Although a work of nonfiction, writing the life of Warren Zevon presented its own challenge: he was the smartest man in any room he entered, and although the chronology of his life is already documented, he was, nonetheless, the very meaning of unpredictability.

With his life and work now documented to the best of my ability, I feel comfortable enough to offer a few humble thoughts on the man and the artist that has provided me with both an inspired soundtrack and needed personal strength during the better part of the last decade.

To put it succinctly, Warren was a conflicted man *and* artist due to the fact that he was always three separate entities of self-expression: while born a musical prodigy, his most internal passion was directed toward his writing. His musical virtuosity, like the gifts of all geniuses, was ancillary to his lifelong literary ambitions. Only confusing matters further, he was drawn toward the adrenaline of rock and roll, which provided both a logical means of fusing words and composition (he had survived for many years as a jingle-writer and studio session "cat"), and fueled a substance addiction that was, more than likely, hereditary.

During the course of research, my appreciation for Warren's work and admiration for his personal strength only deepened. While it may have deprived the world of some of the most intelligent and thought-provoking rock music of the twentieth century, I can't help but believe that he may have been a significantly happier man—and perhaps finally attained the "quiet, normal life" that forever eluded him—had he remained on the career path that Igor Stravinsky and Robert Craft had attempted to lead him to in his youth: a career in professional classical composition and performance.

Once Warren became sober in March 1986, he'd shaken the most violent of monkeys off his back—but his unfinished symphony remained perched there until his dying day. In combing through as many published interviews as attainable, the pattern of Warren's fluctuating willingness to speak on the subject of his symphony throughout the years seemed to indicate a form of sadness, or guilt—most likely at the ambitious work's lack of completion. When the subject came up in his final interview with *The New York Times,* Warren told Jon Pareles that following his youthful exchanges with Stravinsky, he'd decided that classical music "wasn't for him," explaining, "I felt that it was music of another time . . . I couldn't add anything, and it wasn't necessarily so relevant anymore."

Nothing could have been further from the truth. Warren worked on his symphony for the better part of two decades, only later choosing to downplay its importance in his life and overall musical legacy. More than likely, however, he was saving face as he'd never completed it. While on the PR junket for *Life'll Kill Ya,* Warren gave perhaps the final honest update on the project's status to David Bowman of *Salon. com*. "Didn't you go to Juilliard?" the journalist had mistakenly asked.

"No," Warren had answered "softly." "I didn't finish high school."

Difficult words for a reputed former classical prodigy to have to utter. When Bowman asked what had come of the orchestral piece that Warren had completed in 1996 with the intention of taking it "on tour" by way of regional city symphonies, he had tersely responded, "Nothing," then quickly segued the conversation back to the album he was there promote.

Warren had indeed dropped out of high school as soon as the music industry beckoned; anything would have been better than the turbulence and abuse of his home life. But in moving to Los Angeles and becoming part of the drug scene at such a formative age, Warren had also cheated himself out of any future classical training, or potential scholarships, which could have kept him on course.

And while he never hocked his God-given talents for a porcelain monkey, the cerebral nature of Warren's rock-and-roll output consistently kept him at odds with both audiences and record labels. Dave Barry had put it succinctly during our interview, observing, "[Warren] was never going to be a big 'pop' success—my argument has always been that most people aren't smart enough for Warren Zevon. Most people don't want cerebral—they want what's catchy. Warren wasn't going to be just that. He could have been, but he wasn't going to be . . . The lyrics that he is best remembered for, the ones most quoted, [are] funny—cosmically funny—but they're lyrics that he also *lived*."

Warren remarked more than once that one of his greatest heroes had been Glenn Gould; no doubt, had circumstances been different, Warren could possibly have become Gould's heir apparent. I'm quite sure, deep down, Warren knew it, too.

When I say that Warren lived two lifetimes that is an observation that only came once the interview process was near its end. Every single person who was willing to share their own stories and recollections of Warren did so with the kindest and warmest manner; but half had to be convinced of my intentions and agenda.

Those who knew the Warren Zevon of his younger, wilder days were expectedly guarded at first, protective of the legacy that so many offerings of bad press had worked to tarnish. I was very fortunate that my own intentions toward documenting Warren's work and preserving his legacy eventually became apparent enough to gain the needed trust. However, in the case of Warren's friends and colleagues who knew him after 1985—well, quite frankly, most couldn't wait to tell me all about their happy and exciting experiences with the legendary Warren Zevon. In these recollections, his generosity, productivity, creativity, and humanity always won out. Most admitted to me that, if they hadn't known Warren before his sobriety, they'd never be able to imagine that those well-documented mistakes of his past were even true. He had, I was told more than once, become a different man.

And so, my complex subject had become more complex: he was a man who had, indeed, led two consecutive lives. Although mainstream superstardom forever eluded him, critical recognition never did. And for whatever bargain he had made within himself to live long enough to become sober, he had achieved it. Warren lived long enough to make amends, to the best of his ability, with his family and friends—and to reach an artistic level of excellence and maturity that could safely match his own standards. When faced with his own mortality, Warren slipped off the wagon one final time—just long enough to remember how strong he could be, and how crucial his family, his friends, and his art were in summoning that strength.

During his heyday of the late 1970s, a large amount of the press coverage Warren received either made reference to his addictions or, more frequently, made it their focus. What was almost always left overlooked—until his final press junket in 2003, the "living funeral"—was the rare strength he had shown in 1986 by conquering those addictions. Having watched heroes like Jim Morrison and Jimi Hendrix and friends like John Belushi succumb to their own personal battles, Warren had slain his dragon, with little else than an Olympian demonstration of willpower and his own intelligence. A lesser man would have been found dead by 1986. But not Warren.

I'm too old to die young, and too
young to die now.

And too strong to die a coward's death.

∞

In his three-part epic elegy for Warren, "Sillyhow Stride," Paul Muldoon warmly addressed his friend, reminding the "young John Donne who sets a Glock on his dish in the cafeteria" that in both life and in death, "two graves must hide"—

> *So break off, Warren, break off this*
> *last lamenting kiss*
> *As Christ broke with Iscariot . . .*

On Sunday, September 7, 2003, Warren indeed "broke off"—bravely displaying only strength, gratitude, and appreciation for the second chance at sobriety and, ultimately, life that luck—*good* luck—had finally granted him. As for regrets—the sins of his past, for which he had spent the second part of his lifetime paying in full—he had broken off from those, too.

"I got to be the most fucked-up rock star on the block, at least on my block," Warren had said only a few months before his death. "And then I got to be a sober dad for eighteen years . . . I've had two very full lives."

DISCOGRAPHY

Compiling a comprehensive discography for Warren Zevon proved to be a trickier task than I had anticipated. While the various labels that he was signed with for an almost forty-year span kept professional documentation of their recordings, Warren's abilities led him into the studio even more times than he would often make mention—his early years as a session "cat," in particular. As a huge fan myself, it was enlightening and exciting to learn of rare recordings, demos, bootlegs, and the little-known instances when Warren would be a sideman for other performers. However, this made chronicling his work slightly difficult and posed the question: what would be considered canon and what would be left out? Plus, many such albums are, sadly, out of print, despite the Zevon connection. This left me with the additional task of researching the technical specs for work that people seemed to have largely forgotten.

An artist's "canon" is not a position that I feel I have the authority to determine, so the following list is, safely, presented *by medium of release and in complete chronological order of Warren Zevon's participation and street date;* bootlegs and memorial albums have not been included. All other recordings are given the fullest amount of detail as was attainable. Any sessions that were revealed to me during the interview process yet couldn't be authenticated as 100 percent accurate—as was the case of Warren's participation with the Underground All-Stars, et cetera—have not been included here.

Special thanks to Warren's cohorts for their aid in compiling this list—in particular Bones Howe, Kim Fowley, and David Marks—and to *Goldmine* magazine and the WZ fans of his official website, www.warren zevon.com, for their own efforts to authenticate Warren's full career.

In effect, every effort has been made to make this the most accurate discography possible.

—CMK

12" ALBUMS

The Turtles, *Happy Together,* White Whale Records, 1967.
Recorded at Sunset Sound Studios, Hollywood, 1966–67; released April 29, 1967.

Phil Ochs, *Pleasures of the Harbor,* A&M Records, 1967.
Recorded 1967; released October 31, 1967.

Smokestack Lightnin', *Off the Wall,* Bell Records, 1969.
Recorded 1968–69; released 1969.

Various artists, *Midnight Cowboy—Original Motion Picture Score,* United Artists, 1969.
Recorded, released 1969.

Warren Zevon, *Wanted Dead or Alive,* Imperial, 1970.
Recorded 1969 at Sunset Sound, Hollywood; released 1970.
(Note: Credited to "Zevon." Reissued by Pickwick Records, 1979.)

The Everly Brothers, *Stories We Could Tell,* RCA Victor, 1972.
Released March 1972.

Phil Everly, *Star Spangled Springer,* RCA, 1973.
Recorded June 1973; released January 1, 1973.

Phil Everly, *Mystic Line,* Pye Records, 1975.
Recorded August 1974; released January 1, 1975.

Warren Zevon, *Warren Zevon,* Asylum, 1976.
Recorded 1975 at Elektra Sound Records, California, and Sunset Sound, Hollywood; released May 18, 1976.

Excitable Boy, Asylum, 1978.
Recorded 1977 at the Sound Factory, Los Angeles; released January 18, 1978.

Bad Luck Streak in Dancing School, Asylum, 1980.
Recorded 1979 at the Sound Factory, Los Angeles; released 1980.

Stand in the Fire, Asylum, 1980.
Recorded at the Roxy theater, Los Angeles, and mixed at Record One; released December 26, 1980.

The Envoy, Asylum, 1982.
Recorded 1981 at Record One, Los Angeles; released July 16, 1982.

Don Henley, *I Can't Stand Still,* Asylum, 1982.
Recorded and mixed 1981–82 at Record One; released August 13, 1982.

Warren Zevon, *A Quiet, Normal Life: The Best of Warren Zevon,* Asylum, 1986.
(Note: Compilation of selected Asylum recordings.)
Mastered by Dennis King at Atlantic Studios, New York, New York.
Recorded 1975–82; released October 24, 1986.

Sentimental Hygiene, Virgin, 1987.
Recorded 1987 at Record One Studios, Hollywood, California; A&M Studios, California; Cheshire Sound, Atlanta; released August 29, 1987.

Transverse City, Virgin, 1989.
Recorded A&M Studios, Hollywood, California; Broken Arrow Ranch, La Honda, California; EMI Abbey Road Studios, London, England; Le Club Front, San Rafael, California; Mad Hatter Studios, Los Angeles, California; Paisley Park, Minneapolis, Minnesota; Red Zone Studios, Burbank, California, 1989; released 1989.

Hindu Love Gods, *Hindu Love Gods*, Giant, 1990.
Recorded 1987 at Record One Studios, Sherman Oaks, California; A&M Studios, Los Angeles, California; released October 5, 1990.

Warren Zevon, *Mr. Bad Example*, Giant, 1991.
Recorded Dodge City, Glendale, California; the Sound Factory, Los Angeles, California, 1991; released October 15, 1991.
(Note: Vinyl LP release in Germany only; the final Warren Zevon album to receive an industry-standard vinyl record release.)

The Odds, *Bedbugs*, Zoo Entertainment, 1993.
Recorded/released 1993.

CD ALBUMS

Warren Zevon, *Learning to Flinch*, Giant, 1993.
Recorded Live to DAT, June 24, 1992–October 13, 1992; released April 13, 1993.

Mutineer, Giant, 1995.
Recorded at Anatomy of a Headache, Los Angeles, 1994; released May 23, 1995.

I'll Sleep When I'm Dead, Rhino, 1996.
(Note: Two-disc anthology of selected Asylum and Giant recordings.)
Recorded 1976–1996; released September 17, 1996.

Various artists, *Kerouac: Kicks Joy Darkness*, Rykodisc, 1997.
Released April 8, 1997.

Warren Zevon, *Life'll Kill Ya*, Artemis, 2000.
Recorded at Anatomy of a Headache, Los Angeles, 1996–1999; Fort Apache Studios, Cambridge, Massachusetts, 1999; released January 25, 2000.

My Ride's Here, Artemis, 2002.
Recorded at Anatomy of a Headache, Los Angeles; Ed Sullivan Theater, New York; Pilot Studios, New York; Private Island Studios, Los Angeles; Spike Recording, New York; released May 7, 2002.

Genius: The Best of Warren Zevon, Rhino, 2002.
(Note: Compilation of selected Asylum, Virgin, Giant, and Artemis
    recordings.)
Recorded 1976–2002; released October 1, 2002.

Michael Wolff, *Christmas Moods,* Artemis, 2003.
Recorded and released 2003.

Billy Bob Thornton, *The Edge of the World,* Sanctuary Records, 2003.
Released August 19, 2003.

Warren Zevon, *The Wind,* Artemis, 2003.
Recorded at Sunset Sound, Hollywood, California; Anatomy of a
    Headache, Los Angeles, California, 2003; released August 26, 2003.

Warren Zevon: The First Sessions, Varese Sarabande Records, 2003.
(Note: Compilation of Warren Zevon's earliest recordings as a member
    of lyme and cybelle.)
Recorded 1966–1967; released March 2003.

Reconsider Me: The Love Songs, Artemis, 2006.
(Note: Compilation of selected Asylum, Virgin, Giant, and Artemis
    recordings.)
Recorded 1978–2003; released January 31, 2006.

Preludes: Rare and Unreleased Recordings, New West Records, 2007.
(Note: Compilation of previously unreleased recordings and demos.)
Recorded 1974–1976; released May 1, 2007.

45 RPM SINGLES

"Follow Me" / "Like the Seasons" (lyme and cybelle) (1966)
White Whale 228

"If You Gotta Go, Go Now" / "I'll Go On" (lyme and cybelle) (1966)
White Whale 232

"Hasten Down the Wind" / "Mohammed's Radio" (1976)
Asylum 45356

"Werewolves of London" / "Roland The Headless Thompson Gunner" (1978)
Asylum 45472

"Lawyers, Guns and Money" / "Veracruz" (1978)
Asylum 45498

"Johnny Strikes Up the Band" / "Nighttime in the Switching Yard" (1978)
Asylum 45526

"Werewolves of London" / "Lawyers, Guns and Money" (1979) ("Spun Gold" reissue series)
Elektra 45091

"A Certain Girl" / "Empty-Handed Heart" (1980)
Asylum 46610

"Gorilla, You're a Desperado" / "Jungle Work" (1980)
Asylum 46641

"Lawyers, Guns and Money" / "Werewolves of London" (1981)
Asylum 47118

"Looking for the Next Best Thing" / "The Hula Hula Boys" (1982)
Asylum 69966

"Let Nothing Come Between You" / "The Hula Hula Boys" (1982)
Asylum 69946

"Werewolves of London" / "Jesus Mentioned" (1986)
Asylum 69509

"Leave My Monkey Alone" (1987)(Latin Rascals Dub)
Virgin 99440

"Reconsider Me" / "The Factory" (1988)
Virgin 99370

"Werewolves of London" / "Roland The Headless Thompson Gunner"
(1978, promo-only picture disc with die-cut cover)
Asylum AS 11386
"Nighttime in the Switching Yard" (1978, same on both sides)
Asylum AS 11395

"Werewolves of London" (1986, same on both sides; with picture cover
promoting *The Color of Money*)
Asylum ED 5185

"Sentimental Hygiene" (1987, LP Version) (Edit)
Virgin PR 2033

"Leave My Monkey Alone" (1987) (Latin Rascals Mix 10:31) / (Latin
Rascals Edit 5:45, Latin Rascals Dub 5:51)
Virgin DMD1053

"Detox Mansion" / "Leave My Monkey Alone" (1987)
Virgin PR 2062

"Boom Boom Mancini" (1987, same on both sides)
Virgin PR 2133

"Reconsider Me" (1988, same on both sides)
Virgin PR 2216

COMPACT DISC SINGLES

"Gonna Have a Good Time Tonight" / "Narrator" (Hindu Love Gods—
uncredited) (1986)
I.R.S.-52867

"Sentimental Hygiene" (1987, LP Version) (Edit)
Virgin PRCD 2038

"Reconsider Me" (1987)
Virgin PRCD 2216

"Run Straight Down" (1989)
Virgin PRCD 2987

"Splendid Isolation" (1989, LP Version) (Edit)
Virgin PRCD 3157
"Finishing Touches" (1991, Edit)
Giant PRO-CD-5017

"Searching for a Heart" (1991)
Giant PRO-CD-5171

"Rottweiler Blues" / "Poisonous Lookalike" / "Mutineer" (1995)
Giant PRO-CD-7483

"I Was in the House When the House Burned Down" (Clean House
    Version) (Album Version) (2001)
Artemis ARTCD-10

"Hit Somebody! (The Hockey Song)" / "For My Next Trick I'll Need a
    Volunteer" (2001)
Artemis 751069-2

"Basket Case" (2002)
Artemis ARTCD-133

"Knockin' On Heaven's Door" (2003)
Artemis ARTCD-203

"Disorder in the House" (2003)
Artemis ARTCD-208

"Keep Me in Your Heart" (2003)
Artemis ARTCD-209

SOURCES

INTERVIEWS

Mitch Albom (December 12, 2016)
Duncan Aldrich (December 6, 2011)
Kevin Avery (July 28, 2012)
Dave Barry (October 5, 2012)
Niko Bolas (October 7, 2011)
Julie Bowen (January 8, 2013)
Kim Fowley (December 15, 2011)
Anita Gevinson (January 31, 2012)
Merle Ginsberg (February 5, 2012)
Danny Goldberg (January 9, 2012)
George Gruel (June 7, 2012; October 5, 2012)
Billy Hinsche (September 26, 2011)
Barney Hoskyns (January 31, 2012)
Bones Howe (January 11, 2012)
Howard Kaylan (January 15, 2012)
Laura Kenyon (April 11, 2012)
Paul Q. Kolderie (July 13, 2017)
Gary Mallaber (January 5, 2012)
David Marks (January 20, 2012)

Julia Mueller McNeal (October 24, 2012)
Craig Northey (January 1, 2017)
Annette Ramos (February 4, 2012)
Ryan Rayston (June 20, 2013)
Sean Slade (July 11, 2017)
Noah Scot Snyder (April 24, 2012)
Waddy Wachtel (January 26, 2012)
Crystal Zevon (December 27, 2011)
Lawrence Zevon (January 9, 2012)
Sandford Zevon (January 6, 2012)

ARTICLES

Albom, Mitch. "Singer Zevon's Life Anything But Gray." *Free Press*. September 9, 2003.

Allan, Marc D. "Warren Zevon Hopes to Perform His Classical Music with Local Symphonies." *Indianapolis Star and News*, Knight-Ridder/Tribune News Service. March 11, 1996.

Bedell, Sally. "All-Rock Cable-TV Service is a Hit." *New York Times*. August 2, 1982.

Billboard. "Warren Zevon—*Excitable Boy*." *Billboard*. February 4, 1978.

Billboard. "Warren Zevon—*A Quiet, Normal Life*." *Billboard*. November 1, 1986.

Billboard. "Inside Track." *Billboard*. November 22, 1986.

Bowman, David. "Warren Zevon: The Man Who Brought Us 'Lawyers, Guns and Money' Talks About Everything But." Salon.com. March 18, 2000.

Branton, Michael. "Warren Zevon's Mystery Dance." *Bay Area Music*. March 7, 1980.

Browning, Boo. "Warren Zevon's Turning Point." *Washington Post*. April 18, 1980.

Browning, Boo. "Warren Zevon, All Shook Up." *Washington Post*. January 9, 1981.

Cantin, Paul. "Warren Zevon Deconstructs Elvis." *JAM! Showbiz*. March 10, 2000.

Charone, Barbara. "Warren Zevon: *Excitable Boy.*" *Sounds.* February 18, 1978.

Christgau, Robert. "Onward to Sarcasm." *Village Voice.* June 23, 1987.

Christgau, Robert. "Warren Zevon: *My Ride's Here.*" *Rolling Stone.* June 6, 2002.

Cocks, Jay. "Tales of the Neon Underworld." *Time.* March 13, 1978.

Cocks, Jay. "Album Review: Warren Zevon: *Bad Luck Streak in Dancing School.*" *Rolling Stone.* March 6, 1980.

Considine, J. D. "Warren Zevon Finds Singular Success with Solo Tour." *Baltimore Sun.* May 17, 1993.

Correa, Nina. "Waddy Wachtel: Creating 'Werewolves of London.'" Waddywachtelinfo.com. 2008.

D'Agostino, John. "Solo Sparseness Helps, Hurts Zevon at Belly Up." *Los Angeles Times.* August 14, 1992.

Doino Jr., William. "Warren Zevon's Secret." *First Things.* September 16, 2013.

Engemoen, Chip. "Record Review: '*Excitable Boy*' Rockets Zevon." *Woodside World.* April 7, 1978.

Fenton, James. "Between a Rock and a Hard Place." *Guardian.* September 19, 2003.

Fergus, Jim. "After the Storm." *Rocky Mountain Magazine.* December 1981.

Ferman, Dave. "It's Not the Big Time, But It's Zevon's Way." *Sun-Sentinel.* January 26, 1996.

Ferris, D. X. "Ray Manzarek on Working with Roy Rogers, Robbie Krieger, Sly Stone and Warren Zevon." *Ultimate Classic Rock.* October 18, 2011.

Fremer, Michael. "The Fast Lane is History: Don Henley Has Found His Thrill Down at the Grill." *Music Connection.* March 14–17, 1985.

Fretts, Bruce. "He Puts His Licks on 'Route 66': Rocker-Turned-Scorer Warren Zevon." *Entertainment Weekly.* June 4, 1993.

Fishell, Steve. "Waddy Wachtel: Rock Sideman, Pop Producer, Touring Guitarist." *Guitar Player.* October 1979.

Forte, Dan. "RX: Then Add Waddy Wachtel." *The Record.* February 1983.

Gallucci, Michael. "The History of Warren Zevon on 'David Letterman.'" *Ultimate Classic Rock.* May 19, 2015.

Gans, David. "Waddy Wachtel: Confessions of a 'Mafia' Guitarist." *Bam: The California Music Magazine*. March 7, 1980.

Garry, Mac. "Warren Zevon." *ZigZag*. October 1976.

Garry, Mac. "Behind the Scenes with Warren and Jackson (and Waddy Too)." *ZigZag*. December 1976.

Gevinson, Anita, and Jonathan Valania. "Rock 'n' Roll: Rittenhouse Square's Excitable Boy." *Philadelphia Magazine*. May 8, 2008.

Gilbertson, Jon M. "Warren Zevon, *Life'll Kill Ya*." *No Depression*. February 29, 2000.

Giles, Jeff. "How a Warren Zevon Jam Session with R.E.M. Turned into 'Hindu Love Gods.'" Ultimate Classic Rock.

Gilmore, Mikhail. "Warren Zevon Takes Control." *Rolling Stone*. September 16, 1982.

Goldstein, Patrick. "Elektra Suffers New Shock." *Los Angeles Times*. February 27, 1983.

Goldstein, Patrick. "Joe Walsh Jumps Elektra's Ship." *Los Angeles Times*. April 10, 1983.

Goldstein, Toby. "Warren Zevon: Life in the Mental Combat Zone." *Cream*. August 1980.

Gregory, Sinda, and Larry McCafferty. "Thomas McGuane: The Art of Fiction, No. 89." *The Paris Review*. Fall 1985.

Hasted, Nick. "Life'll Kill Ya." *Uncut*. September 2002.

Heim, Chris. "Hindu Love God Just One Reincarnation For Zevon." *Chicago Tribune*. December 21, 1990.

Heim, Chris. "No More Mr. Sensitive Nice Guy For Warren Zevon." *Chicago Tribune*. January 10, 1992.

Hessel-Mial, Michael. "Paul Muldoon: Surging Forward, Looking Back." *Emory Scholar*. March 6, 2013.

Hilburn, Robert. "Elektra's Comeback Kid: Bob Krasnow Turns Once Foundering Label into a Powerhouse." *Los Angeles Times*. February 12, 1989.

Hilburn, Robert. "The Key to Success Lies in the Mix." *Los Angeles Times*. April 2, 2000.

Hinkley, David. "Zevon Takes Musical Detour with New Album." *Sun-Sentinel*. December 26, 1990.

Holden, Stephen. "Warren Zevon at the Ritz." *New York Times*. October 1, 1982.

Holden, Stephen. "Warren Zevon." *New York Times*. June 5, 1986.

Holden, Stephen. "Nightmares of the Future As Seen by Warren Zevon." *New York Times*. February 14, 1990.

Hughes, John. "Rock's Mr. Bad Example On Lawyers, Sons and Money." *Sun-Sentinel*. January 25, 1992.

Kinsey, Tara Christie. "Rave On, John Donne: Paul Muldoon and Warren Zevon." *Yellow Nib*. Spring 2013.

Kot, Greg. "Ups and Downers: Warren Zevon Is Just As Carefree As He Ever Was." *Chicago Tribune*. February 18, 1990.

Kutina, Scott E. "Waddy Wachtel." *International Musician and Recording World*. February 1981.

Lannert, John. "Warren Zevon Kicks Off U.S. Tour with Carefree Show." *Sun-Sentinel*. May 22, 1992.

Locey, Bill. "Tour de Farce: The Good Humor Man of Rock, with a New Batch of Backup Musicians, Is Coming to Ventura." *Los Angeles Times*. November 8, 1990.

Mabe, Chauncey. "Warren Zevon Captures Spirit of a Dying Era with Album, Tour." *Sun-Sentinel*. October 30, 1987.

Marcus, Greil. "Warren Zevon: *Excitable Boy*." *Village Voice*. March 6, 1978.

Marsh, Dave. "Warren Zevon on the Loose in Los Angeles." *Rolling Stone*. March 9, 1978.

Miller, Judith. "Song Inspired by Habib Urges, 'Send the Envoy.'" *New York Times*. November 3, 1982.

Milward, John. "Rehabilitation Enriches Warren Zevon's Music." *Philadelphia Inquirer*. September 26, 1987.

Mitchell, Justin. "Warren Zevon Ready to Record Again." *Chicago Tribune*. August 22, 1985.

Nelson, Paul. "Warren Zevon Comes Out of the Woods." *Village Voice*. June 21, 1976.

Nelson, Paul. "Album Review: Warren Zevon: *Excitable Boy*." *Rolling Stone*. March 23, 1978.

Nelson, Paul. "Warren Zevon: How He Saved Himself from a Coward's Death." *Rolling Stone*. March 19, 1981.

Newman, Melinda. "Zevon Revels in His Own Studio." *Billboard*. April 22, 1995.

Nugent, Frank S. "'Werewolf of London' (1935) at the Rialto." *New York Times*. May 10, 1935.

O' Connor, Rob. "That's Life." Launch.com. December 29, 1999.

Palmer, Robert. "The Pop Life: Warren Zevon Album: Live, Raw, and Powerful." *New York Times*. January 16, 1981.

Palmer, Robert. "Warren Zevon's Checkered Career May Take a Happy Turn." *New York Times*. July 18, 1982.

Pareles, Jon. "Warren Zevon." *New York Times*. September 28, 1987.

Pareles, Jon. "Somewhere Between Irony and Identification." *New York Times*. July 18, 1995.

Pareles, Jon. "An Excitable Werewolf, Still Howling." *New York Times*. March 21, 2000.

Pareles, Jon. "Warren Zevon's Last Waltz." *New York Times*. January 26, 2003.

People staff. "Picks and Pans Review: *Bad Luck Streak in Dancing School*." *People*. May 19, 1980.

Pollack, Andrew. "Music on Cable TV Provoking a Debate." *New York Times*. November 29, 1982.

Pollak, Sally. "Unplugged in Peacham: Ariel Zevon Builds a Life in NEK." *Burlington Free Press*. May 29, 2014.

Powers, Ron. "Zevon Likes Solo Touring." *Spokesman-Review*. March 9, 1983.

Reid, Graham. "Warren Zevon: Tales from the Darkside." *New Zealand Herald*. September 1992.

Robertson, Sandy. "Warren Zevon: *The Envoy*." *Sounds*. August 7, 1982.

Rolling Stone staff. "Browne Remembers Zevon." *Rolling Stone*. September 19, 2003.

Roeser, Steve. "Warren Zevon: Left Jabs and Roundhouse Rights." *Goldmine*. August 18, 1995.

Roos, John. "Zevon Puts Excitable Days in Perspective." *Los Angeles Times*. March 29, 2000.

Rosen, Craig. "Azoff's Imprint Taking Giant Steps." *Billboard*. October 12, 1991.

Silverman, David. "Warren Zevon's Idea of Vacation Makes for One Refreshing Evening." *Chicago Tribune*. November 18, 1988.

Stewart, Andy. "Meanwhile, Back at the Ranch." *AudioTechnology*. Issue 53.

Sullivan, Jim. "Warren Zevon Flinches at a Life Without Humor." *Boston Globe*. 1993.

Tarson, Steve. "Zevon's Musical Parchment Leans Toward the Madcap." *Sun-Sentinel*. August 1, 1986.

Thelen, Christopher. "Learning to Flinch." *Daily Vault*. March 7, 1993.

Thompson, Hunter S. "Champions Roy and Zevon." ESPN.com. May 28, 2001.

Valania, Jonathan. "An Excitable Boy, They All Said." *Philadelphia Weekly*. November 20, 2002.

Washburn, Jim. "Over-Amped Zevon Can't Make Up the Distance." *Los Angeles Times*. March 26, 1990.

Weingarten, Marc. "A Literary Answer to Lyricist's Block: Musician/Bookworm Warren Zevon Recruits Famous Authors for Lyrics on a New Album." *Los Angeles Times*. May 16, 2002.

Willman, Chris. "Zevon Back on the Satire Trail." *Los Angeles Times*. June 11, 1987.

Wolff, Carlo. "Zevon Takes Shots at Guns, Politicos." *Akron Beacon Journal*. October 12, 1987.

Zeller, Craig. "Warren Zevon: *The Envoy*." *Cream*. November 1982.

BOOKS

Avery, Kevin. *Everything Is an Afterthought: The Life and Writings of Paul Nelson*. Seattle: Fantagraphics, 2011.

Brown, Garry. *Colorado Rocks!: A Half-Century of Music in Colorado*. Portland: Westwinds Press, 2004.

Christgau, Robert. *Rock Albums of the '70s: A Critical Guide*. Da Capo Press, 1990.

Christgau, Robert. *Christgau's Record Guide: The '80s*. Da Capo Press, 1994.

Christgau, Robert. *Christgau's Consumer Guide: Albums of the '90s*. New York: St. Martin's Griffin, 2000.

Cohen, Mickey. *In My Own Words: As Told to John Peer Nugent*. Prentice-Hall, 1975.

Davis, Stephen. *Gold Dust Woman: The Biography of Stevie Nicks*. New York: St. Martin's Press, 2017.

Fink, Mitchell. *The Last Days of Dead Celebrities*. Miramax, 2006.

Gevinson, Anita. *You Turn Me On, I'm a Radio: My Wild, Rock 'N' Roll Life*. Self-published, 2012.

Goldberg, Danny. *Bumping Into Geniuses: My Life Inside the Rock and Roll Business*. New York: Gotham, 2009.

Griffin, Kathy. *Kathy Griffin's Celebrity Run-Ins: My A–Z Index*. New York: Flatiron Books, 2016.

Gruel, George. *Lawyers, Guns and Photos*. New York: Big Gorilla Books, 2012.

Hjortsberg, William. *Jubilee Hitchhiker: The Life and Times of Richard Brautigan*. Counterpoint, 2013.

Hoskyns, Barney. *Hotel California: The True-Life Adventures of Crosby, Stills, Nash, Young, Mitchell, Taylor, Browne, Ronstadt, Geffen, the Eagles, and Their Many Friends*. Wiley, 2007.

Hoskyns, Barney. *Waiting for the Sun: A Rock & Roll History of Los Angeles*. Backbeat Books, 2009.

Kubernik, Harvey. *Canyon of Dreams: The Magic and Music of Laurel Canyon*. Sterling, 2012.

Nolan, Tom. *Ross Macdonald: A Biography*. Scribner, 1999.

Priore, Domenic. *Riot on Sunset Strip*. Jawbone Press, 2007.

Ronstadt, Linda. *Simple Dreams: A Musical Memoir*. Simon & Schuster, 2013.

Tereba, Tere. *Mickey Cohen: The Life and Crimes of LA's Notorious Mobster*. ECW Press, 2012.

Thornton, Billy Bob, and Kinky Friedman. *The Billy Bob Tapes: A Cave Full of Ghosts*. William Morrow, 2012.

Torry, Beef (ed.). *Conversations with Thomas McGuane (Literary Conversations Series)*. University Press of Mississippi, 2006.

Walker, Michael. *Laurel Canyon: The Inside Story of Rock-and-Roll's Legendary Neighborhood*. Faber & Faber, 2007.

Yandolino, Frank. *Frank & Charli: Woodstock, True Love, and the Sixties*. Skyhorse Publishing, 2016.

Zevon, Crystal. *I'll Sleep When I'm Dead: The Dirty Life and Times of Warren Zevon*. Ecco, 2008.

MISC.

Ancestry.com
Archive.org
Federal Bureau of Investigation file, William Zevon, 1970–1991.
Warren Zevon Video LP, Sony, 1982, VHS.
VH1 (Inside) Out—Warren Zevon: Keep Me in Your Heart, Artemis Records, 2004, DVD.

ACKNOWLEDGMENTS

Only in seeing this project completed am I fully aware how many friends, family members, and enthusiastic advocates played crucial roles in its completion—and I am humbled and surprised to find that they are not only my own, but Warren Zevon's, as well. In no short order, I would like to thank the following people who, over the course of seven years, aided and abetted this first-time author in bringing his hero's story to light:

First and foremost, my parents, only one of which is here to see this volume's completion; thank you, Dad, for your unending encouragement and advice—and my love of music; this book is dedicated to my late mother, who was the greatest influence in inspiring and fostering my love of writing and the arts; I hope you'd approve of the final work. My brothers, Sean and Brandon, sister Leyla, and nieces Kylah and Sera; my second parents, Aunt Deedee and Uncle Bill, and their children, who are my own second set of siblings, Michael and Megan.

Outside of my relatives, the list of friends who both humored and inspired my project's progress is composed of names that may as well be siblings (and are my own bandmates): Albert, Allen, Ben, Dan, Danie, Derek, James, John, Ricky, Rob, Russ, little Sloane (who better be hard at work using my old typewriter), Terry—and both Phil and Sal, the publishers who gave me my first byline at fifteen years old.

Although my sources section lists the names of Warren's friends and family who had unending patience for my questions and appeals for help and guidance, I must take this opportunity to bring their names front and center here, as well. My absolute gratitude to Mitch Albom, Duncan Aldrich, Kevin Avery, Dave Barry, Niko Bolas, Julie Bowen, the late Kim Fowley, Anita Gevinson, Merle Ginsberg, Danny Goldberg, the incredible George Gruel (who answered many phone calls and emails for added assistance in re-creating some of Warren's most excitable years), Billy Hinsche, Barney Hoskyns (whose interviews were not only incredible, but, as the founder of *Rock's Back Pages,* provided some of the greatest and rarest of Warren's early interviews and press write-ups), Bones Howe, Howard Kaylan, Laura Kenyon, Paul Q. Kolderie, Gary Mallaber, David Marks, Julia Mueller McNeal, Craig Northey, Annette Aguilar-Ramos, Ryan Rayston (the "guardian angel living next door," who took more calls than anyone else in guiding my representation of Warren's wiser, more spiritual, and better self), Sean Slade, Noah Scot Snyder, Waddy Wachtel, Crystal Zevon, Lawrence Zevon, and Sandford Zevon.

And finally, I would like to express my gratitude to the two people whom Warren truly valued the most in all the world: his children, Ariel and Jordan, both of whom gave their blessing and kindest of words at the start of my project nearly a decade ago. My greatest hope is that you both approve of my representation of your father—the artist and the man.

As for my own advocates and greatest champions: a very special thanks to the three personal heroes who made this book actually *happen*—my agent, William Clark, whose infinite patience is only matched by his diligence and understanding; my amazing editor (and dare I say friend) Ben Schafer at Da Capo, who still doesn't believe that I consider him a greater rock star than the ones he often edits; and finally, my first hero in life and career, Elmore "Dutch" Leonard, who made me want to be a writer, and to take the work seriously. In writing this book, I was fully aware of every lesson he taught me about good writing through his letters when I was a teenager . . . Dutch, I only hope that my writing doesn't sound too much like writing—and that you'd forgive my necessity for both a prologue and the usage of the phrase "all hell broke loose." It was, after all, the name of Warren's 1980 tour and, therefore, I hope appropriately justified. However, I adhered to your other eight rules with conscious deliberation.

And to the beginning of everything . . .

My timeless muse and audience of one—who intentionally made me a better writer, unintentionally made me a better man, and accidentally made them one and the same; my gift from God, my dreamer, my fire—my Nina:

> *Your every word spoken*
> *and every glance like a crescendo*
> *all its own.*
> *If there is such a thing as an ecstasy*
> *that builds like kindling—*
> *you hold the warmth of a glow*
> *and the dance of a flame.*

—CMK

INDEX

Abdul, Paula, 237
"Accidentally Like a Martyr" (Zevon),
　91–92, 189, 335
ADAT machine, 314, 324
addiction, Warren's discussion of own,
　255, 362
adolescence, 11–26
　alcohol use during, 15–16
　living with father, 16–17
　as musical prodigy, 12–14
　Santangelo and, 17–26
Adult Contemporary genre, Warren
　assigned to radio as, 301–302
Aguilar-Ramos, Annette, 259–263,
　272, 274–275, 276, 277, 293–294,
　337
　song for, 342, 347
"Ain't That Pretty at All" (Zevon),
　172, 276
Akron Beacon Journal, 240
"Alabama" (Young), 135–136
Albom, Mitch, 319, 320–321, 326
Alcoholics Anonymous, 55, 220, 248,
　250, 256, 262, 272, 273, 275, 277,
　345
alcoholism, Warren on, 238
alcohol use, Warren's, 27, 58, 63, 83,
　85, 107, 344, 345

as adolescent, 15–16
arguing with Crystal over, 52,
　54–55
correlation with Warren's obsessive-
　compulsive disorder, 248, 250
as creative stimulant, 50
on tours, 47, 74, 76, 102–104
violent episodes and, 76
Aldrich, Duncan "Dr. Babyhead," 244,
　286, 322, 337
　Learning to Flinch and, 286–288
　Millennium Paranoia Tour and, 265
　Mutineer and, 296–297
　new recording technologies and,
　　225–226, 285–286
　as road manager, 218–219
　on *Sentimental Hygiene* sessions,
　　228
　Transverse City and, 252–253, 254–
　　256, 257, 262–263
　on Warren's complaints of
　　loneliness, 296
　on Warren's dissatisfaction with
　　career and end of relationship,
　　307
　on Warren's interest in literature,
　　293
Allan, Marc D., 301, 311

All Hell Is Breaking Loose Jungle
  Tour, 152, 163, 176
"All I Have to Do Is Dream" (Bryant),
  43
The Allnighter (Frey), 196
all-star cameos on Warren's albums,
  57, 64, 142–143, 226, 253. *See
  also* individual artists
Alternative Chorus Songwriters'
  Showcase, Warren at, 56–57
Amis, Martin, 293
"Anatomy of a Headache" (Zevon),
  293
Andersen, Eric, 84
Anderson, Ken, 312–313
"Angel Dressed in Black" (Zevon),
  259
Apatow, Judd, 310, 356
Apple, Fiona, 358
Arista, 58
Arngrim, Stefan, 220, 272, 274–275
Arnold, Eddy, 269
arrests for drunk driving, 55, 58–59
Artemis Records, 306, 312–313, 317,
  334, 335, 354
Asbestos Disease Awareness
  Organization, 354
Asher, Peter, 166, 271–272, 297, 327
The Association, 34, 41, 49
Asylum Records, 41–42. *See also*
  Elektra/Asylum
The Asylum Years (Waits), 221
Atkins, Chet, 43
Atlantic Records, 42, 306
Audio Technology (magazine), 259
Auman, Lisl, 322–323
Austin, Michael, 212
Austin City Limits Studios, interview
  with Warren, 355
Australian tours, 264, 290
autobiographical nature of Warren's
  music, 65, 70, 236, 251, 347, 359
Avery, Ken, 74
Ayeroff, Jeff, 222, 225, 236, 238
Azoff, Irving, 196–197, 198, 209,
  269–270, 271–272, 275, 299, 327

"Backs Turned Looking Down the
  Path" (Zevon), 65–66, 216–217
"Bad Karma" (Zevon), 220, 227, 235
bad luck, Warren's fear of, 220, 350
"Bad Luck Streak in Dancing School"
  (Zevon), 128–129
Bad Luck Streak in Dancing School
  (Zevon), 116
  Billboard ranking, 156
  Calderón and, 118
  critics on, 146–149
  design and marketing of, 144–145
  European leg of tour, 159, 163–164
  recording sessions, 122–123, 126–144
  singles from, 145–146
  tour for, 150–154, 155, 156–157
  writing songs for, 120, 121, 122
Baez, Joan, 52
baglama, 235
Baker, Chet, 263
"The Ballad of Bill Lee." *See* "Bill
  Lee" (Zevon)
Baron, Diana, 349
Barr, Brigette, 327, 332–333, 334, 335,
  338, 339, 348
Barry, Dave, 319–320, 321–322, 344,
  361
Barry, Michelle, 322
Battin, Skip, 36
Beacon Theater, 240, 247, 264, 265
Beastie Boys, 271
The Beatles, 26
Beck, Greg, 240
Beckett, Samuel, 134
"Bed of Coals" (Zevon and Burnett),
  143
Behind the Music (VH1), 338, 339
"Bell-Bottom Blues" (Clapton), 129
Belushi, John, 73, 170, 362
Belzer, Richard, 101
Benben, Brian, 308
benefactor, Warren's need for, 17
Bennett, Tony, 263
Berry, Bill, 213, 227, 228, 231, 236,
  269, 270
Berry, Chuck, 152

Big Gorilla Books, 355
Billboard charts
   Bad Luck Streak in Dancing School
     on, 156
   Color of Money soundtrack and
     compilation album on, 221
   The Envoy on, 174
   Excitable Boy on, 98, 106
   "Follow Me" on, 25
   hindu love gods on, 270
   Learning to Flinch on, 291
   Life'll Kill Ya on, 317
   performance of singles from
     Sentimental Hygiene on, 245
   Sentimental Hygiene on, 245
   Stand in the Fire on, 158
   The Wind on, 349
Billboard (trade magazine), 99, 196,
   222, 293, 298–299, 338
"Bill Lee" (Zevon), 135, 139–141, 145,
   146
birth of Warren, 7
Black Angus (Thornburg), 136
Blade Runner (film), 254
bleeding tracks, on *Transverse City*,
   254–255
The Blue Mask (Reed), 174
blues, Warren's knowledge of, 46
"Bo Diddley" (Diddley), 158
Boehm, Mike, 282, 285
Boettcher, Curt, 49
Bolas, Niko, 225–227, 228, 237, 273
Bond, James, Warren's fascination
   with, 2, 163, 168, 171, 335
Bonoff, Karla, 92, 122, 265
The Book of Tao, 307
"Boom Boom Mancini" (Zevon), 213,
   215, 228, 229–232, 239, 245
Bork, Robert H., 240
Born to Run (Springsteen), 72
Bortnick, Bob, 294
Boston Globe, 290–291
Bottom Line (club), 73, 102, 192, 217
Botts, Mike, 173
Boucher, Geoff, 343
Boulder (band), 152–154, 156–157, 282

Bourguignon, Serge, 21
Bowman, David, 361
"The Boxer" (Simon), 138
boxing theme, "Boom Boom
   Mancini," 229–232
Boyce, Gloria, 286
"Boys of Summer" video, 229
Braheny, John, 56
Brando, Marlon, 161
Braudis, Bob, 323
Brautigan, Richard, 162
Brelsford, Barbara, 49, 54, 112
Brelsford, Clifford, 49, 54, 112,
   155–156
Brelsford, Crystal Ann, 44
   addressing own addiction,
     272–273
   Ariel's relationship with father and,
     156, 202–203, 204
   birth of Ariel, 74
   birth of Ariel's twins and, 349
   confirming Warren's admiration for
     Dylan, 233
   disintegration and end of marriage
     to Warren, 123–124, 126, 150
   domestic abuse from Warren,
     50–51, 63, 76, 84–85
   domestic solace with Warren,
     106–107
   early relationship with Warren,
     47–48, 49–50
   "Empty-Handed Heart" and, 148
   Excitable Boy tour and, 102
   foster children, 50, 55, 56
   I'll Sleep When I'm Dead (memoir),
     355
   Las Vegas wedding, 56
   as most dominant muse of Warren's
     career, 347
   move back to L.A., 217
   new life abroad, 182
   pregnancy, 63, 71
   rescuing Warren in Casablanca, 76,
     77
   seeking help for Warren,
     108–109

Brelsford, Crystal Ann (*continued*)
  separations from and
    reconciliations with Warren, 53,
    54, 55, 83, 86, 189
  song for, 131, 145, 148
  suggested threesome with Warren
    and Gevinson and, 190
  trip to Ireland, 116–117, 120–121,
    122
  trip to Spain with Warren, 60–62
  vacations in Hawaii with Warren,
    116
  Waddy Wachtel and, 44, 48–49
  Warren after Life at Least Tour and,
    197–198
  Warren's alcohol use and, 52, 54–55
  Warren's confession of his
    infidelities, 188
  Warren's rehab at Pinecrest
    Rehabilitation Center and, 4,
    110–113
  "Werewolves of London" and, 88
Bridges, Jeff, 162
Brodeur, Scott, 265
Brown, Randy, 177
Browne, Jackson
  Ariel opening for, 356
  Ariel's fourth birthday party and,
    155
  Bad Luck Streak in Dancing School
    and, 131, 148
  Crystal's plea for help and, 94–95
  death of wife, 72, 73
  at demo sessions, 57
  early relationship with Warren,
    51–52
  Elektra/Asylum and, 197
  Enjoy Every Sandwich and, 354
  Excitable Boy and, 86–96, 189
  "Excitable Boy" and, 91
  folk-rock and, 279
  follow-up to *Warren Zevon* and, 78
  Geffen and, 41
  Goldberg and, 312
  "Gorilla, You're a Desperado" and,
    142
  Grammy Awards' tribute and, 353
  on Lankford, 172
  Main Point and, 187
  at memorial service, 351
  message about recording contract to
    Warren in Spain, 61, 62
  Nelson and, 74, 104
  "Play It All Night Long" and,
    136–137
  recommending acupuncture
    treatment for Warren, 180
  response to Warren's diagnosis, 336,
    337
  reunion with Warren at benefit for
    Yvonne Calderón, 305–306
  romanticism of, 141
  Running on Empty tour, 129
  setting Warren up in L.A. after
    rehab at St. Mary's, 214
  skipping *Excitable Boy* tour, 101
  Warren and benefit shows with,
    83–84
  Warren as opening act for *Pretender*
    tour, 75–76
  as Warren's emergency contact, 212
  Warren's intervention therapy and,
    4, 112
  on Warren's karate-on-speed
    period, 157
  on Warren's music, 357
  Warren Zevon and, 62–72, 78–80
  "Werewolves of London" and, 88
Browning, Boo, 146–147, 158
Brubaker (film), 342
brucellosis, 135, 136
Buck, Peter, 209, 210, 212–213, 227,
  228, 236, 269, 300
Buckingham, Lindsey, 57, 64, 66, 68,
  81
Buckley, Jeff, 300
Buckley, William F., Jr., 177
Building the Perfect Beast (Henley),
  196, 209
Bukowski, Charles, 59, 67
"A Bullet for Ramona" (Zevon), 36
Burke, Howard, 73, 97, 125
Burnett, T Bone, 57, 137, 143, 343
Burns, Michael, 20

Butler, Rosemary, 70
The Byrds, 236

Calderón, Jorge, 59, 118, 256
    Bad Luck Streak in Dancing School
        and, 131, 132
    collaborations with Warren, 81–83,
        92, 118, 141–142, 278–279,
        315–316
    contract with Inside Recordings,
        357
    The Envoy and, 172
    Excitable Boy and, 87, 88–89
    Grammy Awards' tribute and, 353
    "Mr. Bad Example" and, 278–279
    Mutineer and, 297
    My Ride's Here and, 327
    nagging Warren to see doctor, 333
    "Porcelain Monkey" and, 141–142,
        315–316
    Sentimental Hygiene and, 226, 228,
        235
    video for "Werewolves of London"
        and, 129
    visits to Warren's home studio, 313
    Warren's intervention therapy and,
        112
    on Warren's physical and mental
        condition during illness, 346
    Warren Zevon and, 64, 68, 69
    The Wind and, 336–337, 341–348
Calderón, Yvonne, 305, 333
"California Dreamin'", 22
Californication (television series),
    using Warren's music on, 356
Campbell, Mike, 234, 262, 343
cancer diagnosis, Warren's response
    to, 333–335
"Can I Get to Know You Better"
    (Turtles), 29
Cantin, Paul, 316
Capitol Records, 358
Capone, Al, 8–9
Cardosa, David, 16
Carefree Theatre, 286
"Carmelita" (Zevon), 47, 64, 69, 215
Carroll, Jim, 300

Carter, Elliott, 242
Casablanca, Warren in, 76
Casady, Jack, 258
Cash, Johnny, 216, 234–235
Cates, John, 16
Catlin, Roger, 281
CBS Orchestra, 310, 321, 325
CD single, 222–223
"A Certain Girl" (Toussaint), 130
"A Certain Girl" (Zevon), 131, 145,
    146, 156, 157–158, 225, 265
Chacon, Bobby "The Schoolboy," 230
Chandler, Len, 56
Chandler, Raymond, 40, 100, 105, 144,
    149
charitable shows, Warren and, 83–84
"Charlie's Medicine" (Zevon),
    169–170
Charone, Barbara, 98
Chateau Marmont, 105–106, 117,
    118–119, 126, 170
Chicago Tribune (newspaper), 215,
    217, 219, 252, 253, 267, 268,
    270–271, 281
Childs, Karen, 240
Chopra, Deepak, 335
Christgau, Robert, 72, 147, 158, 175,
    221–222, 235, 263–264, 267, 326
Clapton, Eric, 129, 130, 221
classical music, Warren and, 13–14,
    15, 133–135, 238–239, 255–256,
    311–312
Clinton, George, 237
cocaine, Warren's use of, 150
Cochran, Eddie, 216
Cocks, Jay, 108, 147–149, 160
Cody, Phil, 307
Cohen, Jerry, 103
Cohen, Leonard, 104, 130, 187
Cohen, Mickey, 9
Cohen, Steve, 323
collaborations, songwriting
    with Browne, 94–95
    with Burnett, 143
    with Calderón, 81–83, 92, 118,
        278–279, 315–316
    with Henley, 216

collaborations, songwriting (*continued*)
  with Hiaasen, 300
  with McGuane, 161–163, 168
  with Muldoon, 323–324, 326,
    337–338
  with Rock Bottom Remainders,
    319–322
  with Souther, 215, 310
  with Springsteen, 137–138
  with Thompson, 323, 326
  Warren and, 79
Collins, Ruby, 38
color, Warren's preference for
    monochromatic, 24, 242, 346
The Color of Money (film), 221, 310
Coltrane, John, 33
Condos, Jennifer, 265
Cooder, Ry, 52, 341, 342
Cook, Bryan, 213
Copland, Aaron, 64
Corea, Chick, 252, 257, 263
Corneal, Jon, 36
Cowsill, Barry, 57
Cowsill, William "Bud," 49
"The Crack-Up and Resurrection of
    Warren Zevon" (Nelson), 223
"The Crack-Up" (Fitzgerald), 141
Craft, Robert, 13–14, 360
Cramer, Floyd, 43
Cream (magazine), 175
creative process, Warren's, 47, 222
critics
  on *Bad Luck Streak in Dancing
    School,* 146–149
  on *Bad Luck Streak in Dancing
    School* tour performances,
    153–154
  on *The Envoy,* 174–175
  on *Excitable Boy,* 98–100
  on *Excitable Boy* tour, 102–103, 104
  on *Life'll Kill Ya,* 316
  on Live at Least Tour, 192
  on live performances, 217–218
  on *Mr. Bad Example,* 280–281
  on *Sentimental Hygiene,* 235, 238
  on *Sentimental Hygiene* tour,
    240–241
  on *Stand in the Fire,* 158
  on *Transverse City,* 256, 263–265
  on *Transverse City* tour, 265–266, 268
  on *The Wind,* 349
Crocker, Glenn, 16, 33
Cromelin, Richard, 281, 328
Crossfires (band), 20
Cruise, Tom, 221
Crumley, Jim, 162
cummings, e. e., 21
cyberpunk music, Warren and, 256

Daily Vault (music review site), 291
dance remix, for "Leave My Monkey
    Alone," 237
Daniels, Joe, 177
Dante, Alighieri, 145
David, Marty, 66
Davis, Clive, 58
Davis, Miles, 229, 263
Davis, Sammy, Jr., 339
D-Doe, Ernie, 130
death
  as theme in *Life'll Kill Ya,* 316
  Warren's, 350–351
death wish, Warren's seeming, 1–4, 51
debut album. *See Warren Zevon*
    (Zevon)
Dekker, Desmond, 67
Dell, Gene, 44
del Toro, Benicio, 323
DeNiro, Robert, 117
Depp, Johnny, 299
DeShannon, Jackie, 25
"Desperadoes Under the Eaves"
    (Zevon), 50, 68, 70
The Detangler (A. Zevon), 356
"Detox Mansion" (Zevon), 213,
    215–216, 233, 234–235, 238, 245,
    291
DeVito, JoAnn, 129
Diddley, Bo, 269
Die Another Day (film), 335
digital audio tape (DAT) machine,
    285–286
digital computer editing, for
    Transverse City, 253

digital editing suites, 325
digital music technologies, Warren and, 219, 255, 263
"Dirty Life and Times" (Zevon), 341
"Dirty Little Religion" (Zevon), 315
"Disorder in the House" (Zevon), 342–343, 353
doctors, Warren's fear of, 332–333
Dodge City studios, 276
Donahue, Jerry, 73
Double Fantasy (Lennon), 174
Dr. Zhivago (Pasternak), 339
dream of shooting himself, Warren's recurring, 1–4, 107
Dream On (television series), 308
drug use, Warren's, 27–28, 33, 63, 179–180, 194
Drug Wars (film), 294
Dubliners (pub), 60, 61
Duchovny, David, 356
Dugmore, Dan, 275
Duino Elegies (Rilke), 339
Dunn, Kevin, 205
Duvall, Robert, 117
Dylan, Bob, 25–26, 36, 104, 138
    covers of Zevon's songs, 335, 354
    Sentimental Hygiene cameo, 233, 258
    Warren's admiration for, 25, 80, 192, 229, 232–233, 279
    Warren's covers of Dylan songs, 130
Dylan, Jakob, 233, 357–358

The Eagles, 41, 52
early life/childhood, 7, 8, 11–12
Eastwood, Clint, 109, 124, 150, 160
Ecco Books, 355
Eddy, Duane, 216
Edlund, Richard "Darkroom Dick," 36, 40, 51
Edwards, Blake, 169
Edwards, Kenny, 93, 96, 173
"El Amor de Mi Vida" (Zevon), 342, 347
Elektra/Asylum, 42, 51, 175–176, 195–197, 198, 221
Eliot, T. S., 113, 122, 140, 145
El Rayo-X, 265

"Empty-Handed Heart" (Zevon), 131, 145, 148
Engemoen, Chip, 98
Enjoy Every Sandwich (Zevon memorial album), 354
Entertainment Weekly (magazine), 328, 335
"The Envoy" (Zevon), 168
The Envoy (Zevon), 163, 288
    critical reception of, 174–175, 267
    recording sessions, 165–174
    singles off of, 174–175
    tour supporting, 176–179
    Warren on challenge of, 164–165
    Warren's secret agent fantasy and, 170–171
Erwin, Wayne, 30
"Even a Dog Can Shake Hands" (Zevon), 235–236
Everly, Don, 42, 56, 57, 58, 64, 65, 84
Everly, Ike, 43
Everly, Phil, 42, 57–58, 59–60, 62, 63, 64, 65, 67, 87
Everly Brothers
    lessons learned from, 282–283
    Warren on tour with, 26, 42–43, 45–46, 50, 52–54, 279
    Warren's work on *Stories We Could Tell*, 52
"Everybody's Talking" (Nilsson), 37
"Excitable Boy" (Zevon), 71, 79, 90–91, 98, 177
Excitable Boy (Zevon), 83, 299
    cover design, 97
    critical reception of, 98–100
    Gevinson's relationship with Warren at time of, 188–190
    listening party for, 93–94
    marketing campaign, 97–98
    recording sessions, 86–96
    tour for, 101–103
extended family, Warren's relations with, 152–153, 207–208, 220, 243–244, 274
Extremely Heavy! (Underground All-stars), 35
"Eye in the Sky" (Parsons), 146

"The Factory" (Zevon), 216, 218, 232, 233

Fairfax High School (Los Angeles), 17–18

Farkas, Sam, 9

fear, Warren and, 107, 332

Fear and Loathing in Las Vegas (Thompson), 314

Feigin, Ted, 20, 21–22, 25

Felder, Don, 131, 142

Fergus, Jim, 162

"Fiery Emblems" (Zevon), 36

"Finishing Touches" (Zevon), 277

Fitzgerald, F. Scott, 81, 138, 141, 162, 236

Five Easy Pieces (film), 55

Flea (musician), 226, 237

Fleetwood, Mick, 87, 88–89, 343

Fleetwood Mac, 49

Flies (band), 33

flip-side racket, 29–30

folk-rocker persona, Warren's, 275–276

folk-rock genre, *Mr. Bad Example* and, 279–280

"Follow Me" (Zevon), 23–25, 25

"Folsom Prison Blues" (Cash), 216, 235

Fonda, Peter, 162

Fong-Torres, Ben, 148

"Football Takes Its Toll" (Zevon & Souther), 310

For Everyman (Browne), 66

Forman, Steve, 173

40 Watt Club, 210, 213, 215

Four Quartets (Eliot), 113, 122

Fowley, Kim, 34–36, 38–39, 127, 296, 356

Frampton, Peter, 101

"Frank and Jesse James" (Zevon), 64–65, 82

French, Toxey, 36

"The French Inhaler" (Zevon), 57, 67–68

Fretts, Bruce, 328

Frey, Glenn, 64, 67, 69, 140, 142–143, 144, 173, 196, 212

Friedman, Barry (Frazier Mohawk), 51–52

From Russia with Love (film), 335

Front Line Management, 197, 200, 212, 271

"Frozen Notes" (Zevon), 71, 93

Full Moon Fever (Petty), 275

Funny People (film), 356

Garcia, Jerry, 106, 254, 258

Garfunkel, Art, 25

Garofalo, Bryan, 75

Gavin, Bill, 26

Gaye, Marvin, 25

Geffen, David, 41, 52, 62, 79, 80, 95, 175, 196

Geller, Arnie, 50

Genesis, 223

"Genius" (Zevon), 325, 326, 339

Gevinson, Anita, 347
    on Ariel's message to Warren, 197
    Ariel's visit to Philadelphia and, 202–203
    career in radio, 188, 191
    on composition of "Piano Fighter," 204
    relationship with Warren, 187, 188–190, 190–191, 195, 204–205, 214
    on Slater, 210–211
    on Warren and Mancini fight, 230–231
    on Warren and politics, 241
    on Warren finding he'd been dropped by Elektra/Asylum, 198
    on Warren's addictions, 194
    Warren's European tour and, 200–203
    Warren's rehab and, 209, 211–212

Giancana, Sam, 9

Giant Records, 269–271, 281–282, 285, 289, 291–292, 298, 301

Gibson, William, 251, 254

Gilbertson, Jon M., 316

Gilmore, Gary, 193

Gilmore, Mikal, 165, 171

Gilmour, David, 253, 255
Ginsberg, Merle, 223–224, 242, 247–251, 259, 347
Glaub, Bob, 65, 67, 92, 171, 254, 262, 277, 278
Gold, Debbie, 310, 311
Goldberg, Danny
  Browne and, 305–306
  final sessions and, 343
  Grammy Awards' tribute and, 353
  memorial album and, 354
  My Ride's Here and, 318–319, 326–327
  Preludes: Rare and Unreleased Recordings and, 355
  record contract for Warren and, 312–313
  on sales of *Life'll Kill Ya*, 317
  Warren on *Letterman* appearance, 339
  The Wind and, 334, 335, 336, 338–339, 342, 345, 349
Golden, Stan, 333
Goldmine (magazine), 289, 298, 299, 310
Gold Mountain Entertainment, 306
gold records, Warren's, 37, 105–106
"Gonna Have a Good Time Tonight" (Berry), 213
Good Clean Fun (Fowley), 35
"Good Times" (Easybeats), 213
Gore, Al, 339
"Gorilla, You're a Desperado" (Zevon), 36, 132, 141, 142, 145, 147
Gould, Glenn, 316, 361
Graceland, 316
Gradney, Kenny, 240
Grammy nominations, for *The Wind*, 353
Grand Canyon (film), 280
Grateful Dead, 106
Green, Richard, 230
green, Warren's stephen lyme persona and, 24
Greene, Graham, 60, 163
"Gridlock" (Zevon), 259, 274

Griffin, Kathy, 308
group therapy, at St. Mary's Hospital, 211
Gruel, George, 310
  on all-star cameos, 142–143
  Ariel's fourth birthday party and, 155
  Bad Luck Streak in Dancing School and, 128, 131, 138, 144–145
  Bad Luck Streak in Dancing School tour and, 153, 154
  on "Charlie's Medicine," 169–170
  on donating T-shirts from tour to mental hospital, 159
  on European tour, 163
  Lawyers, Guns & Photos, 355
  photos for *The Envoy* and, 174
  relationship with Warren, 125–126, 198–199
  subduing O'Hare, 160
  visit from Bill Lee and, 139–140
  Warren, Lankford, and, 151, 180
  on Warren in studio, 149
  on Warren meeting Buckley, 177
  Warren's debut on MTV and, 179
  Warren's grudge against Browne and, 193
  on Warren's love of classical music, 133
"grunge classical," 318
guitar, Warren and, 13, 15, 231, 315
gunfire, inclusion in *Bad Luck Streak in Dancing School*, 128, 129
Gunnels, Gene, 43, 57
guns
  in album photos, 97, 145
  critics note of Warren's fascination with, 99, 100, 101
  Warren's dream of shooting himself, 1–4, 107
  Warren's fascination with and collection of, 69, 83, 97, 107
  Warren's use of, 107–108, 110, 113
"Gunslinger" (Diddley), 158

Habib, Philip, 165–166, 168, 171
Haeny, John, 72

Hall, Daryl, 188
Hammett, Dashiell, 105, 149
Hannah, Daryl, 214
"Happy Together" (Turtles), 29
Harlot's Ghost (Mailer), 328
Harper, Bill, 312
Harris, Bob, 152
Harris, Emmylou, 353
Harris, Jordan, 222, 225
Harrison, George, 31–32, 33
Hartford Courant (newspaper), 281, 289
"Hasten Down the Wind" (Zevon), 43, 64, 66–67, 75, 79, 192, 193, 267
Havens, Richie, 84
Hawaiian vacations, 95–96, 116, 122, 168–169
Hayward, Richie, 240, 254, 262
Haywood, Doug, 73, 149
"Heartache Spoken Here" (Zevon), 279
"The Heartache" (Zevon), 236–237
heavy metal folk, 215
Heim, Chris, 281
Hemingway, Ernest, 81, 138, 144, 162, 229
Hendrix,, Jimi, 362
Henley, Don, 63, 196–197, 220, 221, 357
    appearances on Warren's recordings, 64, 67, 93, 142–143, 144, 168, 173, 216, 226, 233, 341
    Slater and, 209, 271
heroin use
    Arngrim's, 274–275
    Warren's, 150, 180
Hiaasen, Carl
    on making of Warren's final album, 337
    Mutineer and, 297, 298, 299, 300–301
    relationship with Warren, 309, 334
    Rock Bottom Remainders, Warren, and, 319, 326
    on Warren's business card, 351
    on Warren's drinking and drug use during illness, 346

Hiatt, John, 346
Hilburn, Robert, 192
hindu love gods, 213
hindu love gods (album), 269–270, 275, 285
Hinsche, Billy, 70–71
"Hit Somebody!" (Zevon and Albom), 320–321, 325
Holden, Stephen, 72, 177–178, 217–218, 264–266
Holiday, Billie, 263
Holy Bible, Warren and, 339, 346
home studio, Warren's (Anatomy of a Headache), 292–293, 306, 313, 314, 324–325
The Honey War, planned theatrical stage musical, 338
Hooker, John Lee, 32
Horn, Jim, 91, 93, 169
Hornsby, Bruce, 298
Hot Space (Queen), 167
Houghton, Jim, 160
Howe, Dayton "Bones," 31
    connecting Warren with Fowley, 34, 35
    connecting Warren with Geffen and Asylum Records, 41–42
    contracts with Imperial label for Warren and, 40
    as lyme and cybelle's producer, 21–22, 23–24, 25–26
    Midnight Cowboy soundtrack and, 37
    Warren's second album and, 40
Hughes, John, 277
"The Hula Hula Boys" (Zevon), 168, 174
"Hurricane" (Dylan), 138

"If You Gotta Go, Go Now" (Dylan), 25–26, 28
"Iko, Iko" (Crawford, Hawkins, Hawkins & Johnson), 130
"I'll Go On" (Zevon), 26
I'll Sleep When I'm Dead (Crystal's memoir), 355

"I'll Sleep When I'm Dead" (Zevon), 68, 75, 79, 81, 179, 340
Imperial Records, Warren and, 34, 40
Indianapolis Star and News (newspaper), 301, 311
"The Indifference of Heaven" (Zevon), 290, 293–294, 296
infidelity, Warren's, 188, 276, 296
Inside Recordings, 357
Insides Out (J. Zevon), 354
"Interlude No. 1" (Zevon), 132–133, 135
"Interlude No. 2" (Zevon), 135, 140, 145, 146
intervention therapy, 4, 110–113, 115–116
Ireland, Crystal's trip to, 116–117, 120–121, 122
Irish Times (newspaper), 120
Ironside, Michael, 256
I.R.S. Records, 213–214
"I See the Lights" (Zevon), 28
Isham, Mark, 262–263, 280, 311
Ishmael Music, Warren's association with, 24–25, 28
Island label, 199
"Israelites" (Dekker), 67
"It Ain't Me, Babe" (Dylan), 21, 22
"It's True" (Zevon), 58
"I Walk the Line" (Cash), 234–235

Jackson, Michael, 168
Jagger, Bianca, 117, 118
Jam! Showbiz, 316
Japan, Warren's travelogue of journey to, 85
"Jeannie Needs a Shooter" (Zevon & Springsteen), 137–138, 145, 146
"Jesus Mentioned" (Zevon), 169, 171, 229, 315
Joan Jett and the Runaways, 35
"Johnny B. Goode" (Berry), 152
"Johnny Strikes Up the Band" (Zevon), 89, 98, 277
Johnson, Robert, 269
John Wesley Harding (Dylan), 80, 279

"Join Me in L.A." (Zevon), 69–70, 152, 154
Jones, Quincy, 168
Jonny Spielt Auf (Krenek), 89
The Jon Stewart Show, 298
Jordan, Mark T., 75
journalistic research for Warren's songs, 82
"Jungle Work" (Zevon), 131–132, 137, 145, 153

Kasdan, Lawrence, 280
Kaylan, Howard, 20–21, 24, 29–30
K-Doe, Ernie, 269
"Keep Me in Your Heart" (Zevon), 346, 347, 348, 353, 356
Keith, Ben, 143
Kennedy, John F., 335
Kenyon, Laura (Violet Santangelo), 27, 28, 337
    early relationship with Warren, 17–19
    lack of songwriting credit for collaborations with Warren, 23, 24
    lyme and cybelle and, 21–26, 28–29, 30–31
Kerouac, Jack, 80–81, 299
Keys, Bobby, 67, 68, 70
Kicks Joy Darkness (Kerouac memorial album), 299–300
Kim, Duk Koo, 230
King, B. B., 221
King, Carole, 56
King, Stephen, 319, 321
Kingston Trio, 25
Kittredge, William, 161, 162
Knigge, Robert, 43, 45
Knobs, Claude, 163
Knots Landing, Lankford and, 142, 160, 180
Koepf, Michael, 162
Kolderie, Paul Q., 313–315
Kortchmar, Danny, 87, 89, 92, 173
Krasnow, Bob, 196–197
Kravitz, Lenny, 271
Krenek, Ernst, 89

Kristofferson, Kris, 52
Kuhn, Bowie, 139
Kunkel, Russ, 87, 89, 90

Ladanyi, Greg, 127, 128, 131, 155, 225
Landau, David, 118, 266
    appearances on Warren's
        recordings, 158, 165, 167, 168,
        173
    touring with Warren, 101, 151, 152,
        154, 156–157
Landau, Jon, 72, 108, 137
Lankford, Kim, 347
    The Envoy and, 174
    People profile of Warren and, 179
    relationship with Warren, 131,
        142, 149–151, 156, 159–160, 169,
        179–181, 193
    Warren's songs for/about, 172, 173
Lannert, John, 286
La Rochefoucauld, François de, 282
The Larry Saunders Show (television
    series), 308, 310
Larson, Larry, 177
Lasseff, Lee, 20, 21–22, 23, 25
Late Night with David Letterman
    McNeal and, 295–296
    substituting for Paul Shaffer on,
        309–310
    Warren's final appearance on,
        339–341
    Warren's guest appearances on,
        176–177, 239, 298, 308–310
Launch.com, 316
"Lawyers, Guns and Money" (Zevon),
    95–96, 98, 116, 173, 189, 201, 335
Lawyers, Guns & Photos (Gruel), 355
Learning to Flinch (Zevon live album),
    286–288, 290–292, 299, 311
"Leave My Monkey Alone" (Zevon),
    237
Ledner, Jamie, 167
Led Zeppelin, 306
Lee, Bill, 138–141
Lennon, John, 46, 174
"Let Nothing Come Between You"
    (Zevon), 172, 174

Letterman, David, 135, 143, 158, 163,
    166, 308–310, 321, 340, 341.
    *See also Late Night with David
    Letterman*
Levin, Tony, 234
Lewis, Jerry Lee, 168
Licata, Nicolo, 38
"Licked by a Stranger" (Zevon), 310
"Life'll Kill Ya'" (Zevon), 306
Life'll Kill Ya (Zevon), 360
    critical reviews for, 316
    Kolderie and Slade and, 313–315
    recording sessions for, 314–316
    solo tour promoting, 317–318
"Like the Seasons" (Zevon), 24,
    29–30
Lindell, David, 60, 61, 76, 90, 92
Lindell, Lisa, 60
Lindley, David, 84, 265
    appearances on Warren's
        recordings, 57, 64, 65, 67, 130,
        137, 144, 148, 226, 235, 277, 279,
        297, 343
lip-synching, on European tour, 163
listening parties, 52, 93–94
live albums
    Learning to Flinch, 286–288,
        290–292, 299, 311
    Stand in the Fire, 156–159, 160, 220,
        286, 299
Live at Least Tour, 181–183, 191–195
live performances
    critics on, 73–74, 253, 318
    with Odds, 282
    See also solo performances/tours;
        tours
Live Rust (Young), 154
Livingston, Marilyn "Tule"
    birth of son Jordan, 37
    death of, 354
    move to New York, 58
    relationship with Warren, 33–34,
        35, 38–39, 47, 48, 50, 220
    songs written for, 131
Livingston, Mary, 37, 58
The Lloyd Thaxton Show, 25
Locke, Sondra, 160

"The Long Arm of the Law" (Zevon), 256, 257, 266
"Looking for the Next Best Thing" (Zevon), 173, 175
Los Angeles counterculture, Marks and Warren and, 32–33
Los Angeles Times (newspaper)
  Calderón on Springsteen's appearance at final sessions in, 343
  interviews with Slater, 209, 271
  interviews with Warren, 275–276, 284–285, 300, 316, 319, 323, 328
  on Krasnow and changes at Elektra/Asylum, 196, 197
  reviews of Warren's work in, 235, 236, 237, 266, 281, 289–290
Love at Large (film), 263, 280
luck, Warren and, 220, 350, 363
Lukather, Steve, 172
lyme, stephen, 24, 31
lyme and cybelle, 21–26, 28–29, 30, 31
Lynyrd Skynyrd, 135–136

Mabe, Chauncey, 227, 238
Macdonald, Ross, 60–61, 74, 104, 149, 221, 222, 299
"Macgillycuddy's Reeks" (Zevon & Muldoon), 324
Mad Love (Ronstadt), 166
Mailer, Norman, 105, 138, 193, 229, 299, 328, 359
Main Point (club), 187–188
Major, Phyllis, 72
Mallaber, Gary, 66, 68–69
"Mama Couldn't Be Persuaded" (Zevon), 65
Mamas and the Papas, 22
Mancini, Ray "Boom Boom," 230, 232, 278
Mann, Michael, 294, 311
Many, Gregory V., 7–8
Manzarek, Ray, 338
Marcus, Greil, 98, 99, 100
Marinell, LeRoy, 57, 87–88, 89, 90–91, 112, 113, 172–173, 279

Marks, David, 219, 269
  drug use, 27–28, 32, 80–81
  introducing Warren to Phil Everly, 42
  relationship with Warren, 31, 32–33, 36, 39, 40, 60, 337
Marley, Bob, 106
Marotta, Rick, appearances on Warren's recordings, 93, 96, 101, 130, 131, 132, 136, 137–138, 142, 148, 165, 171
Marsh, Dave, 100–101
Martin, Billy, 177
Marvin, Lee, 142
Mauceri, John, 75
May, Brian, 167
McCartney, Paul, 146
McDonald, Joe, 84
McFarland, Danny, 55, 67
McGee, Mickey, 73
McGuane, Thomas, 152, 160–163, 168, 179
McLane High School (Fresno, California), 15–16
McNeal, Julia. *See* Mueller, Julia
McQueen, Steve, 161
McVie, John, 87, 89
memorial album, 354
memorial service, 351
mentor, Warren as mentor to Odds, 282–284
mesothelioma, Warren's diagnosis of, 333–334
Midnight Cowboy (film), 37, 39, 106
migraines, Warren's, 293
Millar, Ken, 105, 106, 109, 119–120, 121, 145, 233
Millennium Paranoia Tour, 264, 265–266, 268
Miller, Judith, 166
Miller, Lesley, 37
Mills, Mike, 210, 213, 227, 228, 236, 269
Milward, John, 228, 238, 241–242
The Missouri Breaks (film), 161
Mitchell, Joni, 41, 63, 91
Mitchell, Justin, 217

"Mohammed's Radio" (Zevon), 68, 75, 143, 240, 284

Mondale, Eleanor, 276

"Monkey Wash, Donkey Rinse" (Zevon), 297, 298

"Moondance" (Morrison), 68

Morlix, Gurf, 275

Mormonism, Warren's mother and, 10, 11

Morrison, Jim, 32, 35, 143, 288, 362

Morrison, Van, 68–69

Moss, Ron, 214

Mr. Bad Example (Zevon), 135, 270, 299
  public and critical response to, 280–281
  recording sessions, 276–280
  tour supporting, 282–285, 286–290

"Mr. Bad Example" (Zevon & Calderón), 278–279

MTV, 176, 178–179, 195

Mueller, Julia, 277, 294–296, 297, 337, 347

Muldoon, Paul, 323–324, 326, 337–338, 363

muses, Warren's, 347–348

music theory, Warren's interest in studying, 13, 14

music videos, Warren's, 129, 229, 237. *See also* MTV

Mutineer (Zevon)
  Hiaasen and, 299, 300–301
  recording, 293–294, 296–298
  Warren's hopes for, 301
  Wolff and, 299–300

"The Mutineer" (Zevon), 335, 339, 354

My Ride's Here (Zevon), 324, 338
  critics on, 326
  promotional tour, 326–327
  recording sessions for, 324–325

"My Ride's Here" (Zevon & Muldoon), 324, 354

Mystic Line (Phil Everly), 58, 62

The Naked and the Dead (Mailer), 328

"Narrator" (Berry), 213

Nash, Graham, 52

National Council on Alcoholism, 208

National Public Radio, 302

Native Tongue (Hiaasen), 300

Nebraska (Springsteen), 80, 279

Nelson, Paul, 148
  fear Warren would come to tragic end, 141
  helping with Warren's addictions and rehab, 4, 108–109, 110, 111–113, 117–118, 119–120
  on importance of *Symphony No. 1* to Warren, 133–134
  profile of Warren for *Rolling Stone*, 124, 147, 181, 223
  relationship with Warren, 73–74, 104–105, 124, 159–160
  reviews of Warren's work, 74, 99–100, 154, 158
  Warren on his own self-denial, 139
  Warren on playing the Roxy, 157
  Warren on resisting temptation of drugs and alcohol, 121–122
  Warren relating first meeting with Lankford, 150

"Networking" (Zevon), 253

Neuromancer (Gibson), 251, 254

"Never Too Late for Love" (Zevon), 174

New Cyber Punk magazine, 256

Newman, Melinda, 293, 298

Newman, Paul, 221

New West Records, 355

New York Dolls, 104

New York Times (newspaper)
  interviews with Warren, 166, 171, 338, 343, 360
  Letterman on Warren in, 340
  reviews of Warren's work, 72, 153–154, 177–178, 217–218, 240, 247, 318

The New Zealand Herald, 290

Nicholson, Jack, 55, 161

Nicks, Stevie, 57, 64, 68, 70, 222, 234

Night Cafe (Van Gogh), 119

"Nighttime in the Switching Yard" (Zevon), 92, 98

Nilsson, Harry, 37

Nirvana, 306
Nitty Gritty Dirt Band, 52
"Nobody's in Love This Year"
     (Zevon), 262, 280
No Depression (magazine), 316
Nolan, Tom, 120
Norris, Aaron, 150, 160, 207
North Dallas Forty (film), 310
Northey, Craig, 283–284
"Norwegian Wood" (Lennon-
     McCartney), 26
Noura Café, 278, 300
"Numb as a Statue" (Zevon), 342

Oates, Joyce Carol, 283
obsessive-compulsive disorder (OCD)
     Rayston and, 331, 332
     Warren and, 242–243, 247–248, 250,
     261, 346
Ochs, Phil, 31
O'Connor, Rob, 316
Odds (band), 282–284
O'Hara, John, 66
O'Hare, Michael, 160
Old Waldorf (club), 194
Olsen, Keith, 49
Ono, Yoko, 174
organized crime, William Zevon and,
     8–9
"Outside Chance" (Zevon), 29
"The Overdraft" (Zevon &
     McGuane), 162–163, 168, 177
overdubbing, on *Transverse City,* 253,
     254

Palmer, Robert, 153–154, 172, 174, 221
Panama (McGuane), 152, 161, 162
Pareles, Jon, 240, 318, 360
Park West Club, 182
Parsons, Alan, 146
Pasternak, Boris, 339
People magazine, 147, 149, 175, 179,
     338
perfectionism, Warren and, 78, 80, 128
Petty, Tom, 275, 343
Philadelphia Inquirer (newspaper),
     228, 238, 239, 264, 265, 298, 318

piano, Warren and, 12–13, 55, 231
"Piano Fighter" (Zevon), 204, 290–291,
     298
Pinecrest Rehabilitation Clinic,
     therapy at, 4, 110–113, 115–116,
     119, 140
Pinon, Roberto, 152
Plant, Robert, 306
"Play It All Night Long" (Zevon),
     135–137, 192
Pleasures of the Harbor (Ochs), 31
Poe, Edgar Allen, 89
"Poisonous Lookalike" (Zevon), 297
political edge, to Warren's stage
     banter, 240–241
Ponder, Eddie, 57
"Poor Poor Pitiful Me" (Zevon), 57,
     67, 354
Porcaro, Jeff, 92, 168, 169, 172, 277
"Porcelain Monkey" (Zevon &
     Calderón), 141–142, 171, 315–316
posthumous albums, 354–355, 356
Pound, Ezra, 145
Powers, Ron, 192
*Preludes: Rare and Unreleased
     Recordings* (Zevon), 355
"Prelude" (Zevon), 238
Presley, Elvis
     Howe and, 22
     "Jesus Mentioned" homage to, 169,
     171, 229, 315
     "Porcelain Monkey" homage to,
     141–142, 171, 315–316
The Pretender (Browne), 72, 75, 84
Prince, 240, 269, 270
"Prison Grove" (Zevon), 342
Prophet, Chuck, 315
Pro Tools, 325
Purgatorio (Dante), 145
Pynchon, Thomas, 251

Queen (band), 167
A Quiet Normal Life (Zevon), 221
The Quiet Sound of Disappearing
     (Rayston), 357
"Quite Early One Morning" (Zevon),
     279

Rachlis, Kit, 72
Radiohead, 313, 314
Radner, Gilda, 153
raga rock, Warren and, 23
Raging Bull (film), 220
Raitt, Bonnie, 64, 70, 317, 354
Ramones, 104
"Raspberry Beret" (Prince), 240, 269, 270
Rayston, Ryan, 331–332, 345, 347, 349–350, 357
Reagan, Ronald, 165
"Reconsider Me" (Zevon), 213, 216, 217, 222, 228, 234, 236, 245
recording sessions
    for *Bad Luck Streak in Dancing School*, 122–123, 126–144
    for *The Envoy*, 165–174
    for *Excitable Boy*, 86–96
    for *Life'll Kill Ya*, 314–316
    for *lyme and cybelle*, 24
    for *Mr. Bad Example*, 276–280
    for *Mutineer*, 296–298
    for *My Ride's Here*, 324–325
    for *Sentimental Hygiene*, 224–229, 233–237
    for *Wanted Dead or Alive*, 35–36
    for *Warren Zevon*, 63–71
    for *The Wind*, 339–348
Record One studios, 166, 225–226
Red Zone studios, 252, 253, 255, 292
Reed, Jerry, 57
Reed, Lou, 174
rehab
    Pinecrest, 4, 109, 110–113, 115–116, 119, 140
    Slater in, 271–272
    St. Mary's Hospital, 205, 208–209, 211–212, 214
Reid, Graham, 290, 291
Reinhardt, Elmer, 15–16
relationships with women
    Annette Aguilar, 259–262, 263, 272, 274–275, 276, 277, 293–294
    cavalier attitude toward monogamy, 276
    Eleanor Mondale, 276

as his muses, 347
    Julia Mueller, 277, 294–296, 297, 337, 347
    Merle Ginsberg, 223–224, 242, 247–251, 259, 347
    Ryan Rayston, 331–332, 345, 347, 349–350, 357
    See also Brelsford, Crystal Ann; Gevinson, Anita; Lankford, Kim; Livingston, Marilyn "Tule"
R.E.M., 213
    hindu love gods and, 269–270, 275, 285
    members backing Warren, 210–211, 212–214
    Sentimental Hygiene and, 226, 227, 228, 236, 239
    Slater and, 210
"Renegade" (Zevon), 135, 279
Revolver (Beatles), 289
Rhys, John, 57–58, 59
Richmond, Fritz, 72
Rilke, Rainer Maria, 339
Rimbaud, Arthur, 80
The Rise of Life on Earth (Oates), 283–284
Ritts, Herb, 229
Rivers, Johnny, 34
Roberts, Elliot, 41
Robertson, Sandy, 175
Rock and Roll Hall of Fame, 197
Rock Bottom Remainders, 319–322
Rockefeller's (club), 216
Rocky Mountain Magazine, 162
Roe, Tommy, 57
Roeser, Steve, 298
"Roland Chorale" (Zevon), 290
"Roland the Headless Thompson Gunner" (Zevon), 82, 90, 131, 240, 265, 290, 340
"The Rolling Coconut Review," 84
Rolling Stone (magazine)
    Ginsberg and, 223, 224, 249
    interviews with Warren in, 163–164, 165–166, 171, 338
    Marsh's profile of Warren for, 100–101

Nelson's profile of Warren for, 107, 124, 147, 181
rejection of Warren's travelogue, 85
reviews of Warren's albums, 72, 99–100
on Warren being dropped by Elektra/Asylum, 198
The Rolling Stones, 46
Ronstadt, Linda, 41, 52, 73, 94, 166, 187, 197
  appearances on Warren's recordings, 91, 132, 148
  covers of Warren's songs, 66, 69
Roos, John, 316
"The Rosarita Beach Café" (Zevon), 40
Ross, Stuart, 242–243
Rossellini, Isabella, 160
"Rottweiler Blues" (Zevon & Hiaasen), 298, 300
Route 66 (television series), 312
Roxy (club), 73, 102, 105, 155, 156–157, 192–193
"Rub Me Raw" (Zevon), 347
Rudolph, Alan, 263, 280
"Run Straight Down" (Zevon), 255, 256, 257, 267
Rust Never Sleeps (Young), 118

St. Mary's Hospital (Minnesota) substance abuse program, 208–209, 211–212, 214
Salon.com, 361
Sandford, Madeline, 208
Sandler, Adam, 354
Santangelo, Violet. *See* Kenyon, Laura
"Save the Whales" concert, 84, 241
Schiff, David, 242
Schmidt, Tim, 353
Schoenberg, Arnold, 134
Schopenhauer, Arthur, 339
Schramm, Rudolf, 44
science-fiction genre, Warren and, 251–252
scoring assignments
  for film, 310, 311 (*see also* soundtracks)
  for television, 310–311, 312

Scorsese, Martin, 160, 194, 220–221, 310
Scott, Ridley, 254
"Searching for a Heart" (Zevon), 262, 263, 277, 280, 302
Sea Witch (club), 30
Seay, Davin, 175
Sebastian, John, 84
self-loathing, Warren's, 85, 107
"Seminole Bingo" (Zevon & Hiaasen), 300
"Sentimental Hygiene" (Zevon), 227–228, 229, 265
Sentimental Hygiene (Zevon)
  recording sessions, 224–229, 233–237
  singles' performance on *Billboard* charts, 245
  tour supporting, 238, 239, 241–245
Setzer, Brian, 226, 233
Shaffer, Paul, 178, 309, 321, 340
Shandling, Gary, 308
Shapiro, Ben, 16
Sharp, Sid, 68, 70, 130, 132, 135, 138
Shatner, William, 312
Sheldon, Stan, 101
"She Quit Me" (Zevon), 36, 37, 106
"She's Too Good for Me" (Zevon), 341
Sick 'Em Dogs on Me Tour, 251, 253
Siegel, Bugsy, 9
Sierra Club, 255
Silk Cut cigarettes, Warren and, 241, 242–243
"Sillyhow Stride" (Muldoon), 363
Silverman, David, 253
"Similar to Rain" (Zevon), 299
Simmons, Ellsworth Blythe, 7, 10, 11–12
Simmons, Helen Nicholson Cope, 7, 10, 11–12
Simmons, Warren Cope, 10, 11
Simms, Frank, 265
Simon, Paul, 25, 138
Sinatra, Nancy, 53
singing voice, Warren's self-consciousness about, 189

"The Sin" (Zevon), 157
sitar on "Bad Karma," 235, 236
Sklar, Leland, appearances on
    Warren's recordings, 89, 130, 131,
    132, 136, 137–138, 142, 168, 226,
    237
Slade, Sean, 313–315
Slash (musician), 343
Slater, Andrew
    as co-producer, 224–229, 239,
        252–253, 254, 259, 305
    demos for Warren and, 212–214
    Ginsberg and, 223, 224
    hindu love gods and, 269–270
    Millennium Paranoia Tour and, 265
    PR savvy of, 217, 218
    relationship with Warren, 209–211,
        219–220, 271–272
    Virgin Records deal and, 222
    Wallflowers and, 233, 357–358
    on Warren's obsessive-compulsive
        disorder, 243
    Young and, 292
Smith, Joe, 72, 95, 102, 105, 111, 145,
    196
Smith, Joseph, 10
Smith, Patti, 300
Snyder, Noah Scot, 324–325, 337,
    342–343, 348
Sobriety, Warren and, 150, 209,
    219–220, 222, 247, 272
solo performances/tours, 163, 245
    in 1985 and 1986, 214–219
    in European after being dropped by
        Elektra/Asylum, 200–203
    Life At Least Tour, 182–183,
        191–195
    to promote *Life'll Kill Ya*, 317–318
    review of, 289–290
    Warren on, 284–285
    See also live performances
Song Noir, 257
songwriting
    Warren as house songwriter, 22–23,
        24, 28, 42, 51
    Warren's insistence on sole credit,
        23

Warren's royalties as songwriter,
    29–30
Sound Factory, 87, 96, 276, 277
"The Sound of Silence" (Simon), 25
Sounds (magazine), 98, 175
soundtracks, Warren's inclusion on
    film, 37, 39, 106, 263, 280, 294,
    356
South, Joe, 57
Souther, J. D., 41, 81, 84, 113, 279, 357
    appearances on Warren's
        recordings, 64, 142, 172, 262
    collaborations with Warren, 215,
        310
    visit to Warren in Philadelphia, 203,
        205, 233
"Southern Man" (Young), 135–136
Southern Rock genre, Warren and,
    135–136
"So You Wanna Be a Rock 'n' Roll
    Star" (Byrds), 236
Spice Girls (band), 309
Spillane, Mickey, 104
spiritualism, Warren and, 307
"Splendid Isolation" (Zevon), 253,
    259, 265–266, 267
sports-inspired compositions,
    138–139, 229–232
Springsteen, Bruce, 72, 73, 108, 194,
    232, 260–261
    appearances on Warren's
        recordings, 342–343
    collaboration with Warren,
        137–138, 146
    cover of "My Ride's Here," 354
    on "Disorder in the House,"
        242–243, 353
    Nelson and, 74, 104
    Warren's admiration for, 80, 279
Squire, Billy, 188
"Stand in the Fire" (Zevon), 157
Stand in the Fire (Zevon live album),
    156–159, 160, 220, 286, 299
Star Spangled Springer (Phil Everly),
    57
"Steady Rain" (Zevon), 40
Steel, George, 163

Stein, Burt, 95, 189
Stevens, Wallace, 221
Steward, Andy, 259
Stewart, Rod, 52, 104
Stinger, Marty, 152
Stipe, Michael, 210, 213, 226, 227, 235
Stone (club), 215
Stories We Could Tell (Everly Brothers), 52–53
Stravinsky, Igor, 13, 14, 32, 120, 133, 148, 231, 360
Strummer, Joe, 300
"Studebaker" (Zevon), 40, 354
Suddenly Susan (television series), 308
Sullivan, Jim, 287
"Summertime Blues" (Cochran), 216
Sundays and Cybèle (Bourguignon), 21
Sun-Sentinel (newspaper), 227, 238, 239, 276, 277
Sunset Sound, 336, 341
Sunset Studios, 24
superstitions, Warren and, 242–243
"Suzie Lightning" (Zevon), 278
Swan Song Records, 306
"Sweet Home Alabama" (Lynyrd Skynyrd), 135–136
Swordfishtrombones (Waits), 199–200
Symphony No. 1 (Zevon), 14, 51, 127, 130, 132–135, 255, 360–361. *See also* classical music
synthesizer, Warren's use of on *The Envoy*, 167

Tadouye, Wayne, 167
Tales from the Crypt (television series), 312
Tan, Amy, 319
Tarson, Steve, 239
Technicians of the Sacred (Valin), 242
TekWar (television series), 312
television
    scoring assignments for, 310–311, 312
    use of Warren's songs in, 356
    Warren's guest spots on, 308–309
temper, Warren's, 18–19, 38–39, 51, 103

"Tenderness on the Block" (Zevon & Browne), 94, 95
Theaker, Drachen, 36
Thelen, Christopher, 291
There's Nothing Too Good for My Baby (Phil Everly), 57–58
"They Moved the Moon" (Zevon), 254, 258, 262
Things to Do in Denver When You're Dead (film), 310
"Things to Do in Denver When You're Dead" (Zevon, Wachtel, Marinell), 279
Thompson, Hunter S., 85, 105, 299–300, 314, 322–323
Thornburg, Newton, 136
Thornton, Billy Bob, 279, 341, 343–344, 353, 354
Thriller (Jackson), 168
Times Arrow (Amis), 293
Tom Horn (film), 161
tours
    All Hell Is Breaking Loose Jungle Tour, 152, 163, 176
    Bad Luck Streak in Dancing School tour, 150–154, 155, 156–157, 159, 163–164
    The Envoy tour, 176–179
    European tour after being dropped by Elektra/Asylum, 199–203
    Excitable Boy tour, 101–103
    To the Finland Station Tour, 176–179
    Live at Least Tour, 181–183, 191–195
    Mr. Bad Example tour, 282–285, 286–290
    Sentimental Hygiene tour, 238, 239, 240–245
    Sick 'Em Dogs on Me Tour, 251, 253
    Transverse City (Millennium Paranoia Tour), 264, 265–266, 268
    Warren Zevon Acoustic Trio, 275–276
    See also live performances; solo performances/tours

Toussaint, Allen, 130
"Transverse City" (Zevon), 254, 256, 257
Transverse City (Zevon), 299
    budget for, 252–253
    concept for, 251–252, 254, 256–257
    critical reception of, 263–265
    failure on *Billboard* charts, 267–268
    tour, 265–267
Travolta, John, 129
tribute album in Warren's honor, Browne's suggestion of, 336
"Trouble Waiting to Happen" (Zevon), 204, 213, 215, 233
"Tule's Blues" (Zevon), 36, 93, 355
"Turbulence" (Zevon), 257–258
The Turtles, 21, 24, 25, 29–30, 31
Twice Nicely (band), 44, 49

U2, 201
Ukranian pogroms, Warren's family and, 7–8
The Unbelievable Truth (film), 294
Underground All-Stars (band), 35
USA Today (newspaper), 338
Uzi, on back cover of *Bad Luck Streak in Dancing School*, 145

Valania, Jonathan, 318
Valin, Jonathan, 242
Van Gogh, Vincent, 119
Vedder, Eddie, 299
Velvet Underground, 104
Venture, Jesse "The Body," 323
"Veracruz" (Zevon & Calderón), 81–82, 92–93, 192
VH1 documentary, 338, 339, 348, 349–350, 353
Village Voice (newspaper), 72, 98, 104, 158, 235
violence
    Warren and, 8, 12, 76
    William Zevon and, 12
Virgin Records, 222–223, 225, 239, 268–269
Volman, Mark, 20–21, 24
von Webern, Anton, 134

Wachtel, Harry, 44
Wachtel, Jimmy, 44, 170
    album design/photos and, 97, 144–145, 158, 163, 174, 280
    Warren's intervention therapy and, 112
    on Warren's preference for monochrome gray, 242
Wachtel, Rhonda, 43–44
Wachtel, Robert "Waddy"
    at Alternative Chorus Songwriters' Showcase, 56–57
    Bad Luck Streak in Dancing School sessions and, 131, 132
    Bolas and, 225
    Crystal and, 44, 48–49
    early life, 43–44
    Enjoy Every Sandwich and, 354
    The Envoy and, 165, 166–174
    Excitable Boy and, 86–96, 93–94
    on *Excitable Boy* tour, 101
    Mr. Bad Example and, 270–271, 276–280
    musical career, 44–45, 78
    on reception of *The Envoy*, 175
    relationship with Warren, 45–47
    Sentimental Hygiene and, 226, 228, 234, 237
    Transverse City and, 262
    as Warren's collaborator, 46
    Warren Zevon and, 64, 66–67, 69
    on "Werewolves of London" as single, 98
Waits, Tom, 41, 67, 170, 187, 199–200, 221
"Wake Up Little Susie" (Everly Brothers), 26, 43
Walecki, Fred, 125, 149
Wallace, Ian, 265
Wallflowers (band), 233, 357–358
Walsh, Joe, 131, 138, 142, 148, 197, 212, 276
"Wanted Dead or Alive" (Zevon), 356
Wanted Dead or Alive (Zevon), 35–36, 39
Warner Bros. Records, 212, 306
Warner Music Group, 42

Warnes, Jennifer, 91, 237
Warren Zevon Acoustic Trio tour,
    275–276
Warren Zevon (album)
    cover photo, 97
    critical reaction to, 72–73
    postproduction, 71–72, 78–79
    pressure for follow-up effort, 77–78
    recording sessions, 63–71
    singles released, 75
    tour supporting, 73–74
Washburn, Jim, 266
Washington Post (newspaper), 146, 158
The Waste Land (Eliot), 145
Waters, Muddy, 32, 269
Wayne, Don, 43, 53
Weill, Kurt, 89
Weingarten, Marc, 300, 319
Weir, Bob, 126
Weir, Frankie, 126
Wenner, Jann, 85, 108, 197, 249
Werewolf of London (film), 87
"Werewolves of London" (Zevon), 71,
    87–89, 90, 98, 102, 187, 213
    on *Color of Money* soundtrack,
        221, 310
    on *Enjoy Every Sandwich*, 354
    grudge against Browne and
        reworked lyrics to, 193
    on *Learning to Flinch*, 287
    video for, 129
Westwood Musical Instruments, 125,
    149
Whiskey A Go-Go (club), 31
White Whale Records, 20–21
    lyme and cybelle and, 21–26
    Warren's songwriting for, 22–23
"Why'd I Let You Get to Me Again"
    (Zevon), 92
"Wild Age" (Zevon), 143–144,
    173–174
Willman, Chris, 235, 238
Wilson, Carl, 64, 70, 71
Winding, Jai, 67, 234
"The Wind" (Zevon), 354
The Wind (Zevon)
    Grammy nominations, 353

    recording sessions for, 339–348
    sales and critical reception of, 349
    Warren's drug use during making
        of, 343–345
Winwood, Steve, 222, 268
Wolff, Carlo, 240
Wolff, Michael, 299–300
Wood, John, 177
"Worrier King" (Zevon), 290
writer's block, Warren and, 78, 116

Yardbirds, 130
Yes I Can (Davis), 339
Yoakam, Dwight, 279, 341
"You Don't Know What Love Is"
    (de Paul & Raye), 263
Young, Neil, 118, 135–136, 154, 265,
    279, 280, 292
    appearances on Warren's
        recordings, 226, 228–229, 253,
        258–259, 308
"You're a Whole Different Person
    When You're Scared" (Zevon &
    Thompson), 323
"You Used to Ride So High" (Zevon),
    40

Zack, Larry, 65, 67
Zapata, Emiliano, 82
Zeller, Craig, 175
Zevon, Al (uncle), 8
Zevon, Ariel Erin (daughter), 122, 190
    birth of, 74
    birth of twins, 348–349
    compilation album and, 356
    The Detangler, 356
    father's final album and, 347–348
    father's illness and, 332, 346
    Grammy Awards' tribute and, 353
    with grandparents, 117
    living abroad with her mother, 182
    mother's alcoholism and, 273
    pregnancy, 348
    relationship with father,
        155–156,197, 202–203, 217, 220,
        273–274, 295
    song written for, 95

Zevon, Beverly Simmons (mother), 7,
    10–13, 15–16, 103, 307
Zevon, Dan (cousin), 244
Zevon, Hymie (uncle), 8–9
Zevon, Jordan (son), 220
    birth of, 37
    compilation of *Preludes: Rare and
        Unreleased Recordings* and,
        354–355
    on *Enjoy Every Sandwich*, 354
    father's alcohol and drug use during
        illness and, 345, 346
    father's death and, 350, 351
    Grammy Awards' tribute and, 353
    on *Mr. Bad Example*, 277
    relationship with father, 58, 103,
        155, 168–169, 192–193, 219
    "The Hula Hula Boys" and, 169
Zevon, Lawrence (cousin), 153, 207,
    208, 244–245, 341
Zevon, Lou (uncle), 8
Zevon, Madeline (Sandford Zevon's
    wife), 14, 208
Zevon, Murray (uncle), 8
Zevon, Paul (cousin), 208
Zevon, Rubin (grandfather, Ruven
    Zivotovsky), 7–8

Zevon, Sadie (grandmother), 8
Zevon, Sandford (cousin), 8, 9, 24
    relationship with Warren, 14, 153,
        207–208, 244
    Warren's illness and, 333, 334–335,
        341
Zevon, William "Stumpy" (father)
    boxing career, 229–230
    death of, 307
    financial support for Warren, 59,
        62
    immigration to United States and
        childhood of, 7–8
    living with during Warren's
        adolescence, 16–17
    marriage to Beverly, 7, 10–13
    move to California, 9–10
    pride in son's successes, 37–38
    as professional gambler, 7, 65
    response to Kenyon, 18–19
    ties to organized crime, 8–9, 38
    Warren repairing relationship with,
        274
Zevon-Powell, Augustus Warren and
    Maximum Patrick (grandsons),
    348
Zirngiebel, Zeke, 152